Bruce

June 1973

JAPAN DIARY

MARK GAYN

Japan Diary

WILLIAM SLOANE ASSOCIATES, INC.
Publishers   *New York*

For Sally

CONTENTS

PREFACE

This book is an eyewitness report of what has happened in Japan and Korea under our Occupation. It is also meant to be some other things. It is the story of that extraordinary figure, General Douglas MacArthur, and the men around him. It is the story of the way our foreign policy operates in one segment of the globe. It is the detailed story of the plot and counterplot which went on behind the Japanese throne in the years of war, and of the subsequent conspiracy to thwart the Allied purposes. It is the story of the common people in two Oriental lands. It is finally the record of my education.

The entries in this book are much as they appeared in my half-million-word diary. What changes have been made are few and minor. Some names have been altered, some dates reshuffled, some entries compressed for the sake of brevity, and, whenever it seemed necessary, background information added. This information has been drawn from a million words of diverse material, ranging from the diary of the emperor's closest aide to the printed records of the U.S. Strategic Bombing Survey.

It is difficult to give proper credit to the men and women in Japan and Korea who have helped me in my work—and my education. There are too many to be named, and many, I am sure, would prefer to remain unnamed. They range from members of the Japanese Parliament to Korean terrorists to American generals; from sharecroppers to brothel operators to revolutionaries, from U.S. Army officers who were anxious to "let the people back home know the truth," to a *kamikaze* pilot who expected to join the U.S. Air Force in the coming war, to a Korean general who was getting an American subsidy to run a Nazi-patterned "School for Leaders."

My thanks must also go to the group of brilliant reporters

with whom I have worked, and sometimes pooled information —William Costello, of the Columbia Broadcasting System; Joseph Fromm, of the *U.S. News* and *World Report;* Robert Cochrane, of the Baltimore *Sun;* Gordon Walker, of the *Christian Science Monitor;* Carl Mydans, of *Time;* Margaret Parton, of the New York *Herald Tribune,* and many many others equally able.

Finally, and most of all, my gratitude goes to Sally, in daily letters to whom this book was conceived, and who later, with patience and understanding, shared many of my experiences. She had gone with me deep underground to talk to Japanese coal miners. When other accommodations were lacking, she lived with me in a Japanese bordello. She traveled with me thousands of miles by jeep, train, and plane, helped me to question villains and reformers, and sometimes, on her own, undertook lines of useful inquiry. This book is for her.

Salonika, Greece
July 1, 1948   Mark Gayn

SEASON OF PROMISE

December 5, 1945   TOKYO

Around noon, we sighted Japan's coastline. It lay clear beneath us, a stretch of green earth ringed with the thin white line of surf. The land looked peaceful and unpeopled— no smoking chimneys, or trains, or traffic on the narrow ribbons of roads.

We landed at Atsugi. Its runway was pockmarked with filled bomb craters. Along the edges stood clusters of Japanese aircraft, torn and dented where our bombs had caught them. The wooden hangars, half burned down, were being repaired by apathetic Japanese crews. And over all this chaos, blew clouds of thick, suffocating dust.

Later, we drove along a narrow and twisting road to Tokyo. The countryside looked well enough—men working in the fields, children playing, radishes drying in the sun, a middle-aged man pushing a cart with a shriveled old woman in it. The buildings were shabby and their paper panels were torn, but they were buildings and there was life and warmth within them.

But the closer we came to Yokohama, the plainer became the gravity of Japan's hurt. Before us, as far as we could see, lay miles of rubble. The people looked ragged and distraught. They dug into the debris, to clear space for new shacks. They pushed and dragged carts piled high with brick and lumber. But so vast was the destruction that all this effort seemed unproductive. There were no new buildings in sight. The skeletons of railway cars and locomotives remained untouched on the tracks. Streetcars stood where the flames had caught up with them, twisting the metal, snapping the wires overhead, and bending the supporting iron poles as if they were made of wax. Gutted buses and automobiles lay abandoned by the roadside. This was all a man-made desert, ugly and desolate and hazy in the dust that rose from the crushed brick and mortar.

There was plenty of traffic, but all of it was American and military. The Japanese trudged by, swallowed in the dust, and seeming not to care. Even the Ginza, once one of the world's most beautiful streets, had not escaped. Its trees and buildings stood blackened with fire, and the stalls, which made every night a country-fair night, were gone.

We turned off toward the Imperial Palace, and drove up to a massive six-story gray building, spared by war. Formerly the head office of the Dai-Ichi Insurance Company, this was now General MacArthur's headquarters. I went in to look for the Public Relations Office. The first familiar face I saw was that of Dick Lauterbach of *Life*.

"Hi," he said, "we've been expecting you."

December 6, 1945   TOKYO

My first night at the Press Club—a tired, old, five-story building that once was a restaurant. It stands in a narrow lane, now known as *Shimbun* (Newspaper) Alley, and lined mainly by roofless shells of office buildings. A punctured main sends out tiny, gurgling rivulets into the ruins, and there is a rusty mess of iron safes, metal bars, and reddish earth. But once the doors of the club close, the chaos is far away, and you are in a warm, busy, and polyglot world, filled with that air of international camaraderie and high intrigue that Hollywood likes to inject into its movies of spies and foreign correspondents. Men whispering in a corner with a mysterious Japanese. A French correspondent with his arm around an exquisitely beautiful Eurasian. An American with his German mistress, who once, with the same fleshy charms, entertained a Nazi gauleiter. A tall, lean Japanese war criminal in crumpled tweeds speaking to a New York newspaperman, who conceivably might help him to escape arrest. A Chinese talking to a Japanese who studied at Amherst, worked for the Japanese Naval Intelligence, and married an Indian princess. Other correspondents drinking, arguing, boasting of distant points on the globe which they have just left, or soon intend to see. A British correspondent making a telephone date with a WAC captain, in a voice that resounds through the building. American colonels being plied with raw Japanese whisky.

The crowd talks in the mixed jargon of war, journalism logistics, and sex. The Japanese boy busily swings the glass doors open for arrivals and departures, and there is a constant roar of motors outside.

The club is crowded, and last night I had to sleep in the ballroom, behind a paper screen. At six this morning, the Japanese room boys began to wrestle on the other side of the screen and woke me up. I showered and went down to the ornate dining room, with its tiled and pretentious pillars. The waitresses are small, plump girls, most of whom had previously worked in offices. Their English is momentarily limited to, "Very sorry," which they employ promiscuously. The food is good, and I see no need for apologies.

After breakfast, I walked down the main boulevard to the Public Relations Office which I found housed in Radio Tokyo. The Imperial Hotel is now short a wing, but the rest of it is still as handsome as when Frank Lloyd Wright built it. Like the Press Club, it stands self-consciously in the midst of ruin, and in its carpeted lobby the rubble crunches underfoot. There is some Japanese traffic on the boulevard: a few decrepit trucks with charcoal burners, emitting puffs of sooty smoke, and a few noisy street cars, with the broken windows boarded up with tin and planks and with the overflow of passengers hanging on to the steps and ledges.

Radio Tokyo is a huge block of concrete, painted in the jet black of the camouflage fancied by the Japanese. In a huge news room, I appropriated a vacant desk next to Frank Kelley, of the New York *Herald Tribune*, and then called on Brigadier

General Frayne Baker, Public Relations Officer. He is stout, laconic, and surly. I have already been warned that he has little affection for special correspondents, with their annoying habit of independent thought and inquiry. Baker feels that the job of reporting Japan can be done adequately by the news agencies alone.

Although I intended to file no stories for a couple of weeks, until I had a chance to look around, I found myself tonight writing on the latest order for the arrest of major war criminals. Some of these are ghosts out of my own journalistic past— the wilful men behind the war on China and the regimentation of Japan. Two men especially interest me. One is Prince Fumimaro Konoye, a tall, spare man related by marriage to the imperial house; thrice premier; and an ambitious politician, who fluctuated between glib phrases of democracy and the concepts of the feudal age. The other man is Marquis Koichi Kido, an opportunist who, as Lord Keeper of the Privy Seal, was the emperor's brain and voice.

The order for the arrest, the newspaper *Mainichi* said, ended "three days of melancholia and acute agony" in the Diet. This worthy institution, packed with Tojo's followers, has already contributed twenty-four men to the prison in the past four days, and its work has been completely disrupted by fear of new arrests.

Late at night, after filing the story, I walked back to the club. The moon was hidden behind a cloud, and I kept stumbling in the deep holes. There was no one abroad, and the darkness and silence were eerie. I passed a tall building of which nothing remained but the front wall. I looked up through the windows, and where the ceiling and the lights should have been, I saw stars.

This is an exciting place at an exciting time in history. I made my rounds of various Headquarters' sections, and nearly everyone I talked to was engaged in what probably will be known as one of the greatest experiments in our history—the reshaping of a beaten nation. Men's enthusiasm is infectious. They fought a hard war, until they were sick of its foulness. Now they feel as if they are cleansing themselves and the enemy. Headquarters is full of "reformers." Lights burn late in the buildings where these young men work on a blue-print for a new Japanese democracy. Most of the bars on civil liberties already have been shattered, and with them the enforcing agencies—including the Thought Control Police. Now Americans are working on new directives which will end the savagery of feudal sharecropping, break up the huge financial empires, or *zaibatsu*, end the stranglehold of the Shinto Church on the State, cleanse the processes of education, give women suffrage, make labor free. There is wrecking aplenty, but this is a feudal land, and no democracy can rise here until the old structure is demolished.

Ed Pauley, the California oil man who heads the U.S. Reparations Mission, today issued a long statement indicating that the physical disarmament of Japan will keep pace with the rebuilding of spirit and institution. There was one striking passage: "Because Japan surrendered without a last-ditch stand, many people have assumed that she is now helpless industrially. The superficial appearance of many bombed cities encourages this easy view. The fact is that Japan's industrial equipment was overwhelmingly designed for war. *Despite all the destruction, Japan still retains in workable condition more plant and equipment than its rulers ever allowed to be used for civilian supply and consumption even in peaceful years.* That surplus must be taken out."

Pauley gave one illustration: In steel, machine tools, and other machinery made of steel, Japan still has in workable condition more than double the facilities she had on the day she invaded Manchuria fourteen years ago.

Pauley recommended that the following industrial potential be removed from Japan, and apportioned among the victors— and the victims—: half the capacity for making machine tools; between 350,000 and 400,000 machine tools; the equipment of 20 shipyards, and all steel capacity in excess of 2,500,000 tons (Japan still has an eleven-million-ton capacity, compared to 2,300,000 in 1930).

It will be interesting to watch the scramble that develops for this industrial wealth. I shall also be curious to see what the Air Force will say to Pauley's claim that most of Japan's industrial plant had survived the pounding from the air. The Air Force boys are very sensitive.

At noon, walking from the Diet, I was picked up by a major in a jeep. He said he was Graf Boepple, a former advertising man, who was now working with the Civil Information and Education Section. His special job was to prepare a series of broadcasts, "Now It Can Be Told," the first of which will go on the air next Sunday. Before we had gone another mile, he invited me to attend a dress rehearsal.

It was a fantastic show. The incidental music blended tunes from Hollywood's "Gone With the Wind," with the strumming of native *samisen*. The actors, struggling with "March of Time" eccentricities, included professional *geisha*, in gay kimonos and two-story, heavily oiled hairdresses. This was Japanese history, but the taskmasters were American officers, speaking in tones of command.

The broadcast was opened by a Japanese narrator. "We, the people of Japan," he said in the best dramatic voice of the American radio, "know now who was responsible for the crimes committed against us."

"Who? Who are they?" other voices asked.

"Give me time," said the narrator. "I'll tell you. I'll give you some of their names. Above all, I'll give you the facts so you can draw your own conclusions."

With these words, the narrator moved into the case history of Japanese aggression. He told of the devices used by the army to usurp power, of the suppression of free speech, of the 59,000 persons arrested between 1933 and 1936 for dangerous thought. In flashback technique, the broadcast reminded the Japanese people of police terror. In ten easy lessons, it would tell the people the whole unsavory story of Japanese aggression, beginning with the conquest of Manchuria.

The only thing that disturbed me in the broadcasts, as well as in the series of twenty newspaper articles starting tomorrow, was their politics. They described the timid Premier Kijuro Shidehara as a courageous foe of militarism; they concentrated their fire mainly on men of the sword, to the exclusion of such obvious war criminals as the emperor or the heads of the super-trusts; they naïvely interpreted, or even distorted, some of the recent Japanese history.

This is a time when accents and omissions are almost as important as plain words of command, for the Japanese seek eagerly for hints of what and whom we dislike, and what we would like to see in a new Japan.

Later, I watched a sergeant trying to make a date with one of the *geisha*.

"Hello, baby," he said with a broad smile. "How's about you and me stepping out tonight?"

The *geisha* smiled back, and walked past him. "That's the way it is," said the sergeant. "Every day the same thing. They look bright, but they don't understand nothing."

A Japanese newspaper editor who now works for me as a tipster told me of two signs of the new democracy: the 70,000 policemen in Japan will have their swords replaced with night sticks; the image of the emperor in the schools from now on will show him as a civilian and not as a military man.

The editor also brought me a copy of a secret report submitted by Prince Konoye to the emperor seven weeks before the attack on Pearl Harbor. The 5,000-word report, which forecast war with the United States, until now has rested in the palace vault. It will appear serially in a Tokyo daily in two days, in a subtle move by Konoye to save his skin by representing himself as an implacable foe of the army.

The report blamed the military for sabotaging Konoye's

effort to reach an understanding with the United States. A prefatory note also will berate those who assailed Konoye as a pacifist during the war, and now clamor for his arrest as a warmonger.

In his country estate, Konoye must feel like a trapped fox. As a historic figure, he cannot allow himself to be arrested as a war criminal, and yet his nimble mind can find no way out. The time is running short. Konoye has only nine days of freedom left.

In the club lobby tonight, while reading translations of Japanese newspapers, I suddenly realized that this was the fourth anniversary of "a date which will live in infamy." I mentioned it to my neighbors, and discovered few of them had remembered it.

The newspaper *Yomiuri* said editorially: "The present pitiful predicament of the nation began on this day four years ago. Cursed is this date."

December 8, 1945   TOKYO

In the morning, went up to the Diet building to see what defeat has done to Japan's lawmakers. The huge, gray structure, towering over the city, has escaped damage, but the years of war have been unkind to it. The building was cold and run-down, the plush looked tired, and there was a musty smell of an old attic. In a large, dark committee room, two-score old men, who resembled undertakers in their black suits and stiff collars, were discussing the proposed Constitution. The speakers droned on, and most of the listeners looked as if they were asleep.

I watched the men below me, and wondered at the whole affair. These, I tried to remind myself, were the rulers of a beaten nation which had promised to become a democracy, and this was the fourth month of defeat. Was it ignorance or supreme insolence that spoke through their mouths?

Here was Dr. Joji Matsumoto, a member of the cabinet, a prosperous *zaibatsu* lawyer, and the principal drafter of the new, democratic Constitution. He was saying:

"Democratic government is said to be government based on the will of the people. But government *by* the people who happen to be in the majority tends to impair popular liberties and rights. There is a need of a government *for* the people."

Here was Premier Shidehara himself, a plump and feeble septuagenarian. "Democracy," he said, "is a government based on and reflecting public opinion. In the United States, it is known as a government of the people, for the people, and by the people. In Japan, the government must be run under his Imperial Majesty, and around the Diet which reflects the will of the masses."

I looked at my official guide out of a corner of my eye. He caught my glance. "Very instructing," he said with conviction. "Very much democracy. Japan very happy."

After lunch, Lauterbach, Darrell Berrigan of the New York *Post*, and I drove out to what is bound to be a historic event—the first large postwar rally of the Communist party. When the U.S. Army opened the jail doors four weeks ago, some 150 Communists walked out as free men. Today, the party claims 1,200 members, but its paper, the *Red Flag*, has a circulation of 19,000 copies, and its sympathizers, especially in the transport and coal miners' unions, are estimated at 100,000. No one doubts that the Communist movement will grow tremendously in the months to come. The land is in agony and frustration, and the moment favors men with extreme solutions.

There were a few white Military Police jeeps in front of Kyoritsu Hall, where the meeting was being held. In the lobby, some Counter Intelligence agents were questioning the youths selling Communist papers. The meeting had not yet started, but the huge, dark hall was packed to the rafters. The audience was of a pattern—male, middle-aged, poorly dressed. It hummed with impatience.

In a dressing room behind the stage we found Yoshio Shiga, one of the party's top leaders and editor of the *Red*

Flag. He was a slim, handsome man, with a high forehead, a Roman nose, and a smile that could not quite decide whether to be sardonic or kindly. Under his coat, he wore a homemade sweater.

There were two things that interested us in Shiga—the man and the program. Life among the communist Old Guard ran to a common mold. If we knew something about Shiga, we would understand other leaders better.

Shiga said he was born in Moji, in 1901. He was one of nine children of a seafaring and Buddhist captain. His first revolutionary landmark came in 1918, when he took part in the famous Moji rice riots.

In 1923, while studying sociology at Tokyo Imperial University, he joined the Communist party. For the next five years, he helped to organize Communist "cells," became a member of the party's Central Committee, and edited a magazine called *Marxism.* He earned a very meager living by writing for leftist publications.

Shiga spoke in a clear, loud, happy voice, and when he felt the interpreter was not doing him justice, he made corrections in fair English. ("I learned it from a missionary named Dr. Daniel C. Buchanan, who is now in Washington, D.C.") He gave an impression of energy, alertness, and a thorough knowledge of the Marxist jargon.

"I was once married," he said. "My wife was arrested together with me. But she had no courage. One day in 1933, under torture, she renounced communism. I could not forgive her. That day I gave up my wife."

The police, he said, tried other means to break his spirit. "I'm deaf in one ear." He pointed. "The jailers used to slap me on this side, until I lost my hearing. My eyes are bad from malnutrition. But the reactionaries failed. I've spent seventeen years in jail. I've come out alive."

Shiga listed for us the main points of the Communist program. It ranged from the establishment of a republican government and the affirmation of all civil liberties, including "the right to strike and to hold street demonstrations," to the dissolution of the *zaibatsu,* the encouragement of medium and small businesses, and the confiscation of land held by "parasitical absentee owners, including the emperor."

Shiga talked the universal language of revolution. But all of us thought that for a man who had spent seventeen years in solitary, who had lost his wife, who had been slapped into deafness, he was amazingly restrained.

We saw Shiga in a more fiery mood on the stage. By now the audience had had three hours of speech-making. But the climax—the indictment of the war criminals—was yet to come, and Shiga was to deliver it. He stood behind the pulpit, gripping it with both hands, and watched the applauding thousands below.

"The time has come," he cried, "to name those guilty; to list the men who brought Japan to ruin, who made her a place of terror and oppression. Our list is long. It has 1,300 names. There are 357 members of the Lower House, who voted as their task-masters ruled. There are 165 members of the Upper Chamber. There are 168 murderers and ruffians, who masked their crimes with patriotism. There are 130 generals and admirals; 86 men of the *zaibatsu*, who made war pay profits; 114 leaders of the so-called labor unions, formed to do the army's bidding. There are 70 journalists and 50 scholars who betrayed science and journalism. There are 23 officials of the Court."

He listed some of the names—the one-eyed Admiral Kichisaburo Nomura and the diplomat Saburo Kurusu, who helped to lull us in Washington while the navy prepared for its attack on Pearl Harbor; Shidehara, who was now premier; Tsuneo Matsudaira, who served as ambassador to England and who has come back to stand next to the emperor's ear. The crowd cheered and shouted after these names.

"We must add more names to the list," said Shiga. "We want to put on it all the adult members of the imperial family. Including Empress Nagako. She led Japan's womanhood on the path of reaction and feudalism. She is a symbol—a symbol of the half-slave status of our women. But not including Prince Yamashina. He is crazy."

The crowd laughed. Shiga waited. The silence spread and grew taut.

"We now come to the last name—the name of the emperor . . . "

The crowd cheered and shouted and stamped its feet. The whole cavernous darkness of the hall was now filled with sound and with fury, and they beat against the stage and the thin figure behind the pulpit.

I caught Shiga again, on a rebound from the hall. He was tense and excited. I wanted him to tell me more about his life in prison.

"The jail was not too bad," he said. "News was smuggled in from the outside, and we directed the Communist movement from prison. We had one easy technique of communication. The prison authorities allowed us to get books from the outside on a narrow range of subjects. My subject was the imperial system." He laughed. "Today I'm the greatest expert in Japan on the emperor.

"My friends were sending books on the imperial system to me, and on the margins, in starch, they wrote reports or requested instructions. We then pretended we had hurt ourselves, and asked the infirmary for iodine. We used the iodine to bring out the starch writing. Then, when we had to return the books, we did two things. We urinated on the books, to dissolve the iodine, and we used a flour paste for writing our own messages. Very simple.

"When Tokuda (Kyuichi Tokuda, the party's ranking leader), who was in the opposite wing of the prison, and I wanted to communicate with each other, we used mirrors and the Morse code. There was a Communist in a cell below me, and I used to tap messages to him. Once, when the text of the new Stalin Constitution was smuggled in to me, I tapped for three days steadily until I passed on the entire text. It was the hardest job I've ever done.

"Many of the guards were very bad. But we talked to them, and some of them were converted. So many had become our friends that the prison authorities had to change the guards frequently. But even that did not help. The guards had to take examinations a couple of times a year, and I tutored some of them in mathematics. In exchange for that, they brought in messages, or gave me food.

"When the prison authorities wanted to punish us, they put a leather belt on us and handcuffed our arms to it, so that our arms remained crooked for two and three days at a time. But, on the other hand, we were put on the Prison Grievance Committee, and we were able to do a lot of good.

"When we were finally released on October 10, all of us had accumulated so much property in jail, we had to bring seven trucks to cart it off. We even had a sewing machine."

The last touch struck me as being a bit fanciful. "Is that a fact?" I said. Shiga looked surprised. "Of course, it's a fact. You, Americans, facts, facts, facts . . . "

December 9, 1945   TOKYO

In the morning, moved from the ballroom down to a room on the second floor. There are four of us sharing it, and my corner does not even have an electric light. Yet, I am happy. My standards of comfort are certainly changing.

Spent the day in a variety of places, from Headquarters to the bustling black market behind the Shimbashi Railway Station. Later, I marvelled at the range of the accumulated hodge-podge in my notebook.

Sardines are a dozen for Y.10, or 66 cents. So are small oranges. A second-hand suit of ersatz cloth costs $80. Ten yen is a day's salary for many a good man nowadays.

Conductors are having difficulty with men who smoke in street cars, despite "No Smoking" signs. The men say, "Do we have democracy, or don't we?"

With just a few days left in this session, the lame-duck Diet is continuing to sabotage the three major pieces of legislation before it—compulsory sale to the government of all land in excess of twelve acres per owner, legalization of labor unions, and a revised election law. The latter has been revised so skillfully that only the familiar names of old-time politicians are likely to find a place on the ballots in the next election.

While these three bills are being kicked around, the Diet is engaged in a vigorous debate. The subject: Is the emperor a God? The premier's answer: "He is not a god in the western conception of the word, and yet he is not human."

Men in the Government Section tell me General MacArthur is about to crack down on the Japanese government, but meanwhile precious time is being wasted.

The Japanese Government has sent out a trial balloon, and now it is waiting for the American reaction. It has set the date of Japan's first postwar elections for January 20, 1946. Elections, of course, are a democratic procedure, but it is doubtful if this particular election will prove anything except that the old political machines are supremely strong. The politicians may live in constant fear of arrest. But most machines are impersonal. If one candidate is arrested, another can be found to run in his stead. Democratic forces need years, not months, to grow in the parched Japanese soil. It is naïve, at this early hour, to expect them to have a strong leadership or the political organization required by modern elections. Five months will have done little to root out old fears and habits. All this is precisely what the Japanese government is counting on in insisting on a prompt election.

At the same time, the old-timers are crawling out of obscurity with growing boldness. The only change is in the slogans. The rabid nationalists of yesterday are today's champions of democracy—"Japanese style."

The other morning, early risers were greeted by posters announcing the formation of a new political party, the *Tenguto*. Translated loosely as the "League of the Long-Nosed Goblins," *Tenguto* is named after the legendary characters who taught swordsmanship to *samurai*. But Japanese friends tell me *Tenguto* is amusing in its name alone. It is an offshoot of the murderous ultranationalist bands once dominated by the Black Dragon Society. The posters said the new party will fight for "absolute support of the imperial system by the common man," through "justice enforced by strong-arm men."

This is not an isolated case, but part of a rash spreading over Japan. A Japanese informant today gave me a list of thirty-eight new political parties. Some of them are legitimate. But most have nothing to do with democracy. Something called The Emperor's Self-Governing Subjects. The Japan Renovation Party, the Great Japan Revolutionary Party, the Great Japan State-Socialist Party. The Judicial Japanese Masses, the Japanese People's Cause. All high-sounding titles, and behind them some of the most sordid figures of the ultranationalist movement.

Here, for instance, is the Japan's Working Masses Party. Its president is head of the defunct Tokyo Munitions Company, Ltd., and its real brain is a former official of the Black Dragon Society. The party is well organized, with such sections as Cultural, Diplomatic and Women's. It has a "defense corps," headed by a former naval officer. It has a Funds Section, staffed with officials of various financial and industrial firms. Recently, the party advertised for members. Nearly 2,500 men replied, and 300 of them are now dues-paying members. But the party is run by a handful of nationalists, ex-servicemen, and businessmen. The party's constitution states flatly, "The emperor is the source of all," and "Let the universe be a simple house ruled by the emperor."

I am constantly amazed by the uses to which the admirable machinery of democracy can be adapted by scoundrels.

But, of course, not all the parties are fraudulent. There are four major parties which will hold the front of the stage in the coming election. A State Department expert today briefed me on them.

The biggest party is the Progressive, whose backbone consists of 270 members of the so-called "Tojo Diet." This party speaks for big business, wealthy landlords, and bureaucrats who, only a few months ago, happily worked with the Japanese Army. It is a party of fear and guilty conscience. Nearly two score of its members already have been branded by General MacArthur as war criminals. Others live in dread of arrest.

Next in line is the Liberal party, which is as illiberal as the Progressive party is unprogressive. The only difference between the two is that the liberals won their Diet seats without an official endorsement from Tojo's iniquitous Imperial Rule Assistance Association. The real driving force behind the party is the 72-year-old Ichiro Hatoyama, whose platform rests solidly on two planks—war on communism and support of the emperor. Under attack as a Fascist, Hatoyama last week explained that he both (a) spent the war years farming and (b) has done "more than any other man to bring the war to an end."

The third largest is the six-weeks-old Social Democratic party, born of a wedding of small prewar leftist parties. The marriage is unhappy, and there is constant squabbling among its various factions, from near-Communist to near-Fascist. For the moment, however, this is a party of intellectuals. Last week, the students of two Tokyo universities picked it as "the party I'd want to succeed." It is also the only one of the big parties with a rational program for Japan's revival, based on land reform and the nationalization of key industries. Right now, the biggest bone of contention is the imperial system, with most of the factions favoring the emperor's retention.

The Communist party is the smallest and the most aggressive. Only 300 strong seven weeks ago, the party hopes to have 10,000 by election day. Its main problem today is the training of organizers, most of whom were killed off by the police. The only Communist "cell" that remained active through the war was in Osaka, where a few-score Communists worked in war factories. The party's leader is Tokuda, a 51-year-old native of Okinawa, who has spent a third of his life in jail. He is sick, and one of his hands is deformed from a police beating. The party is waiting for the arrival of Susumu Okano, who fled from Japan nearly fifteen years ago, lived in Moscow, and spent the last years of war in the underground in China. He is now making his way back home across Manchuria and

Korea, and there is much excitement over his imminent return. Curiously enough, the excitement has infected even the foes of the communists. The Social Democrats are planning a welcome for him.

December 10, 1945   TOKYO

In the morning, walked over to the Japanese Liaison Office, through which our orders are funneled to the government. Went up in an elevator, and discovered that, for the sake of economy, electric lights bulbs have been removed. It was an eerie feeling to be riding an elevator so dark I could not see my hand before my face. But the offices were not much brighter. There were a few lights which, like magnets, drew the people towards them. Everyone was working in an overcoat. After four years of war, and seven of rationing, very few people have warm clothes left, and they go around in December bundled up in their spring topcoats, worn over all their available clothing.

While being introduced to someone, I realized, with a start, that the only warm hands I have shaken thus far in Japan belonged to Americans. The Japanese do not have much of a chance to thaw out, and their hands are cold and red.

Heard of the first instance in which American Military Police have broken up a Japanese demonstration. The incident occurred two days ago at Matsuyama, in Japan's extreme south. A crowd of 1,000 Japanese gathered in front of the City Hall to protest inequities in the distribution of food and clothing. As some offices of the U.S. 24th Division were housed in the building, it was decided that the demonstration was interfering with their work. Military Police were called out, and quickly dispersed the crowd. Apparently as an afterthought, the divisional headquarters announced that the U.S. Army had "not entered the dispute." The mayor of Matsuyama admitted the inequities, and said that in the future the destitute will have a priority on the supplies.

General MacArthur today ordered the government to have a genuine land reform law ready by March 15th next. To make sure that the government and the Diet cease their deliberate dillydallying, the directive outlined the problem, and then set down some of the remedies.

The directive has had an interesting career. Originally, the job of drafting it was assigned to the Natural Resources Section in Headquarters. But the section's experts were professional agronomists and geologists, who refused to get hot under the collar over social reform. The crucial order was bandied around until, late last month, Brigadier General Ken Dyke, Chief of the Civil Information and Education Section, was delegated to do the job. He passed it down to his own Plans and Operations Division, headed by an able ex-newspaperman, Captain Arthur Behrstock. According to rumor, Behrstock and his assistant, a former radio writer, Captain Bernard Fisher, received very simple instructions from Dyke, a former advertising man: "boil it down," and "keep it quotable for the press." The boys minded their order. Like virtually all other MacArthur directives, this one was filled with quotable clichés, such as "the dignity of man," "centuries of feudal oppression," "economic bondage," and "fruits of their labor." The officers who drew it, however, knew that these clichés would have an explosive effect on the Japanese.

The directive was finished in a week. It next went to General MacArthur, who two days later called Dyke in and said it was the best staff study and directive he had seen. And though there was not a single man in Dyke's section, including the two authors of the directive, who knew anything about Japanese agriculture, Dyke was given a large share in the administration of the land reform. But the errors, the clichés, and the rich prose were unimportant. What was important was that behind them lay the lean body of a revolutionary change.

The directive first outlined the premise:

More than three-fourths of Japan's farmers are partially

or wholly sharecroppers, paying half or more of their crop to the landlords;

Nearly half the farm households in Japan till less than one and a half acres each;

Less than half the farmers manage to make ends meet, once they pay the interest on their debts.

Against this picture of rural distress, the directive ordered the Japanese government to write a land reform into its law books. Under this law, the government would purchase all land in excess of a relatively small acreage per household, for resale to sharecroppers at reasonable prices.

The directive produced a shock in the Diet, where the old-timers thought they could get away with the mild law drafted by the Japanese Ministry of Agriculture, then emasculated by the Cabinet, and then ripped into shreds by the Diet.

The Japanese people apparently hear a little of what is going on. The other day a delegation of farmers appeared on the doorsteps of Prince Higashikuni's house, deposited gifts of fertilizer, goats, and rice, and asked the prince to see to it that the emperor stopped the Diet's sabotage of land reform. The prince accepted the gifts, fertilizer and all, and said he would see what he could do.

This is a strange time and place. I filed my story on the land reform directive, and felt exhilarated by the sense of being on the sidelines of history. Then I went back to the Press Club, and was equally exhilarated by being able to find a lamp for my corner. Now at least I shall be able to read at night.

After dinner, Berrigan and I began to work on the itinerary of a two-week trip we want to take into the country to the north. Decided to start the journey at Sendai, 220 miles north of here, where Brigadier General Frank "Pinky" Dorn is in temporary command of the 11th Airborne Division. "Pinky" has served in China, where both Berrigan and I have worked, and we count greatly on his help.

The first strikes are breaking out. None of us doubts that there will be a rash of them, for Japan is headed for a post-defeat slump in which labor will be one of the main sufferers.

This morning went to a suburban railway station to talk to men who are going on strike later today. The line is owned by the Kawasaki family, one of the great *zaibatsu* earmarked by us for destruction. With an interpreter I walked down an endless subterranean passage, much like the subway tunnels in New York, even if there were no tiles here and the dirty walls sweated muddy drops. We finally reached the station, to discover that the strike was already on.

A little old man was at the turnstile, waving his arm to the waiting passengers, and saying, "Come on in. It is free today. We are working for the people today, and not for the Kawasakis."

We told him we wanted to talk to the strike leaders, and he readily abandoned his post and took us down the gloomy, dark platform to the switch house. The office was small, cluttered with instruments and aged furniture, and heated by a small charcoal *hibachi* (brazier). There were two middle-aged men there, both in black railway uniforms. One of the men had straw sandals on, and I noticed that one of his big toes was missing. I passed cigarettes around, and told them the American people wanted to hear of the strike.

I soon realized that if the Americans were not particularly interested in Japanese strikes in general, they might well be interested in this one. It had a novel twist. The strikers had not quit work. The trains were still running on schedule. The only thing that happened was that the workers were giving the commuters free rides. The Kawasakis did not feel like appealing to the police for help, for they themselves were not too sure they would not be hauled off to prison as war criminals. The police did nothing on their own, for they were worried that General MacArthur might not like a display of old-fashioned roughing-up.

The men had a clear idea of their grievances.

"You know how much we're earning?" said the toeless man. "Our wage scale ranges from 80 sen to Y.2.40 (6 to 16 cents) a day. We also get allowances and bonuses that about equal our salary. But even then, what can you do on five yen (33 cents) a day?"

"I've been with the company for fourteen years," said the old man. "I get Y.1.80 (12 cents) a day, and 5 yen a month for each of my nine children. I couldn't keep my family alive on this were it not for my little garden. I sell the vegetables in the black market, and that keeps us going."

"You see my sandals?" asked the toeless man. "It cost me four days' salary. And I can't even think of buying clothes for my children. We're asking for a five-fold raise in our salary. It sounds like a lot, but it isn't. The prices have increased much, much more than that. And yet, the Kawasakis never missed their 8 per cent dividend from this railway."

They sat and smoked my cigarettes. There was a faraway look in their eyes.

"We'll fight until we win," said the toeless man. "Back in 1926, we tried to form a union, but the police quickly broke it up. The same thing happened in 1930. We were so afraid we didn't try again. Until a week ago. Now General MacArthur says we can have a union, and we'll have a strong one."

I left them a few cigarettes, and walked back to the turnstile. There was a small crowd of passengers just outside of it, standing in obvious indecision. I asked a woman with a small boy why she didn't go in. She said in a low, frightened voice:

"They say I don't have to pay. I don't understand how that can be. The police won't like it."

While the railroad workers were beginning their "ride-free" strike, another unusual strike was being settled elsewhere in Tokyo. This was the 90-day dispute on the *Yomiuri*, Tokyo's largest daily, which through the years of aggression and war spoke with the army's harsh voice. The owner and publisher of the *Yomiuri* was a chauvinist and former Tokyo police chief, Matsutaro Shoriki.

Eleven days after Japan's surrender, some fifty staff members, including seven editorial writers, presented Shoriki with a memorandum which must have sent his blood pressure soaring. The staff wanted a "democratization" of the paper, the dismissal of the editors responsible for the *Yomiuri's* jingoism, and improved working conditions.

Shoriki promised to "democratize" his paper, but rejected the other demands. The editorial writers were warned to make no reference to Court or *zaibatsu* officials as war criminals. At one meeting, Shoriki himself denounced an assistant editor for a news story dealing with the breaking up of the *zaibatsu*. When two American correspondents interviewed the emperor, the *Yomiuri* news editors were ordered to carry no word of the interviews which might have seemed to doubt the emperor's divinity.

Two months ago, the dissidents took their next step. They formed a "Society for the Study of Democracy," and sent word of it to Shoriki. The following day, Shoriki announced that anyone who joined in this "cowardly tactic" would be fired. He also declared that the paper was his, and he was free to close it down, or publish it in any form he desired.

In writing the story of the dispute, I realized that it could not be explained in terms of American normalcy. Some day I myself hoped to publish a paper in some small town, and I knew that like Shoriki I would resist any efforts to tell me what I could, or could not, write in my paper. But in this dispute, as in so many other events in Japan, the normal yardstick was useless. For one thing, we had come to Japan with the conscious purpose of extensive social wrecking, so that a democracy could rise on the ruins. For another, the *Yomiuri* was one of the principal mouthpieces of warlike Japan. We certainly could not allow the concept of an inviolate private property to stop us from changing the tone and nature of the paper. The employees who bearded Shoriki in his own building were our allies.

Eighteen days ago, the employees held a mass meeting, decided to form a union, and sent a counterdemand to Shoriki: "In view of your role in the war, resign immediately, with all your assistants." In a fantastic display of self-confidence, the group gave Shoriki twenty-four hours to make up his mind.

He did. He fired five of the ringleaders. Another rally was then held, the union was formally inaugurated, and it announced that it was "in a state of war" with Shoriki.

Shoriki appealed to the government, and it summoned nine leaders of the union for five days of questioning. But by this time, the conflict on the *Yomiuri* had become a symbol. This was the old order fighting the new one, a struggle between entrenched nationalism and democracy. Employees of other newspapers began to hold mass meetings. Union workers came to demonstrate before the fire-gutted *Yomiuri* building. Public opinion turned against Shoriki.

The final decision came from the outside. General MacArthur's Headquarters looked into Shoriki's record, shuddered, and ordered his arrest as a suspected war criminal. After that Shoriki gave in. Yesterday he agreed to resign as president, and dispose of 30 per cent of his stock. Tsunego Baba, a tall, cadaverous-looking essayist regarded as a liberal, was nominated by Shoriki as publisher. Tomin Suzuki, leader of the dissidents, became editor. A committee, on which the union was represented, was set up to guide the daily, and to improve working conditions.

Delighted officers in Headquarters told me this was the first recorded case of collective bargaining agreement. I was interested even more in the fact that for weeks the daily has been run not by its owner, but by the employees. The circulation has gone up tremendously, to reach nearly 1,700,000 copies daily.

Shoriki, incidentally, just made it. He is to enter prison tomorrow.

December 12, 1945   TOKYO

Early in the afternoon, Lauterbach, Alfred Eisenstaedt of *Life*, and I went to the Imperial Theater to see a modern French play, *Toulon*. The Imperial must have been resplendent two or three generations back. Now it is run down and unheated, and the audience sits huddled in overcoats and scarves.

Toulon is remarkable for its career if for nothing else. Its theme is the scuttling of the French fleet in 1942, and its author is a Frenchman, Jean Richard Block. It was written in 1944 in the Hotel Metropole in Moscow, smuggled to Tokyo by a Japanese correspondent, and translated into Japanese for presentation here. The producer padded the French patriotic play with angry allusions to the Japanese militarists. The revolutionary speeches were made doubly piquant by the fact that both General MacArthur and the emperor are virtually within shouting distance of the stage.

Most of the actors wore red wigs. That, and the breath billowing like steam every time the players opened their mouths, provided serious distractions. The hero of the play was an old French admiral, torn between his loyalty to Petain and Laval and his hatred for the enemy. His daughter, a breasty young woman in a red wig, kept dashing on and off the stage, to deliver her lines in a high, shrill voice. French navy orderlies came in, received curt orders, and retired with a *sodesu* or "that's so." Every few minutes the telephone rang, and the admiral grabbed the receiver, and said *mashi-mashi, mashi-mashi* (hello, hello). There was much scurrying about the stage, wild gesturing, and patriotic speeches, delivered to the accompaniment of explosions off stage.

The play ended with the fleet sinking, and the admiral, his daughter, and sundry other citizens gathering in the hills to organize a Maquis unit. But, to me, the climax came a little earlier, when the admiral finally made up his mind to scuttle the ships. He made a speech, stuck one arm out in the classical manner of a departing ham actor, and rushed out. On his lips was the traditional cry of French admirals going to their death: *Banzai! Banzai!*

Whatever my own reactions, *Toulon* impressed the audience. To them, this was obviously a message and a symbol—a message of the revolutionary changes already wrought, and those yet to come. I watched a young student a row ahead of me. He barely breathed, and his tensed body looked as if it was about to leap out of his seat. This was probably the first open, dramatic attack on the old order he had heard, and he was taking in every word of it.

But the wrong of the play was also plain. Suddenly I knew of what the actors and their shrill speeches reminded me. They were presenting this drama of violent social conflict as if it was a traditional play dealing with gods, demons, and *samurai*. Beneath their red wigs and French uniforms, they were still *kabuki* (classical drama) players, with the centuries of training in speech and gesture behind them. The Japanese theater will have to develop a new tradition before it can tackle themes of social stress.

After the theater went to the secondhand book stalls in Kanda ward. The shelves are still filled with the literature and philosophy of chauvinism—textbooks on nationalist ethics, discourses on Japan's "mission," treatises on the emperor's divinity. But there is already a new crop of books by American and European authors, and they are snapped up by the buyers. A dealer told me one university has just "found" some five hundred books on Marxist philosophy and liberal thought which the Japanese government ordered destroyed early in the war. The university cannily hid them in a basement. I am also told that General MacArthur's Headquarters is swamped with applications for permission to translate American works. Among them are Owen Lattimore's *Solution for Asia* and Joseph Clark Grew's *Japan Diary*. But the list is topped by that classic, *Gone with the Wind*. The best comment on it is supplied by the *Nippon Times*. Declaring that what Japan needs most is factual books on the workings of democracy, the Times adds acidly:

"Scarlett O'Hara can wait. Why should the Japanese worry about Scarlett having nothing to eat but sweet potatoes and about the black market prices in Atlanta? The average Japanese can tell a better story about such matters from his own experience."

Got my first batch of letters from Sally.

Also a wire from General "Pinky" Dorn, welcoming Berrigan and me to Sendai.

I have known all along that Japan's rice harvest this season was poor. I did not know how poor until I talked to Major W. H. Leonard this morning. Leonard is a trained agronomist from the Middle West, slow and cautious.

"How bad?" he said. "I'll tell you how bad. Last week, Kyoto was down to 3.3 days' supply of food. Tokyo was down to four days' supply. We figure we'll get along through February. But March 15 is our danger point. After we reach it, we can expect rice riots. Our troops might be jeopardized. We're taking secret precautions."

Leonard is using Japanese official statistics, which show the harvest at 215 million bushels, instead of the average 300 millions. Japan's surplus belt lies to the north of Tokyo, in the area Berrigan and I are planning to tour later this month. This is the granary that feeds the cities. But this year, the rice belt has had all kinds of trouble, from floods to frosts. Things are made worse by the concealment of surplus rice. A shrewd farmer refuses to surrender his rice to the government for Y.30 ($2) a bushel, for he can sell it in the black market for five and ten times that much. Thus, the farmers are in cahoots with local officials to misreport the anticipated yield, and as the false estimates multiply, the cumulative error for the nation becomes staggering.

There is also a sharp argument on how much food a man needs to survive. The Japanese say an average person requires a minimum of 2,160 calories a day. By February, they claim, the ration actually will be down to 1,325 calories. Headquarters thinks the Japanese are deliberately alarmist, and predicts that the average man will continue to get 1,800 calories. The Japanese are pleading for the import of 3,400,000 metric tons of cereals. General MacArthur has tentatively approved three millions.

I want to know if the land reform, just ordered by General MacArthur, will affect the picture.

The major snorts. "Land reform indeed! All it's doing is obstructing the difficult job we experts are trying to do here. The best mission you, as a newspaperman, can perform is to tell the people back home to stop these ill-considered reforms. You can't, and shouldn't, change a system that has survived a thousand years of trial."

December 15, 1945   TOKYO

Today saw another milestone passed in Japan's postwar transformation. The event was the directive separating the Shinto religion from the State. The news was given to us by General Dyke a bare two hours after the directive was handed to the Japanese government.

We sat in the conference room, and I think the same idea was in all our minds: If the Japanese are to rebel against the drastic changes being mapped out for them, this is the test. If they do not rebel when the base is being knocked out from under their religion, they will not rebel at all.

Shintoism is the religious man's weirdest invention—a belief in the emperor's divinity and in the "mission" of the Japanese people to rule the world; a faith based on mythology and embracing a minimum of eight million deities headed by the Sun Goddess Amaterasu, from whom the emperor has descended; a religion of ancestral worship, filial piety, patriotism, and of some watered-down Confucian virtues which would ensure loyalty and obedience to the state.

In discard for centuries, the religion was revised when Emperor Meiji came to power in 1867. It was done deliberately and shrewdly. The makers of modern Japan needed a handy political instrument, and Shintoism supplied it. Shinto priests were brought under government control, a new ritual was drawn up by the government, school children were required to visit shrines, and money was granted for the bread and *décor* of the new state religion.

As Japan's nationalism grew, Shintoism became its handmaiden. It was useful to soak the little man's mind in the belief that he himself was semidivine, that gods expected him to rule the world, and that the path to greatness lay in loyalty and obedience. As more men died in Japan's wars, they joined the expanding list of deities, and with undiminished ingenuity, mediaeval ritual was adapted to the uses of modern aggression.

By the outbreak of the war, Shintoism had become a tremendous power, with 300 national shrines (including the 13,000-acre Ise Shrine to which the emperor repaired to commune with the spirit of his ancestress, Goddess Amaterasu), 129 special soldiers' shrines, 50,000 provincial and local shrines, and 60,000 private shrines. It made one shudder to think of the money and effort that went into Shintoism.

Now General Dyke, a slim, handsome, earnest man, sat here calmly and talked of liberating the people from a religion which "has contributed to their war guilt, defeat, suffering, privation, and the present deplorable condition," and of the "masterly job of promotion" done by the men who put Shintoism to the uses of nationalism. And by his side sat an equally slim and earnest man, Lieutenant William K. Bunce, U.S.N., who drafted the directive and who used to be dean of Otterbein College in Westerville, Ohio. I watched them and wondered if five years ago either one of them could have dreamt that he would celebrate the Christmas of 1946 by wrecking an ancient religion.

Opening with the explanation that it meant to free the Japanese people from the need to believe in a religion designated by the State, the directive ordered:

1. End of the doctrine holding that the emperor, or the people, or the islands of Japan, are superior to all others;

2. Closure of publicly supported schools teaching Shintoism;

3. Removal of all god-shelves and other Shinto symbols from all offices, schools, and public buildings;

4. Cessation of formal visits to Shinto shrines by officials "to report" various events of note.

So far so good. But as Dyke and Bunce finished, doubt began to creep into our minds. The cornerstone of Shintoism is the belief in the emperor's divinity. Will the end of Shintoism also make the emperor human? Dyke said he could not answer "at this time." "The emperor," he said, "is still the spiritual head of Japan." Then this exchange took place between Dyke and me:

"Will the emperor be allowed to make such visits to the Ise Shrine as the one in which he recently reported the end of the war to Goddess Amaterasu?"

"Yes."

"But since *official* visits to shrines are banned, who will be the judge of whether the emperor is paying an official or a private visit?"

"That's a matter for his own mind."

"Will the State officials be allowed to accompany him?"

"Yes, if they travel in their private capacity."

"Will they themselves be judges of whether they are officials or private individuals?"

"Yes."

"Will the press be allowed to report and photograph such visits?"

"Yes."

Shintoism has been dealt a very heavy blow. But I kept wondering if we had not laid a solid foundation for a campaign of sham and let's-pretend, in which things will go on more or less as they always have, with the emperor and his retinue of courtiers, government officials, mayors, village elders, reporters, and photographers traveling to various shrines, and then explaining glibly to us that they were only private individuals, enjoying their right of free religious worship. I also wondered if the farmers, accustomed to seeing the emperor commune with the gods, understood that the emperor was now worshipping not as emperor but as a private individual.

I do not know what the answer is. Certainly, as a free people, we cannot proscribe a religion. But by removing a religion from the public trough, and yet leaving huge loopholes for violations, we stand a fair chance of failure.

December 16, 1945   TOKYO

Last night, a few hours before the deadline for his appearance at Sugamo Prison as a suspected war criminal, Prince Konoye gave a party at his luxurious home in a suburb of Tokyo. Among the guests were some high Court officials and a number of relatives. There was much talk of politics, and of Japan's future. The guests later insisted that Prince Konoye did not seem to be especially distressed by the prospect of entering jail.

Shortly after one o'clock this morning, Konoye retired to his bedroom—a simple Japanese-style room. His bedding was already on the floor. A few minutes later, the prince summoned his second son, the twenty-three-year-old Michitaka, and gave him a long memorandum.

"This note," he said, "will explain the stand I've taken on various problems in the past few years."

The memorandum read: "I have been most deeply concerned over the fact that I have committed certain errors in the handling of State affairs since the outbreak of the China incident [1937]. I cannot, however, endure the humiliation of being arrested and tried by the American court. I cannot but feel especially responsible for the outcome of the China incident. For this reason I tried my best to secure an understanding between the United States and Japan, in the belief that such an understanding alone could solve the China problem.

"It is indeed a matter of great regret that I have been named as a war criminal by the United States with which I wanted and tried to work together for a peaceful settlement of Pacific affairs. I believe my real intentions are even now understood and appreciated by my friends including not a few in the United States."

After Michitaka read the memorandum, Prince Konoye talked to him at length on his, Konoye's, career in politics. Michitaka later said his father made three distinct points:

1. Although he, Konoye, labored hard, he had failed to settle the China affair or bring Japan and the United States together at a "peace conference table" before the war. He said he wished to apologize to the emperor and the people for his failure;

2. Shortly after the Japanese attack on Pearl Harbor, he had written two reports—one on the prewar U.S.–Japanese negotiations and the other on the Tripartite Axis Pact. He hoped the world would judge his record on the basis of these two reports;

3. He had made every effort to protect Japan's "national polity" or structure. Because of their kinship to the imperial family, the Konoyes had a special obligation to safeguard the peculiar political fabric of old Japan.

Michitaka left his father around 2:00 A.M. If he had any misgivings, he admitted none later. At six o'clock this morning, Mrs. Konoye entered her husband's bedroom, and found him dead. Next to him was a low table with a vial of poison on it. She promptly telephoned Prince Konoye's secretary, Tomohiko Ushiba. When Ushiba arrived at six-thirty this morning, the prince's body was still warm.

When the first American investigators arrived later this morning, they were assured no one had expected Konoye to kill himself, though Ushiba did say that "looking back, it's obvious now that Prince Konoye never intended to give himself up to the American authorities." Yet, what little evidence I could find persuades me Konoye's death surprised no one. I am convinced that the men and women who were Konoye's guests last night, sat quietly today and waited for word of his death. I am just as sure that Michitaka, receiving his father's last testament early this morning, knew that he would never see his father alive again.

Later, Americans came and disturbed the family's mourning, and rummaged through the prince's bedroom, study, and the veranda where he kept his English books. Among them was a well-read volume of Oscar Wilde's *De Profundis*, with passages underlined with a red pencil. One read:

"Indeed my ruin came from not too great individualism of life but from too little."

Another said: "Society as we have constituted it will have no place for me, has none to offer; but nature whose sweet rains fall on the unjust and just alike will have clefts in the rocks where I may hide and secret valleys in whose silence I may weep undisturbed."

After a while, family retainers came into the bedroom, replaced Konoye's foreign pajamas with a white ceremonial kimono, and covered the body with a white sheet. At the head of the body, they placed a small table with a cup of "sacred" water. Beyond the table, concealed by a screen, stood an ivory statuette of Kwang Yin, the goddess of mercy.

It was in this same house that the penultimate act of Japan's tragedy was played in the fall of 1941. Both Konoye, who was a central figure, and some of his antagonists have now supplied enough detail to permit a reconstruction of the historic drama.

The theme of the tragedy was the sharp struggle that wracked the ruling group through the summer of 1941. The issue was war. Even today, the knowledge of this conflict is helpful to us in assessing the balance of forces in Japan, past, present and future.

On July 2, 1941, Japan's civilian and military leaders, in the emperor's presence, decided to advance south, even if it meant war with the United States and Great Britain. In making this decision, the conference overrode the views of the foreign minister who wanted to take advantage of the German attack on Russia to invade Siberia.

But the decision did not mean unanimity of view. The army was eager to plunge southward. Its spies worked well, and it knew it would encounter no real opposition. Part of the navy command sided with the army. Its views were put to the emperor by the Chief of the Naval General Staff in these words:

"If things go on as they are, we shall steadily lose the game, but there will be hope of recovery if a drastic operation is undertaken. By that I mean war."

But there was another clique within the navy which opposed the war. It was worried by Japan's lack of oil and other strategic resources. It was concerned with the strength of the U.S. Fleet, and particularly its submarine branch. This faction was led by the Commander-in-Chief of the Japanese Navy, Admiral Isoroku Yamamoto, who later talked so bravely of dictating peace in the White House. Yamamoto told Konoye:

"If I'm told to fight regardless of consequences, I can run wild for the first six to twelve months. But I shall utterly lack confidence if the war goes into its second and third year. . . . I hope you will seek to avoid a war with the United States."

Konoye did not want war with the United States—not yet. He was as intent on Japan's expansion as any of his ultra-nationalist cronies. But he felt it was a mistake to start another war until the conflict in China was ended, and he was not prepared to laugh off American strength. He thought that by playing the army against the navy, he could delay the war. The navy was willing to be used, provided no one accused it of cowardice.

But the generals, led by Tojo, were made of tougher fiber than Konoye. They pounded tables, shouted, and threatened. When necessary, they arranged a border diversion against Russia or China, to force Konoye's hand. They also made full use of the young and murderous fanatics in the army and navy. Through the summer, in the highest counsels of State and Court, there was talk of a "civil war," provoked by the so-called "younger officers' clique," if the government did not embark on new aggression. The generals dropped hints of their inability to control the fanatics. The government leaders lived on a worried diet of rumor and threat, and doubled and quadrupled the number of guards at their homes. Konoye's mettle was unequal to this pressure. He gave in.

On September 6, 1941, at a highly secret imperial conference, Konoye undertook to bring the talks in Washington to a successful end by October 10. If he failed to meet the deadline, the conferees agreed, "Japan would make up her mind to war on the United States and Great Britain."

The deadline came and passed—without a settlement. On October 12, the Ministers of War (Tojo), Navy, and Foreign Affairs met at Konoye's home, to see what he intended to do about his pledge. The Navy Minister cagily withdrew from the debate by declaring the decision was up to Konoye, as premier. The Foreign Minister thought an agreement could be reached with the United States, if Japan agreed in *principle* to withdraw her troops from China. Tojo, blunt and belligerent, kept rejecting all suggestions for a peaceful settlement.

"We can accept no compromises on principle," he said. "After all the sacrifices we've made in China, the army won't agree to any withdrawals. No army morale could survive it."

Konoye pleaded weakly for continuing the talks in Washington. Tojo turned him down. The impasse continued the next night, when the four men resumed the conference.

By the following day, a virtual hysteria gripped the government and the court. Marquis Kido recorded in his diary the fear of an immediate military *coup d'état*. The words "civil war" recurred in the conservations. At the very least, the civilian officials feared that the young fanatics would provoke an international incident that would quickly develop into a full-scale war with the United States. The waves of fear lapped the throne, and that afternoon the emperor summoned Kido and discussed with him the wording of an imperial rescript declaring war on the allied powers. If the hotheads did provoke an incident, the throne would be ready with its blessings.

On October 14, 1941, Konoye—frantic with worry and unable to cope with the army—invited Tojo to his house. They sat in the study and argued, Konoye passionately, Tojo with rising anger. Although the conservation did little to change the course of events, it belongs to history. This, probably, was the turning point of the great controversy.

Konoye began with a reference to Japan's past. When the war with Russia seemed imminent in 1904, he said, the Japanese government sent an envoy to President Theodore Roosevelt, to seek his services as a mediator.

"What hopes do you, General Tojo, have of bringing the war with the United States and Britain to a close once you begin it? This, I believe, is the only point from which our negotiations with America can be considered."

Tojo rejected the argument. "Even if my job depended on it," he said sharply, "I couldn't order the withdrawal of our troops from China. What America wants is hegemony in the Far East. Once we make a concession to her, there's no telling what she will want next."

Konoye pointed to the vast human and material resources of the United States, and argued that because of these, Japanese victory was far from a foregone conclusion.

"There was no certainty of victory in the war on Russia in 1904, or on China," Tojo replied angrily. "There is a large number of people of German descent in America who won't fight against their mother country. Nor can one ignore the possibility of widespread strikes in American war plants once the war starts. The premier of Japan should have enough courage to jump off the veranda of the Kiyomizu temple."*

"If this concerned me alone," said Konoye, "I would not hesitate to jump off the Kiyomizu veranda. But we are considering not the fate of an individual, but of a nation with a history of three thousand years. We cannot go into reckless national adventures as if they were private exploits."

This was the last discussion of policy the two men had. After this night, Tojo refused to see Konoye again. "If I see him," he had said, "I may not be able to control myself."

But in this game, in which Japan's future lay at stake, Tojo was the bolder and the shrewder player. He no longer regarded Konoye as a serious obstacle to his war plans. Now he was ready to tackle a tougher opponent.

Late that afternoon, an emissary was sent to the Secretary of

* Kiyomizu temple, in Kyoto, stands on the edge of a cliff. Proverbially, an ability to make quick decisions.

the Cabinet. "There are rumors," the emissary said, "that the navy doesn't want war. If it comes out openly in favor of a peaceful settlement, the army will bow to its wishes. After all, it's the navy and not the army that would have to fight the United States."

Konoye promptly sent a secretary to one of the navy policy-makers with a plea for a forthright statement against war. The admiral turned down the request. The navy was playing an intricate political game, in which it could not admit cowardice. The best that the admiral could offer was a statement that the navy would abide by the premier's decision.

The same night, a general arrived at Konoye's residence, announced that he was calling in Tojo's behalf, and demanded that Konoye resign. The next afternoon, Konoye rushed to the palace to see his friend and protege, Marquis Kido. Kido refused to interfere. He, too, was playing a game. But Konoye saw the emperor, presented a long and emotional review of the great debate on war and peace, and reported Tojo's demand for a new cabinet. The emperor, who was swinging over to the belief that victory over the United States was possible, offered no comfort.

The following day—October 16, 1941—Konoye resigned. It fell to Kido, the canny and treacherous politician operating behind the throne, to select the new premier. Overriding the views of the Senior Statesmen, he chose Tojo.

Konoye retired to his home, to sulk, to plot revenge with high conspirators and low, and to struggle with his conscience.

Much of what is above has been jotted down by Konoye in his notes, and published in his memoirs. Some has been told by him to his friends, who have been active in the campaign to whitewash him.

But Konoye cannot be whitewashed. I was in Shanghai in the fateful summer of 1937, when the Japanese Army struck at China, and Premier Konoye sanctified the rape with pious statements on justice, sincerity, and Japan's "mission." I was still there in the fall of 1938, when he announced that Japan would join the two Axis powers in establishing "a new order for Asia and the world." This was the time when the moody premier was under the influence of military hotheads, and felt with them that the decadent western world could not halt Japan's progress. However, the mood changed. In 1941, Konoye no longer felt the world could be grasped with impunity.

But this vain and impressionable man, subject to alternate fits of melancholy and exaltation, could not resist the strong men of the army. Together with Japan, Konoye drifted into the war. Even in his last hours, Konoye was no more master of his decisions than he was at the height of his career. He could not stand trial as a criminal because he was an intimate of the throne and a member of a ranking feudal clan. A sentence of hanging against him would have been a sentence against that feudal Japan of which he had for so long been a spokesman.

Nor could Konoye tell the international court the story of Japan's drift to war without incriminating the emperor, and upsetting that "national polity" which he wanted his son to uphold. Truly, I thought, the hand that held the vial of poison was not Konoye's; it was the hand of historic circumstance.

December 17, 1945   TOKYO

In a study in Konoye's house, his son Michitaka and an old friend today worked on a eulogy for the prince's funeral.

As yet, no couriers have come to the family from the Imperial Palace, to bring a message of condolence. The emperor, unsure he would not himself be brought to trial as a war criminal, will not blacken himself by sympathy for a man upon whom for so long he had depended for guidance.

The emperor is not the only one to display callousness. Japan's press and leaders had a field day today heaping abuse on the dead man. Typical is the attitude of the *Asahi*, a leading daily, which, after professing reluctance "to whip Konoye's body," proceeded to do exactly that. "The prince," said the

Asahi, "was not fond of war. His weak character, however, made the advent of war easy. In a government leader, weakness of character is a State crime. Therefore, it is obvious that the prince was a war criminal." The politicians are also doing their best to smear Konoye, in the apparent belief that the blacker they can make him appear, the less guilty they themselves will look.

The peers alone displayed grace on this gray, rainy day. In a special meeting, the Upper House voted to send condolences to Konoye's family.

Keith Wheeler of the Chicago *Times* moved out today, and I inherited his bed, table, bookcase—and window.

December 18, 1945   YOKOHAMA

Drove to Yokohama for the first trial of Japanese war criminals on their native soil. These are not the Class A criminals, who plotted wars and imperial intrigue. These are the small fry of aggression—the soldiers and sergeants who translated the high policy of aggression into acts of individual savagery. There is a force of 200 American lawyers back in Tokyo wading through the mass of evidence, and at least 300 suspects will stand trial here. The purpose of the trials, I am told, is less to punish the guilty than to give the Japanese people an object lesson in the futility of aggression.

I thought it ironic that the stage chosen for this historic tragedy was a shoddy, small courtroom in the Yokohama courthouse, and the principal actor a man who will be known to posterity as "Little Glass Eye."

When I found my seat in the press box, bedlam already reigned in the room. "Little Glass Eye," a small, thin bespectacled man of twenty-eight, sat stiffly in a chair, and all around him milled American photographers, flashing bulbs in his face, and turning him this way and that. The powerful klieg lights were on, casting a ghastly white light on the spotty paint and the rickety furniture. In the back, a thin trickle of Japanese was filing in, to occupy the few seats reserved for the Japanese press and public.

The look of bewilderment on the face of Tatsuo Tsuchiya, alias "Little Glass Eye," deepened when the trial began. He was made to rise, sit down, and rise again. While a translator mumbled in his ear, Tsuchiya stared stonily at the nine army judges.

As evidence was unfolded, doubt vanished that this mild-looking ex-farmer was a sadist, who delighted in inventing cruelties to be inflicted on the prisoners in the camp in which he was a guard. On numerous occasions, he lined up American and British prisoners in two ranks, and ordered them to slap each other until he was bored by the spectacle. In company with other guards, identified as "Mushmouth," "Punk," "Mickey Mouse," and "Rivet Tooth," he beat the prisoners with clubs and knotted ropes, and made them stand naked in the snow. It was in this manner that an Illinois boy by the name of Robert Gordon Teas was murdered before the eyes of his comrades.

But we all felt embarrassed watching the prosecutors handle the case. They were miscast for their historic role. They were handicapped by inability to bring witnesses back from the United States. Their entire case was built on affidavits, some of which would not have passed the scrutiny of a police reporter, let alone a court of justice. The affidavits argued with each other, one picturing Tsuchiya as a five-footer and another making him half a foot taller; one making him a hundred-pounder, another guessing his weight at 165; one placing his glass eye in the left socket, another in the right. There were actually two "glass eyes" at the camp, both equally bad, but I was never sure which of the "glass eyes" was involved. We snickered, but being civilized people, with American ideas of justice, we felt uneasy and ashamed.

The difficulties of the prosecution were compounded by the excellence of the American defense counsel. An amiable Floridian, Lieutenant Colonel John Dickinson, who used to be a county prosecuting attorney, supplied what little gloss the trial had. He knew his law and his courtroom tactics, and as he paced the floor between "Little Glass Eye" and the judges, ripping into the prosecutors' arguments, a touch of drama entered the case. It was not yet a performance to match the historic significance of the trial. But at least it was a good U.S. county court case.

Not even Dickinson doubted that "Little Glass Eye" would be found guilty and sent to prison. Thus, one war criminal in a small way would pay for the indignity and pain to fellow-man. But his experience would not produce what, above all, it was meant to yield—a dramatic lesson to his people. Tsuchiya may be hanged, or rot in jail, or remain imprisoned until we leave this land. But not one Japanese will be impelled by this example to display humanity and fairness in the next war.

December 19, 1945   TOKYO

Democracy, it seems, has not yet made much of a dent in the old Japanese habit of obedience. A report came in today from Oita, Kyushu Island, of a sudden wave of traffic offenses. The entire vehicular traffic—trucks, buses, automobiles —had speeded up to the point where it was no longer safe to walk on the narrow streets.

It appeared that the Provost Marshal of the U.S. 32nd Infantry Division had just posted signs: "35-mile Speed Limit," and the unhappy but obedient Japanese drivers were doing their best. The incident was cleared up after a local Japanese daily came out with an editorial, conceding that democracy was fine, but was it necessary to drive that fast?

December 20, 1945   TOKYO

Last night had dinner at the club with several State Department and Headquarters men, and when we were through, we repaired to the lobby, to drink, to watch the parade of correspondents, officers, and mistresses, and inevitably to discuss General MacArthur. Although he strives to keep himself apart from, and above, the scene, General MacArthur's presence is always felt, and few nights pass at the club when there is not a heated debate on him and his policies. The place is still filled with war, rather than foreign, correspondents, and it is MacArthur's generalship rather than his political record in Japan that is being argued. Many of the correspondents have served with the Navy, and share its acute distaste for the general. I must have heard at least a dozen times of the order issued by General MacArthur's Public Relations Office on the day of victory at Leyte. The order banned Navy broadcasts, with the explanation that "this is the commander-in-chief's day." Other correspondents, ridicule General MacArthur's posturing, his prose, the men around him. Still others, who reflect some of the bitterness of the average GI, call him "Dug-out Doug."

But there was no talk of war last night. We agreed that the occupation was not the unqualified success that was painted by General MacArthur's publicity officers. But we also agreed that the fault frequently did not lie with General MacArthur. Most of us felt that an error had been made in operating through Japan's unreformed government. There are many indications that it has done its worst to sabotage our objectives, and to "protect" the Japanese people from the new democratic ideas. Some of us also feel the retention of Emperor Hirohito was a bad blunder, for the imperial myth will hold together that old, feudal Japan which we are trying to splinter. But if these be errors, they are not of General MacArthur's making. They were made elsewhere.

But no calm discussion of General MacArthur is possible in Tokyo. Some of his most passionate critics are the men who served under him during the war. Now they raised their voices and charged into the argument. The rest of us, they said, did not know or did not understand what was happening within General MacArthur's Headquarters.

While the outsiders, they said, get an impression of a co-ordinated and knowledgeable effort, the fact is that General MacArthur and his aides are confounded by the immensity of the problems before them. General MacArthur's views depend on whom he has seen at lunch, or on what the American press has said that morning in praise or condemnation of his actions. The various sections of his Headquarters are floundering on their own, with no guidance from above. Frequently, the only measuring stick of an important move is the publicity it might bring. Many of the measures for which General MacArthur has claimed credit have actually originated elsewhere. Thus, the action to pick up the war criminals was initiated by a non-American official. The directive on civil liberties was born in Washington.

Apart from all that, the critics said, a dramatic cleavage has developed within Headquarters, dividing all policy planners into two warring camps. One of these believes that Japan should be reshaped drastically. The other opposes fundamental changes, on the ground that a conservative Japan is our best ally in the coming struggle with Russia, and that all that is needed in Japan is a slight face-lifting.

A few days ago, the conflict between the two camps broke into the open. The occasion was a hush-hush conference called on the sixth floor of the Dai-Ichi Building to consider a draft directive purging war criminals from Japanese political life. Representatives of all the sections in Headquarters were present, and a split developed almost at once.

The opponents of the draft brought forth a variety of arguments:

(a) A sweeping purge would throw Japan into chaos, and even conceivably produce a revolution;

(b) If a purge is necessary, it must be carried out gradually, to give the Japanese a breathing spell after each blow; and

(c) Only the highest leaders should be purged, for discipline calls for obedience to orders, and subordinate officials have no choice but to obey.

The opposition to the purge included a solid phalanx of the four military staff sections, spearheaded by spokesmen for

Military Intelligence. Siding with them was one of the State Department's representatives. The main support of the purge came from the Government Section, with scattered backing from other Headquarters branches. Unscheduled aid came from a young lieutenant, who was sent to the meeting by the Natural Resources Section which apparently could find no one else interested in the purge.

Sharp words were traded during the four-hour debate, and a lot of red herrings were dragged across the table. But in the end, compromises were made, and the original purge directive emerged in a greatly watered-down form.

After the conference, Major General Charles Willoughby, Chief of Military Intelligence, sent out a long memorandum on his position. It opened with an expression of support for the purge "in principle," and then devoted pages to demolishing the directive with criticism. The Government Section, under Brigadier General Courtney Whitney, promptly issued a sharp rejoinder, pointing out that the early concurrence in Willoughby's memo did not tally with the rest of it. If the type of purge favored by Willoughby were carried out, the rejoinder said, Japan would have a government of "interpreters and mistresses."

A few days ago, the entire correspondence was deposited on General MacArthur's desk, and he sided with Whitney and the Government Section against Willoughby.

We all listened to the story of the purge directive, and we said, O.K., the conflict is significant enough, and it will probably get worse, but for the moment we have to judge the record not by what happens in the closed meetings, but by the product that emerges.

Most of us thought the crop of reform directives that has come out since Japan's surrender has been good. August was a month of basic directives on Japan's disarmament. In October came the orders on man's elemental liberties—the purge of the Thought Control Police, removal of the last restrictions on political and civil rights, a firmly worded reminder to the Japanese that we expected a strong labor movement, and the dramatic release of political prisoners. In November and December came the orders on such fundamental reforms as the redistribution of land, a broad relief program for the unemployed, separation of Shintoism from the State, and dissolution of the great family trusts, the *zaibatsu*. Speech and assembly were free, and in Hibiya Park, cater-corner from General MacArthur's own office, thousands flocked to listen to hoarse and passionate speeches by Communist orators, and Tokyo newspapers voiced opinions running the gamut from the extreme left to rabid nationalism. Labor union organizers were busy around the clock, and the labor movement was growing so fast that labor officers in Headquarters lagged weeks behind in their statistics. Even rural Jápan, tradition-bound and conservative, was waking up, and organizers were criss-crossing the countryside, bearing the news of the imminent land reform and arguing people into joining the Farmers' Union.

We agreed that these demonstrations of freedom were as yet scattered, and the broad masses of Japan remained lethargic. We agreed that the great body of reform was still woven of words, as yet largely untranslated into action. But the words of the directives formed a thrilling pattern of a new democracy-in-the-making of which Americans could be proud.

Learned today that General MacArthur has decided to issue a directive postponing the elections, and defining the minimum standards which the government must observe if the election is not to be a gigantic fraud.

For three days, rumors of the imminent directive have kept the political scene in a turmoil. Japanese politicians became so worried that the directors of the majority Progressive party, packed with war criminals, were actually planning to meet tomorrow to discuss the party's dissolution.

The order is admittedly a direct intervention in Japanese politics—something which General MacArthur has been reluctant to do. However, the need for such a move has been evident for weeks. But for such intervention, there was every sign that the next "democratic" Diet would be dominated again by unrepentant nationalists. Such a Diet could effectively wreck General MacArthur's entire program for a reborn Japan.

December 21, 1945 TOKYO

Had a hectic day today, packing, getting yen for the trip, obtaining Army Travel Orders, filing a batch of stories.

In the morning went to an interview given to the Japanese press by Colonel Crawford Sams, Chief of the Public Health and Welfare Section. Sams's dander was up. There has been a well-directed "whispering" campaign in recent weeks alleging that Japan is on the brink of a famine, that hospitals are packed with starvation cases, and that scores have died nightly of hunger at the Ueno Station alone. Sams charged the Japanese government with deliberate falsehood and misrepresentation in an effort to compel the United States to furnish more food to Japan.

The winter, Sams said, will not be an easy one, but there will be no famine. The hospitals are now crowded with cases of malnutrition. What few men starve to death are indigents or transients, who never did well in Japan. There is enough food in Japan, Sams said, to maintain an average daily intake of well over fifteen hundred calories through the worst months —April and May. This is more than the Germans will have, and not much less than the Japanese Army allowed its people even back in 1942.

Most of us have had the story of the Japanese campaign for weeks, but it is good to see General MacArthur's Headquarters come out and slap down the guilty. Meanwhile, Headquarters has placed all Japanese restaurants out of bounds to Americans. No Japanese nationalist will be able to say that American appetites are responsible for the meager Japanese ration.

Japanese sabotage is not confined to rumors. Our patrols scouring the countryside are constantly running into caches of military supplies. In the south, on the island of Shikoku, one patrol discovered concrete pillboxes camouflaged as houses, complete with sliding panels. The forts contained large stores of war materiel. Another patrol found ammunition hidden behind a pile of rice straw in a school. A third patrol found airplane parts, a crated glider, antiaircraft searchlights, and an underground fuel dump with 40,000 gallons of gasoline. In other schools, patrols discovered wooden rifles still in use by the students, and one dumbfounded American Education officer watched a life-sized military parade by students, marching under the orders barked by a Japanese in an army uniform.

At night, driving past General MacArthur's Headquarters, saw a huge "Merry Christmas" sign go ablaze with a thousand lights. The sign cast light over the outer wall of the Imperial Palace, and was reflected in the rippling water of the wide moat. I thought of the symbolism inherent in this American light thrown on the darkest Japanese institution; on the debris piled up like monuments in lots which once contained the heart of the Japanese financial empire; on the steady procession of U.S. Army jeeps and trucks; and on the shivering Japanese girls soliciting GI custom at the entrance to Hibiya Park, "Very good, Joe, very cheap."

I thought of this great city, which today contains little but rubble and an obstinate will to live, of a city in which I could travel for ten and twenty and thirty blocks at a time and see nothing but shattered brick, a few chimneys, and a score or two of abandoned safes that had crashed down through the floors of burning buildings. The men and women who had once made Tokyo the world's third largest city have now gone into the countryside, or moved into the few surviving buildings, three and four families to a room. And countless thousands have built shacks from rusty sheets of iron, or moved into the railroad and subway stations. In the morning, one can see smoke rising from what looks like a pile of junk and iron, but in reality is a home. Men still go to work in unbelievably crowded offices, and huddle close to the small warmth given out by a charcoal brazier.

This city now is a world of scarcity in which every nail, every rag, and even a tangerine peel has a market value. A cupful of rice, three cigarettes, or four matches are all a day's ration. Men pick every grain of rice out of their tin lunch boxes; there are too few to be wasted. And on a sunny day men hang out of windows and try to light their cigarettes with magnifying glasses. It can be done when there is no choice.

Like the rest of Japan, Tokyo is a world of illicit trading. Close to each of its railroad stations, in lots made vacant by bombs, there are now black markets, with thousands haggling over the price of a long-dead fish, apples, rice or chipped china.

On the Ginza, once the show street of Tokyo, the big show now is in the windows of U.S. Army Post Exchanges. Here fascinated crowds stare at GI sweaters, towels, battle jackets, and sturdy shoes made of real leather, and hungry kids and young women beg for gum and chocolate and peanuts from soldiers waiting in line.

Some day, if the city planners have their way, the Ginza will be a compound of the Atlantic City boardwalk and Chicago's Merchandise Mart. Right now its pitted, dusty length is lined with dead buildings and piles of rubbish. Some of the department stores have bravely resumed business in the lower two or three floors, but the floors are covered with rubble, and the showcases are filled with cheap crockery and worthless junk. The stories above are nothing but concrete frames, still black where the flames had licked them.

Customers do most of their shopping along the curb where peddlers display their wares on straw mats. There are shoddy silk kerchiefs heavy with fiber, badly printed postcards, crude wooden figurines, and fountain pens that will not work for long. The prices are high, and the quality pathetically low, but the GIs buy readily.

"What the hell," they say. "It ain't money. It's only yen."

Not far from the Ginza there is a huge lot covered with a range of metal mountains. It is the metal donated by the Japanese people to the army to fight the war. There is a mountain of radiators ripped from every office in Tokyo, a mountain of brass charcoal braziers, a mountain of candlesticks, a hillock of temple bells and urns. There is a fence to keep the Japanese out, but U.S. Army colonels in sedans and GIs in trucks come here to rummage for treasures. It will take many months of rummaging to cut down these mountains of useless sacrifice and suffering.

Small groups of people squat by the curb near the entrance to a subway station. They have been unable to get inside for a night's rest and now they try to keep warm by building small bonfires. Near the club, three waifs beg for cigarettes. One correspondents suggests that the boys wash themselves. They refuse; they say they make Y.300 a day ($20) begging for gum and cigarettes, and they will not endanger their begging appeal by cleaning up.

It is a Merry Christmas in Tokyo. It says so on a dance hall near the Ginza: "Merry Christmas, GI, we will soon open here with beautiful hostesses." And even the girls at Hibiya Park know it. Some now say, "Merry Christmas, Joe. Very good, Joe. Very cheap."

At eleven, Berrigan and I, with our new interpreter, George Kimura, drive out to the Ueno Station, pick our way gingerly among the thousands of passengers sleeping, or waiting their turn for train space which may not come for days, and board a night train for Sendai. Our car is packed with GIs returning to their stations from leave in Tokyo. We all retire early to our short, narrow berths, and try to keep warm under a thin blanket. A cold wind blows through the cracks in the window frame, and pretty soon there is a thin layer of ice on the ledge. The train rides softer than the trains back home. Through the haze of near-sleep I hear the sound of Japanese voices and running feet when we stop at stations, and the sharp, short whistle of the locomotive.

Was awakened at six by a young Japanese porter. He told me I could not smoke in my berth. When I told him I was not in the habit of smoking while fast asleep, he said simply, "Please give me cigarettes." Startled by his direct approach to the problem, I gave him cigarettes and forgot to get angry. But it was too cold to fall asleep again.

At the first station, I went out for a look at the train. There was heavy snow on the ground and the wind burned my face. Apart from the two cars for Allied personnel, the train consisted of one second-class hard-seat car for the privileged Japanese, and a long string of run-down third-class cars for the unprivileged Japanese. These cars were packed to the last inch. The windows were broken, and people on the platform were trying to push more children and bundles through. Silently and desperately, men fought for a foothold on the steps and couplings, and those who could not get even that much space stood in a solid line along the station platform and swayed as newcomers tried to push their way forward. The station building itself has been damaged by bombs. It was dark and wind-swept, and packed with people waiting for other trains. Some slept in the dirt on the floor, and the crowd moved over their twisted bodies.

We arrived in Sendai two hours late. Apparently General Dorn had not received our wire, and there was no one to meet us. We hitched a ride in a U.S. Army truck to Dorn's Headquarters in a former Japanese Navy arsenal. Dorn was out inspecting troops, and we waited in his office and talked to his chief of staff.

When he finally did arrive, Dorn proved to be as impressive an officer as I have seen. He has been in the Army for twenty-six years, and looks not one year over thirty-five. He has a keen face, a muscular body, and a friendly manner. This is the first time I have met him, though I have known of him since the Burma campaign, when he was one of General Joseph Stilwell's white-haired boys. Many people regard him as one of the most intelligent American officers to have served in China.

We had lunch with him and Brigadier General Robert Soule, chief of Military Government for the area and a professional soldier with a gruff manner and a talent for storytelling. The lunch was at the old Japanese Naval Officers' Club—a cheerful barrack, with an extraordinary number of Japanese waitresses who bowed low at every opportunity. One does not have to be here very long to discover that both the Americans and the Japanese know who won the war. We do not show the arrogance the Japanese Army displayed in conquered China, but there is a cold and impersonal firmness and a considerable disrespect for the way the Japanese do things.

In the afternoon, General Soule took us to the Military Government to talk to his key officers on food, brothels and the underground, on cabbages and kings.

Theoretically, Miyagi Prefecture should be better off than most of Japan. It grows its own rice, and it ranks third in fish yield. Actually, it will go hungry next spring, and the Military Government is girding itself for possible riots. The villages eat better than the cities, but in this prefecture only one out of every five farmers owns the land he tills. The other four rent some or all of their land. In this time of black markets, the sharecroppers have done uncommonly well, trading rice and radish for the used clothes and utensils being peddled by the hungry white-collar employees. But even "uncommonly well" means little by our standards. The sharecropper is still a pauper.

But it is in the cities that the distress is deepest. Soule gave me a stack of translations from the local press.

"I've been an official for twenty years," said a typical letter to the editor. "Yet my total salary is Y.140 a month ($9). I must feed my family of seven on that. I cannot go about my work, because my head is filled with tomorrow's food problems. Does the government realize that we are paying 70 sen (five cents) for a small sardine and Y.3.50 (25 cents) for a cuttlefish?"

A pessimistic Military Government report summed it up:

"The middle class is being liquidated. In the months to come, it will provide leadership for an uprising of the urban proletariat, combined with the impoverished government employees."

But as yet, there is no unified underground. All that the U.S. Army can see is a flock of small nationalist parties—and a great deal of bitterness on which an underground can grow fat. At night, posters appear on the fences warning Japanese girls against fraternization with the GIs, "Maintain the dignity of Japanese womanhood."

In the late afternoon, Soule took us to the house he shares with Dorn. The two generals live not in ruined Sendai, but in a requisitioned hotel at the summer resort of Matsushima, one of Japan's most beautiful scenic spots. It was a twenty-mile ride of constant skidding and lovely sights. A narrow, snow-covered road hugging a mountainside. Gnarled pine trees, an occasional skier, fishing smacks, ducks rising from behind a hillock, and fresh deer tracks. The hotel has been redecorated and repainted for the generals, and it was full of warmth and good smells and servants and a Japanese chef in a gleaming white cap. I was given a bedroom for myself, with an ancient wardrobe, a built-in marble sink, and a striking view of mountains through the French doors. There was even hot water in the shower, and I thawed myself out, shaved, and put on a clean shirt for dinner.

The food was good, and so was the conversation. The things which are a rumor and a shadow in Tokyo are solid substance here. The dozen Americans around the table spoke without bitterness, like doctors discussing a hopeless case of cancer. The Japanese, they said, were sabotaging every directive whenever they had the opportunity, and the local American commanders, operating under rigid orders from above, could do nothing but file reports which produced no action.

Specific directives have been issued to the Japanese to remove all Thought Control officers and those police chiefs who were clearly war criminals. In neighboring Yamagata Prefecture, five high Thought Control officers resigned. The next time they were spotted, all five were high police officials. Yet, not even General Dorn had the authority to throw them out. In Aomori Prefecture, in the extreme north of this island, the U.S. Command objected to six high police officials. They were promptly fired. It was not long before the U.S. Military Government found three of them back at work—in other towns.

The limitations on the authority of American commanders in the field extend into practically all spheres. A commander, I learned, cannot, for instance, on his own authority close up a brothel that is infecting his men. All he can do is either put the establishment off limits to his men, or request the Japanese police to close it. Soule's aide told us of a dance hall started recently in Sendai, right across the street from the regimental billets.

"They came to us and asked for permission to build a big dance hall for American troops. We said, 'No prostitutes!' They said, 'Oh, sure, no prostitutes. The whole thing will be very respectable.' So they go ahead, buy up lumber and brick that are needed to rebuild Sendai, and furniture, and fuel for the hot water. Well, just before the place is formally opened, we find some fresh VD cases in the unit. The boys say they've been visiting the girls at the dance hall. So General Soule promptly puts the place off limits. A whole procession of Japanese then comes in—the owner, the mayor of Sendai, the police chief. They all plead the owner's case—he has put a fortune into the place, and he has imported 127—count them—waitresses and dancers, and it would be unfair to these lovely gals to leave them jobless now. Well, General Soule is firm. The place is closed up, and nine hundred homeless people from Sendai move in, and everyone is happy.

"A few days ago, a Japanese came in and said he wanted to open a club for our officers at Shiogama, about halfway between Sendai and here. We said, O.K., provided it's a dance hall, and no bedrooms upstairs. The other day, we went through Shiogama, and saw the Japanese manager of the club. We asked him how many girls he had there, and he said very proudly, 'One hundred and twenty-seven.'"

The fault, of course, does not lie with the generals here, or with Lieutenant General Robert L. Eichelberger, who commands the Eighth Army. The fault—if it is one—rests with our policy of working through the existing Japanese government. Here, as in Tokyo, we have limited ourselves to charting the broad course we expect Japan to follow, and then we let the Japanese themselves operate the ship. The American observers can only report that the ship is being operated by what is largely the old gang, and that there appear to be major deviations from the course. But the observers can do nothing on their own.

I suspect that the debate on whether we were right in working through the Japanese government, or should have wrecked the entire rotten Japanese machinery and operated through our own Military Government, will rage for decades. I am not convinced that the Military Government personnel I have met would have been capable of running a nation as complex as Japan. But I also doubt the wisdom of trying to enforce revolutionary changes through men who detest these changes, and fight them tooth and nail. You pays your money —especially if you are an American taxpayer—and you takes your choice.

But the lack of authority, enforced on men used to authority, has had curious results. Throughout Japan, from what I hear, American officers find themselves compelled to take short cuts to achieve results. When a high Japanese municipal official, in a great city in the south, continues to ignore American demands that the streets be kept clean, he is brought forcibly to the front of the Military Government headquarters, given a broom, and told to sweep. When a prefectural governor fails to put a dilapidated building in shape to house an American general, he is summoned to the building, and ordered to remain there until the house is cleaned and painted. The desired results are achieved. The streets are kept clean. The building is painted.

The Japanese have not yet discovered that the conquerors lack authority, or, what is more likely, with their habit of obedience to the man in uniform, they choose not to argue with the American Army. And in continuing to obstruct our orders and reforms, they do so through devious means, through delay and prevarication.

But the necessity of operating extralegally has unfortunate effects on the minds of men, both American and Japanese. The Americans grow cynical, and the need for exceeding their orders does no good to the discipline or morale. The Japanese, whom we are to teach through our own example the benefits and delights of democracy, feel instead that basically there is little difference between their military and ours.

December 23, 1945   SENDAI

In the morning, the Japanese prefectural governor received a peremptory order to wait for us in his office. We found him in a large room, together with half a dozen of his subordinates. It was cold and dark, and there was an air of polite hostility. The governor said he had attended Princeton University. From what we gathered, he remembered no English.

Helped by his aides, he recited his difficulties for us. The rice crop is a third below that of 1943. The population, on the other hand, is now swollen with 200,000 refugees from Tokyo. Uneasily, the prefecture now waits for the return of as many ex-servicemen. The soldiers already back have gone into the black market and racketeering.

The governor stared at the tiny fire in the charcoal brazier. "This is a difficult time for Japan," he said. "The defeat has broken the hearts of my people. Our spirits are low. Our initiative is gone. We keep trying to speed up the recovery, but the red tape of war years binds our hands. It takes four months to get a license from Tokyo to start a new factory. We are helpless. And the months ahead will be filled with bitterness."

The governor is an earnest man, laden with frustration and the sadness of defeat. He is also a man totally unfit for his job. Nine out of every ten men in his prefecture work in the fields. Yet neither he nor any of his assistants can tell me what taxes a farmer has to pay, or how much. He lives in Sendai, and he is full of its miseries and problems, and what happens without the city limits happens in a far-off land.

The governor received another peremptory order—to have Count Okimune Daté wait for us at his home. I found the order vastly amusing. The Datés are one of the great feudal clans of Japan. For centuries they owned a broad strip of North Japan, from the Pacific to the Japan Sea, and their vassals brought them a rich tribute. Seventeen generations ago, in defiance of orders from his suzerain, the famous Count Masamune Daté even sent a retainer to Rome to learn the inner secrets of the Catholic faith. Like other feudal lords, the Datés went into a decline about eighty years ago. But the old men and officials still remember with reverence that all of this prefecture had once been Datés' own.

With the governor's secretary for a guide, we drove to Daté's comfortable mansion, took off our army boots in the snow, and then trooped into the living room. The count was waiting for us—a man in his middle forties, who looked like a playboy who had played a bit too hard. Behind his chair stood a thin, straight, old man, with the tight skin and the ageless look of an Egyptian mummy.

We asked Daté a few questions on his land holdings. He pointed at the man behind him. "This is my *karei* (family retainer). He manages all my affairs. He will answer all your questions on my financial affairs."

For a moment, Berrigan and I forgot all about the count. The old man, we learned, belonged to a vassal family which for four centuries had fought for and served the Datés. He told us of himself with a stern face, which only once showed any emotion. This was when, with a smile, he said:

"My father's sword was presented to your President Theodore Roosevelt."

Quickly the smile vanished, and the wrinkled parchment of his skin was smooth again.

We talked to the count for two hours, and many of the questions we asked were of the kind that could be asked only in a defeated country. Daté took them all with good grace, and the old man answered them in detail. Daté, we found, still had two hundred sharecropper families working for him. He expected the land to yield him this year an income of $11,000. During the war, he also operated a factory making airplane wheels. Now the plant was turning out agricultural implements.

Daté doubted that there would be a famine next spring, but at the governor's suggestion he was setting up a mill to produce loaves made of fish, tree bark, dry leaves, and mud. "It doesn't taste bad," he said. "Like brown bread." We gathered that he and the governor were cronies.

Right now, the count said, he was trying to get tractors from General MacArthur to be used on his land. "Mechanized agriculture is feasible in Japan," he said. A little sharply, we asked him how *he* would know anything about it, and discovered that he was a graduate of the Tokyo Agricultural College. He added that he was in favor of land reform and low-interest loans for sharecroppers. "I myself lend money to them," he said, "at . . . at . . . " He looked back at the old man.

"Ten to 30 per cent a year," said the vassal.

The formal part of the interview was now over, and we were walking around the room, admiring priceless ivory and brass figures. Warm sake was brought in, and soon the count, loud and voluble, was describing to us the treasures collected by thirty-two generations of the Datés, and now kept, in part, in this house. The count urged us to stay for lunch, but we begged off. We rose to go, and the old man disappeared briefly, to return with small boxes for Berrigan and me. I thought of the priceless antiques around us, and of my resolution to take no gifts from the Japanese, and I kept pushing the box back into Daté's hands, and he kept saying he wanted me to have a remembrance of the visit. Finally, the scene began to get a bit ridiculous, and I took the box and thanked the count profusely.

We drove off, and in the street curiosity overcame me. Carefully I unwrapped the box, and pulled out a tiny doll. The governor's secretary looked at it with admiration. "It is very beautiful," he said. "It must be very rare. Count Daté's dolls are famous. All of them rare."

The doll, in its red kimono, was nice. I turned it upside down and looked at the base, and discovered that the count had forgotten to remove the price label. In very large, brazen letters it said: "Yen 1" (six cents).

We had a magnificent steak dinner, with pie à la mode, and more conversation, and then Dorn helped me to work out my itinerary. Berrigan decided to go deer hunting tomorrow morning, and then return to Tokyo with Dorn and Soule to see the Christmas football game. I am going off by myself, with George. But General Dorn is issuing instructions all down the line to help me with accommodations and transportation. To-morrow, I shall take a local east-west train, across Japan, to a town called Sakata, and from there I shall travel north into the big town of Akita, and small towns and hamlets to the north of it.

December 24, 1945   EN ROUTE TO SAKATA

After four hours of sleep, was awakened at six thirty. It was still dark. I shaved, packed, and went down to look un-happily for a jeep to take George and me to the Sendai station. General Dorn was sitting in his sedan, waiting for me. So I rode in comfort, and listened to Dorn talk of Japan. His feeling is that few changes as yet have taken place, and Japanese offi-cialdom is giving us nothing but an appearance of cooperation, in the knowledge that we will soon be out of Japan, and the old men and institutions will take over where they left off on the day of defeat.

It was about three minutes before train time when we reached the street leading to Dorn's Headquarters. He stopped the car, said he would walk to his office, and ordered the driver to make speed. So off we went, with the horn honking, the brakes screeching, and hundreds of GIs saluting the general's car. As I got out of the automobile, the driver handed me a huge package of sandwiches—"compliments of the general and the chef." Only a minute behind, George's jeep roared to the station. We made the train just in time.

We rode in half a car assigned to Allied personnel. The window panes were broken, and snow kept coming in through them. There was no heat. The other passengers were half a dozen GIs, returning from leave in Sendai. The conversation was purely biological.

We reached Yamagata, where we were to take a connecting train, on time. But when we stepped out of the car, there was a trim, young lieutenant asking me if I was Mr. Gayn, and there was a message from General Dorn, and the colonel was expecting me to lunch.

"That's very nice of the colonel," I said, "but I have to board the connecting train."

"Don't you worry about that," said the officer. "The train is going to be a bit late."

So George and I got into the automobile, and went to Dorn's billet in Yamagata—the loveliest Japanese home I have yet seen, with a tremendous living room, thick Tientsin rugs, a piano, recent books, and warmth.

All through the lunch I kept looking surreptitiously at my watch, for there is only one train a day to Sakata, and I did not want to miss it. An hour had gone by, and I was getting worried. Finally, I brought the subject up.

"Oh, don't let it bother you," said the colonel calmly. "We told the sergeant at the station to hold up the train until you got back."

My host kept his word. After lunch, a captain drove me back to the station. The train, with its five hundred Japanese passengers, had been kept waiting. The captain escorted me to my car, the sergeant in charge shouted a command, the relieved Japanese station master signaled, the whistle blew happily, and we were off. We were now an hour late, but the sergeant told me word had been sent ahead, to Shinjo, to hold up the connecting train.

I was now in what was virtually a private car. On both sides of it, the cars were packed, with men standing on the platforms and hanging off the steps. From time to time, some of them tried to enter my car. They were stopped by the conductor. "For Americans," he would say. Each time I waited for an argument. But these were magic words which barred both passage and disagreement. The men retired. This was a defeated nation and, in my uniform, I was one of the conquerors, subject to the laws of victory and defeat. Millions of Japanese were on the road, bound for new jobs, for cheaper rice, for families long unmet. Japan was gasping for more transportation. But in Japan this day, there must have been scores of empty cars like mine; or even private trains like the one that was bearing "Pinky" Dorn, Berrigan, and a few hundred GIs to a football game in Tokyo.

But though I had the car all to myself, I was anything but comfortable. Most of the glass panes were missing, and the windows were now covered with old boards, cracked plywood, and bits of tin. The storm forced the snow through the wide cracks, and it piled up on the seats in smooth, unmelting mounds. More snow came billowing through the spitoons built into the floor at even intervals.

We arrived in Sakata late, and had to wait at the station, around a hot potbelly stove, until a jeep came to pick us up. Skidding crazily, we drove to a Japanese inn where there was a reservation. It looked lovely and warm with its bright lanterns, translucent paper walls and deep, bluish snow shovelled off the doorsteps. Lieutenant Robert McHardy, the garrison commander, was waiting for me. He was a small, compact, handsome youth of about twenty-two with a barrel chest and a firm jaw.

"Welcome to Sakata," he said. "I've invited a few friends to meet you. Wash up, and join us at the reception hall. We'll chew the rag a while."

I found four other young officers in the room. One of them was Lieutenant Marcus, McHardy's second-in-command. The other three were from neighboring towns. They were now sitting around a *kotatsu*, a contraption which consists of a charcoal brazier, covered with a thick comforter. Their feet were against the brazier, their bodies up to the waist under the comforter, their upper bodies swathed in warm kimonos. The men made room for me, and I stuck my legs under the blanket.

It was warm and friendly. We drank beer, chewed on the remainder of Dorn's sandwiches, and talked. The boys, I discovered, were shrewd but green. They had fought a hard war, and now they could not understand why the Japanese were so complacent about the Occupation. They were filled with contempt for Japanese subservience, and with suspicion. They kept saying that when the big blowup came, it wouldn't catch them unprepared. "No, sir, I'm never more than an arm's length from my automatic." Vaguely, they talked of their nonmilitary mission. There were important tasks to perform, but no one was quite sure what they were. After a while, I had a strange sensation. This was a political never-never land, in which these boys wandered, a bit puzzled, a bit worried and suspicious, very curious, and quite disturbed because the gun on which they relied in the previous three or four years seemed no longer dependable.

December 25, 1945   SAKATA

At seven-thirty on this gray Christmas morning, an old and wrinkled maid in a dark kimono shuffled in with live coals for the charcoal brazier. She also brought in a basin with hot water and a three-foot-high mirror, which she set on the floor mats. I raised my three heavy comforters, and peeked out. A strong wind was blowing through the papered windows. Unhappily, I saw there was nothing between me and the snow but two thicknesses of oil paper. I pulled on my clothes, shaved kneeling before the mirror, and then waited for a jeep to move me to the Army barracks.

Beyond my windows, along the edge of a bay, lay Sakata, shivering in the raw wind blowing in from the Sea of Japan. I listened to the howling wind, and thought of the things that brought me to this town.

It was not by accident that I had come here. In Tokyo, before leaving on this trip, I had scouted the land. Sakata, I thought, met most of the answers I sought about Japan in defeat. It was a conservative town that would resist the influx of new ideas. As an old stronghold of militant nationalism, it would offer fertile soil to an antidemocratic movement. A small, solid, rural town, it would be a good testing place for our policies, and for Japan's readiness to democratize herself.

Last, but not the least important, reason for my visit was a family named Homma.

Sakata is a bustling little town of 45,000 people, of one- and two-story houses, of a few industries—gun barrels, army uniforms, ships, magnesium—now shut down by defeat. It is a seaport (a couple of small freighters sunk by our bombers still stick out of the water near the shore), and its business is partly the business of the sea. But to a much greater degree, its mind is on rice and land. For Sakata is where the farmers of Western Yamagata Prefecture come to shop for their nails, and fertilizer, and split-toe sandals. Yamagata is Japan's fourth largest rice producer, and in Sakata, too, rice dominates all thought and talk. Even the social structure is built on rice, for a man's importance is measured not by his ancestry or intellect, but in the acres of land he owns.

Yamagata is a typical prefecture, no richer and not much poorer than the other forty-five. Only a third of the land can be cultivated; two-thirds are mountains. Of every ten men who work on land, eight wholly or partly are sharecroppers. As in the rest of Japan it does not take much to be a landlord. A man with an acre can have a couple of sharecroppers working for him. In the whole prefecture, there are only forty-four men who own more than 250 acres apiece.

The biggest landlord of them all—of Sakata, of Yamagata Prefecture, of entire Japan—is the Homma clan. Many centuries ago, the Hommas had been noblemen, a little north of here. Their feudal suzerain was the Lord of Sakai, for whom they fought, and to whom later they lent money.

The Hommas are older than the United States. They came

to Sakata and sent their roots into its soil years before the May-flower left Plymouth. Slowly, they branched into land owner-ship. Three quarters of a century before our Declaration of In-dependence, the Hommas owned seventy-five acres of land. But with each drought and economic crisis, the crafty Hommas bought up the land of their neighbors, and let them stay on as sharecroppers. By 1925, they were Japan's largest landowners.

The lords of Sakai also survived the test of time and feudal throat-cutting. They, too, settled in Sakata, and went into banking, ship-building, and industry. The name of Sakai is an honored name in Sakata. But land is now a man's measure, and in the new social scale the Hommas stand above the Sakais, and throughout Japan, Sakata is known as the Homma's town.

McHardy's tiny garrison of thirty-odd men is housed in the offices of a defunct shipbuilding company, owned by Baron Sakai. McHardy has installed stoves in the tall wooden building, insulated the bedrooms, built shower stalls. The billet is spa-cious, airy, and fairly cheerful. I found McHardy in the presi-dent's office, his feet on the big desk.

He showed me a letter he had just received from a man named Masanosuke Ikeda, a member of the Diet from Yamagata Prefecture. Ikeda reported that the Homma family, in violation of Allied directives, had hidden a tremendous hoard of gold and securities in its warehouses. Ikeda volunteered to provide all the information needed for a raid.

I thought Sakata's social structure was cracking at the joints when its member of parliament was ready to squeal on the powerful Homma-Sakai political machine. I said, "Ikeda is not due here for another day, and you probably won't raid the Homma warehouses for two. How about coming along with me today when I interview the Hommas?"

It was the most martial interview I ever had. Orders were sent ahead to the Hommas to hold themselves in readiness for me at three in the afternoon. Then McHardy and Marcus strapped pistols against their chests, and we went off in a jeep with an armed GI driver.

The office of the Hommas was housed in a long, one-story,

weather-beaten building. Across the street, a tall brick wall and a magnificent gate concealed the Homma mansion in which the three current heads of the clan lived. The office was shabby and dark, with a grimy counter running the length of it, and with a dozen clerks busily brushing figures into rice-paper ledgers.

The three Hommas waited for us outside. They were courteous, but their faces were hostile. Hostility and name were the only things common to all three. The oldest, fifty and effeminate, resembled a small-town banker in his dark suit and stiff celluloid collar. He was the head of the loan and land companies, which formed the kernel of the Homma empire. Next to him was a bespectacled, partly bald man in a suit of greenish ersatz cloth too tight for him. This was the politician of the clan who presided over the all-important Sakata Agricultural Association and the Sakata City Council, chose the candidates of the Homma political machine, and handled relations with the sharecroppers. The last of the trio was a man in his late thirties. Ostensibly, he was the junior member of the team, who ran the domestic affairs of the clan. But I had heard that this round-faced, handsome man was actually the brain behind the Homma policies.

The three men escorted us to a tiny office, where we all grouped around a brazier. McHardy and Marcus put their feet on it, and focussed fierce stares on the Hommas.

I shall never know why the Hommas told me as much as they did. Perhaps it was the presence of the two armed officers. Perhaps it was because the Occupation was young, and the Japanese still did not know how much they had to tell a uniformed American, and how much could be concealed.

The clan, the man in the celluloid collar told me, now had one principal and fifteen branch families. The dominant voice in the clan passed to the three men earlier this year, on the death of the great Mitsumasa Homma. ("He left no heirs. Just a daughter.")

All together, the clan owned 4,100 acres, cultivated by 5,150 sharecropper families. Each sharecropper paid the Hommas between a third and a half of his crop. Out of the remainder, he paid taxes, bought tools and fertilizer, and tried to keep his family—an average of seven persons—alive. A good sharecropper earned about $117 a year, of which the Hommas took $47. The remaining $70 was a year's reward for a sharecropper family.

The picture of distress was so plain that the three Hommas began to look troubled. "You must realize," said the politician, "that we have the friendliest of relations with our sharecroppers. Most of them have worked on this land for three, four, and six generations. When the times get hard, we don't press them for payment. We are like fathers to them, and they love us like children."

"Indeed," said the celluloid collar, "four generations ago Ko-obi Homma left a testament which we still follow. He said 'Love your sharecropper, and preserve family-like bonds with him.'"

The young policy-maker now spoke up: "It's too bad about the land reform bill you Americans want. Over a period of three centuries, we've established a balance of relations with our tenants. The new law will disturb this balance. What is worse, the policy cannot succeed. Twenty years ago, when the government proposed that the sharecroppers buy the land they cultivated, our sharecroppers refused to break with us. Suppose they feel differently now. A man and wife working together can cultivate at most seven acres. If the man dies, his wife cannot run the farm alone. Nor can she afford to hire a helper. She has no choice then but to return the land to the landlord. No, it can't succeed."

"It's an error," said the politician. "We know a great deal about farming. Now we are allowed to keep only seven and a half acres apiece. Our skills are being wasted. If we could only keep about ten per cent of our land . . . "

I figured the sale of their land would bring the Hommas about Y.90 million, or six million American dollars. The Hommas said they had not decided what to do with the money. "We'll probably go into food processing," said the celluloid collar.

But though they hated to admit it, they were more than landlords. The truth kept baring itself with each question. The Hommas said they had never traveled outside of Japan.

"Never?" I asked.

"Never," said the celluloid collar. "Except once, when I went to Manchuria."

"What were you doing in Manchuria?"

"Just a visit."

"Nothing but a visit?"

"Well," he said reluctantly, "also to inspect the head offices of the Manchuria Food Producers' Bank which we own."

We paused. I said, "Apart from Manchuria, you have visited no other country outside of Japan?"

"No," he said. "Except for a visit to Korea."

"What were you doing there?"

"I visited the head office of the Korea Food Producers' Bank, which also belongs to us."

Slowly, the information kept coming out. The Hommas owned three rural banks. They had a sizable investment in the Kawasaki Heavy Industries. They were interested in the Sakata power plant and power transmission. Not the least profitable of their enterprises was their own loan company, to which five hundred of their own sharecroppers were in debt.

By now it was cold and dark in the room. The faces of the three men were gray with weariness. They all sighed deeply when I thanked them for "volunteering" information to me. They walked us outside, and stood framed in the doorway, between long vertical signs hung alongside the doors. I asked the interpreter to read the signs to me. One said: "Agents for Meiji Life Insurance Co." The other read: "Agents for Fukoku Chohei—insurance for servicemen and their families."

McHardy said, "These birds don't miss a trick." The Hommas bowed low as we climbed into the jeep. As we turned the corner. I looked back. All three men were still there, bowed slightly in a gesture of courtesy.

Spent the day putting my notes in order, and waiting for Ikeda, the member of Parliament turned informer. He is not yet back in Sakata.

In the afternoon, talked to the principal of one of the high schools. He was a pitiful little figure—ragged, frightened, blue with cold. He talked about the Hommas. "They have presented gifts to our schools and they helped to open the town library. They're Sakata's first citizens."

If he is a typical educator, I know why Japan got into the war—and then lost it. *He* thought Japan lost the war because she was not properly prepared for it. The army, he felt, was all right, and Tojo and his associates alone were to blame for the defeat.

He admitted all of his twenty-five teachers had been appointed with the army's blessings. But when I asked him if he intended to purge any of them he said with amazement: "Why? They haven't done anything." I asked then if he felt the men hand-picked by the military were equipped to teach concepts of democracy to Japan's youth.

He said with conviction: "Of course! As soon as we get orders from Tokyo."

At seven a little Japanese boy in U.S. Army shoes three sizes too big for him came in to stoke the potbelly stove. When I opened my eyes, he said politely, "Excuse prease." McHardy was already gone. A little later I found him in his office, arguing with the Sakata police chief over a sheaf of bills. The bills represented the month's expenses for McHardy's force of thirty-seven men. Once approved by McHardy they would go to the Japanese government, to be applied against the costs of Occupation. The Japanese, I was told, were employing every possible trick to run up the costs, in the hope of being able to argue at the peace conference that Japan had already paid through the nose for the Occupation, and therefore should not be penalized further.

"Look at this old fraud," McHardy said irritably. "In the past month, he has charged me three different times for painting the same water drum. If you don't watch out with these Japs, they will steal your pants off you, and then charge the labor against the Occupation costs."

The chief's face was blank. I said, "I want to talk to him when you are through." "Sure thing," said McHardy.

Whether from good will or fear, the chief talked—not of himself, but of others. He talked of the Hommas and Baron Sakai; of the small band of leftists "liquidated" by the Thought Control police during the war, and of the hundred odd Socialists who had reappeared in Sakata since surrender; of the 4,100 unemployed men and women—seven hundred of them ex-servicemen—for whom no form of relief had yet been provided; of the troublesome Chinese community, and the still more difficult black market, in which both the Chinese and the ex-servicemen were especially active. He also talked of the ultranationalist movement, which once prospered in Sakata, and which, I suspected, might rise once more.

"The last big nationalist meeting we had here," he said, "was after the war—about two months ago, when 20,000 people came to a near-by town to hear Lieutenant General Kanji Ishihara."

The name rang a bell. I had heard of Ishihara for the first time in China ten or twelve years earlier, when he was known as the *wunderkind* of the Japanese General Staff. He served in Manchuria, drafted blueprints for Asiatic conquest, allied himself with the fire-eating "younger officers' clique," led the East Asia League, whose rabid jingoism had won over two of the emperor's brothers, and eventually made at least two futile attempts to murder his rival, Tojo.

The rally, the chief said, was held on September 19, 1945— *thirty-six days after Japan proclaimed her surrender*. It was more than a chance rally called to hear a free-lancing ultranationalist. It was a major morale operation, backed by the Japanese government. In a month of utter chaos, the Ministry of Railways somehow managed to get together special trains to bring Ishihara's followers from every corner of Japan. These thousands, on a balmy September day, heard Ishihara blame Tojo for leading Japan to defeat.

"We didn't lose because you lacked courage," he told the vast crowd. "We lost because our false leaders took us into a war for which we were not ready. They had betrayed the emperor, as they had betrayed the land. Now we must start all over again, by building an Asiatic Co-Prosperity Sphere anew. This time we must do it not through force, but by making friends with other Asiatics. But soon—perhaps in ten years—we shall be back."

Japan was getting more than a new Messiah. She was also receiving a happy explanation of the causes of the defeat: the villains were the few men, led by Tojo, who were now in Sugamo Prison, awaiting trial as war criminals. No others—the emperor, the great industrial houses, the political wire-pullers, the generals like Ishihara himself, the people—were to blame. It was a happy explanation which salved pride, eased conscience, and —like a fairly similar theory in Germany after the first World War—would make it easier to wage a war of revenge a generation later.

From Ishihara, the conversation shifted over to the Thought Control police, which used to put people in jail not only for talking out of turn, but even on suspicion of "subversive thought." The chief was visably unhappy. "I'm a policeman," he kept saying, "I don't know anything about these things. We had a Thought police unit here, but it was headed by an officer sent from the prefectural capital."

"What happened to him?"

"He was purged. Way back on September 23rd. All Thought policemen were fired."

"Where's he now?"

With a look of complete innocence, he stuck his finger out toward the window. "There. See that man sitting by the gate, near the American sentry? That's he."

I looked. There was a tough, youngish man sitting on a bench.

"What's he doing here, in a U.S. Army billet?"

"He's the liaison officer for contacts between our people and the American Army here. He was appointed on September 24th."

"Do you know what's happened to the other members of the Thought police here?"

"Yes. There were six agents here. Three of them are now with the Liaison Office, assisting the American detachment."

McHardy, who had been silent through the conversation, growled: "Does that mean that every Japanese who wants to see me has to be passed first by these characters?"

"Of course," said the police chief blandly. "If men come here with complaints which really don't deserve your attention, the liaison officers turn them back at the gate. We don't want you to be disturbed unnecessarily. We want your stay here to be pleasant."

Early in the afternoon, McHardy, three sergeants, an interpreter, and I piled into two jeeps. We were going on a school raid. Through the years of Japanese aggression, the schools had been the breeding grounds of rabid nationalism. Now, in all parts of Japan, small groups of Americans were searching schools—for caches of arms, for airplane parts, for posters extolling the virtues of war, for books dealing with Allied barbarism and spiritual inferiority.

It was a day straight out of a Christmas tale. The sun was bright, the air crisp, the snow so white it hurt our eyes. Heavy icicles, hanging from the red and green curved eaves of fragile, picture-book houses, dripped happy tears. The children tossed snowballs, or pulled sleds filled with other laughing children. Husky boys slid past us on skis. It was peace on earth, and our jeeps and tommyguns and the heavy pistol on McHardy's chest were obscene and incongruous.

We all felt out of place when we awkwardly dismounted at our first stop—a girls' kindergarten. If anything, the uncomfortable feeling grew, for we were now in the center of a crowd of tots in bright kimonos. They chirped gaily, and bowed to us, and giggled when we were not looking. The laughter was clear and sharp in the cold air. "Christ," said one of the sergeants, "ain't it pretty? Just like a *real* Christmas."

We went into the school, feeling ashamed and self-conscious. With exaggerated courtesy, we exchanged greetings with the principal, and McHardy did not have the courage to tell him this was a raid. After all, this was Christmas, and we were in a kindergarten. "We have a correspondent with us today," McHardy said, "and we wondered if he could take a look at your school." Then the sergeants, with their tommy-guns clanging, scattered through the building, and McHardy and I looked at the cold, clean classrooms, at the childish drawings of houses and trees and boats in the harbor, at the unsteady scribbling of *kana* characters on the blackboard. There were a few toys there, a few balls, stacks of tiny dumbbells.

In the corner there was a large wooden crate. I raised the lid. Inside, in two tight rows, lay handgrenades. When I picked up one, I knew they were not real. They were made of clay, or some other heavy substance. But they were lifelike, in shape, size, weight, and color.

"What's this for?"

The principal said, with a perfectly straight face: "For exercise. The girls do like this. . . . " He flexed and unflexed his arms. "We want our girls to be healthy and strong."

We took the handgrenades with us. None of us said a word as we walked out of the school. After all, it was Christmas, and this was a kindergarten, and the little girls outside looked so lovely. And didn't each grenade carry a little sticker, "Approved by the Board of Education"?

When we returned to the billet, I called the former Thought Control chief in from his post at the gate, and asked him about General Ishihara and his East Asia League.

"The general is a great man," he said. "The society has 600 members in this town, and about 1,500 all told in the prefecture. It's quite busy. Why, only last night, the executive staff of the society met about forty miles from here to discuss plans. About a hundred men, mostly farmers."

I dismissed the man, but he lingered in the room. "What's on your mind?"

"Well," he said, "I think the chief of police told you I headed the Thought Control police in town. Technically, it's true. But I was working under the chief himself. *He,* in the last count, was the head of all the police branches, including Thought Control."

December 28, 1945   SAKATA

When we had just about given up hope, Ikeda, the Diet member now turned informer, showed up. He was a small, intense, shaggy-haired man with hot black eyes. For the benefit of the Thought Control man, who followed him from the gate, Ikeda said he had come to pay his respects. But as soon as McHardy sent the Thought Controller out, Ikeda said impatiently:

"When will you search the Homma warehouses?"

"Take it easy," said McHardy. "Where's the evidence?"

What McHardy got was not what he expected. Despite all our efforts to cut it short, Ikeda gave us a two-hour lecture on the history of feudalism, the nationalist movement in this area, and the Hommas. He finally maneuvered himself next to the large wall map, where, with a stray chopstick, he illustrated the historical course of the Homma clan.

"The Hommas," he said, "made feudalism pay. First they made money out of loyalty to the Lords of Sakai. Then they began to buy up land, and rent it out at exorbitant rates. Finally, they went into usury, trade and industry, into banking and colonial ventures. Generation after generation, they've been swelling the Homma fortune, until today it must run into hundreds of millions. And the Hommas were shrewd. When they didn't invest in land or industry, they put their money into gold. That's why they have their wealth, while others have lost it.'

I said, "How do you know it's hidden in the warehouses?"

"Where else could it be? That would be the safest place."

I said to McHardy, "Lieutenant, this bird is just guessing. If I were you, I'd put the raid off until I had better information."

"It's too late," McHardy said unhappily. "Headquarters has already ordered me to proceed with the search. We're going this afternoon."

It was a springlike day, and by three o'clock in the afternoon, when our three jeeps took off on the raid, the wide, unpaved streets were covered with slush. As we went by, clanging our snow chains and splashing the passersby, people stopped and watched us. There were twelve of us, and our Tommyguns must have given us a very businesslike appearance.

The Hommas did not expect us. McHardy went in with an interpreter, and demanded the keys to the warehouses. When he rejoined us, the Hommas were trailing him. Their faces were bleak. Eventually, the Homma in the celluloid collar asked for the reason for the search.

"We have a report that you're hiding gold in your warehouses," said McHardy.

The three Hommas looked at each other. "We wish we had gold," said the celluloid collar.

From the outside, the warehouses looked like two-story, shabby, wooden barns. But when the door of the first one was finally unlocked, we discovered that the boarding concealed a foot-thick wall of asbestos brick. The warehouses were as neat as the proverbial Dutch housewife's closets. The floors were covered with well-kept straw mats. The walls were lined with hundreds of cedar boxes. We opened a few. They contained nothing but records—land titles, ledgers, promissory notes by the Homma sharecroppers. Before us was the depository of the combined grief—the mounting debt, the backbreaking labor, the enormous rent—of thousands of families through a score of generations. We walked out, leaving behind muddy footprints on the neat yellow mats.

The celluloid collar fumbled with the large key at the second warehouse. In the history of the Hommas, the interpreter said, none but the head of the family was allowed to pass these doors. This time, the search was more productive. In one corner we found a hundred sword hilt guards, with incrustations in gold and silver. In another corner, we found two ancient *samurai* swords. These were heirlooms, and the Hommas had permits to keep them.

Suddenly there was a shout from the darkness upstairs, where a sergeant was searching with a flashlight. "I got something." He came down, with a small can in his hand. McHardy looked at the can, and said angrily to the eldest Homma: "What in hell are you doing with percussion caps?" The celluloid collar looked blank. I looked at the can.

"Hold it, Lieutenant," I said quickly, "read the label." In small type, the bottom line read: "Made in London, To the Order of the Ottoman Empire."

"What in the hell is an Ottoman Empire? said the sergeant.

"This must be one of the things our great-grand-uncle brought from Europe last century," said the celluloid collar.

Eventually, we did find gold—a tiny cloth bag of it, with a few ounces of the yellow dust. By now, McHardy was disheartened. "What's this supposed to be?" One of the Hommas explained that the family once prospected for gold in a stream it owned, and this was a sample of the gold produced. The project was abandoned fifty years ago. Like almost everything else in this huge, dark warehouse, the gold really should have been in a museum. Almost the only exception was a thick bundle of Japanese war bonds. They totalled Y.900,000, or $60,000, and for lack of better booty, McHardy seized it.

But there was still another warehouse to be searched. When it was finally unlocked, we saw a large, clean room, with nothing in it but six packages resting side by side. Each package, about six feet long, was wrapped in coarse silk. One of the GIs began to unwrap a package. Under the silk, there was another layer of cloth. The GI pushed his hand down. The surface yielded.

"What in hell . . . ?" he said. The Hommas looked sad. Finally the celluloid spoke up. "From time to time," he said, "members of the imperial family come to Sakata and stay with us. When that happens, we take these . . . "—he swept the six bundles with his hand—"We take these to the big house. They are imported innerspring mattresses."

Coming back, we were all subdued. We knew our raid had failed. No one knew it better than McHardy, who had impounded the war bonds and the keys to the warehouses, and was wondering if Headquarters would approve.

While McHardy was telephoning the colonel at the prefectural capital, I talked to the former Thought Control man at the gate.

"Do you know this man Ikeda, the Diet member who was here this morning? Is he a friend of the Hommas?"

"Oh, no." He chuckled at my question. "They are no friends. They've been fighting each other for twenty-five years."

"Why?"

"It all started way back, around 1920. At that time, the Hommas decided to build a shrine for the spirit of one of their ancestors. But they didn't want to pay for it themselves. So they invited all the city elders to a great feast, and when it was nearly over, they suggested a 'voluntary tax' for the construction of the shrine. The guests agreed it was an excellent idea. So the tax was imposed, and, in 1921, a beautiful shrine was built in the city park. Ikeda fought the new tax, but he failed, and the Hommas made it difficult for him to work. So Ikeda made friends with General Ishihara and other nationalists, and in the 1942 elections he defeated the Homma candidate, and became a Diet member. And he still hates the Hommas."

When I returned to the office, McHardy was giving instructions to the sergeant: "You take these bonds and keys back to the Hommas, and tell them we made a mistake. Be polite with them."

Akita was a happy sight—busy, undamaged, packed carefully, like a Christmas gift, in thick wads of cottony snow. Behind the store windows, frosted along the edges, lay a better variety of goods than I have seen in Tokyo, and the stores seemed crowded. The children looked sturdier and gayer.

We drove through a maze of alleys, lined with prosperous homes. Then we turned a corner, and saw in the distance three figures in violent red. When we came closer, I saw that they were servants in red liveries. Behind them loomed the athletic figure of Colonel Lukas E. Haska, who is my host in General Dorn's absence.

At lunch, Haska told me the story of the liveries. It appears that Dorn, distressed by the shoddy appearance of the servants, decided to get them uniforms. His aide, an imaginative young man, proceeded to the local Catholic convent and ordered some bright red cowboy outfits. Feeling that these might give his residence a musical comedy touch, Dorn vetoed them. On his next try, the aide produced the red hunting liveries. Dorn finally gave in.

I spent the bulk of the day with the Japanese—mostly politicians and newspapermen. The Japanese say that Akita has been a garrison town for 1,200 years, ever since a force was sent here to beat back the Ainu tribes. Now the Ainus have been pushed to a small corner of the island to the north, where they are of no interest to anyone except photographers for American illustrated magazines. Akita no longer has a Japanese garrison, and it lies buried under snow and worries about the food shortage in the coming spring. They are even saving tangerine peel here, though I doubt if anyone will eat the stuff. This is a rice-growing prefecture, with roughly a million and a quarter people. Of every five persons in Akita prefecture, three work on land, and of all the farmers, 86 per cent are sharecroppers. The remainder is small owners who barely make a living. There are only about fifty landlords.

My first talk was with an editor of the local daily. He is a small, mousy man in badly patched shoes and one of the few clean white shirts I have seen in Japan. He gave me a general political roundup, which yielded these tidbits:

(a) General Ishihara's East Asia League, into which I ran in Sakata, has about 4,000 members in this prefecture, and is now busily recruiting more. It does so in the guise of "teaching the farmers to use yeast." Ishihara, I am assured, is "crazy about yeast."

Ishihara delivered a bitter speech here five weeks after Japan's surrender, and 2,000 people came to hear him. He blamed Tojo, Admiral Kantaro Suzuki, who was then premier, and the Japanese press for the defeat, and added that this was one of his last speeches.

"I shall have to go underground for a while," he said, "perhaps for five years."

(b) The Social Democratic party here has become a catchall, including everything from Communists to Fascists. Its head is one of the wartime organizers of the totalitarian Imperial Rule Assistance Association.

(c) Even though nothing has yet been done to enforce the land reform law—which will break up the large estates and make it possible for the sharecroppers to buy land—there have already been at least a hundred violations. The big landlords are splitting their holdings into small parcels, which they distribute among "dummy" owners—their cousins, servants, and children newly born.

When we finished the talk, the editor invited me to come to his newspaper, the *Akita Sakigake Shimpo*. He promised to produce the political boss of the town, and also one of General Ishihara's lieutenants here. "By a coincidence," he said, "this man will be in our office on business this afternoon."

We sat in a large room under a sign saying, "Peace for East Asia, 1940." Girls brought in platters of apples and tangerines, and two *hibachi* with glowing charcoal. Then a mob of men began to move in. They examined me out of the corners of their eyes, and settled down in a circle around the room. I tried to look unconcerned. Eventually the editor came in and said these were the sub-editors, who wanted to interview me and to watch me interview the political boss. I promptly began to ask *them* questions. I was especially interested in learning when they began to feel that the war was being lost. The editor said he knew defeat was certain when the Japanese lost Guadalcanal. Three of his subordinates all said they knew Japan would lose the day Pearl Harbor was attacked. I was in the middle of this question, when the political boss came in.

His name was Suzuki, and he was a pillar of conservatism and respectability in Akita. He was an old, baldheaded codger in a black cutaway, striped pants, a shaggy brown bearskin vest, and knee-high rubber boots. We talked for an hour, and I discovered that he had once served as mayor of Akita, had always been an intrepid fighter for democracy, wished to run for the Diet as a service to his people and his country, and thought the food problem could be settled easily by importing 75 million bushels of rice. He was opposed to the Social Democratic party, because it consisted of men who owned no property and therefore had no qualifications for leadership.

I kept asking him questions, and he kept skirting around them with clichés as his armor. Finally, I decided I was wasting time. So I thanked the old man, and he promptly picked up an apple and began to munch on it. That done, he settled deeper in his chair and closed his eyes.

Now I wanted to see General Ishihara's lieutenant, and the editor was sending messengers to all parts of the building, without much success. While this was being done, the newspapermen were questioning me. The ony subject they seemed to be interested in was women's suffrage. The climax of the interview was reached when I said that in the last election Sally and I probably voted different tickets.

"You mean your wife voted for a different candidate?"

I nodded.

They were exchanging remarks of wonderment when a messenger came back to whisper to the editor, and the latter said the man we were looking for was gone. The editor did not know whom General Ishihara's lieutenant was visiting on the paper, nor did he know the man's address, nor did he think it would make much sense to look for him in Akita. I was getting a runaround, and I did not like it one bit. The newspapermen were all munching apples and waiting curiously to see how I would react. A sharp remark I began was arrested by a thin, high sound I could not identify. I looked around. The political boss and the champion of democracy had fallen asleep, his mouth was open, and he was snoring.

December 30, 1945   AKITA

Colonel Haska, a West Pointer whose face bears marks of four years of boxing, believes in punctuality. He was in the dining room at seven-thirty on the dot, trim, alert, and exquisitely courteous. For breakfast, we had an omelet with red peppers which burned the inside of my mouth in no time. But the peppers were not the only thing hot. The colonel smiled and said to the lieutenant down the table: "Oh, Lieutenant, I hope that you'll honor us with a shave. Say, before noon." The lieutenant's young, blond growth turned red, and he said, "Yes, sir."

The colonel is leaving for Tokyo today in a private train, with all the men who can be spared from their tasks here, to see the New Year's football game.

After breakfast, I drove to the Military Government building on Akita's main street. The local detachment is commanded by Lieutenant Colonel Borden, a Lincolnesque Alabama county judge who is returning home soon to enter politics. He is far above the common run of Military Government officers I have met thus far, and he should do well.

Before I left the building at five, I had talked to most of the Military Government people here and learned something of their problems. The men are frustrated and unhappy; they think we are bungling our job in Japan; and nearly all of them want to get out of here at the first chance.

A directive from General MacArthur has ruled that U.S. forces have no right to give orders to Japanese officials, except on the matter of Japanese demobilization. "How can you get these people to do what you want them to do without authority?" asked one of the men. "I've observed no improvement here. The old gang continues to run things. And the Military Government, instead of being what its name implies it is, and enforcing General MacArthur's directives, can only chew its nails."

There were other complaints. The Japanese get the texts of the American directives through their official channels much quicker than we do. Sometimes, requests to American officers to check up on compliance with directives arrive before the directives themselves reach the outposts.

"You see this book?" asked another officer. He waved a little green folder. It was the familiar file of directives reprinted by the *Nippon Times*, the mouthpiece of the Japanese Foreign Office. "Everyone of us has a copy. This is where we find our directives. We also subscribe to the *Nippon Times*, to learn what our policy for Japan is."

"Our objectives in Japan, from all we can gather, are O.K.," said still another officer. "What is wrong is that there are no checks, or balances, or authority. We are told to check up on Japanese compliance. The only thing we can do is go to the Japanese here, and ask them polite-like, Do you teach military science in your schools? What about Shintoism? Today, we are responsible to our local U.S. Army tactical commander. If we find a flagrant violation of some directive, we can talk to him, and figure out some extralegal way to get the Japanese to reform their ways. But on January 1, all Military Government units will go under the direct command of the Corps commander, who is hundreds of miles away. It will take months of time and reams of paper to decide on some local action.

"I don't care whether the Military Government has power or not. But I say, give this power to somebody—any American organization at all—before the Japanese make a farce of all our objectives."

The last word came from one of the key men in the unit.

As I was putting my heavy coat on, he said: "For a year I've been dreaming of being able to come home and say with pride, I was with the Military Government in Japan. But I'll be damned if I'll mention the fact to anyone now."

December 31, 1945   KOMORO

In six hours it will be a new year, and I am lonely for Sally, and homesick. I am writing this in a shabby upstairs barrack room in a town I shall call Komoro. The room holds four army cots, a black coal stove in the center, a couple of machineguns and a *samurai* sword next to me, and a collection of photographs of prostitutes who, at one time or another, had visited here.

There is a garrison of a dozen men here, led by a man whom I shall call Lieutenant Hartley. He is a nice, carefree boy of twenty-six who knew what to do with his unit in the war and fought well, but who is perplexed by the problems of political directives, a coldly hostile Japanese town, loneliness in peacetime, and a unit in which the disciplined men of a wartime army are being replaced by 18-year-olds who were still children when this war started. Komoro is n miles into the Japanese nowhere, and Hartley, sitting here without guidance and without newspapers, feels that he has been left to his own devices, and he understands neither the nature of the danger nor the precautions he must take. He takes help where he can find it, and in Komoro he can find it only among the Japanese villains, and his uneasiness mounts because he is aware of their villainy. He tries to pretend that he is free and gay, but his anxiety is ill-concealed.

Tonight, Hartley is giving a big New Year's Eve party. He has invited a large number of guests. There will be the Japanese minister from the small local church, his young wife, and some of his more solid parishioners. There will be the present chief of police, and his predecessor, who was dismissed for being a Thought Control man, and who apparently still runs this town. There will be four women described as "*geisha*," three Japanese women described as "girl friends," and four others about whose profession no one makes any pretence. There is a big Christmas tree in the playroom, and an improvised bar, with some bad Japanese whisky, a lot of Japanese beer, and some punch for the minister and his flock.

We had an early dinner. When it was over, Hartley rose and addressed his unit. "Men," he said, "we're having a party tonight, and I want it to be nice, just like the party we had Christmas eve. If anyone gets plastered, I want two other boys to take him outside to sober up, and then put him to bed. If anyone wants to take a woman upstairs to see some Japanese etchings . . . " He smiled. " . . . Well, don't drag her by the hair. Take her by the hand, and lead her up quietly. We're going to have the minister here tonight, and his wife, and some nice people, and we don't want them to think badly of us. And, for God's sake, don't forget your prophylactic kit. We don't want any VD in this unit."

When he got through, I went upstairs to reread Goodrich's *Delilah*, which I had found under the bed.

At eight Hartley came in to invite me down. The party had started. "Oh, my aching back," he was saying, "something is wrong but I can't figure out what it is." I went down. The playroom was crowded. All the women were sitting primly on one side of the room, and the Japanese men on the other. The GIs were at the bar, getting drinks for themselves and the women. The minister was making frequent trips to the women's side, to talk to two lovely and thoroughly frightened women. They were his wife and a cousin. The rest of the women were middle-aged and heavily made up with a white paint and rouge. The Thought Control man was in the middle of the room, turning tentatively under his own finger stuck on top of his head. He was not drunk, but he pretended he was. There was little talk. The GIs knew no Japanese, and the Japanese knew no English. The "proper" Japanese would not talk to the "improper" ones. I had a glass of beer and went upstairs.

By ten o'clock there were shouting men and giggling women dashing by my door, and the sound of merriment was coming from the playroom. I went down. Now the picture had changed. Everyone was drunk, and everyone was talking—with the listener often unable to understand, but refusing to let this bother him. The Thought Control man was doing a hunter's dance. His quarry was the minister, who was also very drunk. The police chief was in a corner, with an arm around one of the uglier prostitutes. The minister's wife and cousin were in the adjoining room, next to the stair landing, where they were playing pingpong with a very young GI. Both were sober, and unhappy. Occasionally, they had to get out of the way, to let by a soldier taking a woman upstairs. The boys were not yet dragging them by the hair, but they were dragging them nevertheless. Each time a couple rushed upstairs, the minister's wife and cousin pretended they saw nothing. Their faces looked strained.

I joined the pingpong game, and tried to cheer the women up. Hartley came by. I said, "Look, will you tell the minister to take his women home. I don't want to play watchman, and there's going to be trouble." Hartley said miserably, "I tried to tell the old fool, but he is having a fine time. I'll try again."

I was in the middle of a game with the minister's wife when she looked past me. I turned. The other woman was gone. There was only one door there, leading into a long corridor with store rooms. The corridor was empty. I found the girl in the third store room. In the dim light coming in behind me, I could see her kneeling, with a man wrestling with her. The man was an American visitor. I grabbed him by the shoulder and pulled. He looked up. His face was completely blank. As he released his embrace, the girl rose and scampered out of the room. The man walked out slowly, without saying a word.

The game was on again. I went into the playroom, took the minister by the arm, and led him to George. "You tell him," I said, "that I want him to get his coat, and take his women home. Right now." The minister looked at me, smiled, and said in English, "OK." I waited until he left the building, stumbling a bit in the snow, and walking ahead of the two women, as befits a well-mannered man in Japan.

The party broke up about eleven. I was in bed when Hartley came in. He sat down on his cot, and covered his face with his hands. "Oh, my aching back," he said at last to no one in particular, took his shoes off, and stretched out on his cot in his clothes.

At midnight, I said, "Happy New Year."

Hartley did not answer.

January 1, 1946   KOMORO

I was awakened at eight by Hartley's shouts into a field telephone. He was talking to a neighboring town. It appears that earlier this morning a GI reported to Hartley that the Japanese town hall, right across the street from us, had run up the "meatball" (Japanese flag) in violation of all known orders. Hartley promptly dispatched a sergeant to tear the flag down. The Japanese police chief explained that he put up the flag with the permission of General MacArthur. Hartley had had trouble before with directives which reached the Japanese long before they got to him, and he suspected that this had happened again. He knew he had lost face, and he had a bad hangover, and he was thoroughly incensed.

Now he was shouting into the phone to check with the neighboring garrison whether the Japanese were lying or not. No, they had heard nothing of it, but the flag was also up in their town. Then the lieutenant in the next town wanted to know if Hartley had heard of a new directive ordering the Japanese to surrender forty-seven specified books on Shintoism. He had picked up a broadcast from Tokyo, but it was disjointed and it did not make much sense. No, said Hartley, he had not heard.

He put the receiver down and said, "I'm just the guy who works here. I don't know nothing."

Downstairs, Sergeant Finley, which is not his name, was exhibiting to me a rich collection of trophies he had gathered in raids on local schools—a couple of machineguns, glider models, war posters, military training manuals. Finley is a compact youth of about twenty-four, who intends to remain in the army and who actually runs the garrison here.

"A couple of days ago," he said, "I went on one of them raids. All by myself, and a horse. Well, I came to a school, and I guess they didn't expect me. In the barn in the school yard I found me a life-size glider, all ready to fly. So I borrowed a sledge hammer in their workshop and busted up the damned thing. I went through the school pretty thoroughly, but I found nothing else.

"Well, I got back and started thinkin'. I just didn't like the way those bastards looked. So yesterday I took another fellow and went back. We came into the yard, and here was all the teachers digging a big pit. And right next to it, waiting to be buried, three brand new airplane engines, airplane tools, instruments and a lot of other junk.

"I say to the principal, What in hell is this? He says it's stuff they had just found. I say I went through the building yesterday and saw nothing, and what did they think they were doing burying it? The principal says they knew they had to melt it down, but they had no equipment for it, and so they were going to bury the stuff until such time as they got the equipment. So I gave them some axes and told them to go to it."

At lunch, Hartley asked me what I would like to do. I told him I wanted to go on some school raids. With Finley, we mapped out a campaign. We agreed that the schools around Komoro had been thoroughly forewarned. But there was a town called Otuki, about two hours' trip away by local train, and no Americans had been there yet. The main thing, we agreed, was to preserve the surprise element. We considered carefully the problem of reserving rooms in the Otuki inn. Finally, Hartley called the Japanese police chief in, said that I was going to visit Otuki for a possible newspaper article, suggested that he, Hartley, might join me, and asked the chief to use the police phone—the only phone line to Otuki in town—to make the necessary reservations for me.

The train was to leave at four in the afternoon, and we had a few hours to kill. But there was no rest for Hartley. Japanese callers began to drop in to convey their New Year's greetings. Among them was an old, thin man with a goatee and oversized black-rimmed glasses, whom Hartley introduced to me as Mr. Muko. Through George, Muko explained that he was a famous philologist and linguist, that he had written books and studied in China, and that he spoke German, English and Chinese. The only comprehensible English words I heard from him were "Sank you," which he used inordinately.

Before long, Mr. Muko had Hartley and me in a corner. He had heard from the police chief that we were going to Otuki, and he wondered if Hartley would take him, Muko, along. It appeared that Muko had a potato farm in Otuki, and if he could just make a trip there, he could bring enough potatoes back to last the family a month. "Oh, my aching back," said Hartley. "I don't know why I talk to this guy." To Muko he said, "O.K., you can come." Muko said, "Sank you."

When Hartley and I arrived at the station, the train—straight out of Toonerville—was waiting for us. The station master, marching importantly ahead of us, escorted us to our private car. A few minutes later, Muko climbed in. Brightly, he said he had used the police line to telephone the mayor of Otuki, and tell him that he, Muko, was bringing his American friends with him, and to be sure that they receive the best of accommodations. Otherwise, Muko said, he would personally feel a sense of shame. Hartley was distressed. "Tell Mr. Muko," he said to the interpreter, "that we appreciate his help, but we don't want the son of a bitch messing up our arrangements."

The Nisei translated the remark to Muko. Muko smiled, shook his goatee, and said in Japanese, "No trouble. Lieutenant Hartley is my friend."

We made the rest of the trip in silence. When we reached

Otuki, it was snowing, in big soft flakes which obscured the view. We left the car and stepped on the station platform. Before us, lined up neatly, stood six men. Two of them wore cutaways, one had a police officer's uniform.

Muko said, "Allow me to introduce: the mayor, the deputy mayor, president of the council, the police chief, the school board president, the station master." The mayor bowed and said "Welcome to Otuki." Hartley said angrily, "You tell this guy we thank him, but Mr. Muko has nothing to do with us. He just bummed a ride off us."

Muko smiled benevolently and said, "Sank you."

The mayor led us outside the station. Before us was a large, horse-drawn sled, with a large boxlike structure on it. For the first time, we learned that the Otuki station lay three miles from the town. Awkwardly, the four of us crawled into the box, and made room for the mayor. There was not a free inch left in the box. The mayor shouted, and the sled took off.

After a while, I began to hear strange sounds. I looked out of the side window. There was nothing but empty fields and snow. I drew up the rear curtain. Behind us, running heavily, was the entire administration of the town of Otuki.

By the time we reached Otuki, a life-size blizzard was raging over the town, shaking its flimsy wooden buildings and whirling the snow. The Otuki inn was a surprisingly large, two-story building. We took our shoes off, and walked up to the rooms reserved for us. We were now in a large, shabby room, empty but for two charcoal braziers in the center and eleven sitting pillows laid out in a wide circle around them.

"What's that?" said Hartley.

The mayor said, "A little banquet. The town of Otuki wishes to welcome the American guests. Mr. Muko—"

Muko was one Japanese word the lieutenant knew. "Goddamned Mr. Muko," he shouted. "Goddamned Mr. Muko. We don't want to hear his name again. We don't want any banquet. We don't want anything. Just let us be."

The mayor looked nonplussed. "You tell him," said Hartley, "that we're tired. All we want tonight is some food and sleep. Thank him, and say we'll have the banquet some other time."

The mayor retired, and the owner came in to say the bath was ready. Hartley and I took ours first. On the way back to our rooms, I thought I heard a familiar voice. I slid a panel aside and looked in. There was a circle of men sitting around a brazier, and drinking sake. Sitting in the host's place was the mayor. In the place of honor, and talking in a high falsetto voice, was Mr. Muko.

January 2, 1946   OTUKI

We rose early, shaved, and waited for breakfast. When it came, with it arrived Muko, beaming happily. We smiled back. We were filled with the secret delight of a hunter about to spring his trap. The Japanese had given us a runaround, but this was our day. We finished breakfast quickly, and brushed off Muko's attempt to pay our bill. Then, in single file, we marched down a path cut through four-foot snow. It was sunny and warm, and the town looked gay in its white dress and necklace of sparkling icicles.

We had not walked two hundred yards when we saw a figure coming towards us. It was a Japanese policeman, with a short sword. He talked to George, and George said the man had been sent ahead *to guide us to the police station.* I said in disbelief, "You're kidding us." "No," said George, "the man says the inn called them up when we left, and the chief sent him out to guide us to the station."

Hartley and I exchanged glances. Secretly we knew we were beaten, but we still refused to give up hope. Perhaps this was just a coincidence, this guide for a visit meant to be a surprise.

We marched up a hill to the police station, which was small and warm, and there was a group of men waiting for us. We knew the police chief and the deputy mayor. The chief introduced the others. They were the principals of the two town schools.

He said, "We thought you might want to visit our schools, and so I asked the principals to come here, and offer to serve as your guides."

Forlornly, we trudged up a narrow mountain path behind the two principals. Both were in cutaways and tall rubber boots, which began to strike me as part of the formal attire in this part of the world. We crossed a gulley, climbed up another mountain, and we were in the school. All preparations had been made for our visit. The teachers in their Sunday best had been assembled in the faculty room, and the women teachers served tea and rice cookies. We felt angry and frustrated, and at the first opportunity we broke away to examine the school. I made the first find. In a classroom for eight-year-olds I found a long shelf with the banned books on "ethics." They were illustrated with pictures of Japanese submarines, men-of-war, and *kamikaze* planes blowing American vessels into smithereens. I asked the principal what he proposed to do about these books, and he said he intended to tell the children to ink out the objectionable portions, but he had been much too busy to have done it as yet.

Slowly we all moved towards the large entrance lobby, lined with book cases, and waited there in indecision. Hartley was walking along the book cases, asking his interpreter the titles of the books, and kicking the drawers below. "What's in there?" he asked. "School records," said the principal. "I want to see them," said Hartley.

The drawer was finally unlocked. In it we saw a collection of airplane instruments, each with a tag. The first one I picked up was a gauge from a British plane shot down in Malaya. Another gauge was labelled, The Pioneer Company, Brooklyn, N.Y., and may have come from almost any battlefield of Southeast Asia.

The principal's face was red, and he kept explaining that he did not know how the instruments got into the school. We were feeling jubilant, and unwilling to listen to his protestations.

We took the drawer out, and ordered a Japanese policeman to take it to the inn. Then we walked back to the inn, our spirits up and our minds busy.

"You know what," I said, "if we could find this stuff in a town that was obviously prepared for us, think of the stuff we could find in an unprepared town. Where could we go from here so that it would be a *real* surprise?"

"It's a swell idea," said Hartley. The train that goes through here goes as far as a town called Mitumine. Let's just get on the train, tell no one where we're going, and then get off at that town. And let's take the police chief along so that he can't warn anyone."

The police chief did not want to come with us. He said he had a bad cold. We were firm, and he finally came. Again we were on a train, and though we knew our mission to Otuki had surprised no one but us, we also felt sure our next raid would be a tremendous success. Surprise, we said to each other, is the essence of a fruitful raid.

We were now on a three-car local, the first train I have seen that was not bursting with passengers. We had not yet told the chief where we were going, and he was now sitting in a corner, sulking. At each station he raised his oversized cap from his eyes, and looked at us. We pretended we did not see him.

It was close to two in the afternoon when we finally reached Mitumine. Briskly we trooped out on the platform. And then, in stupefaction, we watched the bowing men lined up before us. A tall, slim man in a cutaway. Two or three short men in black coats and starched collars. A small, squat police officer with a very long sword. The tall men stepped forward, and said, "I'm the mayor of Mitumine. We welcome you to this town." Dully we acknowledged the introductions, and heard the mayor announce that a visit had been arranged for us to the Mitumine school, and dully we fell into a long procession that started from the station.

Eventually we reached the school. I was warm from the climb, and I did not want to go in. I sat down on the steps and watched the valley below, with its stream, the busy, little village hugging the stream, the children riding sleds on a slope. It was sunny and quiet, and I could hear the children's shouts of delight. After a while, the mayor came to plead with me to go in. I walked dutifully through the beautifully cleaned up school, the bare gymnasium, and the faculty room where women teachers were serving tea. On a shelf, I picked up a book on *Military Virtue*. But I said nothing. We had been defeated, completely and humiliatingly. All that I wanted to do now was to get away, and to find out exactly how we had been tricked.

It was three o'clock, and the train did not leave for two hours. "Perhaps," suggested the mayor, "we could go to Mitumine Inn and have some tea." There was nothing else to do, and we agreed. And it was no shock at all, when we entered the inn, to discover that a banquet had been laid out for us, with a long succession of dishes and gallons of sake.

"There's one thing we can do," said Hartley. "Let's get drunk." He traded cups with the town officials, in a gesture of courtesy, and offered toasts himself. There was an atmosphere of deeprooted good will and understanding. Then young women teachers, kneeling before us, began to serve food. I pleaded indisposition and ate nothing. In the middle of the banquet, the mayor said he wanted to make a speech.

"I've been a champion of democracy all my life," he said. "This is a small town. But it is the spirit and not the number that counts. It's too bad that the U.S. Army does not send its excellent officers like Captain Hartley more frequently to Mitumine, to help us become democratic. We hope that the next time you visit us, you will give us an advance notice."

Hartley said to me, "What in hell do I say?" I suggested that he respond with a statement that our visit must have been somewhat less than a complete surprise, since the mayor had had time to put on his striped pants and order a full-size banquet.

"We can't be sarcastic," Hartley said reproachfully. "The guys are our hosts."

He expressed pleasure over his visit and the indications of a good job of democratizing being done by the mayor. But I was not an official, and I could be objectionable if I wanted. I kept questioning the mayor until I found out that he was by profession a "connoisseur of arts," and that his father had been one of the biggest landlords in the area.

We left the inn at five and walked to the station. We shook hands all around, and the mayor said, "Please come back in the spring. The fishing here is splendid. But, please, no surprise." He smiled coyly, "No surprise." With the Otuki police chief, who was very drunk, we went into the car. There were no lights, but the city fathers of Mitumine put a small charcoal brazier in the aisle.

I sat next to the police chief, gave him a cigarette, and asked him about his cold. He laughed and said sake had cured it. I wanted to know how long he had been chief of police in Otuki. He said he had been there since late August—a fortnight after Japan's surrender—and before that he had been chief of Thought Control in a neighboring town.

"All of us," he said, "were moved around in August and September." I said it was too bad that the Thought Control force had been disbanded for "there's no one now to keep an eye on subversive elements." It was not quite as bad as all that, he explained, because "all Thought Control work will now be under the Peace Preservation Officer and the Administrator of Justice in the prefectural governments."

"I myself," he said "have just come from a conference in the prefectural capital. December 28 and 29. Our former Thought Control chief who is now Peace Preservation Officer gave us new instructions on our work. Especially in the coming elections."

I had just one more question. "How did you know that we would want to see the schools in Otuki, and how did the people in Mitumine know we were coming?"

He laughed. "It was very simple. There is nothing but schools for Americans to see in Otuki. Maybe the flour mill. But we didn't think you'd come all the way from Komoro to see the mill. Then, when you decided to go to some other town and took me along, I just told my assistant to call up every town on the railway line and tell them to prepare for your visit. There are only four towns. We wanted you to enjoy your visit."

I said, incredulously: "Do you mean to say that in every town along this line, there were officials waiting for us at the station, and tea, and banquets? And we just went by and didn't even look at them out of the window?"

The chief nodded. Behind me Hartley said, "Oh, my aching back."

January 4, 1946   EN ROUTE TO TOKYO

This is my second straight day of train travel, and I'll be happy when we get to Tokyo sometime today. The whole trip is a dim, confused memory of cold, snow, interminable delays, spam sandwiches, stations packed with waiting humanity, cat naps, and work with the typewriter on my lap. Once, in the mountains, the wooden car had become ignited by sparks from the locomotive. We pulled the emergency cord, stopped the train, and put the fire out with snow and with chlorinated water from our canteens. Last night we picked up a colonel. Some hours later, at a station, the conductor came in to explain that the coal was so poor he doubted if we would make the steep grade ahead. He thought that if we waited until early this morning, we might get an extra engine. The colonel looked at a passenger train pulling into the station from the opposite direction.

"Where's that train going?"

The conductor said it was going to Akita.

"Uncouple the engine from that train, and attach it to ours," the colonel said. "I'm going to Tokyo on important business, and I can't miss the next connection."

The engine was uncoupled. We made the grade all right, but when it looked as if we would still miss the connection, the colonel sent word ahead to hold up the connecting train. We were three hours late, and the train was held up for us,

At Niigata, George went out to pick up the Japanese papers. They contained the text of a rescript issued by the emperor on New Year's Day, and General MacArthur's comment on it. I listened to George's translation of both with unbelieving ears.

As if nothing had happened in Japan, the emperor began his message with a long quote from Emperor Meiji's "Charter-Oath," describing it as "the basis of our national policy." The five points of the 80-year-old "Charter Oath" purportedly provide for a genuinely democratic regime, with reliance on public opinion and the vigorous participation of "All classes, high and low . . . in the affairs of State." As everyone in General MacArthur's Headquarters knows, Emperor Meiji has become the pillar and symbol of militant nationalism in Japan, and whatever the verbiage of some of his proclamations, a popular government was never practiced in his 45-year reign, nor was it intended to function. Under Emperor Meiji, Japan fought China and Russia, seized Formosa, violated and annexed Korea, and established "special rights" in Manchuria. And it was Emperor Meiji whose rescripts set the narrow feudal mold for contemporary Japan. Yet, here was Hirohito, the emperor of a country which we had marked for democratization, going back to the nineteenth century for the guideposts of a democratic Japan.

"Excessive radical tendencies," Hirohito's rescript said, "are gradually spreading, and the sense of morality tends to lose its hold on the people, with the result that there are signs of confusion of thought. We stand by the people, and we wish always to share with them in their moments of joy and sorrow. The ties between Us and Our people . . . are not predicated on the false conception that the emperor is divine, and that the Japanese people are superior to other races and fated to rule the world."

General MacArthur issued the following comment on the rescript: "The emperor's New Year's statement pleases me very much. By it he undertakes a leading part in the democratization of his people. He squarely takes his stand for the future along liberal lines. . . . "

Returned to Press Club, to find everyone busy at a typewriter. The purge directive, which had provoked an intramural fight in Headquarters, has just been issued. Although there are big gaps in it, I am impressed with it. It removes the top layer of Japanese nationalism—the military men, the bureaucrats who belonged to the Imperial Rule Assistance Association, the men who formed, led, or financed the terroristic or secret societies, the officers of the firms that looted and exploited Occupied Asia, intelligence agents, and the wire-pullers behind the Japanese puppets in Asia. It also requires that all future officials must fill in a questionnaire, showing their activities and affiliations since 1931.

Among the societies marked for dissolution is the East Asia League of my friend General Ishihara.

But I am wiser now that I have been away from Tokyo, with its air of intrigue, excitement, and authority, into the country where the real test of our success will be made. The directive places its enforcement in the hands of the Japanese governmental machinery. Will the men I have seen—the governors, the police chiefs, the political bosses—agree to rub themselves out of political life, to end the hold of this entire wicked, feudal system on the country, just because a paper directive had been issued in Tokyo? The Thought Control men were removed from authority exactly three months ago, under a directive no whit different from today's. Yet, they have survived the storm by changing their labels. Will yesterday's Thought Control chief who is today a Peace Preservation Officer give up his job tomorrow, or will he merely change his title? The Japanese papers predict that most of the cabinet ministers will survive the purge. Actually, it will be up to Premier Shidehara, and the sinister politician named Wataru Narahashi behind him, to decide who is to be sacrificed. Will they sacrifice Foreign Minister Shigeru Yoshida, who helped to draft the notorious plan for the conquest of China known erroneously as the Tanaka Memorial, or Welfare Minister Hitoshi Ashida, whose *Japan Times* plugged for aggression? We all doubt it.

This directive can be a terrific haymaker. Yet, we weaken

the punching power behind the blow by letting the Japanese themselves decide who is to be punched and who is to be spared. The fault belongs to no man; it is the fault of our policy of relying on an undemocratic government to democratize the land.

January 6, 1946   TOKYO

Learned today that the first draft of the emperor's rescript, in which he renounced his divinity, was actually cooked up in General Dyke's office. I can see no objections to putting words in the emperor's mouth. What does amuse— and puzzle—me is that once he uttered these words, we promptly issued a statement lauding his "liberalism" and "democratic spirit."

January 9, 1946   TOKYO

Got up early to write my report on the trip north. Worked steadily, despite all the handicaps of the Press Club. At eight at night they started a movie in the ballroom above me. I finally gave in, and went upstairs. It was "Rhapsody in Blue," with my favorite Gershwin piano concerto played twice through. When the lights went on again, a heavy hand descended on my shoulder. Sure enough, two of the five Russian correspondents here—Boris Gorbatov and Boris Agapov—were behind me. Gorbatov, his clean-shaven head shining brightly, said with mock glumness, *"poidem pit"*—Let's have a drink.

We went to the bar, and proceeded to drink—and argue. As a rule, I dislike arguments. But I find it stimulating and informative to argue with these five Russians, for what they have to say must mirror the top layer of Soviet thought. Boris Gorbatov, who won a half-million ruble Stalin prize for a book called *Taras' Family* (published in the United States as *The Unconquered*), is president of the all-important Union of Soviet Writers, a former Red Army colonel, and one of the most distinguished of Russian war correspondents. To a degree greater than his four comrades, he is a Slav nationalist. In a way, I suppose, he is the Russian counterpart of our mid-Western isolationists. Boris Agapov, who won a Stalin prize for documentary moving pictures, is the most Western of the Russians here. He has lived in France, knows European literature, and has a tolerance for the West. Both are tremendously impressive. You could be in constant disagreement with them but you could not deny them imagination, agile minds, and dynamic power.

This evening, our argument was on the perennial theme: Who won the war?

"We fought Germany," said Gorbatov, "to save the world. In fact, we did save it."

"Hold on," I said. "You didn't get into the fight to save the world. You were attacked. You fought for yourself, your wives and children, your towns, your heritage, your pride. In fighting for all this, you did help to save the world from naziism."

The two faces reddened. The Russians said if they had been fighting for their country alone, they could have made peace with the Germans half a dozen times before Germany's surrender.

Gorbatov said, "Only because we were fighting for the world, we were compelled to march on Germany, on Austria, on Hungary, on the rest of the Fascist satellites."

"Do you know," said Agapov, "that our soldiers went into battle shouting, 'For a free world?'"

Gorbatov at this point produced an unknown historic bit. "I happen to know," he said, "that the Germans made three approaches for peace to Russia in 1942 and 1943. The first one was after the Nazi failure to capture Moscow and Leningrad. Hitler proposed to end the war, with the Germans remaining on the Dnieper River. We turned him down flat.

"The other two overtures were made very late in 1943,

when the German High Command saw the extent of the debacle at Stalingrad. This time Hitler said: 'Let's stop this war, and I'll pull all my troops out of Russia.' We rejected this proposal. He tried again. We turned him down again. That was the end of it. I happen to know this because I have seen the relevant documents, and the German couriers."

We drank. "We turned Hitler down for the sake of the world, for the sake of humanity," said Gorbatov.

At one o'clock in the morning, Konstantin Simonov and Leonid Kudrevatikh joined our party. Simonov, who is probably better known to Americans than any other Soviet writer, looked handsome in his tall Cossack fur hat. Kudrevatikh, a noted correspondent for *Izvestia*, as usual had the air of a good-hearted country boy.

The conversation changed, but the spirit did not. "When our correspondents marched into Berlin with the Red Army," said Simonov, "we went half-hungry, because all the available food was reserved for the foreign press—mostly Americans. They were our guests, and we wanted them to have the best.

"But the trouble is that we find no reciprocal desire to take good care of us. I'll tell you a story. All of us, and a full Red Army general, landed at some airport in Kyushu. The American colonel in command sent his aide to invite us to dinner with him. That was all right. We appreciated the courtesy.

"Around five in the afternoon, we started cleaning up. We wanted to look good at the colonel's party. When we were just about ready, an aide showed up and said the colonel would not be able to keep the engagement. However, he expected us to have dinner at the officers' mess. Well, we could see where a military man might have problems come up that would throw his social life out of joint.

"We don't know much about protocol, but we know enough to see that it was not being observed. Together with our general, we were put at the foot of the table. From our seats we could see the colonel well. He had other guests for dinner: a couple of ill-mannered and noisy girls. In the middle of the dinner, one of the girls got up and sang, and all the officers whistled. Our interpreter said the song was called, 'Will I Sleep Alone Tonight?'

"This was bad enough. But the food was even worse. Real garbage. Some sort of meat. And with it potatoes. I like potatoes. But these were *bashed-up*, completely *bashed-up!*"

January 22, 1946   TOKYO

Had an instructive lunch with four members of the editorial staff of the Army's *Stars and Stripes*. They came loaded with stories censored by the army. The deletions shed a curious light on what the military command thinks the American citizen army should *not* know about Japan.

The censors deleted items dealing with the war role of the emperor, cabinet ministers, government officials, and the *Nippon Times*, the official and shrewd mouthpiece of the Foreign Office. Typical censored facts: that Premier Shidehara belonged to a Nationalist council; that a member of his Cabinet once belonged to a totalitarian party; that the English-language *Nippon Times* advertised itself as "indispensable to understand and appreciate the Leader-Empire."

Items showing that wartime propagandists were now "democratizing" Japan's educational system were killed. Specifically, the censors deleted mention of the author of a book called *The Fundamentals of Training of Imperial Subjects;* of Tojo's friend who had written *Instructions for Behavior on the Battlefield;* and of a professor who was decorated by Benito Mussolini, and who later played host to a Fascist educational mission to Japan.

Finally, no further critical reporting is allowed of a man named Toyohiko Kagawa, known as a Christian social worker.

Kagawa, for the moment, is an important star in the Tokyo political constellation. It is known that last month many important officers in Headquarters considered him the best candidate for the premier's job. Kagawa's progress, however, was blocked momentarily by the publication of his wartime record in the *Stars and Stripes*.

To me, as probably to millions of other Americans, Kagawa until recently stood for selfless effort. Born fifty-eight years ago in a wealthy family, and educated at Princeton, Kagawa could have chosen some comfortable career. Instead he had gone into the slums, to become one of the world's best known social workers. When he had visited the United States to lecture, great crowds came to honor him.

I saw Kagawa for the first time this morning, in a two-hour interview. He impressed me with his shrewdness, if with nothing else. Physically he is unprepossessing—a small, birdlike, old man in unkempt clothes. But his mind was sharp, and he dodged with skill and alacrity my questions on his recent record.

He said he stood for control of wealth, redistribution of land, and abolition of feudalism. But though he was against feudalism, Kagawa was for the emperor. "We need him," he said strongly. "In recent years, five premiers have been assassinated. The parties keep quarreling with each other. What we need is an arbiter. Hirohito is a man of tragedy. I sympathize with him. The nation and the Diet are responsible for the war. He is not."

The word "peace" was Kagawa's shield. He said he was imprisoned for three weeks in 1940 "for my part in the peace movement." He said he visited the United States in 1941, and on return told the Diet that President Roosevelt was a man of peace.

Kagawa admitted that he attacked the United States in 1945. "I did it intentionally," he said, "because American radio stations said I'd be premier after Japan's defeat, and they were destroying my influence as a Christian."

He spoke warmly of General MacArthur. He said: "General MacArthur has done a wonderful job. Even the conservatives are now praising his intentions."

I asked Kagawa the sources of his income. "I get up at 3:00 A.M. to write fiction," he said. "Currently I have three serials running in newspapers and magazines. All of them have a Christian theme. I'm also an adviser on crystography to an electric company, owned by an elder of my church." He spelled crystography out for me. "It's a science of crystals. Mathematical crystography is a hobby of mine."

But the man's portrait was incomplete. Some things of which he spoke did not tally with other evidence. Of many things he said nothing. Was he, like so many other liberals, caught in the nationalist hysteria? Had the pressures become so great he could not resist them? Was he so anxious to preserve his standing as a Christian leader that he stood ready to sacrifice some Christian principles?

If the questions of motivation remained unanswered, the record was clear on everything else.

On his return from the United States, Kagawa addressed the Foreign Affairs Committee of the Diet October 4, 1941. The speech has been removed from the Diet records. It was noted, however, that he spoke on "The Division of Public Opinion in the United States." The speech was reprinted in a magazine. It did not, as Kagawa claims, deal with President Roosevelt as a man of peace. Its comforting theme was the strength of American isolationism, from something called "The Vanguards" and "The Copperhead Club" (comprising, according to Kagawa, 90 per cent of America's 2,900 commercial pilots) to Charles Lindbergh, Burton Wheeler, and Herbert Hoover. Typical was this passage:

" . . . . Many of America's chief war advocates are Jews. Even the people in America who never before had discriminated against the Jews, were now indignant at the conduct of the Jews. . . . This was told me by Mr. (Alf) Landon, 1936 presidential candidate. When I heard this, even I felt this indignation. Up to that time, I had always been as sympahetic as possible towards the Jews but after hearing Mr. Landon's tale I couldn't help entertaining the same unpleasant feeling as Mr. Landon, because the Jews had certainly gone too far."

I strongly doubted if Mr. Landon would say anything of the sort to a Japanese visitor.

This was the beginning of a propagandist's career. In 1942, in a voice broadcast intercepted by our monitors, Kagawa said: "Today I see America as a white grave. I cannot believe that the Almighty God of all the earth will permit the success of their inordinate ambitions for world domination. . . . Ah, woe to America for so degrading the name of Christ by this butchery."

In 1944, Tokyo Radio quoted Kagawa as saying in a sermon: "Babylon fell . . . Rome fell, and America, too, is about to fall into ruins due to her self-love. . . . American children amuse themselves with the bones of dead Japanese officers and men. President Roosevelt takes pride in owning a book-knife made from the bones of a dead Japanese soldier. . . . "

In May of 1945, ten weeks before Japan's surrender, he was quoted as declaring that the San Francisco conference was "indicative of an inordinate ambition of the United States to dominate the world."

Kagawa lent other efforts to the war. On the signed testimony of Japanese fellow-Christians, he visited China to seek the end of Chinese resistance. He composed a war song. Together with a notorious racketeer and army agent (who is now in Sugamo Prison), he served as an adviser to Premier Higashikuni, and jointly with the racketeer sponsored a "peace meeting."

But the most interesting exhibit in my Kagawa file was an affidavit signed by a man named Kan Majima.

"I've been associated with Dr. Kagawa for twenty-five years," Majima said. "I was sadly disillusioned with him shortly before the war. I had mentioned to him that the militarists were driving toward a war with America. Much to my surprise, Kagawa said: 'If the war starts, I'll support it.' When I wanted to discuss this with him, he called me a coward. About a year after the war started, Kagawa told me that Japan is very strong and on the road to victory, and that we must do everything we can to help her win. After that we became estranged, and I did not see him until April, 1945. . . . My hospital had been burned to the ground and I told Kagawa that Japan had lost the war and that we as social workers should explain to the people that the war must be stopped. I told him that he, as a famous leader, should and could speak out against the war. A fierce argument broke out and Kagawa said that we must fight on, if necessary, even if we have to fight with bamboo poles."

The affidavit was signed in the presence of American witnesses, and Majima was photographed signing it. So were the other men who wrote other damaging affidavits.

Presumably the evidence on Kagawa was available to the colonels who wished to install him in the premier's residence. What was it that made them ignore the record? And what was the reasoning which led the army censors to bar knowledge of Kagawa's background from the GIs?

January 24, 1946   TOKYO

Today completed plans for a five-day trip to Nagano Prefecture next week, to join a team of farm union organizers on a tour of villages. The junket was organized by a magazine writer named Ono, a square-shouldered young man with an impassive face and unruly hair. Ono used to be an editor of a leading literary magazine, whose entire staff was arrested during the war for running a "subversive" article. Ono spent two years in prison. Our plan is to go to Nagano City, 130 miles to the northwest of here, pick up a noted publicist named Hirokichi Hayashi, and then travel on foot with the organizers. Nagano Prefecture is famous for its silk, apples, and progressive farmers, and the trip should be exciting.

At night had another session with the Russian correspondents. Gorbatov told me of Ilya Ehrenburg, whose impassioned articles formed the greatest single literary influence on the Red Army. "Everything that Ehrenburg wrote," Gorbatov said, "became a commandment to our troops. I'll give you an example. Kudrevatikh and I entered Berlin with the advance units, after the final battle. Few buildings remained intact, and many of them were guarded by our sentries. One night we were walking past a building, and here was the sentry, very busy. He had arranged an easy chair before the building, piled up paper and twigs against the wall, and carefully set them afire. Then he sat down, stretched his legs out, and began to warm himself.

" 'Comrade,' we shouted, 'Comrade, what are you doing? You're destroying the building.'

"The soldier was very calm. 'Comrade Ehrenburg said that we must destroy the Nazis and their property.'

"So we had to reason with the man, and explain to him that the war was over, that we were also writers, and that, anyway, Comrade Ehrenburg had now changed his mind.

" 'You're not lying?' he said. 'I mean about Comrade Ehrenburg.'

"We said, No, we had talked to Ehrenburg just before we left Moscow.

" 'Well,' said the soldier, 'in that case . . . ' "

January 27, 1946   TOKYO

A gang of us went over to Hibiya Park to watch a mass meeting honoring Susumu Okano, the Communist who has just returned from Red China and has now dropped his underground pseudonym to become Sanzo Nozaka. The park is a bald patch of ground circled by trees. For this occasion, a platform, decorated with red and white bunting, had been erected, and the welcoming committee sat solemnly on it.

I have not yet had a satisfactory explanation for Nozaka's popularity with non-Communists. It may be that his fame as an underground fighter had reached wartime Japan. It may be that there is such a paucity of leadership that the Japanese are ready to turn to any leader, regardless of his political hue. Whatever the explanation, this was a non-partisan meeting, with right-wingers sitting next to Communists.

The first thing we saw was a column of about five-hundred transport workers, with posters, running into the park in ranks and chanting *Wassho, wassho, wassho*. They all ran in step, old men and young, and the effect was that of color, movement and melody, as in a well-directed movie. Then smaller groups began to flock in, some marching with a song, some running in.

We placed ourselves behind the platform, and intercepted all who looked interesting. One of these was a young woman-organizer, a sturdy girl with bright eyes and gay laughter. She was a graduate of the ultra-exclusive Peeresses School, had been arrested in January, 1945, for organizing a girls' circle to study current conditons, and was released the day of Japan's surrender. "My father," she said merrily, "is a politician. That means he has no political ideals. But I think I'll change him yet."

Then, a little apart from the crowd, I saw an old couple, sitting on a bench. The man was small and unshaven. The woman had a large, plain face made almost beautiful by its expression of inner contentment. They talked readily, or rather, the woman talked and the man nodded. She said her husband was a tailor, neither of them was a Communist, and they came to the meeting because "we love democracy." She pulled at my sleeve. "Come with me." She led me to the edge of the platform where there was a cluster of flags. She pointed to a silk banner with a yellow fringe. "Feel that," she said. "Real silk. My husband and I made it. For democracy."

Nozaka was a slim, quiet man with a professorial manner. He spoke calmly, with no oratorical frills. "Sixteen years have passed," he said, "since I left Japan, but not for a minute have I forgotten my land, or ceased to fight for humanity. Even before I left China, I heard that Japan was destroyed, and no one was giving thought to the rebuilding. Now I find that people's very livelihood is in danger. They lack homes and jobs. Most of the people are hungry, while a few hoard vast wealth. The returned soldiers are having a hard time. The *zaibatsu* and the war criminals remain in power. Democracy is yet far away, though people yearn for it."

He wanted the government to be replaced by a coalition cabinet, which would give people food, jobs, and houses, purge war criminals, give land to the sharecroppers, revive industry, and help the returned soldiers.

"During the war," Nozaka said, "we were called traitors and defeatists. But we can ask now: who are the real betrayers of Japan? Look at the destruction around us. Look at the discouraged faces. The people who did all this are not the Communists, but the emperor, the militarists, the politicians. And no one can say that we, Communists, have not died for our country. After the Manchurian incident alone, hundreds of Communists were killed by the Japanese police. Those of us who have survived will now help in rebuilding the country."

Once the meeting ended, the people began to pour out of the park onto the main boulevard a block away from General MacArthur's Headquarters. There were three thousand of them, and they came out thirty abreast, both men and women, and mostly young. They had locked their arms, and marched with a song on their lips. The crowd had its own marshals, who kept the human stream in line. From time to time, the column broke into a trot, to the accompaniment of the electrifying chant, *wassho, wassho, wassho*. When the demonstrants reached the main intersection, they were turned left towards the Diet. Once again they ran in a solid mass, chanting, cheering, singing, waving posters, and swallowing within them onlookers who had decided to join in.

I crossed the street to the building of the U.S. Provost Marshal for Tokyo. A colonel was watching the parade from the steps. His face was wrinkled with thought. "Goddamn them," he said. "It's the most impressive sight I've seen in this country."

February 3, 1946   IIYAMA, NAGANO PREFECTURE

This is my third day on the road. I am beginning to feel as if the world I know—the world of warmth and comfort, of cocktail parties, paved streets and motorcars, of American directives and Japanese intrigue—has vanished. This is a world unlike any I have visited—a common man's world, filled with accumulated hopes and hatreds of many generations, a peasant's world in which land and crops are the beginning and the end, a primitive world of villages buried under snow, of elemental passions, of social forces barely awakened. For three days now, I have been tramping the land, visiting hamlets whose names I cannot recall, meeting men whose faces have become blurred, and listening, for sixteen hours a day, to the tragic and hopeful story of rural Japan.

It was three days ago that Ono, the editor, and I stepped out at the Nagano railway station to be met by Hayashi, a writer and an expert on rural Japan. Sometime later we were in a suburban train, crowded and friendly. I talked to Hayashi, and other people joined in, until we had a sort of a mobile village meeting. Some of the men asked me my business, and then told me theirs. We talked of the crops, the heavy snow, the money which had lost its value, of the unmet need for fertilizer, for tools and shoes and kitchen pots.

There was a tough, little ex-serviceman standing next to me. He had with him a bundle of *samurai* swords wrapped in silk. When I reminded him that all the swords had to be surrendered to the Japanese police, he snorted: "What do I care about those orders? Only fools give up their weapons. These swords are too good to be surrendered."

We stayed at the home of a local businessman named Hirai. He was that rare thing in Japan—an industrialist regarded as a friend by the sharecroppers. Hirai owned land and a pine oil refinery. At the same time he had organized the Iiyama unions of consumers and sharecroppers. Back in the early 'thirties he had spent two years in jail for precisely that kind of activity.

Now Hirai and a fiery little union organizer named Washimi, who had walked a hundred miles to join us on our trip, acted as our guides. The first meeting I attended was held in a sharecropper's hut, half-home, half-stable, with a precious cow in it. As the people came in, they knelt in the doorway in a greeting, and then joined the tight, ever-widening circle around the brazier. We ate a lunch of cold noodles dipped in cold soya sauce, and cold *jagaimo* (Irish potato) boiled with radish. As my share, I put in a couple of cans of spam. Everyone had a slice, and complimented the American palate.

Much of what was said at the first meeting—on democracy and on General MacArthur's directives—was obviously said for my benefit. But apart from these asides, the discussion dealt with the farmer's hopes, troubles and grievances. In that particular village, two hundred of the sharecroppers belonged to the union, and they were beginning to take pride in it, and sense its growing strength as a political instrument.

Not everyone at that first meeting was a sharecropper. There was the head of the local landlords' organization, who argued his case with vigor. There was a school teacher, fired years ago for trying to form a farmers' union, and now himself a sharecropper. There was a school principal, and a youth who identified himself simply as "bankrupt and a bankrupt's son." But most of them were genuine sharecroppers, dark-skinned from the sun and the winds, dressed poorly in wartime khaki suits or in tattered kimonos, speaking haltingly but earnestly of the problems troubling them.

There was a pattern to men's minds here, a pattern that most Americans reshaping Japan's future back in Tokyo did not understand. Very few of these farmers knew precisely what kind of land reform the Americans wanted, and they shied away from what they knew. "All it means," they said, "is an opportunity to buy land for which we have no money." While we were trying to buttress the Japanese government, these men spoke of it with anger and derision. "The government," they said, "is always in league with the landlord. What we want is not more Japanese land laws, but an order from General Mac-Arthur. The landlords would obey *that*." But though there was anger, there was little evidence of a coming revolution. Time and again, the farmers told me they felt that even a redistribution of land was too drastic a solution. The sharecropper knew he was being oppressed, and he thought his union might help him. He had not yet gone far beyond that.

What all the sharecroppers wanted with a painful yearning was security from eviction. They kept coming back to it again and again, with tales of landlord injustice and, sometimes, of retaliation. There was the landlord who threw his tenant out after eighteen years of sharecropping. There was another landlord who tried to evict his tenant, but gave it up when no one in the village, save his own family, would speak to him. There was a village where, of seven hundred farmers, only four owned more than thirteen acres apiece. When one of the landlords tried to evict a tenant, the village dared him to use force. He gave up. But the landlord was not alone. As ever, he operated in alliance with the police and the rice collector. When sharecroppers were obstreperous, their quotas of rice to be surrendered to the government were raised. "In my village," said a farmer, "an evicted family nearly committed suicide. All that stopped it was the news of a son's return from Manchuria." Said another: "In mine, a tenant jumped off a bridge because the rice collectors were after him."

These men tilled an average of two acres each, and they agreed a family could not live on less. But they recognized the scarcity of land in Japan as they recognized the floods and the droughts; nothing could be done about it. Their complaint was against the excessive rents, which ran up to half the crop and more. "Cut the rents to a quarter of the yield," they said. "Protect us from eviction. Then we'd prefer sharecropping to any crooked government reforms."

It was a picture of misery, hard work, tired soil, and a wicked system of land ownership. One answer to it lay in the land reform on which Americans were now working. But it would have to be guarded from the Japanese government's machinations, both before and after it was put in the law books. And someone besides the government would have to publicize the new law until every sharecropper knew it.

In the evening, after that first meeting, we were walking across the countryside, and I wanted an unscheduled witness. When we entered a hamlet, I turned off the main path and entered the first hut. It was dark, cold, and dirty. A man and his wife were making rope with crude tools. The woman had a baby strapped to her back; she never turned to look at us. The man remained kneeling.

He said, Yes, he belonged to the farm union. He said, No, he had never heard of the land redistribution law. He said, Yes, he would like to buy the two acres of land he now rented, but at the current prices he would have to work all his life and never earn enough to pay for it. When we asked him how he made up his mind on various public issues, he said simply:

"My neighbor is a very clever man. He gives me advice."

At night, we held private meetings in Hirai's lovely guest room. We sat on pillows around a low table, drank tea, and talked of many things, from recipes to usury.

My host, Hirai, in his low, quiet voice, confirmed some of my conclusions. "People," he said, "have lost confidence in the men in authority. They feel that little has changed in the way things are run—and even less in the personnel. But to this day, most of the people don't know what's going on. You talked to that farmer earlier today. I'd say 80 per cent of the sharecroppers are still in the dark on General MacArthur's directives, including the land reform and Thought Control."

Hayashi agreed, "People are still too browbeaten." Hayashi interested me no less than the sharecroppers. He has the sensitive face of a thinker, and the manners of a courtier. I have heard him discuss fertilizer with the farmers, but one night he talked to me of his great love for Maxim Gorky, and he could name every one of Gorky's works. Hayashi himself had written three books on the problems of rural Japan, and one of them was banned by the Thought police before publication. Someone told me Hayashi had sat in jail as a radical, and someone else told me he had fled to Shanghai for a year to escape arrest. What I do know is that he has a large following among the sharecroppers, and that a week or so ago, two outstanding American experts on Japan had traveled all the way from Tokyo to consult Hayashi on the state of mind in the Japanese countryside.

We were all tired. It was decided that on this, the fourth day of our junket, we would go to Yudanaka, one of Japan's best known winter playgrounds. It was still dark when I crawled out of my sleeping bag and woke up my interpreter. We washed in the open passageway, where we could see fresh snow falling. From the kitchen came the sound of children singing and women talking, the clatter of pots and pans, and there was a painfully pleasant air of domesticity.

Last night I gave Mrs. Hirai some rations for our breakfast —cocoa, canned milk, and canned ham and eggs. But when breakfast arrived, I discovered that the Hirais would have none of that. They brought us freshly made omelets, a soup made of eggs and bean curd, boiled rice, and some dried persimmons.

After breakfast, all my companions came up. After three days with them, I have come to recognize and identify each man. They were as dissimilar as men can be: Ono, a typical Tokyo newspaperman; Hayashi, a man of pure intellect; Washimi, a peasant; Hirai, a businessman. And yet there were strands of common experience and belief which ran through all of them. They had all sat in jail for opposition to feudal ideas and institutions. They were all fired by the concepts of democracy we brought in with us.

This was a pure and luminous fire, the kind I have rarely seen in Tokyo. And I recalled a phrase uttered by a State Department man: "The nicest people in Japan are the former jailbirds." For anyone who had a breath of progressive idea in him was inevitably found out by the Thought police and clamped in prison.

This was as true of Ono as it was of the young teacher who was now asking me for an autograph. He had been jailed during the war for intimating that Japan should have stayed at peace. Now he has organized a youth group which helps the farm union with its work and holds forums to discuss such topics as the meaning of reforms ordered by the Americans.

He stood over me and waited for me to write something significant in his little book, and I could think of nothing terse or pithy to express my feeling that he was the salt of the earth. I finally wrote, "Democracy is no better than the men who shape it. Democracy will be a wonderful thing indeed if there are more men like you." The thin ink in my fountain pen spread and blurred on the rice paper.

It was snowing hard when we started for the station, and this time I had also to carry some of the load of my interpreter who said he had asthma. Between my typewriter, rucksack, and a box of food I must have had sixty pounds, which did not make the walking any easier. It took us an hour to reach the Iiyama station, and then another hour, in a crowded interurban train, to reach Yudanaka.

Yudanaka is one of a series of hot spring resorts nestling in the foothills of the Japanese Alps. It also has some of Japan's best known skiing grounds. The little town, in which every other house is a bathhouse or an inn, was crowded with Japanese skiers and hikers. The snow was three feet deep, but the open gutters steamed with hot water. The town wore a carnival air. The automobile that was to pick us up did not appear, and we started hiking again.

Above us, along a ridge, the villas of the wealthy were strung out. Below us was the wide stream rushing down a steep incline. We passed by small farmhouses, many of them with small pools in which huge carp and foot-long goldfish were swimming around. We walked through villages in which hot water bubbled out of the public hydrants, and women were washing clothes or dishes in the gutters near by. Every village had its public bathhouses, and we could see men and women sitting waist deep in hot water. We crossed a river, and began to ascend again. Our hearts pumped, but no one wanted to stop.

In mid-afternoon, after a final spurt up an almost vertical incline, we reached a small grove of evergreens. Deep within it was a Japanese hotel, consisting mostly of small two-story houses. We were assigned a house in which an imperial princess stayed last summer.

I was put up in the princess' suite on the second floor. The rooms were enclosed by a glassed-in porch, from which I could see the valley below, a range of mountains beyond it, and then, far, far away, the Japanese Alps, their snowy sides glistening in the sun and their tops lost in the clouds. There and then I decided that when Sally arrived in Japan, I was going to bring her here for just a look at this view.

The maids brought live charcoal and a comforter for the *kotatsu*, and told me a small bathing pool downstairs was vacant. The pool was about eight feet square, and hot springs water bubbled at one end of it. It was lovely, except for two things. The water was too hot to get into, and the bathhouse had all its windows knocked out, so that I was out in the fresh air. It was the strangest bath I have ever had, but when I got through dashing hot water on myself I was both warm and clean.

I put on a warm kimono and my trenchcoat on top of that, and slid under the comforter of the *kotatsu*. Gradually the room filled up with my companions and with local union organizers. All of them had taken a hot bath, and now they radiated warmth and good cheer. One by one they slid under the comforter, until there was not an inch of free space left by the fire. We talked of farm problems, and they all repeated the refrains, by now familiar to me, of security from eviction and lower rents.

In the middle of the discussion, the maids began to bring food in. It developed that one of the local sharecroppers had contributed rice for the fifteen of us. I chipped in with some canned pork and beans and cocoa. We were hungry and the food, for a change, was hot, and we ate noisily and much. We complimented the farmer on the quality of his rice, and he smiled proudly and explained that this was the rice he did *not* surrender to the government.

"We keep the good rice for ourselves," he said. "The poorer kind we give the rice collectors."

They all laughed as if this was a good joke, and then vied with each other with tales of how they managed to pull a fast one on the government. These were the typical tales of Asiatic sharecroppers, waging their perennial war on the landlord and the government. Some were tales of cunning, and others of violence. But I was thinking less of what these men had done than of the many decades of usury and oppression that had produced these reactions.

"Oh," said the host, "there is a good story about this house, too. As you know, an imperial princess stayed here last summer, with her suite. The village turned itself inside out to make their stay pleasant. We butchered our cattle and chickens. Though we didn't have too much ourselves, we gave them the best rice we had and vegetables and fruit. The princess stayed here two weeks, and then moved on. Before leaving, she gave the village an imperial purse, in appreciation of all we had done for her. So we picked a date for a special village ceremony, at which we would open the purse. But meanwhile, we all speculated on how much she gave us. Some people said five hundred yen. Others said a thousand. Still others said the imperial family owns thousands and thousands of acres of land in this prefecture alone; there must be at least five thousand yen there. So the day of the ceremony came, and the village headman bowed to the purse, and opened it, and took out the money.

"It was twenty-five yen."

I thought of this two-dollar largesse, and I remembered that Washimi was a Communist. I asked him what he thought of the story and the emperor. Washimi said gravely: "I feel sorry that the emperor has such children."

After the meal we all went to sleep. I had a terrible headache from the charcoal fumes. But when the maid brought fresh coals and woke me up, I felt rested. Again the men came up, and we talked. We stayed there through the rest of the day, and through the evening. From time to time, we broke up and walked up and down the porch, and looked down upon the moonlit valley. But after a brief recess we gathered again, and started with a new subject.

A sharp discussion was provoked by a question on what each of them would do with the emperor. "*Haishi*," said Washimi, "Quit. That's what I want him to do." "*Haishi*," said another organizer who was a Social Democrat. "There are two powers in Japan—the emperor and the people. When you reduce the emperor's power, you increase ours." But not all of them agreed. My guide Ono spoke for several of them when he noted that the emperor's every move, including both the declaration of war and the surrender, was made under duress.

As soon as he said it, two or three of the sharecroppers jumped on him. "Why have a figurehead?" And, "When he was a god, we could believe in him, but now we know he is human, and not too good at that." And, "Whether he was under duress or not, he must bear responsibility for the war. *Haishi.*"

After dinner, Washimi told us the story of his life. He was born a sharecropper in this prefecture forty years ago. At the age of nineteen, he became active in organizing farm unions, and at twenty-three he was arrested. He stayed in jail for six years. While he was in prison, his wife was arrested for organizing silk filature workers, and kept in jail for a year. On his release, Washimi went back to farming, but surreptitiously kept up his union work. The police then forbade him to leave his farm—a sort of a house arrest.

"In 1937," Washimi said, "all social movements were driven underground by the police. All my friends and I announced that we had become nationalists. We met in my house, and continued our old work. When a police agent sat in on our discussions, we talked of Japan's mission and the emperor. But the police remained suspicious. In 1941, after the war broke out, all of us were pulled in and sentenced to six months in jail.

"When finally we came out, a policeman in our village told me to play the fool. 'If you don't,' he said, 'you'll be pulled in again.' So the police watched me, and I stayed quietly on my farm.

"But on August 15 of last year, when I heard the emperor's surrender broadcast, I went wild. I cried and I shouted with joy. I ran to the station and I stood in line for a whole day buying a railroad ticket, and then I went all over Japan. I felt that I had been under arrest for fifteen years, for in jail or out the police never allowed me out of their sight. I wanted to see my country, and I wanted to feel the sensation of being free.

"Then I came back and began to form a union. Today 400 out of the 500 sharecroppers in my area belong to the union."

He paused. "And now," Washimi said, "let's sing." The men sang the folk songs of Japan, their village and their trade. The voices were not professional, and often the lyrics were forgotten. But to me, folk songs are always beautiful. When they halted, I asked for more. It was after one of these requests that Washimi said in Japanese: "And now I shall sing *eye daburyu daburyu* songs I learned before the war."

"What's *eye daburyu daburyu?*" I asked.

"You know!" he said. "The revolutionaries you Americans had twenty-five years ago." With his finger he drew on a damp tea tray the letters I.W.W. And then, in this typically Japanese room, where a Japanese princess stayed not many months ago, in alien words that I could only vaguely follow came the unmistakable song:

"You will eat, bye and bye,
In that glorious land above the sky;
Work and pray, live on hay,
You'll get pie in the sky when you die."

February 17, 1946 TOKYO

Got my Travel Orders today for a trip to southern Japan. I am especially interested in the Kyoto-Osaka area, which is the industrial heart of Japan. I hope to spend about two weeks there, mainly studying the application of our anti-*zaibatsu* policy.

It was a cold, bright morning when we left Kyoto for Osaka on one of the best roads I have seen in Asia. It was wide, smooth, and almost deserted, but for an occasional army jeep and a charcoal-fuelled, smoke-belching Japanese truck. We drove down a beautiful valley, green with rice, and pressing against rugged, snowcapped mountains. There were white stuccoed buildings, and a miniature train rattling in the distance. The young GI driver said, "Jeez, it looks just like California."

We took a sharp curve, climbed up a dyke, and suddenly the scarred and tortured face of Osaka lay before us. There were holes in the long bridge, where light bombs had gone through. Beyond the bridge, as far as the eye could see, lay acres of debris, rusted iron, and an occasional factory chimney. We drove down the streets of what was once an industrial suburb, past the damaged but functioning railroad station, past a black market in hastily built, flimsy houses. Then, suddenly, we were on a broad, tree-lined avenue leading to a cluster of domed, columned, streamlined buildings. This was the heart of Osaka, the nerve center of a vast industrial empire, the home of the great banks which financed Japanese commercial and military expansion.

I moved in on a Major J. C. Milligan, a former Pennsylvania fire chief, who now runs the Public Safety and Rationing branches of the 107th Military Government Detachment. Milligan looks, acts, and thinks like a New York cop. Watching him through a succession of interviews with Japanese officials, I began to suspect he did not always know what he was doing, but that, anyway, he was having an awful lot of fun doing it.

Between interviews, Milligan told me Koreans and Chinese, imported during the war for slave labor, have been raising hell.

"That's just about all I do," he said, "keep telling the Jap police to get tougher with these guys. But the cops hestitate. No one quite knows what in hell these Koreans are—our allies, neutrals, Jap subjects or what. I've been conducting a one-man campaign to get every Jap cop armed. Once they get arms, that will boost their ego."

The biggest trouble with the police, Milligan complained, was that all its top men had been purged for ultranationalism. "It sure raised hell with the police force. If we had them back on the job, we wouldn't have all this mess."

From Milligan sometime this morning, I got the customary refrain of the Military Government: "I'm no reformer. My job is to maintain public safety. I don't care what the guy's politics are as long as he does a competent job."

In his room in Hotel New Osaka, Milligan produced a bottle of Suntory whisky. A few officers came in to say hello. One of them was Major Shaw, assistant chief of the Military Government for the area.

"Don't judge us too harshly" he said, "We work hard enough, but everything here is messed up. Headquarters dreams up directives. These go to the Military Government in Yokohama. Weeks later, the directives filter down to us. Meanwhile, the Jap government rushes its orders down its own channels.

"What happens is this. The Japs here take some action. We give them hell. We say, 'You can't do this.' They say blandly, 'Excuse please, but we can. There is a directive out to that effect.' We start checking frantically with Yokohama, and the next thing that happens is that we are embarrassed no end. The Japs have made us look like a bunch of fools.

"We are called Military Government. It's a misnomer. We govern nothing. We couldn't govern even if we wanted to. We decided we'd let the Japs govern themselves, and we'd just sort of supervise. Therefore, the Military Government was cut down to the bone. Our team is supposed to have direct authority over two prefectures, and supervision over nine others. You know what this area is? It's the industrial guts of Japan. Do you know how many people we have to run this area? Twelve officers, twenty-six enlisted men, and four typewriters. There are eight hundred typewriters stored in a U.S. Army warehouse in Kobe, forty miles from here. All we need is a permit. But we don't seem to be able to get it."

I had lunch with Major Ben Locke, chief of the Industrial and Financial Division. Locke is a good notch above most of his colleagues. He comes of a well-known American industrial family, whose interests he represented in Japan before the war. He knows his way around Japan, and he knows what he wants to do. If this clashes with the professed goals of the United States, too bad for the goals. It is not that Locke is disobeying his orders. It is that the American planners in Tokyo—and possibly even in Washington—have issued conflicting orders. Locke obeys the orders which in his opinion are right.

Six months ago, President Truman listed as an avowed goal of the American people the destruction of the *zaibatsu*. But General MacArthur's planners are also faced with the urgent problem of putting the Japanese economy on its feet quickly, so that the Japanese people have jobs, and don't go into the streets to demonstrate and don't join the extreme rightists or leftist groups. If you are anxious to restore the economy quickly, you do not want to disrupt it, however briefly, by extensive shakeups. It is a real problem: to purge, and have a more democratic economy ten years from now—but pay the cost of dislocation in the next few years; or not to purge, and restore the economy much as it was in 1939, and let the bad boys remain in control—and are they really bad? Locke has made his choice. It is a significant choice, for duplicated in a hundred Japanese cities, it is the pattern of our policy for Japan.

"I may sound pro-Japanese, but I'm not," said Locke. "I fought this war for three years. This is our big chance to win Japan over by letting her keep her industrial machinery and letting her produce and export. Right now we're muffing this job by not knowing what our policy is. Are we to make Japan our economic vassal? Is she to be an agricultural nation? Will we allow her to be self-sustaining? It is easy enough to break up the *zaibatsu*. But, hell, you destroy the old *zaibatsu*, and you get some new form of a *zaibatsu*, for somebody has got to run the Japanese industrial machinery.

"I'm not defending the *zaibatsu*. They were behind the Japanese aggression. Today, they're in control of the Jap government. But what's the alternative? Destroy the *zaibatsu*, and you must have chaos for the next ten years, or have a socialist economy. Wipe out the *zaibatsu* banks, and the entire banking structure goes to pot. Smash the *zaibatsu*, and there'll be no field for our investment in Japan. You know yourself that the businessmen in headquarters in Tokyo want to see old Japan restored. The military people also feel that most of their headaches can be prevented by keeping the *zaibatsu* intact.

"Now, it'd be silly to tell the Japanese: 'For each GI you killed, give us a lathe.' Let them keep their damned machinery, instead of having our salesmen here in a few years, selling them machines which will be newer than ours. Nor is there any sense to giving the Jap equipment to the Chinese or the Filipinos, for they won't use it efficiently, and besides—they'll compete with us.

"And something else. Let's not kid ourselves. We need a strong Japan, for one of these days we'll have to face Russia, and we'll need an ally. Japan is it."

In the afternoon, Milligan and his associate, a Major Kernan, took me to the Wakamatsu jail, one of Osaka's biggest. Together with the police force, the prisons of Japan stand high on our list of reform targets, and I thought this might be a good opportunity to check on our progress.

We drove along the canal, crossed the modern heart of Osaka, and twisted through the maze of the residential district, until we reached a blind alley. Before us was a tall, brick wall, with a sign on the gate: "Wakamatsu Detention House."

In the small front yard, a hundred people—mostly women —milled before a window, where a clerk was issuing visitors' passes. We filed through the office door, declined the warden's proffer of tea, and waited until he got the keys.

The warden was about five feet tall, and he wore a blue uniform, a short sword, and a harassed expression. His assistant, a stocky, little man with a lot of gold teeth, tagged along. The warden knocked on the metal door, it swung open, and we were in the middle of the seventeenth century.

Two things hit us. The first was the stench, thick and nauseating. The other was the muddy color. It started with the damp cement floor, and traveled upward, to the three balconies hugging the tiers of cells, and beyond them, to the indistinct ceiling. Men's faces were of the same color.

There was heavy traffic in the corridors, with one stream of men going out through the small front door, presumably to see visitors or to be questioned, and another stream coming in. The prisoners were of a common mould—sallow-faced, emaciated, dressed in shabby blue or mud-colored gowns. Many wore conical straw baskets covering their faces—feudal Japan's concession to a man's desire to "save his face" from shame.

"Everyone should have a basket," the warden said apologetically, "but during the war they wore out so many we still don't have enough to go around."

Each door had a slot, the kind we use for mail back home. I lifted a flap and looked in. The cell was about eight feet by ten. The large window was heavily barred. There was not a stick of furniture. Just a stack of quilts in a corner—one to a prisoner, to serve both as a mattress and a blanket—and a trench latrine in another corner. There were nine squatting men in the cell, three to a row, all facing the door. They were stonily immobile, as prescribed by the jail regimen.

The warden unlocked the door, and I stuck my head in. The stench was so heady, I quickly backed out. After that, we talked to the men from a distance.

Most of the inmates were in for gambling, which, for repeaters, is a serious offense. Some men have been here for months, waiting for the judge's preliminary investigation. (Under Japanese law, which no one has yet bothered to change, a suspect is first investigated by the police, then by the public procurator, who is a sort of district attorney, and, finally, by the judge. The law allows the judge to keep a suspect in jail for two months for investigation. Then all the judge has to do to keep a man in jail until he rots to death is to keep issuing monthly orders of continuance). Two of the men showed every sign of rotting. It was cold in the cell. Yet, these two feverish cadavers were damp with sweat.

Next to this cell was a row of solitaries, each about five feet wide, for men awaiting hanging. Some of the men were asleep under their quilts. In one cell, a shabby old man, sentenced to death for burglary and stabbing, was scratching violently. When he saw me through the slot, he quickly pulled his hand out of his gown, stretched his arms to me in supplication, and began to wail. We walked down the corridor, and his high toneless cries trailed us.

We left the main block, and emerged into the inner yard. In it, unevenly spaced, were four narrow, round, brick structures, which looked like pillboxes. Each had a metal gate. The warden pulled one of the gates open. Behind it was a second, barred door. Out of the darkness beyond, a face sprang up, and began to shriek in a desperate, highpitched voice. It was a man of about thirty, and he was interspersing his Japanese with English words:

"Macassar (MacArthur), very good. Macassar. Thank you. Help. Help. Very good. Very good."

The warden looked as if he was about to burst into tears. His assistant smiled, and twirled a meaningful finger about his head. In a squeaky voice, the warden said the prisoner was a murderer gone insane. Since Japan has no asylums for the criminally insane, the warden, for curative purposes, put the man in the blockhouse for ten days. We walked off, and the warden shut the metal gate. The prisoner kicked it open. He shook the bars fiercely, and screamed, "Macassar, very good."

I tried the doors of the two gray pillboxes. They were locked. The warden said the cells were for prisoners with communicable diseases. Right now, one of the cells had two smallpox suspects. They were supplied with food in this cement sarcophagus through small slats.

In the filthy, small infirmary, in which the only equipment was a couch and a bucket of cold water, we later looked at the doctor's chart. It showed that of the 850 inmates, 90 had bad colds, 20 had skin diseases, 5 venereal diseases. In six weeks, 18 prisoners died.

In the evening, there was a show for Major General LeRoy Hunt, U.S.M.C., in the dining room of the Miyako Hotel in Kyoto. It was a sorry little show, composed of some *geisha* dances and a third-rate magician. It was put on, according to a printed program, "in appreciation for the Occupation of Osaka by I Corps; Sponsored by the Japan Democracy Association. President, Mr. Kensuke Aoki."

The officers made ribald jokes, and laughed uproariously.

Japan did not surrender blindly. As soon as her rulers decided to give in, they put Japan's entire, closely knit, efficient machinery of government to the job of circumventing the pledges they were uttering to the victors. They made good use of the two-week interval between the announcement of their surrender and the arrival of the first American units. Documents were burned. Government funds were dispersed where they would do the most good. Stocks of valuable material were concealed. Detailed plans were made for keeping the governing apparatus intact whatever the conqueror's orders.

This morning, Lieutenant Colonel Munske, chief of Military Government for the great Kansai industrial belt, supplied more details. He is big and portly, and smiled as he recited Japanese evasions. I smiled too. The joke was on us, but we had all become cynics in this land.

"In one of my prefectures," said Munske, "seven out of the fourteen police chiefs were members of the Thought Control police during the war. Five months ago, we issued a directive purging the Thought Control boys. But somehow they got wind of it. They all resigned just before the directive was issued. The Japanese claim this technically left them with a clean record. The Jap government then promptly appointed them police chiefs. Under the cute setup we have here, all I can do is report. The report is buried in the files in Yokohama, together with other reports on the same thing happening all over Japan. Indirectly, we are told there are 'higher considerations' which make it necessary 'for the time being' to ignore this violation of directives by the government."

His irony was so heavy, you could almost hear the quotes on "higher considerations."

Another detail of the same picture was supplied to me at lunch by Major G. Lewis Schmidt, Economic Officer here.

"There's a lot of talk about reform and reorganization," he said. "In this particular area, our special baby is Sumitomo, one of Japan's three biggest family trusts. Under our directives, they are supposed to be broken up. Especially the Sumitomo Holding Company, which has a capital of well over four billion yen. We ask them for their records. They claim the records were lost or burned in the raids. There is nothing you can do about it. We demand that they reorganize. They reorganize four of their hundred and two companies. We suspect the reorganization is only on paper. But again there is nothing we can do.

"The Jap government in Tokyo submits information to us on the industrial firms here. We find it's shot through with error and omission—down to the name of the company and its product. In one list of a hundred plants we found twenty major errors. A great Mitsubishi plant that had been making aircraft was not even listed.

"Huge companies that once made munitions come to us and ask for permission to reconvert. They say, 'Since we are to help in the conversion to peacetime economy, we'll have to beg off from giving up our machinery to you as reparations.' Then they submit their inventory to us, and it's full of holes. Sometimes they just don't tell us what they have. At other times, we find they moved machinery and raw materials. They stopped it only after we started sending armed patrols into the country to look for the stuff.

"We know for a fact that the Jap Army and Navy issued orders to base commanders to hide their supplies. Between the surrender and our arrival, mountains of supplies were moved out. For example, a few days after surrender, the Jap Army Command in Kyushu gave its fuel dumps away to big firms, contractors, officers, and just friends. We discovered this when somebody, quite by accident, stumbled on a buried fuel dump. Another example: a Korean peddler found a dump of raw rubber in a ravine. A hundred tons. The villagers said it had been hidden on orders from the Japanese Navy base commander near by."

February 26, 1946   TOKYO

Today heard of the Dai-An Club, at which American guests are treated to good food, liquor, and women—on the house. The host, and apparently the only member, is a man named Akira Ando, for whom the club is modestly named—*Dai* for great and *An* for the first syllable of his name. An officer who has visited the club told me that that night Ando was playing host to six parties simultaneously. The officer estimated the cost of his own party at Y.30,000 or $2,000. Ando explains to his guests that he is a devout believer in U.S.-Japanese amity.

Ando's hospitality is not confined to officers. He also owns a cabaret which caters primarily to GIs. Ando told a friend of mine that he loses Y.300,000 ($20,000) monthly on the cabaret, but that "it isn't too much to pay for Japanese-American friendship." Ando is said to be a big-time building contractor, a labor boss, and a racketeer.

Ando belongs in the same pigeonhole with one of the heads of the great Riken industrial combine, who the other day threw a "pornographic party" for two key officers and me. After he had exhibited his priceless collection of mediaeval obscenity to us and treated us to a lavish meal, he began to pump us on any American plans we might know to break up industrial combines and pick up more war criminals.

Both items went into my file marked "subversion." The file already contains such examples as the "virgin girls" offered to the officers of a newly arrived detachment (and sharply rejected) in a town northwest of here. Or, the young prostitutes bought by another town for the entertainment of the officers garrisoned in it. Or, the banquets given to hand-picked generals and colonels by the notorious Prince Higashikuni, whom even the emperor's advisers regard as "too reactionary." Or, the party to celebrate the opening of a Japanese "international cooperation" club, at which an important member of General MacArthur's staff begged a correspondent not to report his presence.

All these belong to one of the most lurid and important stories of the occupation—the story of the shrewd, well-organized and well-financed Japanese campaign to corrupt the Army of the United States. The weapons are wine, women, and hospitality, and the objective is to subvert the starch and purpose of the Occupation.

March 6, 1946   TOKYO

All of us trekked to the premier's residence today, to the office of Wataru Narahashi, Secretary of the Cabinet, to hear the announcement of a new constitution. Narahashi is a stocky, bushy-haired, self-confident man in striped pants, black coat and a stiff wing collar.

"The new Constitution," he said, "is an epoch-making document. . . . In it, the emperor himself proclaims the people sovereign, as provided in the Potsdam Declaration. In it, we declare militarism is dead. . . . Through the adoption of this Constitution, the emperor will become a symbol above the people, and people will also realize this is their government. . . . "

He answered some of our questions in fluent French. "We're in a very dangerous situation," he said, "and in order to avoid a bloody revolution, we must take revolutionary steps, such as this Constitution. Some people say this is a government of peers. But I myself am a coal miner, and I began to work at the age of fourteen. I think I know what the people want."

Later, General MacArthur issued a 450-word statement. It noted "with a sense of deep satisfaction" the decision "of the emperor and government of Japan" to submit to the Japanese people "a new and enlightened constitution, which has my full approval." Grandiloquently worded, it said the new Constitution "severs for all time the shackles of feudalism and in its place raises the dignity of man under protection of the people's sovereignty." It also noted that the foremost of the provisions of the new Constitution is that which "forever renounces the threat or use of force as a means for settling disputes . . . and forbids in future the authorization of any army, navy, air force or other war potential. . . . "

This is the story that went to the four corners of the earth —as yet another proof of Japan's cooperation and rapid advance towards democracy.

But there is a story behind the story, which Bob Cochrane, of the *Baltimore Sun,* and I are now piecing together. Like the new Constitution itself, it belongs to the history of the Occupation.

One night a month ago, key officers in General MacArthur's Government Section were told in extreme confidence that they would have to draft a new constitution for Japan. In an informal session at the Dai-Ichi Hotel, the broad outline of the document was sketched out. The next morning, General Whitney called his entire staff into the conference room.

"Ladies and gentlemen," he said solemnly, "this is an historic occasion. I now proclaim you a constitutional assembly."

A former Manila lawyer, Whitney also is somewhat of an actor. In the speech he made, he alternated between solemnity, pathos, and political harangue. The most pressing issue of the hour in Japan, he said, is a new constitution. All the drafts prepared by the Japanese have been completely unsatisfactory, and the Supreme Commander—he pronounced it "Commahn-der"—felt it was necessary for him to intervene. The Government Section was being given the assignment of drafting a new constitution. Extreme haste and secrecy would be necessary, so as to take the Japanese by complete surprise, and prevent them from organizing an effective opposition.

"I'm greatly flattered," Whitney said, "that the Supreme Commander considered the Government Section capable of drafting the constitution, and in such a short time. I asked the Supreme Commander if he wished to indicate the lines to be followed in drafting the new constitution, and the General replied he would leave the entire job to the expert judgment of this section—but with these three exceptions. . . . "

Whitney recited the three points which General Mac-Arthur wanted to see in the new Japanese constitution:

1. Japan was to renounce war forever, abolish her armed forces, and pledge never to revive them;

2. While sovereignty was to be vested in the people, the emperor was to be described as a symbol of the State;

3. The peerage was to be abolished, and the property of the Imperial Household was to revert to the State.

The men who had taken part in the informal session the previous night were totally unprepared for the first point. All three points, however, provoked numerous questions.

"I assume from Point Two," said one questioner, "that the emperor would not be tried as a war criminal."

Colonel C. L. Kades, Deputy Chief of the Section and a former Treasury Counsel, replied that he agreed with the assumption. General MacArthur, in his opinion, felt that the emperor had atoned for any past errors by his wholehearted support of the Occupation.

"I would consider it a gross breach of faith," Whitney said, "if the emperor were to be tried as a war criminal after all the services he had rendered to the Allies."

Originally, it was intended to draft the new constitution in ten days. General Whitney had expressed his hope that it could be announced by the Japanese on February 22—George Washington's birthday.

At General Whitney's opening "constitutional assembly," teams were set up, each with the job of writing one or more chapters of the constitution. The team captains together formed a steering committee, which was to co-ordinate the work. There was a feverish study of American and European constitutions, but on the whole the new Constitution followed the pattern of the old Meiji Constitution which is to be discarded. Kades and Commander Alfred R. Hussey Jr., U.S.N., took on the job of drafting the preamble. There is good reason to believe that the provision renouncing war and armed forces was originally drafted by General MacArthur himself.

The entire job was finished in two weeks. On February 19, General Whitney sprang the Constitution on the Japanese.

Cochrane and I have been unable to find out whether the meeting took place in the residence of Premier Shidehara or Dr. Joji Matsumoto, the ultraconservative lawyer who was "revising" the old Constitution. General Whitney took Colonel Kades and Commander Hussey along. When the three Americans entered the room, they were met by Matsumoto, Foreign Minister Shigeru Yoshida, and a slippery character named Shirasu, who was now vice-chief of the Central Liaison Office. We believed that Premier Shidehara and his Cabinet Secretary, Narahashi, were also present.

The Japanese apparently had been studying the Matsumoto draft before the Americans came in. Anyway, it was spread on a desk. The Americans later said the atmosphere was one of an anticipated horse trade. General Whitney strode to the table, looked at the papers on it, and said:

"Gentlemen, the Supreme Commander has studied the draft prepared by you. He finds it totally unacceptable. I've brought with me a document which has the approval of the Supreme Commander. I'll leave it with you for fifteen minutes, so that you can read it before we discuss it."

The three Americans then withdrew to the adjoining porch. Through the windows they could see the Japanese huddled over the document. Just about then, a U.S. bomber buzzed the house. It was a well-timed incident, even if General Whitney insisted that it had been unscheduled.

At the end of fifteen minutes, Shirasu came in to summon the Americans. As General Whitney re-entered the room, he said dramatically:

"We've just been basking in the warmth of the atomic sunshine."

The Americans noticed that the Matsumoto draft had been removed from the desk, which now held only General Whitney's draft. The Japanese looked thunderstruck. Shirasu, who acted as interpreter, actually opened his mouth several times, but no sound came out.

The Japanese devoted the next few minutes to fishing for information in an effort to discover room for compromise. They argued that the American draft had gone far beyond anything that they had ever considered, and that it was totally un-Japanese in its tradition. Whitney replied firmly that General MacArthur would not consider any document which did not go as far, although he would be willing to consider minor modifications which did not violate the spirit of the American draft.

"If you are not prepared to sponsor a document of this type," he said, "General MacArthur will go over your heads to the Japanese people. But if you will support a constitution of this kind, General MacArthur will support you."

The Americans left after a few polite remarks. Hussey later wrote a detailed account of the interview for the record, and it was read to the staff at a general meeting. The memorandum emphasized that the Japanese had been taken by surprise, and the Americans therefore enjoyed a marked advantage.

The Japanese are excellent politicians, and the surprise did not last. As soon as they recovered from the shock they began to play for time. Their first move was a plea that since they had seen the new Constitution only in English, they could not properly evaluate it. Therefore, they insisted that the new Japanese Constitution be translated into Japanese. A staff of

Government Section interpreters worked all day Sunday, but when the translation was done, the Japanese claimed that it was "simply not Japanese" in word or spirit. There was some more haggling over the wording.

Time wasted away, and General Whitney finally informed the Japanese that Headquarters would announce the draft on its own, thus denying the government an opportunity to identify itself with the new constitution. The Japanese then capitulated. Today's announcement was the result.

The American Constitution for Japan is not a bad constitution. Despite the double talk of the Japanese officials, it vests sovereign power in the people; it guarantees civil liberties; it provides for checks and balances on the government's actions.

What is wrong—disastrously wrong—is that this Constitution does not come from the Japanese grass roots. It is an alien Constitution foisted on the Japanese government, and then represented as a native product, when any Japanese high school student simply by reading it can perceive its foreign origin.

The Far Eastern Commission has been aware of the dangers of an imposed constitution. During its recent visit here, it insisted on letting the Japanese themselves formulate their basic law, and exacted an assurance from Headquarters that that would be done. Only a few weeks later, this promise was broken. The lame explanation by one of Whitney's aides was that the original undertaking was based on the assumption that the Constitution was a long-range problem, "while the events have proved it a matter of immediate business."

And nothing in the Constitution is more wrong than General MacArthur's own provision for the renunciation of armed forces. For no one who has read the morning papers or studied Japanese history can doubt that as soon as the Occupation ends, the Japanese under one pretext or another will re-create their army. That is as inevitable in Japan as earthquakes. By its very nature, the new Constitution thus invites circumvention. No constitution in which fraud is inherent can survive.

What is more, the new Constitution is being passed on to the Japanese through unclean hands.

What better illustration of this is needed than the fact that Japan's spokesman for a new democratic constitution today was a man who, by his own admission, was an agent of the Japanese Army in China? Wataru Narahashi, who may yet be the premier of Japan, reminded the voters in the "Tojo elections" of 1942 that eighteen months before the attack on Pearl Harbor he "took part in the reconstruction of East Asia, and cooperated with the Japanese Army in North China." Today, by one of those incredible Japanese paradoxes, he decides who among the candidates running in next month's elections is a war criminal.

No one can fathom the motives of the Americans who have tailored the new Constitution for Japan. One motive could be General MacArthur's desire to go down in history as the maker of Japan's basic law. Another could be the military man's belief that anything could be done through a military order—even a democratic constitution. And no one apparently has thought of the contradiction inherent in the idea that any constitution forced down a nation's throat could be democratic.

It is true that Baron Shidehara's cabinet has been sabotaging General MacArthur's orders to draft a new constitution. But the answer to that lies not in having Americans draft a Japanese constitution, but in throwing out the Japanese saboteurs, until a cabinet more devoted to democratic ideals comes to power.

General MacArthur's greatest monument in Japan may not survive his mortal life.

March 18, 1946   TOKYO

With Sally due here in May, I found a house for us today. It is a modern building of glass and cement, sitting atop a wooded hill and overlooking the Tokyo harbor. The place is owned by a Count Watanabe, who speaks fair English, works for a newspaper, and during the war served in Japanese Naval

Intelligence. The house is occupied by some friends of his, and I found it a shambles—crying children, smoking charcoal braziers, non-functioning toilets, filthy walls, and filthier straw mats on the floor. But the shell is there, and the house can be put in good shape. As soon as the tenants are out, I shall have to get a crew in to disinfect, wash, and paint the place.

There is a large living room, a lovely den for me, two bedrooms, a beautiful Japanese room, a sun porch, and a Japanese bathroom with a five-foot deep tiled tub. Characteristically, there is no cold water faucet in the tub and no hot water faucet in the adjoining shower.

There are just two difficulties. One is the large air raid shelter in the garden. Its entrance, on the edge of the hill, is slowly sagging as the timbers give way under the weight of the earth on top. When I insisted that the shelter be torn down, Watanabe said:

"My friends tell me there's another war coming. It would be good to be prepared."

I assured him that there would be no war in the next few years.

The second difficulty was less serious. My neighbor next door is an imperial prince. When Watanabe's house was completed, it was discovered that the windows of one of the bedrooms overlooked the prince's grounds. A police officer called on Watanabe and ordered a permanent obstruction built in front of the window. I told Watanabe I would tear the boards down.

He said: "I think when you do that, you'll have more light." He thought a moment. "Also, more air."

March 21, 1946   ATAMI

From time to time in the past ten years, I have found myself arguing on Japan's future. Like most people who have worked in the Far East, I never doubted that Japan would sooner or later fight the United States and Britain. But what would happen after Japan's inevitable defeat? Could Japan be democratized? Would there by any progressives left who could assume leadership and enforce reform?

In such arguments, it was Yukio Ozaki who was always mentioned as Japan's outstanding democrat. Ozaki was one of the world's great parliamentary leaders. He had sat in the Diet since 1890, and more than once in the years of aggression he rose in the Diet to attack the army boldly for its usurpation of political power.

This morning, I rode out to this seaside resort to see Ozaki. Now eighty-seven years old, Ozaki lives in semiretirement in a villa put at his disposal by a rich publisher. Ozaki was waiting for us in the living room, by a huge window overlooking the ocean. He was an old, old man, with a thin face, a white beard, and a handsome dark kimono that made him look like an ancient Japanese etching.

I sat across a low table from Ozaki, and he gave me a long rubber tube, which had a suction cup at one end and a sort of cigarette mouthpiece on the other. The cup went under my chin, the mouthpiece went in his ear, and the tube stretched between us. Apparently my speech sent vibrations which sometimes reached him. It was an odd feature of an odd conversation.

"Which party do you belong to, Mr. Ozaki?"

"Ito's.

"Ito? Who's Ito?"

"Prince Ito."

I stuttered in amazement. Ito was one of the founders of modern Japan; he was premier some sixty years ago. I said, "No, Mr. Ozaki, I mean more recently." He said, "Well, Marquis Okuma." Okuma was premier just before the turn of this century. "I belonged to all of them," Ozaki said. "When they became majority parties, I led them."

I kept asking him for his social and economic program for a new Japan. He said plaintively, "I don't understand economics." Eventually, he admitted he had a two-point program —elimination of Chinese characters from the Japanese written language, and nationalization of land, but he thought the latter should wait until it had been studied more thoroughly. ("When I was mayor of Tokyo, I learned that reforms profit the wrong people.")

He thought the next Diet would be dominated by "bosses and gangsters," and the next Cabinet will be worse than the present one. He spoke sharply of Hatoyama, the Liberal leader, and warmly of Nozaka, the Communist, though he felt the Communist program was nothing but "a collection of words." He also told me the emperor was "a pretty good man." The Russian correspondents told me that when they saw Ozaki, he called the emperor a war criminal and a useless man who should be "liquidated," and urged that the entire imperial system be put to the test of a plebiscite.

After an hour, I began to feel as if I was butting my head into a soft pillow. Many of my questions never reached him. The ones that did, he answered in generalities. His record proved him to be a liberal. But he was a liberal conditioned by a feudal environment, a man whose mind and memory lagged half a century behind the calendar.

Once again I discovered that I, and many of my friends, had used a wrong set of yardsticks. A decade ago, the measure of a progressive Japanese was his opposition to the army. But now the army was gone, and what was wanted of a progressive leader was an integrated blueprint for social betterment. Yesterday's progressives in Japan could not meet the new test. Like Ozaki, they had served their purpose. New leaders were now needed, and they would have to come from the grass roots.

I rode back to Tokyo with Ozaki's thirty-year-old daughter, who works for *Reader's Digest*. She told me a few stories which showed that within his limits, Ozaki had done a good job. Late in 1940, she said, her father foresaw the coming of the war, and decided to do something about it. He was already being watched by the Secret Police, and his mail was being censored. Thus, he asked his daughter to take a letter to Marquis Kido, and surrender it to no one else. The letter predicted the war if events were allowed to follow their course, and urged the emperor to offer generous peace terms to Chiang Kai-shek.

The young woman handed the letter to Kido. Four or five days later, it was returned to Ozaki by ordinary mail, and with no comment. Ozaki felt that Kido, by letting the army censors read the letter, deliberately tried to put him on the spot.

In 1942, the army warned Ozaki that if he tried to address his constituents at Ise, he might be killed. Defiantly, he went back, and in a speech proceeded to draw the parallel between Tojo's regime and some of the unhappier periods in Japan's history. Every time he did it, a Thought Control man cut him short. Ozaki would then say to the crowd: "If you talk to your children, they'll tell you what I'm not allowed to say. They've studied it in their history textbooks."

That year, by misinterpreting a line of a song Ozaki quoted, the Secret Police arrested him on a charge of *lèse majesté*. He spent a day in the same Sugamo Prison in which Tojo is now confined. Subsequently, the Supreme Court acquitted him.

Ozaki's daughter spoke very caustically of the U.S. Army and its "undemocratic action," such as the requisition of Japanese houses for American use. She had just returned from Manchuria with her husband, who was a Japanese Army officer, and I took some delight in drawing the contrast between the behavior of the Japanese Army in Manchuria and China proper and our own behavior in Japan. We parted on a distinctly chilly note.

March 26, 1946   SAITAMA

At seven in the morning, a crowd of us drove in two jeeps to the Imperial Plaza. The huge square, with its light yellow gravel, was abandoned, except for the usual American sentries and a few parked jeeps with U.S. Military Police.

At seven-fifty, the gates opened and the emperor's Mercedes Benz rolled out across the bridge. With it came four other cars with Japanese policemen and Court officials, and four police motorcycles. The white jeeps of the MPs roared off to lead the procession. The two press jeeps supplied the rear-guard. We drove down almost empty side streets, and at every corner there was a compact figure or two in plainclothes. The men ignored us, but watched the few passersby. At street crossings, the traffic policemen stood with their backs to the procession. The people bowed reverently. With a fine sense of values, they bowed twice: one to the emperor, once to the MPs in the white jeeps.

Eventually we got to the tiny suburban station, where more MPs stopped us at the gate. The press train, they said, had left fifteen minutes earlier. We put on our most important expressions, and brushed by them. "The emperor has invited us to come along." The platform was crowded with Japanese policemen and Court officials. We watched the emperor get into his car, and then marched into the car behind it. It was full of Japanese policemen, with swords and starched white collars. We had just cleared them out of a few seats, when a Court official came in to make explanations in a hurt voice: "There was a press train for you. You are permitted to ride in this train, but the permission is not to be considered as a precedent."

I had seen trains like this at world's fairs back home, but never in active use. It was a beautifully maintained 1890 model, with not a speck of dust on the windows, the metal work, or the seats. The springs, too, were good. After a while, a boy came in with cigarettes and cups of green tea.

The whole countryside had seemingly been turned out for the emperor. (Later, I learned that the orders were issued by the police through the Neighborhood Associations, which control food and fuel rationing.) At every station the entire staff was lined up at rigid attention. At every crossing there was a tight mob pressing hard against the lowered barrier—villagers with flags, school children, groups of women. In the fields, farmers raised their heads to look at the train, and then bowed waist-low. It probably was easy to recognize the imperial train, it was so shiny, and it had the imperial chrysanthemum on the side. You couldn't mistake it for the battered, crowded, windowless trains the common folk used.

Our first stop was at Takasaki. We walked out into the station square close on the emperor's heels. As soon as he emerged, there was a roar of *banzai*—ten thousand years. The emperor bowed and entered a waiting Mercedes—his second. We got into trucks provided by the U.S. Army, which was seemingly supervising the whole affair. As I was getting into a truck, a middle-aged woman thrust her red face near me and yelled *banzai*. She was shrill and excited, and every bit as genuine as some of the women you saw at the wartime meetings in New York. We rode through the town, between two solid lines of cheering children. Imperceptibly we left the town behind, and then we were in the country, with small clusters of shouting people. We came to a halt at a Japanese military hospital.

It was a large, well-swept, bare compound, with lines of dreary one-story wooden barracks. We walked ahead of the emperor, and watched him enter the wards. The patients, in white hospital gowns, were kneeling on their beds or on the floor. They were husky, hard-looking youths, with stony expressions on their faces. But for one amputee, they all appeared to be healthy.

As the emperor walked into the first ward, someone barked a command, and the men bowed. The emperor shuffled forward, with the doctors, policemen, Court officials, American officers, and cameramen bunched around him. The voice barked another command, and the patients raised their heads, staring forward.

By that time, I had had a good look at the emperor, or "Charlie," as we called him. He is a little man, about five feet two inches in height, in a badly cut, gray striped suit, with trousers a couple of inches too short. He has a pronounced facial tic, and his right shoulder twitches constantly. When he walks, he throws his right leg a little sideways, as if he has no control over it. He was obviously excited and ill at ease, and uncertain of what to do with his arms and hands.

At first, he shuffled past the men, stopping occasionally to read the charts. Then he apparently decided the moment called for a few words. He tried several questions, but they all seemed out of place. At last he settled on the simple "Where are you from?" He now walked from man to man, asked his question, and when the patient answered, the emperor said, "Ah, so!" He sounded as if he was surprised to learn that the man had come from Akita or Wakayama or the Hokkaido. His voice was high-pitched, and as time passed, it grew thinner and higher.

The irreverent Americans were now all waiting for the inhuman sound of "Ah, so," and when it came they nudged each other, and laughed, and mimicked the sound. But the joke wore out. We could now see the emperor for what he was: a tired, pathetic little man, compelled to do a job distasteful to him, and trying desperately to control his disobedient voice and face and body. It was hot and hushed, and there were no sounds other than the emperor's shrill voice and the heavy breathing of his escorts.

I do not remember when we left the hospital, or how. We drove along country dirt roads, and choked in the emperor's dust as did the uncounted thousands of children assembled along the route from the entire countryside. The road wound between and around the hills, just touched with the green of spring, and against this green there were these tots in bright kimonos, or in drab school uniforms. They cheered throatily, and their cheers rolled in waves over the countryside, and bounced from one hillside to another.

For lunch we stopped at a silk filature. A U.S. Counter Intelligence agent with us said, "You should've seen the way they've been scrubbing this place for the past three days." The little girls working at the plant also looked scrubbed. Only their hands—looking like overcooked hams from the constant dipping into boiling water where the silk cocoons are kept—betrayed their trade.

The emperor ate alone. The rest of us munched on cold boiled rice, malodorous radish, and little bits of raw fish, provided by the management. From the window, I could see the girls lining up in front of the building, and I went out to talk to them. They giggled shyly, and it was hard to find one willing to answer my questions. But eventually I was told they were "fifteen years old"—the legal age for work—they worked nine and a half hours a day, and made 3 to 5 yen or 20 to 33 cents a day. Then the emperor came out, and they bowed, and cheered at the manager's command, and craned their necks to see the monarch.

Again, we drove interminably. Once we stopped at an airfield converted into a farm. The farmers were lined up with their hoes, and the farm manager stood forward to welcome the emperor as he left the car. We drove up just as the driver flung the door open for the emperor. There was a groan, and the manager stumbled back. He looked dazed, and the blood was pouring down from the gash on his head where the door intercepted his deep bow. They were bandaging his head, and his lips were trembling from pain and shock, and the blood on his green uniform turned black in the hot sun.

The emperor, alone and self-conscious, stood in the middle of a circle watching him intently. He was completely deserted by his attendants, and there was no one to speak to. The tic had returned to his face, and he shifted awkwardly from foot to foot. It was a good ten minutes before the manager's head was bandaged, and he could report to the emperor on the condition of the farm. His voice was surprisingly clear and loud. The emperor asked no questions.

We were now on the last lap of the trip. The town was Saitama—if you could still call it a town. It had been rubbed out with an eraser of TNT and fire until nothing remained but rubble. The rubbish had first been cleared off the roads, and, here and there men had swept clean a patch of land and built a wooden shack. There was a tense and unhappy look about the town. We stopped, and the emperor left his car. We were facing a narrow side street, lined with mounds of rubbish and a few dozen flimsy frame houses. Now the mounds were covered with a dense, silent crowd. The emperor stood at the mouth of the street, watching the crowd. The crowd watched him.

Then, like an injured boxer hearing the gong for a late round, he slowly walked forward, bowing grimly to the people on the flanks. The immense crowd held back until he was well on his way. Then pandemonium broke. The mob surged down from the rubble and closed around the emperor. Children and women were trampled down. Those who could not get close stood on the fringes and wept. Some women moaned, dry-eyed.

I had seen mob hysteria before, but never anything so sudden or so marked. The few correspondents and officers were swept out of the way. My Leica was jammed violently against my chest. I was pushed and twirled around, until I had trouble keeping my balance. I towered over the little men and women around me, but unless I employed violence, I was at their mercy.

It took us half an hour of hard struggle to fight our way out. We caught the last army truck headed for the station. The emperor had yet another stop, but we had had enough. We were now on the emperor's press train—also with the imperial emblem, but with less spit-and-polish on it. Again we were rolling across the Japanese countryside, and everywhere there were waiting crowds. We rolled by them—a few American newspapermen and officers, munching on K rations—and the crowds saw not the men within but the emblem without, and bowed to us as to a living god.

It was a memorable day, for I had watched with my own eyes an act of political face-lifting. The usefulness of the emperor as a god diminished sharply on the day of surrender. Now a group of shrewd old men at, and around, the Imperial Court were manufacturing a new myth—the myth of a democratic monarch keenly interested in the welfare of his people. It was a shameful conspiracy against the Japanese people and against that concept of democracy which we said we would help to establish.

I did not know all the men who masterminded this campaign. From time to time, there was a shred of evidence. Prince Konoye, who took poison some four months ago rather than face trial as a war criminal, was now said by his intimates to have been one of the champions of the Great Metamorphosis. Marquis Matsudaira, the new Minister of the Imperial Household, was another figure in the plot. So was Shigeru Yoshida, the Foreign Minister. Toyohiko Kagawa, the "slum clearer," is a powerful influence in selling the new myth to Japan's Christians. So are the two conservative parties, which have made "Save the Throne" the only plank in their platforms. Their campaign for the elections, now less than three weeks off, will not be hurt by the emperor's junkets.

Forty years ago, Basil Hall Chamberlain spoke with admiration of the boldness and political acumen of the men who made the emperor a god. It requires an even greater boldness to re-shape the myth to meet the new conditions. What Japan's real rulers are trying to do is to find a middle ground between the old myth and the new democratic concepts they read in the Potsdam Declaration, and subsequent Allied statements. The borderline is thin, but the men behind the emperor hew to it skillfully.

It would be interesting to speculate on how much genuine affection there is for Hirohito among these men. My guess is there is little. But for their own good reasons, the men take good care of the emperor. They sent this frightened little man into a narrow Saitama alley, and they allowed the crowd to swarm upon him. But they also sent along a pack of tough, confident, and alert men, each with—strangely enough—a paper clip on his lapel. U.S. Counter Intelligence agents told us on the train the emperor was constantly protected by plainclothesmen, whose only identification was the clip.

The myth-makers took even less of a chance with the Potsdam Declaration. I have just learned that there is an enabling ordinance—the so-called "Potsdam Ordinance"—issued by the Japanese Government on U.S. orders. Signed by the emperor, the Ordinance ordered his subjects to obey implicitly all of General MacArthur's directives.

A few days ago, an officer in General MacArthur's Headquarters told me the Ordinance had never appeared in the *Official Gazette*. It was published, instead, on loose sheets of paper, not many copies of which have been seen around.

The myth-makers obviously want no record of the emperor's compliance with orders from an alien conqueror to mar their future history.

For the past four weeks, I have spent most of my waking hours in a study of the *zaibatsu*, those peculiarly Japanese combines which dominated the nation's life, helped to shape its policies, and made fat profits out of its wars.

In Osaka last month I spent two days with the heads of the House of Sumitomo, one of the four great *zaibatsu*. In a cold and plushy conference room one day, they fed me the history of this fabulous family which translated a visit by an itinerant European trader four centuries ago into one of the world's great fortunes. Taught by the trader to refine copper and silver, the family began to search the land for ore. When it discovered the Besshi copper deposits in 1691, its destiny was made. By last month, the four living Sumitomos had pyramided their empire to no less than 292 firms, from mines and foundries to musical instruments and life insurance, and worth some $600,000,000 at prewar prices.

Since my return from Osaka, I have met at least a dozen American and Japanese experts on the *zaibatsu*. Among them were Mosaburo Suzuki, the Social Democratic leader who spent three years in jail and four under police surveillance for writing exposés of Japan's monopolies; and my friend Shigeto Tsuru, a Harvard economist who now works for Headquarters. From them, and many others, I have had a liberal education in the history, practices, and prospects of Japan's fabulous combines.

Zai in Japanese means wealth, *batsu* means clique. Put together, the two words stand for some twenty families or groups which, for generations, have held Japan's economy in a stranglehold. Though the term should properly be applied to all of Japan's combines, it is now—wishfully and incorrectly—restricted in usage to the four of the richest family groups—Mitsui, Mitsubishi, Sumitomo, and Yasuda.

Among them, the four clans controlled nearly three-fourths of the combined capitalization of all Japanese firms.

In 1941 Mitsui and Mitsubishi together mined 40 per cent of all Japan's coal. In 1937 the banks of the four *zaibatsu* held one-third of all deposits in Japan's private banks; their trusts held three-fourths of all trust deposits; and their insurance companies held a fifth of all life insurance policies. Mitsui, Mitsubishi, and Sumitomo controlled more than half of the copper output, and before our submarines went prowling in the Pacific, half of Japan's mercantile shipping. Mitsubishi enjoyed a virtual monopoly on glass, and Mitsui on paper.

In 1944 Mitsubishi built every fourth of Japan's ships. Between them, the Mitsui and Mitsubishi combines controlled three-quarters of the flour-milling capacity, and came close to shutting out all rivals in the refining of sugar. Before the war, the Big Three owned half the warehousing space in Japan, and conducted a third of Japan's foreign trade.

In 1939 Mitsubishi alone handled $200,000,000 worth of foreign trade. In the prewar days, Mitsui conducted up to a third of Japan's trade in raw silk, raw cotton and cotton textiles. And at the same time, Mitsubishi controlled one of Japan's three large breweries and one of two foreign-style confection factories. But once the war started, Mitsubishi forsook beer and candy to devote its energies to such pursuits as the building of 10,000 planes, or one in seven produced in Japan.

This inventory of *zaibatsu* wealth, I discovered in a day of study of elaborate charts prepared by Headquarters' experts, could be continued *ad nauseam*. The charts showed that last New Year's Day, Mitsui directly controlled 185 and Mitsubishi controlled 285 firms, and there was no field of economic activity which did not yield a crop of yen to one or another of the *zaibatsu*. This extended from rural usury to the making of toys, to the Manchurian soybean, to hotels, to Hawaiian mines, to the building of battleships, to a Sumitomo-controlled firm called "Friendly Talk Co., Ltd."

Thanks to the European vagabond, Sumitomo became the first of the *zaibatsu*. It settled in Osaka, and made most of its money out of non-ferrous metals and the rice trade. Its present head, Baron Kichizaemon Sumitomo, is one of Japan's most spectacular figures—a horsetrader with imperial dreams and a talent for poetry. His henchmen in Osaka assured me he was "a gentleman of an extremely peace-loving nature and of considerable literary inclination." A peace-loving poet, he presided over the Sumitomo Holding Company, and from it ran the vast Sumitomo empire with an iron hand—guns, aircraft carriers, bombers, nitrogen, and all.

Not much younger was Mitsui, the biggest of them all. The founder of the house started as a moneylender to a feudal lord, and then branched out into trade. When, three-quarters of a century ago, a test of strength came between the military usurper and the clique backing the emperor, the Mitsuis gambled on the latter. The emperor won out, and the firm was given a succession of plums, from an agency to handle the government's purchases abroad to the acquisition at a give-away price of Japan's richest coal mine. As their wealth grew, so did their interest in politics.

The Mitsuis took over the powerful Seiyukai, the GOP of Japan, and put their men in the cabinet. Today, the firm is controlled by six major and five minor Mitsui families, whose *personal* income in 1937 totalled $20,000,000. (The imperial family that year earned an estimated $7,000,000.)

The Mitsubishi *zaibatsu*, which belongs to the Iwasaki family, was founded eighty years ago by a shrewd *samurai* named Yataro Iwasaki. Iwasaki's job was to manage the financial affairs of his feudal lord. But the lords lost out in their struggle against the emperor, and Iwasaki took over his lord's assets, including eleven ships. In 1875, when Japan struck at Formosa, Iwasaki was given a contract to carry troops and supplies. To make his task easier, the government bought, and handed over to him, thirty more vessels.

This was the beginning of one of the world's great shipping lines, the Nippon Yusen Kaisha, or N.Y.K. With continued help from a friendly government and court, the Iwasakis shifted to dockyards, in which to build more ships; to coal mines, to produce fuel for their steamers; to marine insurance, to insure their bottoms; and to a bank, to finance the seaborne trade.

In 1890, the government, hard pressed for funds, compelled the Iwasakis to buy wasteland in Tokyo. The Iwasaki luck held.

The tract became the heart of new Tokyo. If the rival House of Mitsui backed the Seiyukai, Mitsubishi put its money into the Minseito, the Japanese counterpart of our Democratic party. Japanese politics became a tug-of-war between the two *zaibatsu* and their political parties.

The last of the four big *zaibatsu*, Yasuda, began as a money-lender late in the last century, and came of age during the Russo-Japanese war of 1904–05, when it lent huge sums to the government. After that it went heavily into colonial enterprises, into hemp and paper and airplanes, but to this day its primary interest is in financing. Unlike the other *zaibatsu*, Yasuda pulled its political wires not through parties but through military and secret societies. Thus, even Japan's murderous ultranationalists, who had often talked of their hatred for the moneyed clique, were made to serve its ends.

The *zaibatsu* were much like the great trusts of the West, and with many of them—from Vickers Armstrong to Tide Water Associated Oil to Westinghouse—they had friendly agreements. And yet they were centuries apart, for the *zaibatsu*, despite their industrial know-how, were still rooted in Japan's feudal past. Again and again, my Japanese informants urged me to study these differences for, they said, "unless you Americans understand them, you'll never destroy the *zaibatsu*."

Although the *zaibatsu* families owned most of the great combines, the latter were usually run by *banto* or managers. *Banto* were a peculiar Japanese phenomenon, based on the concept of a *samurai's* loyalty to his lord. The *zaibatsu* combed their huge staffs and the graduating classes of Japan's best schools for talented young men. These were then assiduously trained for leadership. As they slowly moved up the ladder of hierarchy in their *zaibatsu*, they were farmed out to subsidiary firms.

Sooner or later, the best of them became *banto* in their own right, and trained their own successors. Once a man became a *banto*, he was given great latitude. All the house demanded of him was success and an all-pervading loyalty. Some of the *banto* moved into the pages of history. Many became cabinet ministers, governors of the Bank of Japan—and active planners of war and conquest. But the *zaibatsu* were still feudal organizations, and many *banto* who had risen high, dropped precipitously if the rulers of the house were displeased. One major *banto* who delighted in playing the flute once appeared on a radio program. He was heard by an Iwasaki, who felt the act demeaned the good name of the Mitsubishi. The *banto* was summarily dismissed.

The *banto* were important in this one respect: when one of them managed a subsidiary firm, it did not matter if the *zaibatsu* investment in it totalled 5 per cent or 100. The *banto* saw to it that his company followed the general policies of the *zaibatsu*. Mitsubishi, in its report to Headquarters, listed 285 firms in which it had a controlling voice. In smaller type, it also referred to 451 other companies in which it had "less than 10 per cent investment." The Iwasakis were playing with words. Through the trusted *banto*, they might well control many, if not most, of these companies.

The *banto*, in short, were not hired help. They were feudal family retainers serving their lords.

The second characteristic of the *zaibatsu* was their banks. Japan's credit facilities were limited, and he who did not have ready access to a friendly bank went bankrupt. The big combines had their own banks, which subsidized their expansion. The smaller *zaibatsu*, which had no banks, had to come to the bigger ones, to make alliances—and to seek credits. As the *zaibatsu* banks grew in wealth, the small businessmen flocked in to deposit their money. These funds were used to expand the *zaibatsu*, and often to swallow the business of their own small depositors. The *zaibatsu* banks were ruthless. Competitors were denied credit. Those who did get it often were required to buy their raw materials from the *zaibatsu*, or let it store, ship and market their goods. In years of depression, the banks took over the bankrupt industries and added them to their own *zaibatsu*.

The third characteristic was the intimate bond between the *zaibatsu* and the Imperial Court. The emperor himself is being described now as "a life-size *zaibatsu*." He is certainly Japan's richest man. Thirteen weeks ago, in a report to General MacArthur, the Japanese government valued the imperial property at nearly Y.1,700,000,000. Because of the computing system used, this figure cannot be converted into American dollars. But one Headquarters expert said: "The emperor is worth between half a billion and a billion dollars. The reason for the range is that we don't know, and probably will never know, how much of his assets was concealed just before our arrival."

The imperial family has been a large investor in *zaibatsu* banks, including Mitsui and Sumitomo. For years it has been the largest investor in the N.Y.K. shipping line, holding a larger block than the Mitsubishi, which controls the firm. But with fine impartiality, it also held a huge block in N.Y.K.'s chief rival, the O.S.K. Line. The emperor has been an investor in the Mitsubishi trust and insurance companies; in the Mitsui collieries, paper company; Formosa sugar and shipping; in the Hokkaido Colonization and the Hypothec Banks; and even in the Imperial Hotel which is now a billet for American "Brass."

With 60 per cent of the issued stock, the imperial family has been the largest investor in the Bank of Japan. The remainder, inevitably, was held by the *zaibatsu*. Like the *zaibatsu*, the imperial family shared in the profits of conquest. Thus, on the eve of the war it held 22 per cent of the stock in the Yokohama Specie Bank, whose prime interest was in the exploitation of areas occupied or coveted by Japan. The bank's policies were decided by a board of directors, representing the *zaibatsu*. Together with the *zaibatsu*, the imperial family was a very heavy investor in the South Manchuria Railway Company, that infamous Japanese counterpart of the British East India Company. Millions of imperial yen also were invested in such instruments of colonial exploitation as the Banks of Formosa and Korea.

The imperial family was part of the same pattern with the *zaibatsu*, and it shared with them a common philosophy of predatory business. Because the emperor's advisers selected premiers, the whole feudal system was assured that national policy would conform to this philosophy.

The *zaibatsu*, in their turn, were among the most assiduous builders of the imperial myth. In it they saw one of their most effective defenses from a popular protest against their policies. Few men would go to the Asiatic mainland to fight wars enriching the *zaibatsu*. But millions would do exactly that if told they were serving their emperor. Thus, millions of *zaibatsu* yen went into Shinto shrines, into propaganda, into a campaign to sell the pernicious concept of Japan's "mission."

But the bonds were even tighter than that. The Sumitomos claimed their descent from a branch of the imperial family, the Mitsuis from a feudal clan that provided wives to emperors. Through friendship or marriage, the *zaibatsu* allied themselves to the emperor's advisers and to the whole feudal web. The Sumitomos have been linked with Prince Saionji, for sixty years "the maker of cabinets." The Mitsuis have been closely bound with a succession of Court statesmen, including the last two ministers of the imperial household. Mitsubishi, happily launched with the aid of an emperor's adviser, has since had its own men next to the emperor's ear.

Nearly every *zaibatsu*—and certainly the Big Four—owed much of its wealth to war. Mitsubishi's foundation was laid in a Japanese imperial raid on Formosa. Yasuda became a major concern on the profits of the war with Russia.

The *zaibatsu* agents marched in step with, and often ahead of, the Japanese soldiery. There is ample proof that the *zaibatsu* offices abroad often have been centers of economic and military espionage. The Intelligence web of the South Manchuria Railway Company, controlled jointly by the army and the *zaibatsu*, covered all of Asia. In Shanghai I knew a Japanese newspaperman who doubled as a spy for the South Manchuria Railway. When the Japanese Army attacked China in 1937, the "newspaperman" blossomed out in the uniform of an army major.

But espionage was only incidental to the making of profit. The *zaibatsu* made aggression pay in a variety of ways. For the last fifteen years, they have earned billions on the making of munitions. (Mitsubishi Heavy Industries, capitalized at some $180,000,000 at the prewar exchange rate, in 1944 made a profit of $75,000,000.) The *zaibatsu* banks extended loans to the government. Once the army made yet another advance on the map of Asia, a "development" company was promptly created by the government, with the *zaibatsu* investing the bulk of the money.

The "development" companies were engaged in a systematic looting of the invaded areas.

Parallel with the expansion abroad was the growing *zaibatsu* control over Japan's internal life. This was done in many ingenious ways. One of these was the "control associations" which assigned raw materials, credits, and production quotas to factories. The associations were controlled by the *zaibatsu*, which used their authority to squeeze smaller operators out. *Zaibatsu* friends in the government saw to it that permits to open new plants were issued only to "efficient" firms—which meant the *zaibatsu*.

And once the Munitions Ministry was set up and certain firms were designated as "munitions companies," the *zaibatsu* were granted a guarantee of profits, immunity from certain laws, and the right to recruit labor and to set wages. It was not surprising that of the four munitions ministers, two hailed from Mitsui. And it was even less surprising that at the first opportunity the labor unions were dissolved, a management-labor "patriotic association" came in their stead, and the government announced that "labor shall be the duty of people to the State, and it shall be regarded as an honor to offer labor to the State. . . . An orderly spirit, obedience to superiors and cooperation among the workers should be encouraged."

One of the *zaibatsu* myths, never as useful as now, has been the premise that there was an unbridgeable abyss between the *zaibatsu* and the militarists. The American exponents of this myth in the 'thirties argued that Japan would never go to war with the United States because the business-minded *zaibatsu* would curb the army. Some of our more misguided diplomats in Tokyo even spoke of *zaibatsu* leaders as "our best allies" and "our kind of people." And every time some military fanatics murdered a *zaibatsu* official or plotted to blow up the Mitsui Bank, these friends of the *zaibatsu* said, "See, they hate each other." The men of the *zaibatsu* made full use of this misconception—if only to lull us into the tragedy of Pearl Harbor.

Actually, the *zaibatsu* and the army never had any fundamental conflicts. Like the army, if for different reasons, the *zaibatsu* dearly loved aggression. It gave the *zaibatsu* protected markets, vast loot, and an exclusive source of raw materials. What differences there were, were differences within a partnership. The *zaibatsu* and the army jockeyed for a larger share of political influence and a larger slice of patronage. And from time to time they differed on the *pace* of aggression. When caution was dictated, the *zaibatsu* and their allies at the imperial court pulled the reins on the army. But never could the *zaibatsu* be regarded as anything but the army's teammates in aggression.

Not everyone in uniform had affection for the *zaibatsu*. Many of the junior officers who had come out of the villages, and had seen the steady strangulation of rural economy by the *zaibatsu*, hated them often to the point of mayhem. But this hatred was seldom shared by the generals and admirals. Many of them found comfortable niches in *zaibatsu* firms. Mitsubishi, with its vast shipbuilding interests, preferred admirals. The Mitsuis employed a flock of generals.

And General MacArthur's Headquarters did no more than confirm persistent rumors when it reported the other day that the house in which Tojo tried to commit suicide had been presented to him by the Iwasakis, and that the Tojo family had reputedly received Y.10,000,000—in cash, stocks, and property —from the benevolent head of Mitsubishi.

All of this we knew the day Japan struck. And through the war our determination to break up the vicious economic system grew. On August 29, 1945—a fortnight after Japan's surrender—this determination was put in emphatic words in a statement of policy radioed to General MacArthur jointly by the Departments of State, War, and Navy. The general was instructed to seek a program for the dissolution of the *zaibatsu*, and for the creation of democratic organizations in labor, industry, and agriculture.

When we landed in Japan, not a single industrial wheel was turning. On September 22 the famous Directive No. 3 ordered the Japanese to start producing. ("We feared riots if the factories didn't get to work soon," a colonel explained to me.)

But almost at the same time, word was sent to the *zaibatsu* that they had better start thinking of dissolving themselves.

Representatives of the Big Four virtually camped in Headquarters until a plan was worked out. A part of the plan called for the self-purge of the top *zaibatsu* men. The rest of the plan was translated into an imperial ordinance providing for the creation of the Holding Company Liquidation Commission, to be set up next month. Under this plan, HCLC will take over the securities of the *zaibatsu* holding companies and sell them to the general public. The *zaibatsu* owners will get receipts, which will eventually be redeemed in long-term nontransferable government bonds.

I am assured that the *zaibatsu* are not panic-stricken. For one thing, they are known to have anticipated Japan's defeat, and prepared for it. When it came, vast stocks of raw materials, finished goods, and machinery were concealed, to be taken out again the day the Occupation ended. Another cushion was provided by the so-called "indemnities"—government insurance against war losses of any kind. The government "owed" the *zaibatsu* the fantastic amount of fifty billion yen, of which twenty billion has already been paid in two hurried installments, one just before and one just after the surrender announcement.

But these are not the only reasons why virtually all the Japanese experts I saw thought the present plans to break up the *zaibatsu* futile. The objections are many. The Japanese, for instance, criticize us for regarding the *zaibatsu* as a carbon copy of our own trusts, and ignoring the feudal character of the Japanese combines. They say we are not paying enough attention to the links between *zaibatsu* industry and *zaibatsu* banks. They say we are confused as to whether we want immediate industrial revival or a democratic economy. They, finally, say that it is naïve to expect criminals to reform themselves.

No commentary is more telling than the fact that the government through which we now promote reform is one of the most thorough *zaibatsu* Cabinets in Japan's history. Its premier is Baron Shidehara, married to an Iwasaki and for twenty years known as a political mouthpiece for the Mitsubishi. Its foreign minister is Shigeru Yoshida, who is linked by marriage to one of the emperor's pro-*zaibatsu* advisers and who only four months ago delivered a passionate protest against the dissolution of the *zaibatsu*. The cabinet minister assigned to draft a democratic constitution is Dr. Matsumoto, Japan's highest paid corporation lawyer, who has served the Mitsubishi and Yasuda *zaibatsu* both as a counsel and a director. The Minister of Commerce and Industry is the president of the Tokyo Stock Exchange.

And—this is the part which is most ironic—the Finance Minister who is supervising the breaking up of the *zaibatsu* is Viscount Keizo Shibusawa, head of one of the *zaibatsu* scheduled for extinction. Whatever legislation he might draft will have to be approved by the emperor, whose two closest advisers at the moment are both Mitsui men. I am beginning to understand why the *zaibatsu* are not panicky.

April 4, 1946   CHIBA

On a tip that a Japanese military colony had been set up on an abandoned airfield, drove out to Chiba prefecture in company with Cochrane and a Nisei lieutenant.

We first headed for the prefectural government, where we sought out the Peace Preservation Section chief. It took us an hour of prodding to discover that we were in the wrong place. When the Japanese government decided to surrender last August, it shifted two-thirds of all key personnel and shuffled up the names of the local government sections. This was a canny device, for when the U.S. Army demanded vital information or sought to fix responsibility for noncompliance with its orders, the Japanese officials could say with a straight face, "I wish I could help you, but I'm new here myself." The Peace Preservation Section, we discovered, was the old Economic Section, while the former Peace Preservation Section was now known as Security Section. The section handling ex-servicemen was now labelled Public Welfare.

We spent two more fruitless hours at the last of these. The interview was held in a huge, crowded office, and soon the entire staff was listening to our conversation. There were two Japanese close to us. They wore officers' uniforms, complete to yellow cavalry boots. They pulled up chairs and laughed uproariously as the Section chief parried our questions.

Our next stop was at the local Japanese Army Demobilization Office. We talked to a major general who was the image of Tojo. He told us he combined the functions of an adviser, mother, nursemaid, and King Solomon. Bob and I could not quite figure out if the office was striving to keep the demobilized soldiery together, or was merely trying to help those who seemingly could get help nowhere else.

As an example of the problems he had to tackle the general mentioned soldiers returning from Allied prison camps. Up to now, Japanese soldiers captured by the enemy were officially declared dead, and their wives were proclaimed widows. Even army scouts captured while reconnoitering were subject to ten years' imprisonment when they escaped from the enemy. But now there were twenty-three men in the prefecture who admitted openly they had been Allied prisoners, and thousands more were coming. The general was frankly disturbed.

This also the general told us: there were a dozen "military farms" in the prefecture. He gave us the road directions to the Shimoshidzu farm for which we were looking.

We drove into the drizzle, along a damp ribbon of macadam, edged with cherry trees in bloom. From a hill, the entire countryside seemed covered with these pink clusters, and the air was heavy with their fragrance.

Then we saw the airfield, so vast its other end was lost in a mist, and disregarding a U.S. Army "No Tresspassing" sign we drove in. The closer end of the field was now being used as a dump for Japanese equipment—heavy guns, tanks, trucks, and even a tall mound of helmets rusting in the rain.

We crossed the field, and finally arrived at what must have been the commanding general's headquarters. A worried, middle-aged Japanese came out to greet us. He said he was a Tokyo city engineer attached to the farm as an adviser. We sat in the bare, dusty office, where disobedient springs pushed out of the overstuffed chairs, and talked of the farm and its personnel.

The man told us the farm was "democratized five days ago," after the U.S. Counter Intelligence Corps expressed interest in it. He showed us a copy of a report prepared for the CIC. The report said the farm had a thousand families and 6,200 acres of land—about three times the national average. The farmers included three major generals, 29 colonels, 39 majors, and so on down the line, until one got to two gendarmerie sergeants. Four hundred of the men had been civilian employees of the War Ministry. Until the day of democratization, the colony was divided into eight units, each headed by a colonel. The eight heads formed a general staff, commanded by a major general. Now, the man explained, the council consisted of a colonel, two majors, and six War Ministry civilians.

The door swung open, and a Japanese came in. He had the broad, red face of a farmer and the voice of a drill sergeant, and he made a striking contrast to the meek adviser. He told us he had been a colonel.

On the day of Japan's surrender, the colonel said, her government summarily transferred all military property to the Finance Ministry and all military land to the Ministry of Agriculture. Simultaneously, the War Ministry set up an "Assist and Lead Society." The society issued a call to all military people who wanted to settle on the land.

"The army," shouted the colonel, "screened the applicants, and then sent them here. The Finance Ministry gave us twenty buildings, some equipment, and a loan of Y.6,630,000 [$400,-000]. The Agriculture Ministry gave us this land, and assigned an adviser. . . . " He pointed at the Tokyo engineer. "Last season we raised a crop of sweet potatoes. It wasn't enough to go around, but we'll do better this season."

We wanted to know how much interest the farm paid on the loan.

"Interest?" boomed the colonel. "We pay no interest."

"When do you have to repay your loan?"

"We don't have to pay it back."

"How much rent do you pay for the land?"

"We pay no rent."

Last November, we learned, the U.S. Army finally caught up with the "Assist and Lead Society" and closed it down. But the society had already done its job. Now supervision over the military farms was exercised by prefectural governments, which were in no mood to irritate the ex-servicemen. Less friendly to the colony were the neighboring farmers. The sharecroppers did not see why the military had to have all this rich land, and they objected. After a lot of angry negotiating, the military surrendered 400 of the poorer acres to the neighboring villages. But it took a raid by 200 villagers, organized into a Livelihood Protection League, on the farm warehouses to get a share of the supplies, including seed.

"Communists," shouted the colonel. "Communists, all of them. And the police are in league with them."

After the talk the colonel invited us to have a look at the farm from a military watchtower. We drove across the vast farm, across untouched drill grounds and antiaircraft redoubts still intact. As we drove past a long garage, I saw seven large tanks.

"Tractors," said the colonel. "We took the guns off. Now we use them as tractors."

It was quite a feat, in the strong wind loaded with rain, to climb up the bare skeleton of the tower. But it was worth it. All that we could see in the mist, "from that forest to those hills," was the military farm, and only a tiny portion of it was cultivated. We climbed down, and offered to take the two men home. They said they wanted to walk, and marched off into the rain.

We made Tokyo in time for dinner, which was much better than spending the night in a Japanese inn. After dinner, I spread out my file labelled "Military Underground." To the scores of items I had before, I now added my notes on a skeletal army corps setup going under the name of a farm, marching to work in units of fifty to three hundred men under a colonel's command, living under military discipline, using tanks for tractors, and waging war on the civilian neighbors; and prefectural governments in which evidence of the old order and personnel has been deliberately concealed by a skillful reshuffle.

There were many other items in the file. An intercepted letter to a high official of the Imperial Household Ministry informing him that the writer had done well with the stocks (illegally) entrusted to his custody. A lieutenant general who operated a string of three military "liaison offices" long after he was ordered to dissolve them. A retired lieutenant, who has opened an Institute for the Study of Recent Thought, with forty or fifty ex-servicemen come to learn the latest wrinkles in militant nationalism. There were a dozen orders issued by the Japanese Army and Navy in the dying hours of the war, with stern injunctions to the recipients to burn the documents after reading. But many were careless, and there was a partial record of continued treachery—orders to conceal weapons, burn files, move personnel around, disperse vital raw supplies or vehicles or machinery.

The record betrayed a careful conspiracy. Provisions had been made to finance the military and nationalist groups through the dark days of the Occupation. Army and navy supplies had been turned over to the *zaibatsu*, for money or for love. It was money in the case of a Japanese general who sold 8,000 army horses and pocketed the proceeds. But it could have been love in the fantastic disappearance of 2,500,000 bushels of military stocks of wheat, rice, and horse feed in five months, of the total of 8,250,000 bushels recorded on the day of the U.S. landing in Japan. Banknotes had been distributed by the bale—without accounting. Arrangements had been made with banks and industries to place ex-officers on the payroll.

In a typical order, the War Minister on August 17, 1945—three days after Japan's surrender—instructed local commanders to distribute immediately to the civilian population all army goods, fuel, vehicles, building supplies, ships, clothing, and even land. The War Minister was fully aware of the fact that he was cheating. The document bore the notation: "This order should be burned and completely obliterated before the enemy lands, and proper measures should be taken to assure that it does not fall into enemy hands." The order added: "Records which are involved in (illegal) transfer should be well adjusted, and special care should be taken not to leave any discrepancies which would arouse suspicion and cause trouble in the future."

General MacArthur's Headquarters has been aware of the conspiracy. But suppression has not marched in step with awareness. The Counter Intelligence Corps has been desperately undermanned. Even more of a deterrent has been our dependence on Japanese governmental machinery, to this day run by men who not so long ago served the cause of ultranationalism. Officers in the field who, day after day, run into evidence of planned obstructionism are alarmed. A visitor from an outlying town told me the other day:

"The thing is so big we don't even try to figure out its scope. The clues we follow multiply and lead us into fields we never expected to investigate. We don't know if the time has come to worry, but we can't forget what happened in Germany twenty-five years ago."

April 5, 1946   TOKYO

With General MacArthur in the stellar role, the newly created Allied Council for Japan had a strangely unhappy debut this morning. The conference room in the Meiji Insurance Building was packed early. The four chief delegates sat on two sides of a huge, well-polished table, their aides behind them. The United States was represented by General Marquat, who will be chairman of the Council; the British Commonwealth by the suave and scholarly W. MacMahon Ball, who once headed the Political Science Department at the University of Melbourne; Russia by the powerfully built Lieutenant General Kuzma Derevyanko, a hero of the drive from Kursk across the Ukraine; and China by Lieutenant General Chu Shih-ming, who formerly served in Washington.

This was one of the infrequent public appearances for General MacArthur, and the cameramen were out in force, focusing their cameras on the small speaker's stand.

General MacArthur entered on time, a tall, stooped man with dark hair slicked down to cover a bald spot. He shook hands with the three foreign delegates, smiled at each, and then without delay proceeded to read his speech. He read it well, with the vigorous voice and emphasis of a professional speaker.

Though the speech was in General MacArthur's traditional flowery language, there was no mistaking his purpose. In his second sentence, he made it plain that the Council has only advisory functions, and it would not "divide the heavy administrative responsibility of the Supreme Commander as the sole executive authority." After that, he proceeded to castigate those who were critical of his work, and to praise his own record. He was especially laudatory in his comments on the new Constitution, which he indicated had been drawn by the Japanese themselves, and "widely and freely discussed" by them. He brought up the provision for the renunciation of war (which he has reputedly drawn himself) as a guidepost for the world.

Both General MacArthur's tone and the anxiety it betrays are easy to understand. Under any circumstances, he is not the kind of a man to share authority. The eleven-power Far Eastern Commission has been breathing heavily on his collar, and General MacArthur might well expect its offshoot, the Council, to try and seize some of his powers. Certainly the example of divided authority in Germany is not conducive to a duplication of the same rivalry and confusion in Japan. But there is an added element in the picture. General Mac-Arthur is extraordinarily sensitive to anything that smacks of criticism. It might well happen that perfectly justified inquiries and advice by the Council will be taken by General MacArthur as a reflection on his success and reputation, and he will react sharply. The Council's proceedings will call for the utmost tact and patience. From what we gather, the British delegate is equipped with both. It will remain to be seen if either General Derevyanko or Generals MacArthur and Marquat are similarly endowed. Some of the men who have served in the Philippines recall that eight months before Japan's surrender, American psychological warfare officers were instructed to make no further mention of the Allies in connection with the Philippine campaign. What General MacArthur was reluctant to admit in Manila he may be even more reluctant to admit in Tokyo.

April 6, 1946   TOKYO

The election—billed as Japan's first display of democratic yearnings—is only four days off. Today, I toured an outlying Tokyo area with an "observer team" of a young lieutenant and a Nisei interpreter.

At closer look, the "observer teams" are somewhat less impressive than they seem on paper. The lieutenant's instructions were vague. He was not to interfere in political activity; he was to report on any wrongdoing; he was to unearth what he could of a suspect New Japan party. Neither he nor his interpreter had had any briefing in Japanese politics or history. The interpreter, who has just arrived in Japan, spoke a pidgin Japanese learned in California. With the utmost effort and good will, the lieutenant could not understand what he saw. He was just a puzzled boy of twenty, whose only acute comment was: "The way the Japs live, I don't see how any Americans could live like that."

With a Japanese police guide, we proceeded to a small suburban town to talk to political candidates. It was a lovely spring day, the cherry trees were in bloom, the alleys were sodden with a recent rain, and the whole community, with its trim bamboo fences, gardens, and little homes, looked gay and unreal. The unreality was heightened when we discovered we were following in the tracks of a U.S. Army DDT team. The children chasing our jeep were white-haired from the powder, and the *futan* (comforters) hung out to air looked bleached.

We found our first candidate sitting on the floor of his living room. The outer panels had been removed and the room had become a porch, opening on a small garden with a large cherry tree and a freshly dug up vegetable patch. The candidate was a fat, old man, with a cleanly shaven head and a priest's robe. We did not want to take off our shoes and sat on the edge of the room, with our legs dangling down into the garden. The old man's face was crinkled in a smile. He said he was running on the ticket of the Buddhist party, which would have thirty or forty candidates throughout the country. "Politics are easy," he said with a laugh. "All my work is being done by the temples and Buddhist schools."

I asked him about his platform.

"I'm for democracy."

"What economic problems do you think should be tackled first?"

"Economics?" he said. "I don't know anything about economics. I'm a man of religion." And then, with a touch of pride, "I've studied for many years under the head abbott of our sect."

"What about your campaign expenses?"

"It's my money, but a businessman friend is helping out. He manages me, so to say."

The priest explained that his friend was a manager from the Yasuda *zaibatsu*.

"Did you get that, Lieutenant?" I said.

The lieutenant looked puzzled. "What's a *zaibatsu?*" I explained what the *zaibatsu* were, and why it was noteworthy when they put up a candidate for election. "Oh," said the lieutenant, "I guess I better put it down in my report."

The priest insisted we have tea with him. We waited, and soon an old woman came in with a tray of cups, and ceremoniously put them in front of him. It was all done with the proper decorum, come down through generations. The only new note was the DDT, which lay thick on her hair and was now drifting slowly into the tea.

Our next stop was at the residence of a candidate of the New Republic party. He was a slim, wary, middle-aged man who avoided all questions on his political views. After much prodding he admitted that he and his family owned four companies, dealing in land, farm implements, hotels, and department stores. It was a small *zaibatsu*, which did not want to be identified as such. The man was shrewd and slippery, and we were learning little of his party. I remembered the lieutenant's orders to dig up information on the New Japan party, and changed my tack. Now I wanted to know if the candidate had any serious political competition in the district.

"I don't want to talk of my rivals," said the candidate, "but since you ask, I can tell you about the New Japan party. I think it's an extremist group. Its chief is a gangster in the Ueno District. He started as owner of a school for masseurs. Now he is a black-market dealer. We understand he buys and sells votes. His vice-president is one of Ueno's biggest black market operators. Both are bad men."

I kept questioning the man until the lieutenant had the information he wanted. But I suspected he did not realize he also was getting a picture of an equally unsavory organization known as the New Republic party.

In the evening we had a gala affair at the Press Club—a dinner with the leaders of the four major political parties. The Liberal party, which is expected to win the election, was represented by its president, Hatoyama. The other conservative party, known as Progressive, had one of its directors, an old-timer named Gen Nagai. The Social Democrats had one of the pillars of the party, Komakichi Matsuoka, president of the staid and powerful Japan Federation of Labor. The Communists were represented by one of their Big Three, Nozaka. Burton Crane, of the New York *Times*, presided. Every effort was made to make the evening decorous. The dining room, always trim, was now glistening with glass, silver, and white tablecloths.

We asked the men their party platforms. Nagai, a big, surly man, was the first to answer. "The Progressive party," he said, "stands for no labor disputes. We disapprove of strikes because they represent strife. We also disapprove of such things as Popular Front."

Both Matsuoka, thin and vigorous, and Nozaka, came out

for the nationalization of banks, land reform, and a greater voice for labor. Hatoyama was the last to speak. He surveyed the audience with a confident smile, and said in labored English he was proud to be at the Club. As to his party's program, he distrusted the Popular Front, thought Karl Marx a greater menace than William Pitt, and urged public works as an answer to unemployment.

The next question dealt with the new Constitution and the emperor. Nagai blandly admitted the Constitution was not a domestic product. "We were working on a Constitution," he said, "but on March 6 the Supreme Commander's Constitution came out, and we realized it was much better than ours. So we decided to support it." Matsuoka, the ardent Socialist, spoke of the "love and respect" with which his party regarded the imperial system. Nozaka said the Communists were campaigning for "a Constitution drawn by the people themselves." He thought the American draft left the emperor nine major prerogatives, which should be denied him.

"The reason we object to them," he said, "is simple. We must remember that Hitler came to power using the liberal provisions of the Weimar Constitution. If we retain the emperor virtually unchanged, and create a body much like the present House of Peers, we run great risks. Nor do I think that war can be renounced through a constitution. The militarists have always made war in the name of peace."

Before dinner I had organized a political probe. The suspect was Hatoyama. It may be that correspondents have no business to engage in politics. But I thought this was a legitimate undertaking in every possible way. As an American I wanted to help rid Japan of a ranking war criminal—a man made doubly dangerous by the fact that he is scheduled to be the next prime minister. As a newspaperman, I looked forward to a front-page story.

A week ago, some Headquarters officers gave me the translation of a book Hatoyama wrote in 1938, after he visited Hitler and Mussolini. The book contained admissions that did not sound well from the lips of a prospective premier in a democratic Japan. The officers tried to use the book to have Hatoyama purged. When they failed, they passed the book on to me. Before dinner I tore the book into half a dozen sections and farmed them out to interested correspondents, Chinese, English, and American.

But the first shot was actually fired by Frank Robertson, an Australian working for the International News Service. Somewhere he had obtained a page of quotes from the book, and he now wanted to know if Hatoyama had any comment on his statement in 1938 that "Hitler loves Japan from the bottom of his heart. The Japanese people must increasingly discipline themselves spiritually and must not betray Hitler's faith in them."

After that the probe began in earnest. In a way it was a savage performance, but Hatoyama had no one to blame for his past but himself. He was asked if he still believed that "The Nazi spirit and Japan's *bushido* spirit are similar," or that Japan should "closely follow" the Nazi method of handling labor problems. ("The Fuehrer's totalitarian principles are closely woven into the labor control laws. They prevent class strife.") We shot at him quotations of fulsome praise for Hitler and Mussolini ("The fact that Mussolini pursued a resolute course in spite of all the British propaganda marks him as one of the great heroes of his generation. For Italy, for the Italian people, long may he live!").

The British correspondents wanted to know the details of Hatoyama's conversation with Hjalmar Schacht, in which he suggested German-Japanese exploitation of China to "drive the British influence out of China." Eddie Tseng, of the Chinese Central News Agency, demanded comment on Hatoyama's statement that when he dined with Prime Minister Neville Chamberlain and other Tory leaders, he told them that "China cannot survive unless she is controlled by Japan. . . . "

As the probers closed in, Hatoyama became confused. At first he claimed he could remember nothing. Then, when we showed him the quotations, he said he had lied in his book. The real truth, he said, came out only in his private meetings with university classmates, to whom he confided that "Hitler is a liar, Mussolini a country hick, and Chamberlain a gentleman." We wanted to know if he was sure he was lying then, and not now, and whether he could now go before the Japanese people and admit that he lied to them eight years earlier in helping to push them into further aggression.

The book was not the only weapon we had. As more information came out, Hatoyama became a rattled old man, unable to think fast enough to cope with the hunters. He told Tseng that "when the China affair started, I thought that if it ended with the grant of special rights, Japan would be happy and China would save face, and everything would be fine." He admitted to me he did say four months ago that he was "wholeheartedly for the war up to the capture of Singapore." He admitted he still favored "discipline" for labor.

The final thrust came five hours after Hatoyama sat down to what had promised to be a happy dinner. Some eight years ago he told Hitler that "the time would come when I would organize the Cabinet . . . to carry out my own policies." Now we wanted to know if the views he had expressed tonight were a fair forecast of the policies he would pursue as premier. He had no answer.

It will be interesting to see the reactions of Headquarters and the Japanese Government (which screened and cleared Hatoyama) to tomorrow's crop of headlines.

April 7, 1946   TOKYO

Another demonstration, with an unexpected ending. There was a mass rally scheduled for Hibiya Park. Meetings are so commonplace they no longer make news, and I went down to see it with the feeling I was taking a busman's holiday. There were about 12,000 or 15,000 people in the park, most of them squatting on the dusty ground. The speakers, Communists, Social Democrats and some unaffiliated trade union leaders, demanded Premier Shidehara's resignation and the end of the Y.500 ($33) limit on monthly incomes.

The meeting ended soon after I came. The people rose, dusted themselves off, and began to form into ranks. Ten abreast, they marched out of the park, with flags and posters, with songs and that wonderful chant, *wassho, wassho.*

I joined *Life's* Eisenstaedt taking pictures from a jeep. The procession headed for the premier's residence, and we kept up with it, stopping from time to time to photograph the parade and individual faces. When we reached the Diet hill and looked back, the procession had grown tremendously. It was now a thick, black serpent, speckled with the red of flags, its tail lost behind a distant corner.

The premier's residence is a red brick building designed by Frank Lloyd Wright. It is surrounded by a thick wall, with two broad wooden gates. Now the wall was edged with the heads of policemen watching the approaching procession from inside the compound. We went inside and saw that the gates had been reinforced with thick wooden beams stuck into the ground at an angle.

Kept in ranks by its own marshals, the crowd slowly came up the hill and massed in front of the building. As more people kept coming up, they began to press against the gates. The police summoned by a very excited officer, put their weight against the gate from the inside. The gate held, but the demonstrants began to climb over the wall. Some men jumped down, and were immediately hustled off into the guardhouse. The others merely stood on the wall and on the roof of the guardhouse, waving flags and posters, and shouting to the crowd outside. The police seemed to be uncertain as to what to do. The shouting continued for about ten minutes, while more people kept coming up the hill. Now they were flat against the other gate and pushing it in. Tempers rose. The crowd tossed rocks and wooden staves over the gate. The policemen threw them back. Missiles were coming in now in such a steady shower that Eise and I retreated to the refuge of a porch.

Then, with one great surge, the crowd broke through the gate. Skirmishes broke out all over the yard. Most of the policemen took to their heels. Others fought a rearguard battle. One policeman was caught inside a small hut under construction. The crowd closed in on him and beat him to the ground. A bespectacled demonstrant struck by a policeman, turned around, calmly put his spectacles in an inside pocket, and began to punch the policeman in the face. They were separated by marshals.

Meanwhile, the bulk of the crowd threw itself against the wide front doors of the premier's building. The doors groaned, and glass came down with a crash. Men started throwing rocks into the windows. The fighting continued.

The building stands on a hill, and right behind it there is a sheer, stone-lined drop, with a narrow concrete stairway leading down. The police were now driven down to the canyon below, and we could see them standing there in indecision. Some of the demonstrants tried to follow them, but stopped when the policemen took pistols out of their holsters, and waved them menacingly. Soon a force of 150 police reinforcements came up on the double quick, and the reorganized force began to advance. One of the policemen opened fire, and others followed. The shots sounded thin and sharp, like firecrackers. The crowd milled in one spot, and then began to run back into the compound.

Eise and I were taking pictures over the edge of the drop when the firing began. We took a few photographs, and then, finding ourselves in no man's land, retreated hastily. We stopped behind the thick pillars of a servants' house and watched the policemen come up the stairs. The crowd was ripping up the house under construction, and throwing bricks at them.

When the policemen came up to the top, they stopped firing, and the marshals went out to meet them. Slowly other demonstrators came up behind the marshals. They stood there and yelled at each other. One demonstrant, with his face twisted in anger, was shouting the Japanese equivalent of "lemme at 'em." Others were trying to shame the policemen. "We're not against you," they cried. "You're also people. We're against Premier Shidehara."

It began to look as if the violent spirits would win out, and the marshals told the policemen to go down again. The police obeyed, but they made it obvious they felt it was a loss of face for them.

Eise said: "This is just like the German revolution. Or like the coming of Hitler."

We were still on the edge of the hill when we heard the sound of a jeep driving into the yard. Six American Military Policemen jumped out and began to clear the yard. They were armed with nightsticks, and they beat the demonstrants on the backs and buttocks. Slowly and reluctantly, but with no display of anger, the crowd broke up and began to pour out of the compound. It stood in the street, sang, and listened to speeches by men who stood on the wall, out of the reach of the Americans.

I went down to the entrance of the building. The delegation of thirteen representatives of the demonstration was still waiting at the doors to be admitted. Among them was the Communist leader Tokuda, the Social Democratic leader Kanson Arahata, an editor of the *Yomiuri* and a famous woman novelist. Arahata, who is a slight, quiet man, looked ill. I was told that when he objected to the ejection of the crowd, a husky Military Policeman picked him up by his neck and threw him to the ground.

A tall, young MP lieutenant was urging Tokuda to tell the demonstrants to go home.

Tokuda listened patiently. He is too smart a political leader not to know the value of massed people. He kept saying he could not tell the demonstrants to disperse, for they were waiting for the results of the delegation's meeting with Shidehara.

When the compound was cleared, the Japanese policemen returned, shut the gates, and restored the supporting beams. The guards inside the building then opened the doors, and let the delegation in. Eise and I went in, too. We were still the only correspondents, but there were two or three men from the Counter Intelligence Corps and a score of Japanese reporters and cameramen. The delegates were ushered into a small waiting room and sat down along one side of a long, dusty table.

The cameramen set up their equipment and began to grind their cameras. At last the assistant secretary of the cabinet showed up. He sat across the table from Tokuda, and they traded hostile smiles.

Arahata, who looks like a country squire, demanded that Shidehara resign. The secretary said he doubted if Shidehara would. Tokuda turned red, took the thin, brass-headed farmer's pipe out of his mouth, and began to pound the table with his fist.

"We want Shidehara here," he shouted. "We want a responsible answer."

"Shidehara has an appointment," the secretary said.

"What kind of an appointment?" shouted Tokuda. "We can't tell the people outside Shidehara can't see us. You go out and tell them. We're not children's messengers. Is Shidehara on a vacation? He must've known we were coming. Keeping that crowd outside in order is a terrible job."

Tokuda and Arahata read their statements, while from the outside came the roar of the assembled thousands. By then Tokuda knew the whole thing had fizzled out. But he tried to maneuver for an advantage, for anything that could be used against Shidehara in the future. They all looked like poker players, Tokuda betting on the crowd, the secretary on the American MPs. I did not know it yet, but six American armored cars and six jeeps armed with machineguns already had begun to patrol the street, slowly breaking up the demonstration.

Eventually the secretary said Shidehara would meet the delegates tomorrow afternoon. Tokuda threw his parting shot: "Shall we ask the crowd to wait outside until tomorrow?" We all went out. In the broad, dark lobby, a Japanese police officer was being questioned by Japanese reporters. When he said only two shots had been fired by his men, the reporters jeered. Later in the day the police raised the number of shots to twenty and said eight policemen had been injured, three of them beaten into unconsciousness. There were three hundred policemen in all.

When we came outside, an army sedan drove up, and the MP lieutenant rushed up to report. It was Brigadier General

Hugh Hoffman, of the First Cavalry Division. The lieutenant reported that things were under control, the general nodded in satisfaction and drove off.

Amazing as the whole afternoon has been, it was our own, American, part in it that supplied its most amazing feature, for in that wise document, entitled "Initial Post-Surrender Policy in Japan," sent to General MacArthur for his guidance last August there was this paragraph.

"The policy is to use the existing form of government in Japan, not to support it. Changes in the form of government initiated by the Japanese people or government in the direction of modifying its feudal and authoritarian tendencies are to be permitted and favored. In the event that effectuation of such changes involves the use of force by the Japanese people or government against persons opposed thereto, the Supreme Commander should intervene only when it is necessary to insure the security of his forces and the attainment of all other objectives of the Occupation."

In one afternoon we had seemingly violated this directive on two counts. We had directly intervened in support of the Shidehara cabinet. And we had stopped the people when they were employing force to overthrow what is by all standards a feudal-minded, feudal-bred regime.

After General Hoffman left, I stopped the lieutenant and asked him why he broke up the demonstration. He said gruffly:

"They can demonstrate, but they can't damage private property."

April 8, 1946   TOKYO

Once again to the same small room in the premier's residence to see Shidehara meet the leftist delegation.

This time the room was packed to the last inch. We waited for a long time, and then word came from Shidehara that he did not want to come downstairs, and his own room was too small for the press. Next he objected to the cameramen. The Japanese reporters did some sharp talking, and it was finally agreed to move upstairs to a large room with ornate furniture and huge Japanese paintings of fishermen.

Again the secretary came in to announce that Shidehara objected to floodlights and to having his voice recorded by the newsreel men. The irritated Japanese reporters shouted at Shidehara's secretary: "What kind of a democratic premier is that? Is he afraid to let his people hear him? Is he afraid of bright light? Tell him to resign." When the secretary retreated to Shidehara's office, the newsreel cameramen posted lookouts and began to conceal microphones under the table where Shidehara could not see them.

The delegates watched this with obvious pleasure. There were only twelve of them today. Arahata, who was thrown down by an MP yesterday, was confined to his bed with injuries. But when we kept pressing Tokuda for more details, he refused to talk. The leftists court no trouble with the American authorities.

While we were talking, Shidehara came in. He is an old, old man with a shaking head and trembling hands. He sank into a tall chair facing the twelve delegates sitting in two rows across the table from him, and the violent meeting began, a meeting of abuse and denunciation, of contrast between the old and the new, of politics in the raw. The delegates demanded to know if Shidehara thought the Y.500 limit on monthly income was fair, and whether he lived on it. "Look at you," said Tokuda scornfully. "You're so fat. One can't get far on Y.500. You must be buying food in the black market."

One after another the delegates jumped up, to demand that Shidehara resign, that he repair the rationing machinery, that he end the black market. They were, most of them, earthy, untutored men with callouses on their hands and their speech. They called Shidehara a cheat and a liar. From time to time, the *Yomiuri* editor, Suzuki, cut in with a reasoned attack on the government's policies, or lack of them. But as soon as he ended, the trade union people burst in with speeches of denunciation.

Shidehara sat before them, a pathetic, stout old man, looking at the ceiling, at the reporters, at his hands, and mumbling from time to time, "I don't want to argue." Occasionally his secretary jumped up to say that Shidehara was a busy man and had to leave, but he was shouted down by the delegates.

In the middle of somebody's speech, Tokuda saw a lean, hard man with a bulging coat standing behind Shidehara. The man had a paper clip on his lapel—the badge of secret servicemen.

"There's the man," shouted Tokuda violently, "the man with the gun. Look under his coat. This is our democracy in which the premier will not talk to the people without a gun backing him up."

The delegates turned to us and cried, "Take a picture of the democratic premier and his gunman." A Communist delegate jumped up, ran to the secret serviceman and tried to pull his coat open. The serviceman took a fighting stance, but Tokuda quickly called his man back. There was a great deal of commotion and shouting, and in the tumult Shidehara rose and half ran towards the door. One of the delegates rushed forward and tried to block the premier's path. The secret servicemen pushed him off, and there was a melee. Someone gave Shidehara a shove, and he bounced against the wall. I saw him totter, but he quickly recovered, and his aides whisked him out of the room.

That is about all there was to it—a bit of violent history. In the past two days, the leftists have demonstrated great strength. The streetcars are decorated with posters denouncing Shidehara. By courtesy of the railway workers' union, yesterday's demonstrants were brought to Tokyo from the suburbs free of charge. A truck drivers' union assigned fifty trucks—a large number in present-day Japan—for yesterday's march. A thousand farmers came into town for the demonstrations. As distress mounts, and the government continues to do nothing, the Communists strength in the unions and among the sharecroppers grows.

Spent most of the day covering the last pre-election rallies. Fred Sparks of *Look*, Roy Ozaki, my new assistant, and I started with a vacant lot at the Shinjuku black market, where three meetings were going on at the same time. It was anything but an ideal place for political campaigning. A bomb had obliterated the building that used to stand there, and now the lot was covered with brick and rubble. Gusts of wind raised a thick, brownish dust and banged the loose sheets of iron on the neighboring buildings, drowning out the political oratory.

On one side, against a fence, a former Communist was campaigning for election as an Independent on an anti-Communist program. He was an accomplished actor. He wept on his soapbox, recalling how he had been misguided in his youth; he grew furious, denouncing birth control as a menace to Japan's greatness; he pointed to the callouses on his hands, and declaimed his affinity to the common, working man; and from time to time, assailing the Communists or speaking of the rot eating into Japan's moral fiber, he pounded on the fence with his stout cane and shouted: "Destroy it! Like that! Like that! Like that!" He had the largest audience of the three candidates, and he was warmly applauded.

Next to him, a young man was speaking in behalf of the Communists. There were many red flags flapping in the wind, and school girls were passing leaflets. I watched a minor episode on the edge of the crowd. Two girls, both about eighteen years old, offered a leaflet to a listener. He said no. They asked why? He explained, they retorted, and before long there was a crowd of fifty people around them listening to a long, calm discussion.

The former Communist had finished his speech, and called for three *banzai* for the emperor, and got them. The Communist speaker then called for applause for his party, and that was given, too, though less lustily.

Next to the Communists, meanwhile, the Social Democrats were setting up a soapbox and a flag for the appearance of their stars—Mr. and Mrs. Kanju Kato. Kato is a great labor leader, with a distinguished record behind him. He is seeking a seat in Nagoya, but has come down to Tokyo for a few days to help out his wife. For Mrs. Kato this is a political debut. Until now women have had no suffrage.

Mrs. Shizue Kato, I have discovered in recent weeks, is many things to many men. Depending on whom you talk to, she is anything from a radical to a shrew. In between, she is a Good Woman, in capital letters; an unreformed patrician; an intensely ambitious female; and an unprincipled character who insists on birth control and wishes to destroy that beautiful Japanese family in which Father is all, and women, quite deservedly, are wretched dust.

What the eye can see is a poised and charming woman, looking younger than her forty-nine years. And what the ear can hear is a woman of quick wit in both English and Japanese. Before Shizue married Kato, she was married to a baron, and toured the U.S. lecture circuits as Baroness Ishimoto. The baron eventually deserted her for nationalist pursuits in Manchuria. Both the Katos are my friends, and I hope both win, for they have shown themselves so far, as progressives who could well fight reaction when we pull out of this country.

The soapbox stood against a wall still decorated with a tremendous mural of a Japanese bomber and the slogan, "Boost Plane Production for an All-Out Attack!" Kato climbed atop the box. He is a small, muscular, intense man, born one of six children in a farmer's family. His first job was as a slavey in a dry goods store. He escaped to Tokyo, studied, became a union organizer, and a member of the Diet. (Shizue says, "He's the kind of man whom café waitresses like. He's a man's man, not sweet like candy.")

Now he recited the common man's grievances against the Shidehara Cabinet, wanted to know if his listeners were two weeks behind in their rice ration as he was, and promised reform if the Social Democrats came to power. He spoke for ten minutes, and then walked to the fringe of the crowd, stripped to his shorts, and while young admirers interviewed him, mopped his damp body.

Mrs. Kato's metallic voice was charged with emotion. She

spoke of the need for planned reconstruction, for helping the widows and orphans of the war, for aiding the millions of repatriates come home. Men and women left their black market stalls to join the crowd. They listened first with amazement, then incredulity, then attention. They even shouted, *Yoshi, Yoshi* (Yes, Yes) when she made a good point.

After the speechmaking ended, the people would not leave. They clustered around the box, and asked her questions—on government, the future, birth control. She was courteous, unruffled, and unhurried. When the crowd thinned out, she walked to the station of the Tokyo Loop Railway, on her way to another rally. She said, "I'm very tired and excited, but I can't let down now."

Our next rally in a dockyard, where Nozaka, the Communist leader, was addressing shipbuilding workers. A softspoken, neatly dressed man, Nozaka belies his years in jail and the underground. Now he is regarded as the Communist party's philosopher and long-range planner, while the more dynamic Tokuda is its man of action.

This for Nozaka is a season of homecoming, after fourteen years in exile. The other day he told me the story of his life since 1919, when, as a socialist and an organizer for a conservative labor union, he went to England to study at the London School of Economics. By the time he left England, eighteen months later, he had joined the British Communist party. He traveled through France, Switzerland, and Germany, spent a month in Russia in 1921, and then returned home to help form the Japanese Communist party the following year.

By 1928 he had served three jail terms. He was a sickly youth, had had an eye operation, and "knew more about the peculiarities of the eye than the prison doctor did." When he was arrested in 1928, Nozaka used his knowledge to demand another operation to save his sight. He was finally allowed to leave prison for a month for an operation, on the condition that he stay out of Tokyo. He entered a Kobe hospital, where five doctors conspired for a year to keep him out of jail by claiming that he was suffering from ailing eyes and stomach, constipation, piles, and diabetes.

The police checked daily, but saw nothing to arouse their suspicion. From time to time, other Communist leaders called on him secretly. It was finally decided to smuggle Nozaka out of the country. The Communist "underground railway" worked well. Disguised as a merchant, Nozaka left Japan for Manchuria with his wife, and then crossed the border into Russia. He remained in Russia for nine years, and in 1935 was elected to the presidium of the Comintern.

In 1940 he was ordered into the field. The Japanese Army had overrun much of China, and there was work to do. Disguised as a Chinese, Nozaka operated north of Peiping and in the mountains of western China. Eventually he came to the Chinese "Red Capital" in Yenan, organized the Japanese Anti-War League, and opened schools for the indoctrination of Japanese prisoners. I had heard from members of the U.S. Mission in Yenan that he helped them greatly with information on the Japanese forces in North China, and with advice on psychological warfare.

After Japan's surrender, Nozaka left Yenan for Tokyo. The trip took four months. Part of the way he was given a ride in American and Soviet planes, part of the way he hiked. He crossed all of North China, Manchuria, and Korea before American military police put him on a Korea-Japan ferry.

Now Nozaka was addressing a crowd of about four hundred men, crammed tight into a small hall. People were lined up along the walls, pressing against the stage, squatting on the floor, and packing the entrance. Nozaka spoke like a school teacher: drily, in the simplest words, and shunning oratorical tricks. He said the party did not want to hang the emperor, but it wanted to get rid of the "parasitical superstructure which is crushing you." The Communists, he said, did not want to confiscate all private property: "all of that is the propaganda of our enemies; what we want is to nationalize the monopolies." He listed their names, and the extent to which their tentacles spread over Japan's economy. "This is an important election," he said. "The reactionaries are strong, as strong as they've ever been. It's up to you to break their control." The audience sat still, and the hall was hot with the breath of tightly packed men.

After dinner we went to our last rally of the day—a Liberal meeting addressed by Hatoyama. We came in as Hatoyama was finishing his address. He spoke calmly and with dignity. An audience of five hundred—obviously middle-aged and middle-class—applauded him warmly. The election is only a few hours off, and he has not yet been purged.

April 10, 1946   TOKYO

In the morning, Cochrane, John Luter of *Time*, John LaCerda of the Philadelphia *Bulletin*, and I joined General Whitney on a tour of the polling places. When we arrived at the first place on the list, we found the doors locked. There was much confusion and joking about the "new democratic elections," and we finally left without finding out what had happened to the polling station. It may have been moved at the last minute to another address. After that we decided to ignore the schedule, and the next three places were taken at random. We were persuaded that the election was orderly, and the turnout was heavy.

The American officers seemed very surprised and pleased about this, but what I think they forget is that this is not the first election ever held in Japan. I have watched similar elections in prewar, army-dominated Japan, and they were equally orderly and well patronized. What mattered then, and what probably matters now, is that the political machines that picked the candidates were thoroughly corrupt and reactionary. The only new feature was the presence of women—thousands of them, young and old, and often with babies strapped to their backs. While the women were marking the ballots, the infants' heads bobbed over their shoulders. The fourth place we saw was a "scheduled" stop, and there was a line of voters a quarter of a mile long. We went through the building, and then drove on to a neighboring village. Half an hour later, when we passed by the building again, the line was gone. We suspected that the voters had been held up deliberately, to be exhibited to us, but we had no proof of any wrongdoing.

After lunch the four of us drove out of Tokyo, into the villages. One polling place was a national memorial where Emperor Meiji had once slept, and now two young women were running a small nursery in a side room to enable women voters to mark their ballots in peace.

In another place all voters had to take their sandals off, and there was some confusion when they tried to find their footgear again. The election officials invariably were middle-aged men, most of them in old frock coats. In every place we asked the men if they had run the previous election—the so-called "Tojo election" in 1942—and they all said Yes. When we asked them if there was any difference between the two elections, they said, No, except for the women. I suspect that women's suffrage may be our greatest contribution to Japan.

In the late afternoon spent an hour in Government Section, talking to General Whitney, his deputy, Colonel Kades, and Commander Guy Swope, who used to be governor of Porto Rico. Whitney was jubilant about the manner in which the election was run off. Up to this point almost no violations had been reported. Cochrane and I wanted to know if General MacArthur would call the election off, if, on reading the names of winning candidates tomorrow, he discovers that the bulk of them are war criminals.

Whitney said, "Of course not. You know how the chief works. He takes no rash steps."

The stench from the Dai-An Club, owned by Ando the racketeer, has become so great that the provost marshal has finally put it out of bounds to Allied personnel. Ando promptly reopened it under the name it bore in its pre-Ando, *geisha*-house days—the Wakatombo Club. Cochrane and I learned today that yet another agency of Headquarters is watching Ando. We were permitted to look at the agency's extensive dossier, and it is an eye-opener.

Ando was born on February 15, 1901. At the age of thirteen, he was a messenger at the Tokyo City Hall; at twenty, a member of a traveling show; at twenty-three, the owner of a transport business. Sometime later he operated in Korea and Manchuria. Ando's star soared when the military began to tighten their control on Japan's domestic life. In 1936 he set up the Dai-An Company, which to this day is the key company in his web of interests. In 1941 the Metropolitan Police Board appointed him head of a packing and a lumber company, chairman of the Tokyo Traction Union, and "Guardian of Korean Laborers and Protector of Korean Juveniles." When the war broke out Ando extended his operations. His firm dug tunnels and underground factories, built airfields, installed telephone and telegraph lines, carried war supplies, and moved entire munitions plants to areas less vulnerable to our raids. He was made an adviser to the Ministries of East Asia Affairs and Munitions. When Japan surrendered, he was commissioned to put the battered Atsugi Airfield in shape for General MacArthur's arrival, and completed his job in four days. In 1945, the dossier said, he made a profit of Y.500,000,000 (or $33,000,000).

Ando's chief aide is Ichietsu Machida, a former police official, who boasts openly of persecuting liberals. He has served in China as a military agent. Ando is one of Tokyo's great labor bosses, his gang put at 10,000 workers. Among Ando's enterprises is a chain of eighteen bordellos.

After we studied the dossier, we ran into a captain who had a curious tale to tell:

"Ando is a wonderful guy," he said. "One day he saw me pull out my Elgin watch. He says, 'Boy, that's a beautiful watch. Let me look at it.' He looks at it, and says, 'Please, Captain, sell it to me. I'll pay you any price you want.' I says, 'Hell, I paid only twenty-six bucks for it.' So Ando takes the watch with him, and a couple of days later he sends the dough to me. You know how much? Eighteen thousand yen ($1,200 at the official rate). The guy is a dope. The watch is not worth it."

April 13, 1946   TOKYO

Spent the morning with a Mrs. Tamae Fukagawa, a middle-aged housewife who tried to get elected on an anti-American platform and failed. She spoke in a nonstop flow. When I finally managed to bring up the question of her anti-American speeches, she said it was all a lie; I produced the scripts of her speeches in which she accused GIs of raping Japanese girls.

"I never said anything of the sort," she said. "What I did say was that late at night there are many GIs with girls on their arms. The people don't like it. We don't want any blue-eyed babies in Japan."

The election results are out. As expected, Hatoyama's Liberal party came out on top, with 140 seats in the new Diet. The equally hidebound Progressive party came in second with 93 seats, with the Social Democrats just behind. The Communists took five seats. The Social Democrats polled nearly 18 per cent of the total, and the communists just over 4 per cent. Hatoyama was elected by the largest majority in his district, while Mrs. Kato topped hers. At least 33 other women were elected.

The Tokyo press surveyed the scene without joy. The moderate *Asahi* said: "The old parties (Liberal and Progressive) found their enthusiastic supporters among the industrialists, big and small, who profited by the munitions boom of the wartime years, and the landlords who lined their pockets with boosted prices of farm produce. These feudalistic influences form the greatest obstacle to freedom and progress."

April 18, 1946

For two days now the Allied Council has been engaged in wrangling. This has been done against a background of orders within Headquarters to "talk the Council to death." A typical memo, circulated in a key section, called for "inconsequential items" which "will not hurt us" for presentation before the Council.

The wrangle began yesterday morning, with Headquarters' reply to General Derevyanko's request for information on the reported Japanese failure to comply with the purge directives. The answer was given by General Whitney. He spoke in a peremptory manner, which, one witness said, "skillfully borders on the line between the permissible insult and the point where you get punched on the nose." Whitney asserted that Derevyanko's question endangered the progress of the Occupation. He also defended General MacArthur's record, and especially the recent election, in a manner that produced guffaws in the audience. Among the more noteworthy statements were these:

"[The election] demonstrated to the world a free and honest and orderly election such as few, if any, of the western democracies can boast in more complete degree."

And, "The bare fact that persons subject to . . . the purge are still in office is of little significance. The important fact is that the Japanese Government has and is complying with the directives."

To all of us who have watched the campaign of skillful and determined sabotage of General MacArthur's reforms, and to those of us who could name scores of war criminals in the government, these bland denials were next to incomprehensible.

Surely, it would have been more honest to admit that the Japanese government was engaged in sabotage, and announce corrective measures.

But it got worse. Whitney now embarked on an old-fashioned filibuster. He listed the organizations purged. He read an entire three-month-old 10,000-word directive, already familiar to everyone in the room. Occasionally he stumbled over Japanese names, and reread the passage, or, with exaggerated courtesy, he asked the Council if it wanted the names of the subversive organizations in Japanese as well as in English, or if it desired any other information. It was, I suppose, no worse than some filibusters carried on in Congress. But to us, in this international gathering in which we wanted to take pride in the United States, it was a juvenile, small-time performance. It made us feel as if we were slowly shriveling with shame for an American general. Some filibusters have been known to serve a good purpose. This one did not. If it did anything, it made it plain, in the most discourteous manner, that we did not intend to cooperate with the other Council members.

After lunch Ball and Derevyanko tried to end the filibuster. Ball suggested that it was up to the Council itself to decide how long a witness could speak, and whether the report was to be oral or written. Derevyanko, who apparently was not familiar with American filibusters, proposed that the report be completed in "in fifteen or twenty minutes." Both failed.

General Marquat ruled that it would be unfair to stop General Whitney, who had put so much time into the preparation of the report. Whitney, he said, had come in good faith. Moreover, since General MacArthur was challenged, it was "not within the prerogatives of the Council to interrupt a representative of the Supreme Commander." Ball thanked Whitney for his "frank and friendly way of presenting the report," the audience laughed, and Whitney went on with the filibuster.

The reactions of the correspondents to the whole affair were so strong that I suspect Headquarters will wear mourning tomorrow when the War Department shoots back summaries of stories filed by us. But I also suspect that, to all effective purposes, the Council is dead. Many of us are sorry, for, with a less sensitive Headquarters, the Council could have performed a very useful advisory function. Assured at all times of support from the British and Chinese members, General MacArthur could well use the combined wisdom and experience of the Council. It also could present to the Japanese a front of Allied unity. Now the British and Chinese members have been antagonized; the Japanese have been shown chinks which they will inevitably try to put to their advantage; and a new focus of international friction has been created. And, Lord knows, there are too many points of friction already.

April 22, 1946   TOKYO

Premier Shidehara's cabinet resigned today. Later, it was announced that he had agreed to become president of the Progressive party.

Had drinks with George Atcheson, Jr., political adviser to General MacArthur, who has just been named chairman of the Allied Council, replacing General Marquat. Atcheson returned here last week at General MacArthur's express request —which, I gather, surprised George no end. His treatment by Headquarters up to now has been somewhat less than friendly.

Atcheson's appointment, according to United Press, was caused by adverse press comment on Headquarters' tactics in the Council. There are several indications that a new approach will be tried. Two Headquarters' sections, which originally were ordered to filibuster, have spent the last few days in trimming their reports. One report scheduled to consume three hours now has been reduced to a wieldy half hour. I am also told that a very high British official here has called on General MacArthur to plead for "a more cooperative attitude."

General MacArthur today fully endorsed the election. He declared:

". . . . Given the opportunity for free expression of their popular will, [the Japanese people] responded wholeheartedly; and, rejecting leadership dedicated to the political philosophies of the two extremes, both of the right and of the left . . . they took a wide central course which will permit the evolvement of a balanced program of government. . . . "

General MacArthur's statement does not jibe with the reports flooding the Japanese press. These confirm the impression that the electorate was never allowed to get out of hand. This was achieved through a variety of pressures, from violence to the employment of organizations mothered by the army and untouched by defeat. Among the most important of these are *tonarigumi*, or neighborhood associations, which, during the war, controlled rationing, conducted propaganda, and spied on private lives, and which can still starve a man out with no great difficulty. Typical was the decision of the Tokyo *tonarigumi* early in the election campaign to organize for "the defense of the emperor."

The old political machines continued to function smoothly in key areas, even as many of their bosses awaited trial as war criminals. Neither the war nor the defeat destroyed the machines. They simply waited out the hard times and went to work as soon as the signal was given for a "democratic election."

For many weeks, with irony and disbelief, I have been compiling a list of war criminals who were candidates for election. A few days ago I took it to a colonel in the Civil Intelligence Section, laid it on a table, and said, "What are you going to do about these?" The colonel was liberal and intelligent. "We know most of what you have there," he said. "The point is that we are powerless. Our orders are to let the Japanese government do its own screening. We have committed ourselves to work through it, and now we have to stick to the bargain."

That is a fair enough argument. But whichever way I look at it, I feel we are playing with dynamite. We have already spent eight precious months waiting for the Shidehara government and the old Diet to enforce the reforms we blueprinted for them in our directives. The time was wasted, for only the supremely naïve could expect enemies of reform to put it through. Now we have sponsored elections which, theoretically, should produce a new government and Diet, both imbued with democratic spirit. But the faces of the new reformers are the old faces. We had not given the people—the common man on whom we had publicly pinned our faith for democracy in Japan—enough time to organize, to produce new leadership, to wake up from the lethargy of war years and nationalist training. All we have given Japan is a set of democratic clichés, promptly picked up and used by the old gang. And then, though the great deception is plain and brazen, we have given our blessing to it.

Who are the men who express "the popular **will**" of the new democracy?

Japanese editors tell me there are as many as 180 war criminals in the new Diet. My private blacklist is much shorter, but it includes the leaders of all three major parties.

Hatoyama is one of the prize exhibits, being the leader of the largest party. Cochrane and I met him in the street last night. He beamed at us as if we were his warmest friends, and said he was now preparing the roster of a new cabinet. He might yet be disappointed, for Headquarters, from what I gather, has not quite gotten over the press disclosures of Hatoyama's past.

But Hatoyama apart, the gallery of villains is impressive enough. The untitled leader of the Progressive party at the moment is the swarthy lawyer, Narahashi, who once openly boasted of his service as an army agent. Another leader of this party belonged to the Diet "Committee to Hasten the East Asia Alliances." Still another leader helped to set up a puppet regime in Nanking, and served as its economic adviser.

One of the spokesmen of Hatoyama's Liberal party is a

rabid nationalist with a seventeen-year history of rabble-rousing behind him. In 1931 he stumped the land demanding the occupation of Manchuria; in 1937 formed the "Continental Administration Society"; and in 1941 wrote a book of antidemocratic essays, *The History of Elimination*. Two other leaders, one Liberal, the other Progressive, have been Tokyo publishers, who helped to build up the prowar hysteria in Japan.

Nor is the Social Democratic party any purer. One of its leaders as far back as 1933 joined a dozen army officers in forming the Imperial Way League, which demanded "the spread of imperial rule" and more and bigger weapons. Another leader long before the war led his Proletarian party into the army's warm embrace, and wrote in Tojo's support. Still another, a graduate of the Missouri School of Journalism, served in the South Seas with the simulated rank of rear admiral, getting slave labor for the navy.

These are not the small fry of jingoism. These are the men who will lead the new Diet and speak for the Japanese people; men whose ideas will be imprinted on the democratic legislation; men who will be cabinet ministers and even premiers, when their party's turn comes.

Of violations by smaller men there can be no count. In at last two prefectures purged political bigwigs ran their wives, and had them elected. In dozens, purged bosses ran their henchmen. In Kyoto the elected Diet members included a puffy little man who, I suspect, tried to poison me two months ago in the belief that I had come to arrest him as a war criminal. In 1942 this man wrote in the *Official Gazette:* "First of all, I like the imperial policy of Premier Tojo, who rides horses. I also like the soldiers, who are the treasure of the nation. . . . The Japanese nation must be built in accordance with the Japanese totalitarianism which I advocate. . . . " He was elected as an Independent.

All of us at the Press Club go around with lists of villains we have compiled, and we all say, "Just wait, I'll expose them and they'll be purged." But we get bored with the scores of stories which these scores of villains demand, and our newspapers are bored with our output. What is wanted by our editors is action and "human interest." Sly political villainy is soporific.

After stewing for a couple of days over the records of war criminals in the Diet, Cochrane and I decided to call on Colonel H. I. T. Creswell, Chief of the Counter Intelligence Corps. This is virtually an autonomous organization which, as most hush-hush outfits, has tremendous powers. If anyone could, Creswell could tell us what had gone wrong with the screening of the war criminals who got into the new Diet, and, especially of Hatoyama.

Creswell is a hard-looking, lean man, with a face lined with wrinkled brown leather, and a voice that could be heard across a drill ground. We asked his permission to examine the questionnaires filed by each candidate before the election.

"No," boomed Creswell.

We were taken aback. "Why not, Colonel?"

"This is a matter involving the candidate himself, the Japanese government, and this Headquarters. It's none of your business."

"But, Colonel," I said mildly, "the American people are also interested in what kind of a government the Japanese are setting up here. After all, you know, legally we're still at war with them."

"What happens here doesn't involve the American people," Creswell said firmly. "It is not in the public interest to give out such information."

He paused, and then turned on us. "You boys go around with a chip on your shoulder. All of you come down here and say Hatoyama is this, Hatoyama is that. Each one of you has a pet hate, but all of you together are ganging up on Hatoyama. I'll give you an example of the harm you're doing. Take 'Tokyo

Rose.' We've had her in Sugamo Prison for months, and now we find we have no solid evidence against her. She was just taking orders. Yet we don't dare release her, because we know that you boys will promptly jump on our necks."

Bob and I spoke up together. "You're wrong, Colonel. If you have no evidence, you let her go, and the two of us anyway will say nothing against you."

"You're just saying this now," he said. "But if we let her go . . . "

We argued interminably, courteously, but with an undertone of sharpness. Creswell insisted the records of the men elected to the Diet were of no concern to the American press —or people. We maintained that after four years of pretty bloody effort to change the nature of the Japanese government, the Americans had every right to know what the result of that effort was. Finally I thought I had a brilliant argument.

"Colonel," I said, "you say your home is in California. If and when Robert W. Kenny runs for governor, wouldn't you want to know all there is to know about him, his performance, and his utterances?"

Surprise spread over his face. "Of course not," he said. "I'm a professional soldier. I haven't voted in all my life."

April 27, 1946   TOKYO

What has happened to the Japanese Army? Many of us feel that though it has been disarmed and demobilized, it could be put together again in six months. Some of us wonder if the Japanese have not taken a page out of the history of the German Army after 1919. For so much of what is happening now appears to follow a pattern, as if it all had been thought out carefully beforehand. The evidence, I admit, is not yet conclusive. There are hundreds of little facts, but they can be fitted into several theories. For instance, if it is true that the

Japanese Army is emulating the Reichswehr, where are Japan's Ludendorffs and von Seeckts?

Bob Cochrane and I have done much thinking and digging. We find that, almost as a rule, the generals have left the cities to lose themselves in the countryside. My friend Tsuru tells me the process is only natural: the countryside is more conservative, and if a new ultranationalist movement rises again, it will emerge from the villages. The generals, Tsuru argues, have gone back to their native soil where they can nurture and shape the new nationalism.

This belief is confirmed by the testimony of one of the generals, Ryukichi Tanaka. One of the key men behind Japan's expansion in the past decade, Tanaka gave an extremely frank interview to Kudrevatikh, the Soviet correspondent, the other day. Discount things that a shrewd Japanese general, who wants to play the United States against Russia, might tell a Soviet newspaperman, and his story is still interesting.

"All of us," he told Kudrevatikh, "have become farmers. We bought a little land, and now we cultivate it. There's no opportunity for us in the cities. The land keeps us alive. It also keeps us close to the people. They haven't turned against us; they simply feel that Tojo and his gang have blundered. I bought a farm near Atami, and I spend most of my time there, working. Look at my hands! Those are real callouses. But I also do a lot of thinking—the causes of defeat, the things happening here now, the future. Five years from now, ten at the most, the Occupation will end. I will then return to Tokyo to assume a position of responsibility and leadership."

Tanaka has written a book in which he blames all of Japan's woes on Tojo and company. But Tanaka does not conceal his own part in the expansion. His argument appears to be that *he* did not lose any wars.

I am even more interested in General Ishihara, the brilliant fanatic into whose activities I ran in Sakata last Christmas. Most of my Japanese friends feel Ishihara is the likeliest Fuehrer of post-Occupation, post-MacArthur Japan. He has not been tainted by defeat. He is a clever politician. He is a leader of men.

A Japanese reporter tipped me off that Ishihara was in Tokyo, recuperating from an operation. Cochrane and I finally found him in a hospital.

Ishihara received us in his small room, whose window frames were still buckled from bomb explosions. He is a lean man, with a deeply tanned face, close-shaven head, and hard, unblinking, black eyes which bored into us. He was sitting Japanese-style on his cot, his hands in his lap. Even in a shapeless gown of yellow Chinese silk, his body looked straight as a steel rod. Above him a Japanese scroll stretched across the wall.

We asked Ishihara just two questions: What of Japan in defeat, and what of himself? He answered readily and at length, in a sharp, firm voice. He talked like a man who believed every word he uttered.

"Had I been in active service," he said, "I'd have given you Americans a better run for your money. We could've done much better by shortening our defense lines and lengthening your supply lines, and also by settling the China affair.

"Had our leaders realized the meaning of the Battle of Midway and solidified our lines in the Solomons, the vastness of the Pacific would have been our ally. Even Admiral Isoroku Yamamoto [Commander-in-Chief of the Navy, shot down by U.S. airmen] was wrong, for he didn't know where to make his stand. I knew we had lost the war when I heard of the fall of Saipan.

"I know we could have had peace with China. We had much confidence in *Toa Renmei* [Ishihara's East Asia League]. If its spirit could've been instilled in the Chinese people, we could've ended the war. *Toa Renmei* has always believed in nonaggression. It argued that if China recognized Manchukuo, the Japanese Army could've retired from China. Chiang Kai-shek would've recognized Manchukuo, if it had ever come to a showdown. I've always favored pulling troops out of China, and making Manchukuo a buffer against the Russian threat— though, of course, we had no intention of fighting Russia.

"Tojo and I didn't differ on the China policy. We couldn't, for Tojo is not the kind of man who could have a plan of any sort. He was a smart man in small office matters, but he was useless in such major problems as the China policy. He was also a coward, who never had the courage to arrest me. The fact that a man like Tojo and his henchmen could come to power was one reason for Japan's downfall.

"Tojo was supported by no one but a bunch of rightists. The crowd which put Tojo in his job had no ideology; it was merely riding the crest of a political wave.

"Unfortunately, *Toa Renmei* was dissolved by you Americans. Tojo had also tried to suppress *Toa Renmei*, but it remained powerful in Korea, Manchuria, and even China. When MacArthur dissolved *Toa Renmei* we saw that there was no difference between militarists in Japan and the United States. Yet, it was the only organization which could fight Communist ideas on equal terms.

"Today, we aren't allowed to hold meetings, and my comrades are always under surveillance. Even when my wife wants to visit me, she must obtain a permit from the American military authorities. My mail is censored, and it takes at least three months for a letter to reach me from Tokyo. Under Tojo, the mail was also strictly censored, but it never took more than a week for a letter to get to me.

"When I served on the General Staff, Prince Chichibu [the emperor's brother] was my subordinate. Had he not become ill, the Great East Asia War wouldn't have occurred. Until 1940, the prince served on the General Staff, and he was the only man who could bind the emperor to the people, and thus avert the war. The prince was opposed to the outbreak of the China incident, and later he wanted to settle it along the lines advocated by *Toa Renmei*. Unfortunately, when the China incident broke out, the prince was in Europe and could do nothing to stop it.

"If you've read Prince Konoye's memoirs, you'll recall the conferences held from September to December of 1941. At these meetings, the army faction which started the China incident encouraged the belief that it couldn't be settled without a bigger war. This group consisted of amazingly deteriorated cowards. I'm not a brave man, but had I had Prince Chichibu's support, I would've averted the war."

The door opened softly to let in an old woman dressed in a

drab kimono. She looked worried. "This is my wife," said the general. The interpreter told her we were newspapermen, and some of the anxiety vanished from her face.

"I am fifty-seven years old," said Ishihara. "I was born of a poor *samurai* family in Tsuruoka. There are few rich people there, and those are mostly landlords or shopkeepers. My uncle was a military man, and he saw to it that the army became my career.

"In the army, I was surprisingly popular with the soldiers. Even now many of the men who served under me call on me wherever I might be. But my superior officers always disliked me, perhaps because they disliked all just men and things. In 1928 I was made chief of staff of the Kwantung Army in Manchuria. No one liked the post at the time, because it involved wrangling with the Chinese. We all felt the Chinese were unfair to us, and to our colonists and interests. From the day of my arrival in Manchuria, I knew that sooner or later an incident would break out."

Ishihara, I knew, did not wait for the incident; he helped to engineer it. The men who later went on to shape the fate of Japan, and of Asia—Tojo, his coterie, and even his rivals—had received their inspiration from this statuesque figure before us. Most of them would now stand trial as war criminals. Ishihara, by the happy accident of a feud with Tojo, would escape punishment, and possibly some day return to power.

With Manchuria securely in Japanese hands, Ishihara was recalled to Japan to wider responsibilities. It was his supple mind which originated the plans for the China "incident" itself—the bloody and undeclared war that was to last for eight years.

"I was Chief of Operations until September, 1937," he recalled. "During my two years in this job, I believe I put the Japanese Army on its feet and set the course for it to follow. My main job was to complete military preparations to protect Manchuria from Soviet Russia. Until I accomplished that, the emphasis on the General Staff had always been on maneuvers in China.

"I was removed from the General Staff because I insisted

that our problems with China had to be solved. As a matter of fact, I even opposed the capture of Nanking in December, 1937. My last job was a two-year term as a divisional commander in Kyoto. I was retired in March, 1941. Tojo had no courage to face me openly. So the order to retire came to me from the emperor."

He paused, picked up the book before him (it was a work on the philosophy of the Nichiren Buddhist sect), and looked at it with unseeing eyes. For nearly two hours now he had been pouring out this curious brew of truth and half-truth, prejudices and delusions, all seasoned with a savage and unconcealed hatred of Tojo.

"The real cause of Japan's defeat," he finally said, "was a lack of democracy. Because of the Thought police and the Gendarmerie, the people were always afraid. Just because these police forces have now been eliminated, doesn't mean that Japan is a democracy. But once the secret police was smashed, MacArthur should have let the Japanese themselves carry out the purges. What's happening now is that Mac-Arthur's Headquarters relies, in its actions, on information from people who cannot be trusted. I urge you, as members of the press, to help Headquarters get at the truth."

Ishihara's wife turned to him, and began to speak in a low monotone. He remained silent. We rose and said goodbye. Before we left, I asked Ishihara about the scroll above him. He said it had been written by his old calligraphy teacher. I jotted down the sentence:

"It is time to reveal the true essence of the nation."

April 28, 1946   TOKYO

A week ago four ships loaded with American cotton left U.S. ports for Japan. This is the first installment of the 890,000 bales which will be brought here in the next twelve months under the magic "prevention of disease and civil unrest" formula. Originally, General MacArthur informed Washington that Japan was face to face with "a grave crisis" and asked for a million and a quarter bales. Since virtually the whole world is going ragged, Washington pared down this figure. But even the 890,000 bales are calculated to give every Japanese eight and a half yards of textiles, meet Japan's industrial requirements, and leave enough for export with which Japan will pay for the raw cotton.

This is the story as one gets it from Headquarters. But there is another story which I managed to get from two members of the international Textile Mission now surveying Japan's resources.

The mission has discovered that the canny Japanese had concealed in their warehouses a billion yards of textiles or their equivalent. The Japanese also have enough yarn and raw cotton on hand to keep their mills running for twelve to fourteen months. The Japanese government kept mum about this hoard, and kept bombarding Headquarters with demands for American cotton to "save Japan from a disaster."

Headquarters, according to my informants, began finding the hoard after it sent its plea to Washington. Typical was the discovery of 100,000,000 pounds of cotton yarn in warehouses in Niigata Prefecture. Unwilling to admit that it had been deceived by the Japanese, Headquarters has been trying to keep the matter hushed up. But it has ordered Major F. E. Pickelle, of the Import and Export Division, to Southeast Asia to seek markets for Japanese textiles.

"Headquarters," said one of my informants, "probably wouldn't have asked for that much if it knew how much cotton there is hidden in Japan. But now it's out on a limb—and trying to justify its request to Washington. Actually, the Japanese have more yardage per head than almost any country in Asia or Europe. Now the Japanese are ready to burst into the world markets, and Headquarters is helping it out."

Tonight I got a résumé of the hush-hush report on the dissolution of the *zaibatsu* prepared by the famous "Edwards Commission." The group, sent here by the War and State Departments and headed by Professor Corwin D. Edwards of Northwestern University, spent some months here last year and this, and has gone back to the United States.

The two-volume report is complex and technical. For a layman, its most important recommendations, I thought, were these:

1. The dissolution of all *zaibatsu* combines, the elimination of interlocking directorates, the breaking up of *zaibatsu* family interests, and the end of family control over industry through ingenious holding companies, or *honsha*.

2. Sale of *honsha* securities to stockholders untainted by contact with the *zaibatsu*, to cooperatives, *zaibatsu* employees, labor unions, and new investors. A system of precautions against the purchase of stocks by dummy buyers for the *zaibatsu*.

3. Compensation of the *zaibatsu* from the proceeds of stock sales, paid in the form of bonds maturing in ten years, paying "blocked" interest, and usable only for the payment of taxes or the purchase of State bonds. If no buyers appear, the State will confiscate the *zaibatsu* assets. Public utilities owned by the *zaibatsu* to become publicly owned.

4. Removal of key managerial personnel (*banto*) closely linked with the *zaibatsu*.

5. The end of collusion between *zaibatsu*-owned banks and *zaibatsu*-owned industry.

The two experts who supplied me with the long summary expressed admiration for its thoroughness and wealth of detail. But they also felt that it was "formless and lacking in direction." Said one of them:

"Right now it's got everything from cooperatives to kitchen sinks. I wish it indicated the course to be followed by us, or assigned a relative value to each of its recommendations. The shape it's in now, MacArthur can use it as a basis for admirable anti-*zaibatsu* legislation. But it can also serve as a basis for legislation that would mean nothing at all."

April 31, 1946   TOKYO

Tonight there was a meeting at the Press Club to discuss what appears to be a full-fledged antipress campaign by Headquarters. Signs of it have been multiplying for a week or more. The army motor pool, where we have been getting vehicles, has been closed to us. Those of us who owned our jeeps found it impossible to get gasoline. One correspondent has been denied dental aid. The club has been deprived of the truck in which we have been bringing our food. An "unfriendly" correspondent who was complaining about the continued delays in bringing wives here was told twice to "go home if you don't like it." Another correspondent, serving a string of newspapers, was told that "special correspondents are not wanted here." Those who are bringing their wives here have been informed that they will be unable to purchase food at the army commissary after July 1. The pressure is particularly grave because there are no supplies to be bought in the Japanese market, and all such deals are illegal anyway.

Many correspondents feel that the campaign is an expression of displeasure with our coverage of the Allied Council sessions. But part of the blame must be laid at the door of General Baker, whose definition of a democratic press is seemingly that kind of a press which will publish nothing but his handouts.

The Australian correspondent Jack Percival, who has been critical of some aspects of the Occupation, told us Baker had written to his editor accusing Percival of a variety of journalistic misdeeds. The propriety of such behavior by a Public Relations Officer, whose avowed function is to assist the press in its work, escapes me.

An even more interesting story is told by Bill McGaffin

of the Chicago *Daily News*, just in from China. He reports that both he and Gordon Walker, of the *Christian Science Monitor*, were denied permission to re-enter Japan on the curious ground that the travel space was needed for more essential personnel. Fortunately for him, McGaffin had return Travel Orders. So he simply boarded a plane and flew to Japan. Having no such orders, Walker protested to his paper, which began an inquiry in Washington. Eventually, according to McGaffin, Baker informed the *Monitor* that the Army Command in Korea had objected to Walker's "irresponsible coverage" and that Walker was free to come to Japan, but that his reporting would have to be more accurate. The *Monitor* replied with appropriate firmness. It said it was pleased to hear that Walker could return to Japan, where he could resume his reporting, "with its usual high standards of accuracy."

Tonight's meeting drafted a resolution of protest, and named a committee, headed by Cochrane, to present it to General MacArthur.

May 1, 1946   TOKYO

This is the day of the May Day rally, and after breakfast not a soul remained in the club. By the time I reached the Imperial Plaza it was churning with people, and more columns were pouring in from all directions. They came in singing and waving flags and posters. Some drove up in trucks, and cheers rolled in their wake like waves.

Despite the gray skies, this was a joyous meeting, filled with enthusiasm and more confidence than I have yet seen in Japan. With the speakers' platform too far away and the loudspeakers not loud enough, the vast crowd had broken into small segments, each singing, cheering or listening to its own orators. As my interpreter and I pushed our way through the crowd, men and women called out to us and asked us to take pictures of them, the flags, the posters extolling May Day or lampooning the government.

It took us half an hour to work our way to the speakers' platform, draped in red and decorated with streamers. There were a few familiar faces there: Tokuda, Nozaka, Kato, some of the prominent right-wing labor union leaders. They sat stiffly in their chairs, and all around them milled foreign correspondents, Japanese cameramen, and rally organizers. From the platform I could see a black sea of heads, undulating and restless and humming with impatience. It covered the plaza, and overflowed into the neighboring streets. As far as the eye could see, it was speckled with red, which, in Japan, is the color of the labor movement and not of revolt.

One after another, the speakers rose and shouted into the mike. The loudspeakers magnified their voices, or drowned them in mechanical whines and whistles. When that happened, everyone looked distressed, but the oratory did not halt. There was a uniformity to the speeches, for they all, right-wing or left, dealt with the food shortages and the need for a democratic government.

Tokuda was the last speaker. He stood surveying the cheering thousands with a stern face. He, too, spoke of the short rations, of rice hoarded by the rich and the speculators, of the workers' inability to make ends meet. The crowd yelled its agreement. But the loudest, the most prolonged cheers came when Tokuda, both arms in the air, shouted: "Down with the emperor!"

Behind Tokuda the audience could see the palace buildings towering over the thick, gray walls, and the American sentries standing on guard.

When the speeches ended, the crowd began to unwind itself into four columns. I joined the procession headed for the premier's residence. It had started to drizzle. The paint on the posters spread and ran, and soon the thin, soggy paper itself began to come off the poster frames. But the enthusiasm seemed undiminished. Waving the bare staves of the posters, the men marched briskly, singing the "Marseillaise" and the "May Day Song,"

> *Listen, laborers throughout the world,*
> *To the reverberations of the May Day . . .*

and the "*Akahata,*" or the "Red Flag," with its curiously lilt-
ing tune,

> *The people's flag, the red flag, wraps the bodies of our dead;*
> *Before the corpses turn cold, their blood dyes the flag. . . .*

I stopped a few people at random and asked them why
they were demonstrating. A transport worker said: "Because
I believe that in a democracy power should belong to the people." A mail carrier said: "This is *my* day, and I consider it
an honor to participate." A farmer said, "For me this is the
first May Day in ten years. I'm very excited."

There were two U.S. armored cars, a jeep with a machinegun, and a half-dozen Military Policemen in front of the premier's residence. The gates were open, and there were no more
than a score of Japanese policemen within. Apparently, Shidehara had been assured of U.S. protection. I joined Cochrane
at the gate, and watched the procession flow by in what seemed
an unending stream. It went past us for 95 minutes, at the
average rate of 300 people a minute, for a total of some 28,000.
The marchers made no effort to enter the compound. Only the
younger men, after passing the gate, whirled around in a mad
dance they had learned at shrine festivals.

While we were watching, word came to us that Shidehara,
who will remain premier until his successor is named, was
receiving a May Day delegation. We hurried into the reception
room, and saw what is by now a familiar act, performed by
familiar faces: Shidehara, mumbling his answers; Tokuda,
quick and aggressive; Narahashi, smooth and glib and natty
with his gray, neatly trimmed beard, and a well-cut blue striped
suit.

Tokuda (to Narahashi): "We want to talk of rationing.
But you wouldn't know anything about it. Judging by your
figure, your rice is not rationed."

Narahashi (laughing): "Of course I know of rice rationing. (Patting his round stomach.) I'm simply living on past accumulation."

By now it was raining steadily, but the crowd was still marching and singing. We drove down to Radio Tokyo, and here was the second column, a little longer and even livelier than the first one. A third column was streaming up the Ginza, Tokyo's main street. Colonel Logie, deputy provost marshal, told us the second column, which marched past General MacArthur's Headquarters, took two and one-half hours to pass a given point. He estimated the number of demonstrants officially at 300,000 and unofficially at half a million. My own estimate was a little over a hundred thousand.

In the late afternoon the demonstration broke up into splinters, and as each moved away, it did so with a song. It occurred to me that there were few times during this day when I could not hear singing voices. It was a day filled with a curious kind of joy—perhaps the kind of luminous joy a war prisoner feels on regaining freedom.

But before nightfall, I had heard of many Americans who did not think well of the demonstration. There is apparently an authentic story of a colonel who spent his entire working day by his window, watching the marching thousands with gloomy concentration. Another officer told me at the club he thought "we should've never allowed this Commie meeting." Some of the ultraconservative Japanese labor leaders who sat on the platform this morning would have deeply resented the comment. It also made me feel, for the *nth* time, that the military mind distrusts people in any bulk unless they wear uniforms. The military mind likes discipline and order, in war or peace, and there is certainly little suggestion of orderliness in draft-age men who whirl in a defiant snake dance before the premier's home.

But if the colonel sitting unhappily before his window could think in social rather than military terms, he might have marked this day in happy colors in his calendar. For the great demonstration—the joy, the freedom, the portent—was the best tribute we have yet had to the brand of democracy we had brought to this feudal land.

May 2, 1946   TOKYO

This evening, in a drizzle, Cochrane and I saw Hatoyama waiting for his car before the Liberal party headquarters. He beamed at us happily, and gave us the glad news: his name is being submitted by Premier Shidehara to General MacArthur for approval as Japan's next premier. There is something symbolic in Tojo and Company going on trial tomorrow as war criminals, and Hatoyama, who, on a smaller scale, is equally culpable, waiting to become the premier of a democratic Japan.

May 3, 1946   TOKYO

A few hours before Hatoyama was to be officially designated by the emperor as the new premier, General MacArthur ordered the Japanese government to remove him from the Diet. The special memorandum listed Hatoyama's sins as a war criminal—including the evidence brought out at that tumultous meeting at the Press Club.

At 11:13 this morning in the auditorium of the Japanese War Ministry, on a hill overlooking the ruins of Tokyo, twenty-eight Japanese—two *in absentia*—were arraigned before an International Military Tribunal on charges of planning, preparing, and waging a war of aggression.

As a historic performance, the trial was beautifully staged. For months carpenters and electricians have been working in this huge room, erecting stands and enclosures, arranging a battery of lights, laying rugs. Once the whole setting was rip-

ped up because it was felt that it did not live up to the importance of the occasion. Now nothing seemed to be missing.

The judges sat on a high platform, with their flags behind
them. Below them were tables for the clerks, the prosecution,
and the defense. Across the huge room, on a smaller platform, sat the defendants in two long rows, with four husky
Military Policemen in white helmets guarding them. To the
right was the enclosure for 200 newspapermen, American,
foreign and Japanese. Above the press, a balcony held space
for 300 Allied personnel and 200 Japanese.

The trial began 43 minutes late. First the prosecution filed
in, led by Joseph B. Keenan, a red-faced, compact man, who
once served as assistant attorney general of the United States.
Then the defendants came in through a small door to take their
seats. They entered hesitantly, crowding each other and searching the balcony for familiar faces. Seven minutes later, the
nine judges filed in, solemn, slow, black-robed. The powerful
klieg lights came on, and movie cameras began to purr. The
president of the court, Sir William Webb, a ruddy-faced,
hawk-nosed, large Australian, surveyed the scene benignly
and read his opening statement.

The defendants listened intently. General Tojo, erect in
his military uniform, never took his eyes off Webb's face. Behind him sat Shumei Okawa, the tall, gaunt spy and nationalist philosopher, across whose trail I ran last Christmas in Sakata.
He had come to the trial in *geta* (wooden clogs), and when
ordered to take them off, he also removed his black coat, and he
sat now in a crumpled white shirt.

Matsuoka, the U.S.-reared jingoist who emulated William
Jennings Bryan with a fiery speech on a Japan "impaled on a
cross of gold" when he took the Japanese delegation out of the
League of Nations, sat leaning on a cane. Another man with
a cane was Mamoru Shigemitsu, who began his rise to fame by
losing a leg to a Korean bomb thrower. On his wooden leg, this
tall, thin man marched to the embassies in London and Moscow,
to the Foreign Office, and then to the deck of the U.S.S. "Missouri" where, on behalf of his country, he signed the treaty of
surrender.

To the left of them, still plump and unruffled, sat General Kenji Doihara, one of this century's great political manipulators and secret agents, who was known as "The Lawrence of Manchuria," and whose spies had been scattered over the map of Asia. Ten years ago I saw him in Peiping, drunk with alcohol and power, and busily reshaping the destiny of North China. Here, finally, was a shabby, pinched man with oversized black-rimmed glasses, Marquis Kido, who used the imperial symbol to make himself one of Japan's most powerful men.

To me this was an incredible show, for when I saw them last these men were at the pinnacle of power at the intoxicating moment when they had challenged the world, and heard no word of defiance. Each man now evoked in me a memory of a crime, from a modest beginning in Manchuria to bigger and bigger crimes which involved places as wide apart as California, Australia, and the Red Sea. Some day, I thought, a skilled Japanese biographer would select a dozen of these men, study their motivations, and then weave the strands of their lives into the history of Japan's rise and fall.

That history, I felt, also would serve as a lesson in the futility and danger of letting political power slip out of the people's hands into the eager grasp of the military and big business. For history has a nasty habit of repeating its patterns, so that what was true in Japan yesterday might, with only a few changes, also be true of another land tomorrow.

The history of these twenty-six men in the dock, and a hundred more still in Sugamo Prison, began fifteen years ago, when Japan still had two major political parties; a Diet in which men rose from time to time to speak some of the truth; a press still fairly free; schools in which liberal thought could still be taught; and libraries on whose shelves liberal books could still be found. It was a time when the workers and sharecroppers could still form unions, and men could still speak critically of their government and their army without being branded "disloyal."

But the military-financial oligarchy had not been happy. The *zaibatsu* wanted to expand abroad, to find new markets, to tap new sources of cheap raw materials. They subsidized the two major political parties, and they spoke glibly of civil liberties and their liberal tradition. In fact, they resented and resisted the growth of such institutions as labor unions. The military, too, wanted to expand. They dreamt of military promotions, of imperial glory, of larger appropriations for "defense." But no one in the oligarchy spoke of what was in his mind. What they all talked about was Japan's "sacred mission," the flag, and the urgent needed to halt the spread of communism.

Then, on a warm autumn night in 1931, after months of careful preparation, they blew up a twenty-foot length of a Manchurian railway, called it an unprovoked attack on Japan, and took over a rich chunk of China. The pretext did not matter. It could have been the murder of a military "observer" in Manchuria. It could have been the friction between the Chinese and the Korean settlers, for whom the Japanese Army suddenly found a warm spot in its otherwise cold heart. But when a pretext was needed, a crooked rail sufficed to launch Japan on the road to aggression—and defeat.

Japan had had nothing but victories. But the victories were costly, for each demanded a new effort to protect the gains. Or, as the Chinese said, the appetite came with the eating. To meet the "national insult" of a twisted rail, the army found it necessary to occupy Manchurian towns. To protect the towns, the army pushed north, until it faced the Russians across the Amur, and south, until it looked over the Great Wall. Inevitably, the army said it needed more and bigger weapons to "defend the nation" from Russia. And just as inevitably, the army decided nothing could end the hostile spirit in North China but a new act of aggression. Thus the army marched on, from Peiping to French Indo-China, and then beyond, to Malaya, the Philippines, and the approaches to Australia.

With each aggressive step, the oligarchy tightened its grip on the Japanese people. More and more talk was heard of the necessity of "blocking Communist expansion." The farther away from the Russian border the army moved, the more it talked of the Russian menace. It was ready to sign peace with Chiang Kai-shek if he agreed to a "joint defense of China from Russian designs." It joined Germany and Italy in an "anti-Comintern" pact, which was actually a military alliance directed against us.

With the anxiety to halt communism came proud phrases of Japan's heritage, of "manifest destiny," of the high ideals to be bestowed on the other peoples, of the need for "restoring peace and order." Japan was in the grip of nationalist hysteria, skillfully fanned by the army's propagandists and the *zaibatsu*. With the growth of fear grew the appropriations for more soldiers, more guns, more warships and airplanes. And with each year, as big business made munitions and followed the army into the new areas of conquest, its profits mounted.

"Friendly" regimes were set up from Manchuria to Siam, and they were given loans or warships or military advisory missions to "safeguard their way of life" from British, or American, or French encroachment. But each such action produced a chain reaction. The worried Russians, or French, or Britishers brought up reinforcements. This called for more Japanese arms or credits. The vicious circle was a noose around the Japanese taxpayer's neck.

At home the artificial hysteria grew. Moderation was now called "disloyalty," and moderates in the government were forced out, or even murdered. Men were ostracized, or jailed, or manhandled by ultranationalists for "dangerous thought." A band of hoodlums broke the limbs of a moderate Social Democrat over bamboo poles. And a band of other men, scholars, generals and lawmakers, hounded out of public life a distinguished professor who was disloyal enough to suggest that the emperor was the organ of the state rather than the reverse. Nationalist groups exerted pressure on universities to purge themselves of "disloyal" professors. Libraries were forced to discard "subversive" books. They started with Karl Marx, and inevitably they came to Dreiser, Tolstoy, and Gide.

The number of liberals dwindled. Those who were out of prison kept mum or adopted the terminology of ultranationalism. Japan's moderate newspapers began to speak in strident tones. Matsutaro Shoriki, chief of the Tokyo Police who became publisher of the great daily, *Yomiuri*, made it the open mouthpiece of aggression. Japan's outstanding monthly magazines—the *Harper's* and the *Atlantic Monthly* of the land—were terrorized, and eventually closed up, and their staffs were put in prison.

One by one the dissenting voices were silenced in the Diet. Some were expelled under army pressure. Others were not re-elected by the frightened voters. Reactionary individuals and committees in the Diet now went witch-hunting for the "disloyal." And since these men were the lawgivers, there was no one to draw the line between hysteria and legal process.

Labor and farmers' unions were among the early victims. It started with a purge of Communists, real or imagined, and of the "disloyal." Next was the army-sponsored merger of unions into an official organization. Then came the "patriotic" associations, in which labor and management were happily welded together, strikes were banned, and the officers were recruited from the *zaibatsu* and the totalitarian party.

"Crisis" and "emergency" became household words. They were used to explain why the prices went up, and why it was necessary to send missions to Siam, to "protect herself from neighbors." The Cabinet shrank to an "inner cabinet" of five men, of whom two or three were usually military men, and one or two representatives of the *zaibatsu*. Occasionally, the two factions squabbled, but the marriage was not unhappy. Generals and admirals were given lush jobs in the *zaibatsu;* men of the *zaibatsu* were given key "national defense" jobs in which they were able to divert the war orders to themselves, and kill off the non-*zaibatsu* competition.

Fear was an instrument which helped the army and the *zaibatsu* to entrench themselves in power. But unrelieved fear was not good for morale. Thus the propaganda machine kept reassuring the Japanese people that they were stronger than any foe because their ideals were higher, their civilization deeper, their industry stronger, and their secret weapons more destructive or ingenious than those of any enemy. There actually were secret weapons, and some of them were pretty terrible, such as the poison gas they tested at Ichang in Central China. But what the Japanese military did not realize until it was too late was that destruction did not end a war. Against a determined enemy it created as many problems as it solved. Despite all their weapons, secret or known, the Japanese failed to knock China out.

These twenty-six men before me did not sit down around a table and plot the course of the fourteen years—the conquests, the hysteria, the seizure of absolute power in the State. The spy Okawa did not sit down at a table with Tojo. They had hated each other with an abiding, venomous hate. Marquis Kido, the prissy little man, had nothing in common with the life-loving, hard-drinking General Doihara. Some of the men had actually never met each other until they were arrested. Some were never makers of policy but merely its executors. By a curious mischance, there was not a single *zaibatsu* man in the dock. The Sugamo Prison could have easily yielded a list of policy-makers more important than this group.

But still, this was a fair cross section. And though they may not have been in physical contact with each other, these men were a part of a great and bold and sinister conspiracy, as mad and yet as coldly calculated as Hitler's plot. The great object was national advancement to the outer rim of the map, and the men who individually or collectively hatched the plot were patriots by every known standard.

Yet patriotism in these men was a synonym for a variety of motivations. Tojo was a patriot. He was also a small, bullet-headed man tortured by ambition, and by a desire not to be overshadowed by his father, a famous general. He was a man of petty hatreds, and of an infinite capacity for desk work. When he was made chief of gendarmerie in Manchuria, he found himself. His wife was a shrew who bore him a large family and who nagged him into more intrigue. After Tojo became war minister, Mrs. Tojo summoned press photographers and reporters every time he made a move. The Japanese called her "an Eastern Mme. Chiang Kai-shek" and made fun of her, behind closed doors. The Tojos were social climbers, and they were not above taking lavish gifts from their new *zaibatsu* friends.

Marquis Kido was a professional courtier, born well and reared in an atmosphere of Court intrigue. Slowly he rose through the hierarchy of bureacracy until he reached the Court. He stayed to become a power behind the throne, a maker of cabinets, a man fond of intrigue. He hated Tojo and Tojo's roughnecks. But he understood the bases of power in Japan, and it was he who selected Tojo as premier. Kido knew that Tojo meant war. But to defy Tojo meant to endanger his own power, perhaps to risk a *coup d'état* by the inflamed soldiery.

Okawa was a fanatic, a soldier of adventure, a magnificent ne'er-do-well with imperial dreams. He had served in Manchuria and China as an army agent and a research director for a great business organization. He combined his research with daring and murderous plots to change the political structure of Japan. Among his earlier conspiracies was a plan to break into the Imperial Palace with two co-plotters, kill off the Court moderates, and then, in a dramatic encounter with the emperor, demand his own, Okawa's appointment as premier. What he may not know to this day was that one of his two fellow-plotters intended, at this point, to plunge a dagger in the backs of Okawa and the other companion and have himself chosen as premier. I know because the man told me so himself. Okawa was alternately an ascetic and a sybarite, a brilliant madman, a magnetic personality who could send his followers to sure death without a whimper.

The three—Tojo, Kido, and Okawa—were as dissimilar as men can be. But all three had faith in Japan's destiny and each independently helped to advance the conspiracy which drove Japan into aggression. And as the conspiracy grew and their own influence expanded, they were driven to devise ever new intrigues at home and abroad. All three were drunk with success, with ambition, with the adulation they received as the builders of a Greater Japan.

No one could possibly disentangle personal motivations from the patriotism these men professed. Nor could anyone find the point at which personal motivations ended and the action of the social forces began—the *zaibatsu* craving for new markets and new sources of raw supplies, the pressure of impoverished masses which might rebel if their passions were not diverted into foreign adventures, the inviting weakness of the neighbors, the scarcities of food and coal and raw materials which plagued Japan, and the feudal system accustomed to seeking answers in war and not in social betterment.

In the afternoon the court marshal read the indictment. By this time, two of the defendants who had been abroad had arrived in Japan and joined the other twenty-six behind the enclosure. The men were accused of participating as "leaders, organizers, instigators, or accomplices" in a conspiracy with Germany and Italy to dominate the world. They were charged with being members of a "criminal militaristic clique" which molded the domestic and foreign policies of Japan to promote aggression, to exploit the conquered and to subject the Japanese people themselves to an absolute military control.

The defendants listened, or made notes. Okawa alone was restless. He kept unbuttoning his shirt and scratching his bare, sunken chest. Gradually his unbuttoned shirt slipped off a shoulder, and Webb ordered the guards to button it. As soon as the American colonel behind him buttoned up his shirt, Okawa loosened it again. Gradually the eyes of the audience became focused on this act of comedy, and the indictment was forgotten. After the second or third time, the colonel put his hands on Okawa's shoulders, and whenever he felt motion, he pressed Okawa's arms down. Eventually Okawa turned back and smiled reassuringly at the colonel. Everything was still again, and the reading of the indictment went on.

Suddenly, Okawa leaned forward and hit Tojo sharply on the head with a rolled copy of the indictment. The smack resounded through the room. In a special booth above the defendants, cameramen began to crank furiously. Tojo slowly turned back, and smiled at Okawa. The colonel and some MPs quickly hustled Okawa out, and a recess was called.

Cochrane and I went to the defendants' room. Okawa was

standing behind a desk. With his long, thin body, gaunt face and extraordinarily long arms, he looked like an Oriental Don Quixote. He spoke to us in slow, clear English:

"Tojo is a fool. . . . I must kill him. I'm for democracy. . . . America is not democracy. . . . I don't want to go to America, because she is democrazy. . . . You know what I mean? Demo crazy. . . . I've eaten nothing in seventy-two days. . . . I don't have to eat anything. I get my food from the air. . . . " He stretched his arm into the air to show how he got his nutrition from the air.

"He eats nothing," confirmed an American guard. "He just starves himself. He is sixty, and he keeps saying he must see his mother, who just got into town. The guy's nuts."

After the recess, the trial continued. But it seemed as if the climax had already passed, as if the antics of a demented man, or a man pretending he was demented, had torn the shroud of solemnity off the trial. How many men who saw this historic first session, I wondered, would recall anything of it in another year but the sharp slap on Tojo's clean-shaven head. And would this court of obscure judges and counsel be equal to the demands presented by a trial intended for the pages of history?

As at Nuremberg, so here in Tokyo, new concepts of international law were being formulated. The arguments presented here and the decisions reached, will be codified, and a hundred years hence will be cited in other world courts. This was a place for men not only high in the courts of their lands, but also possessed of a sense of history and drama—a place for an Oliver Wendell Holmes or a Benjamin Cardozo. But at this first session, all that was shown was a very large and photogenic room. Its relative unimportance was betrayed by the first act of inanity.

Two correspondents, unknown to each other, told me today they had been called in by General Baker, who wanted to convey to them General MacArthur's warm thanks for their "fair and impartial" coverage of the Allied Council sessions. Both correspondents told me they were very embarrassed. They had filed stories sharply critical of General Marquat, General Whitney, and General MacArthur. By the time the stories appeared in print to gladden Baker's heart, they had been completely rewritten by the home offices.

Another story is of a radio correspondent who earlier this week contacted his San Francisco office, told it that Tojo was to go on trial, and asked if the network wanted a special broadcast. The San Francisco office explained it had no authority to decide, but would contact New York. Pretty soon came the answer from the alert, newswise editor in New York. "No broadcast wanted tomorrow unless Tojo convicted."

General MacArthur has assured us that no pressure on us was intended, and that henceforth we will be treated "like my own officers." The various restrictions that have hindered our work have magically vanished.

The rapprochment between the State Department and General MacArthur is complete. Atcheson's group here has become a "Diplomatic Section" in Headquarters, and an officer has been assigned to it to teach it how to write army-style: "Subject . . . From . . . To . . . One . . . Two . . . Three . . . Umpteen . . ."

But the liaison is even closer than that. At the last session General Whitney sat at Atcheson's elbow and kept whispering instructions to him at such a rate that Ball, the British delegate, finally stopped in the middle of a statement and inquired acidly if it was all right for him to proceed. When Whitney retired in the afternoon General Baker took his place. What a spot to be in for an American diplomat, and what a commentary on the state of diplomacy in this theater.

May 10, 1946

Ozaki, my assistant, came in today to ask for a week off.

"In my ward," he said, "no rice rations have been issued for ten days. I want to go to my in-laws who are farmers in Shikoku, and borrow or buy some rice. It doesn't matter how much canned food you give me. When we have no rice, we are hungry."

They must be hungry, for Shikoku lies three days' train ride away, and train travel for a Japanese today is a harrowing experience. Apart from the physical strain, a man carrying rice faces constant danger, both from the police and the rice-jackers. Yet hunger, real or illusory, compels men to keep trying. The trains are packed with rice smugglers, and many factories in Tokyo give time off to their employees for food-hunting in the country. If he is lucky, Roy thinks he can smuggle through enough in two suitcases to last his family for two months.

Later I did a little checking on Roy's story. One of John Luter's two assistants in the *Time* office is just out of the hospital. He collapsed a few weeks ago of vitamin deficiency. Sparks's assistant has broken out with ugly sores. He has beriberi.

Malnutrition is upon us. But I hestitate to file the story without more checking. The Japanese government, which has been doing all in its power to make the general picture appear darker than it is so as to win a softer peace and receive more American aid, would be happy to see such stories in print.

So would some officers in General MacArthur's Headquarters, who openly advocate building up Japan into our advance outpost in the Pacific.

It is easy to be emotional about hunger. But, as after the First World War, food is an instrument of high policy. As such, it demands a callous approach. There is no doubt that Japan is not eating well. But the world stocks of food are limited. If Japan is given our wheat, will it come out of Chinese bowls, or the dinner pails of the French, or the Yugoslavs, or the Greeks? Who is hungrier—the Chinese and the French, or the Japanese? And is it not true that the Japanese, who have eaten relatively well during the war on food looted in Asia, have reserves of physical stamina which the Chinese and the Greeks lack?

Anyhow I told Roy to take his week off, and gave him an advance on his salary, some food for the trip, and a few trinkets to trade for rice.

At noon, Colonel Logie, Deputy Provost Marshal for Tokyo, invited Cochrane and me to join Lewis J. Valentine, former New York Police Commissioner, on a visit to the International Palace. We quickly said Yes.

The International Palace fascinates me. It is more than just the world's largest brothel. It is also one of the items of evidence in the damning record of Japan's efforts to seduce the Army of Occupation away from its purposes. The building now occupied by the brothel used to be part of a huge munitions plant. When the emperor proclaimed Japan's surrender, the management of the plant held a conference. Obviously, there would be no more demand for war materiel. Yet, there was the idle plant, money, and managerial talent, all waiting to be reconverted. What would be the commodity most likely to be in demand when the Americans came?

The Tokyo Police supplied the answer. Accordingly, five of the workers' dormitories were converted into brothels. Some of the managers stayed on to provide the benefit of their experience. Some of the prettier girl workers stayed on as prostitutes. Only Allied trade was permitted, and when the turnover became heavy the irreverent Americans began to call it "Willow Run"—because (until it was placed off limits to troops last month) it processed its product on such a huge scale.

We gathered in front of the Provost Marshal's office—Commissioner Valentine, big and amiable, members of his mission, a couple of Army officers, and a guide. We drove southeast, until we could see, rising out of the paddies, a series of two-story buildings with a sign in English, "Off Limits—VD." As we came closer, we saw smaller VD signs, dabbed in red paint on the fence and gate. We drove into the small yard, and at once a crowd poured out of the building toward us. They were all beaming at us and bowing low, like salesmen in a store that has not been doing too well. By the time we parked, the manager of the brothel was out to greet us. He was an oily character, speaking broken English. All I could understand was his opening sentence, delivered in a staccato manner: "Wercome, wercome. I am a Ph.D. in economics from Corumbia University."

Our first stop was at the infirmary. It was a huge, bare room, lined with *tatami* (straw mats). There were about a dozen girls lying on the floor, under thick comforters. Nearly all the girls hid their faces when we entered. A Nisei lieutenant and I began to question a girl in a corner. She said she was nineteen, and had never been a prostitute until she joined Willow Run five months ago. She now owed the company Y.10.-000 (about $660), mostly for the clothes she bought at the brothel store. We got similar stories from the other girls. Most of them had lost their families in the American fire raids. Some had lost jobs in the war industries. A few described themselves as *geisha*, or professional entertainers. They were all in debt to the management, and the debt was growing. We asked them if they had heard of the MacArthur directive which banned contractual prostitution. They had not.

We went through the clinic, in which, the manager claimed, the girls were inspected once a week. Each chair in which the girls were examined had a tiny curtain, to conceal their faces from the doctor. We looked at the two shallow pools in which the girls bathed every other day. We saw their cooperative dining room. We entered the "ballroom," in which about a hundred girls, most of them in ugly Occidental gowns—with nothing underneath—danced with each other. Some of the girls looked no older than fourteen.

It was a dreary place—the red paper streamers suspended from the ceiling, the scratchy old jazz records, the unsmiling women pushing each other clumsily across the floor, as if performing a distasteful duty.

"They are very gay, eh?" said the manager. "But inside are very sad. Very lonely. No GI friends come two, three weeks."

From the ballroom we walked to the girls' room. There were fifty cubicles to a building, each tiny room separated by a low partition, and a thin curtain for a door. Each entrance had a crayon-colored sign reading, "Well Come, Kimi," or "Well Come, Haruko," those being the names of the occupants. The rooms were neat enough, with a stack of comforters in a corner, a tiny make-up mirror set on the floor, and a few yellowed photographs. There was a heavy smell of antiseptic about the whole place.

Off the stairway we saw a long, narrow room with the sign "PRO Station" painted out lightly. This was the room where the Army supplied prophylactics for the GIs until it put the place off limits. Right next to it there were two small, doorless rooms to which the women retired after each visitor.

The odor was so sickening I fled. I walked down to the covered passageway between the houses and sat on a bench, near a company store selling cheap cosmetics and clothes. The manager was right behind me.

"You must meet the officers of our union here," he said. "We have a real union. Democratic."

Behind him stood three young women, one in a bright kimono and the other two in Western tailored suits. "These," said the manager, "are the officers of the Women's Protective League. The president——" he pointed to a girl who smiled prettily, "Miss Akiko Kato, former *geisha*. Miss Sumiko Hasegawa, vice-president, a former typist. Miss Kimi Iijima, a former dancer."

I had visions of a colorful story on the underprivileged women of a brothel rising in arms against the management and demanding higher pay and better working condition. I asked the manager to leave.

The women said they were between twenty-six and twenty-nine years old. They had all come to the International Palace in December, 1945, and now had a debt of between Y.4,000 and Y.6,000 ($266–$400) each. "No," said Miss Kato, "we have no savings. It all goes for clothes and cosmetics, which we buy from the company."

Every twenty-four hours a woman "processed" an average of 15 GIs, each of whom paid Y.50, or $3.30. Of this amount, half went to the management, and the other half was kept by the women. Out of their income, the women paid for their food, medical expenses, cosmetics, and clothes.

I did a rapid bit of calculating. Among them, the 250 women "processed" 3,750 GIs every twenty-four hours. This meant a daily income of $6,200 for the International Palace. Not bad, even for munitions makers!

I said, hopefully: "This union of yours, this Protective League, does it have difficulties with the management?"

They said, with surprise: "Of course not. The management is very friendly. In fact, the union was formed at the manager's suggestion."

"What kind of a union is *that?*"

"It was like this," said Miss Kato. "We were doing well for four months, making friends with GIs and helping to establish firm cultural relations between Japan and the United States. Then, last month, the Army barred the place to the GIs. Since then only eight or ten GIs come in daily, on the sly. So we talked it over one day, and agreed that it was too lonely this way, and not good for the traditional U.S.—Japanese friendship. The management said, 'Why don't you form a union?' We did. Then the new union drafted a petition to General MacArthur.

" 'Your Excellency,' we said, 'now that the International Palace is closed, the GIs are lonely and homesick. Up to now we have felt it our duty to make the GI's stay here pleasant.

Please, Your Excellency, reopen the Palace, and let us cheer up the homesick Americans.' "

May 11, 1946   TOKYO

General Dwight D. Eisenhower, Army Chief of Staff, in town for a few days, today met the press. There was little that was newsworthy in what he had to say. He thought the main problem in the occupied countries was re-education in the ways of democracy. He believed the German occupation, being more complex, would last longer than the occupation of Japan. He expressed his faith in the United Nations. But the import of the meeting, we thought, lay not in what he said, but in how he said it, and in the reaction of the "Bataan Boys" to the visitor.

There were few in the crowded studio in Radio Tokyo who were not impressed with Eisenhower. Many thought there was no one in this military theater to match his quick wit and his friendly manner. All noted his shrewdness, and his sense of public relations. When General Baker tried to intervene, Eisenhower quickly stopped him. Eisenhower stepped on no toes, but in ducking questions, he did it with such good grace and humor that no one begrudged the ducking. He stood smiling before the large crowd, took the questions on the fly, and shot back his answers as if he really enjoyed the whole thing.

But by nightfall, the "Bataan Boys" were out in force, testing our reactions to Eisenhower and putting in a critical word here and there. There is little love for "Ike" in this Headquarters. The official view is that General MacArthur never wanted the European theater anyway, because the number of Allies involved made the job of fighting the war so much harder.

"But," in the words of one of General MacArthur's close aides, "the Old Man would not have given in to the British the way Eisenhower did. Eisenhower in the end became a pawn of the British—and that's why they liked him so much."

The calculating military eye here sees Eisenhower not only as General MacArthur's rival for a niche in the history of the Second World War, but also as a competitor in the coming presidential elections. "Do you think Ike will run?" "Do you think he will make a good president?" "Don't you think he will keep making concessions every time pressure develops, the way he did in the war?"

May 15, 1946   TOKYO

George Atcheson made his debut today as chairman of the Allied Council. I like him, and feel sorry for him. There is no American diplomat who has taken a worse beating than he has—first in China, from General Patrick Hurley, when Atcheson saw the morass into which Hurley's policy was leading us; later in Washington, still from the same crochety, aging Hurley; and finally here, when he and his entire State Department mission were deliberately snubbed by Headquarters. When I landed in Japan six months ago, Hurley was filling the air in Washington with a variety of charges, and I found Atcheson in the depths of depression. He wanted to hit back, but the caution of a career diplomat held him back. Eventually, Hurley grew tired, and Washington grew tired of Hurley, and George could lean back with relief. This is his first real chance to redeem himself.

But the meeting started on the wrong foot. The wrangling this time centered on a Japanese petition presented to General MacArthur and the Council after the May Day meeting. The petition detailed a series of grievances, and asked for their redress. Now General Derevyanko wanted to know what Headquarters had done about it.

"The translators of the document," said Atcheson, "believe that the original composition was drawn in a foreign language, and then translated into Japanese. . . . The United States does not favor communism at home or in Japan, but in both countries the Communist party is free to develop and organize. As a personal opinion, I believe that the document contains unmistakable earmarks of Communist propaganda."

Derevyanko was visibly taken aback. He whispered to his political adviser. "I've attentively listened to Mr. Chairman," he finally said, "But I can't understand what connection there is between all he has said and the question under consideration." The petition, he insisted, was submitted by the people who took part in the May Day rally, and "it would be undemocratic to disregard it on the pretense that it was Communist propaganda."

With his mind still on George's charge that the petition originally had been drawn in a foreign language, Ball said wryly: "Mr. Chairman, *I* am not responsible for the document."

There could be no mistake as to what foreign language Atcheson thought the document had been drawn in originally. He stared at Derevyanko, and the general colored. To all of us this was a big story. It was the first official charge that the Russians were behind the unrest in Japan, and that the protests supposedly emanating from the Japanese people were actually drafted by Russian agents, and then translated into Japanese.

There was only one authoritative agency in Tokyo to which Atcheson could have referred such a translation—the famous ATIS, or Allied Translator and Interpreter Section. Cochrane and I promptly went to the bustling ATIS building, and called on one of its key officers. After we promised to keep his name in confidence, he said:

"Well, this is the way it was. They came to us and said, 'Here's a Jap document. Do you think there is any possibility it's a translation from the Russian?' We studied it very carefully, and we told them, No, there's no possibility whatsoever. The new Japanese Constitution was an obvious translation. Any Jap college student could tell it was a translation from English. But this document is Japanese, good, idiomatic Japanese."

Cochrane and I next drove out to the Communist headquarters, in a shabby two-story school house turned over to the party by its owner. The Big Three—Tokuda, Nozaka and Shiga—were in conference in a tiny room. This was the first they had heard of George's charge, and they looked stunned. We asked them for comment.

Around April 27 or 28, they said, some seventy labor union officials met to discuss the last details for the May Day demonstration. At this meeting it was decided to draft a petition to General MacArthur and the Council, and a committee was picked to draft it. Most of the names on the list shown to us belonged to right-wing Social Democrats and Osaka independent labor leaders. On May Day, the petition was read to the huge gathering, and then a delegation was named to present it to General MacArthur.

Nozaka called in a Communist who was a member of the four-man delegation. The man said:

"There were four of us, two Social Democrats, one Korean Communist, and I. We went over to General MacArthur's Headquarters, but the sentries wouldn't let us in. We then walked over to the American Embassy (where General MacArthur lives), and gave the resolution to a sergeant of Military Police. He said he didn't know anything about it, and we said, you just pass it on to the Supreme Commander.

"We also told the sergeant about one of the complaints in our petition, the one about Lieutenant Angus. It involved a steel company in Kobe. The company has been paying Y.60 ($4) a month to the apprentices and Y.200 a month to men with eight years' experience. Two hundred yen wouldn't keep a family alive for four days. So the union demanded a five-fold increase. But weeks passed, and the management just refused to see the union people or to receive their petitions. The people were getting desperate. Finally they went to the president's residence, and he was obliged to talk to them. But the Japanese police soon came to the house, said they were under orders from Lieutenant Angus, Public Welfare Office for the prefecture, and told the workers to leave.

"The next day the workers returned to the president's house, and argued with him for better wages. While the argument was on, someone found a great deal of hoarded food in the house. In the excitement some property was damaged. Later, American Military Policemen arrested a union leader at his home. They also accompanied company managers, while the managers tore down union posters and told the workers Lieutenant Angus wanted to see no more trouble.

"We told all this to the sergeant, and asked him to pass it on to the Supreme Commander, and he said, Sure. Then we left. But the petition was our, Japanese, petition, and it spoke of our, Japanese, problems."

Cochrane and I went back to the club and discovered a few correspondents had done some checking with Japanese philologists, who reached the same conclusion as the ATIS experts. We gave Atcheson the benefit of the doubt; he was a new man in the job, and he would not prefer a charge of this sort on his own. But we all wondered what agile mind in Headquarters had dreamt up this charge, for what purpose, and who in Headquarters had given final approval to the move.

May 16, 1946   TOKYO

In the morning Cochrane, Luter, Joe Fromm of *World Report*, and I pinned on our official green badges and drove out to the Diet to see the debut of what is described as Japan's "first democratic parliament." The session had not yet begun, and the corridors were packed with guards, in their police caps and frock coats; reporters, messengers, the unmistakable oldtime politicians, and a sprinkling of new faces—including women's.

While waiting, I talked to half a dozen new Diet members. The first was Miss Shizue Yamaguchi, a 28-year-old Social Democrat. Miss Yamaguchi looks like a high-school girl, complete with bobby socks over her stockings. She has a nice, fresh face, and the smooth movements of an athlete. When I first saw her, she was sprinting down the corridor in pursuit of someone. Miss Yamaguchi is the daughter of a rich bicycle manufacturer, in whose factory she formerly worked as a dietitian. Then came the elections, and Mr. Yamaguchi ran his daughter for the Diet. I am told that the women voted for her because she is a woman, and the men voted for her because she is a pretty one, and in the end she won more votes than the Communist leader Nozaka. Talking with animation, she said she would fight for a five-hour workday for women, and for a milk ration for babies.

My next interview was with an ultranationalist I met in Kyoto. He seemed overjoyed to see me, though I suspect that he tried to poison me at our first meeting in the belief that because I wore an army uniform I had come to arrest him as a war criminal. I told him I had been violently ill after our encounter in Kyoto, and described the symptoms. He said, with a sympathetic cluck: "Sounds like poison." He is a small, round-faced man with a sense of humor, and an obvious affection for food, drink, and women. He said his platform consisted of one plank: "Fight the Communists!" We agreed that he would tip me off on political trends, in return for dinners at my house.

As I left him, he shouted after me: "Don't forget the sake. And please don't poison me."

Walking back to the press gallery I ran into Ozaki, "Father of parliamentarianism," sailing regally down the corridor with his retinue. He is generally treated with higher regard than the emperor himself. I stopped him to tell him that the textbooks on basic English he had asked me to get were due any day. He said, "Huh?" and produced an instrument resembling an oversized tobacco pipe—this time a portable hearing aid. He stuck the thin end of it in his ear, and gestured to me to shout into the bowl. I did, several times, but without success. Finally, one of his attendants took over, and the message reached him. Ozaki nodded his thanks, and sailed on. He had expressed a desire to address the Diet today, and the members deferentially agreed.

In his speech Ozaki advocated a new system of electing the House Speaker. He talked for a long time, until the less reverent members began to shout, "Cut it short," and Ozaki's admirers shouted back at the hecklers. Ozaki went on through the bedlam, presumably having heard not a sound. Late in the speech, he turned to the five Communist members on his right and said: "When a democracy advocates a violent revolution, it isn't a democracy any longer."

In a split second Tokuda was on his feet, shouting: "It's not a revolution. It's mass action."

There was much mass action through the day, as there has been for the past month. When we left the Diet, we saw a demonstration by thousands of railroad workers. They had forced their way into the compound of the premier's residence, but were driven out by Japanese policemen, aided by our MPs. Now they were waiting patiently for the return of a delegation that had gone to the Diet to demand better wages, better rations, and a better government.

The unrest is part hunger, part hope, part a growing political consciousness. Rations in the cities have been lagging a fortnight and more. The prices are soaring, while the wages remain frozen at a fantastically low level. Finally, Japan's labor is beginning to flex its muscles. On May 1, there were close to 2,700,000 unionized workers in Japan, or six times as many as Japan had ever had. While thousands never knew why they joined, other thousands had taken to heart General MacArthur's order to Shidehara six months ago to encourage the unionization of labor so that "it may be clothed with such dignity as will permit it an influential voice in safeguarding the working man from exploitation and abuse. . . . "

Shidehara's was a *zaibatsu* cabinet whose ears have never functioned well when labor spoke. Thus, with the competent guidance of Communist and Social Democrat tutors, labor went into the streets. The demonstrations have been a liberal education both for workers and for politicians. For Japan is not accustomed to the sight of working people marching past the premier's windows with demands for a richer life. Nor is she accustomed to hearing the emperor denounced by thousands massed in the Imperial Plaza. And Shidehara's was the first cabinet forced out partly by street demonstrations.

The next step in education obviously is a general strike. Thus far the Communists have been a restraining influence. Tokuda told me they are uncertain of the American attitude should workers in coal mines, utilities and railroads walk out. The doubt is justified. There is a growing feeling in Headquarters that labor in general, and especially the Communists, is getting out of hand. This has already led this month to two warnings by the Chief of Staff.

The wits in Headquarters say that what we want in Japan is a free and vigorous labor movement—"provided it's housebroken."

While labor demonstrated, and Headquarters worried, the Japanese conservative politicians went on with their plans. The incomparable team of Shidehara and Yoshida, known hereabouts as Twiddledee-san and Twiddledum-san, has taken over the two major conservative parties without ever having run for election—Shidehara becoming president of the Progressive party and Yoshida of the Liberal. Early this afternoon, on Shidehara's recommendation, the emperor summoned Yoshida to the palace and ordered him to form a new cabinet.

Like his friend Hatoyama, Yoshida is a case for a political psychologist. He is a small, gray man, who for most of his sixty-eight years has used grayness as protective coloration. Japanese officials who know him say he is made up of fear, ambition, and intense conservatism in equal shares. Superficially, Yoshida's record is respectable. Or respectable enough, anyway, to preclude the possibility of a purge. He has been a professional diplomat nearly all his life, he knows the clichés of democracy, and he is regarded as a member of the "pro-American clique." Best of all, he was arrested by the gendarmes just before the end of the war on charges of conspiring to conclude peace with the Allies, and kept in a cell for forty-five days.

But politics in an era of hysteria are complex. No man could rise in the 'thirties unless he had proved his worth to the ruling oligarchy. A diplomat could not succeed as a diplomat. He also had to be an extreme and vocal nationalist. Admiral Nomura, the "moderate," who negotiated with Cordell Hull on the eve of the war, could point to the eye he lost to a Korean assailant. A diplomat hobbled to fame on a wooden leg replacing his own, lost in a Shanghai bombing. Another diplomat won notice—and promotion—by bashing a more moderate colleague with a bamboo stool. A third became ambassador to Spain via insults to Chiang Kai-shek.

Yoshida was a quiet man who got ahead in this boisterous company. What was it behind this gray exterior which advanced his career? The answer was given to me a few days ago by a tired, old Japanese, who, nineteen years ago, was associated with Yoshida in a project erroneously known as the "Tanaka Memorial."

The year was 1927—the year of Chiang Kai-shek's rise to power, and of the mounting demands among the younger Japanese officers for "positive" action in Manchuria.

On June 27 an Oriental Conference was convoked in the Foreign Office in Tokyo, under Premier Baron Giichi Tanaka. Its purpose was to formulate a new policy for China, with special reference to the Japanese zone of interest in Manchuria and Mongolia. There were twenty-three participants, who met altogether five times. Among the conferees many remain newsworthy figures to this day. Two generals are now on trial as major war criminals. Of the three admirals, one, Nomura, served in Washington just before the attack on Pearl Harbor. One eventually became a leading banker of imperial expansion. A notable figure in this illustrious gathering was the Consul General from Mukden, Yoshida.

Yoshida was important for two reasons. He was known favorably by the army as "an aggressive diplomat." He was also a son-in-law of the emperor's closest adviser.

On July 5, 1927, the conference approved a memorandum entitled, "Basic Japanese Policy toward China." Its theme was expressed in two sentences: "Manchuria and Mongolia are to be considered as separate from China because of Japan's special interests," and "It is Japan's duty to see to the maintenance of peace, economic development, and social stability in these two areas."

The document was not shown to the emperor, since it did not call for his signature. But the following month Yoshida and another conferee proceeded to Dairen, to pass the new policy on to the Japanese officials from Manchuria, Mongolia and North China. Yoshida thus was one of the earliest spokesmen of the predatory policy which convulsed and seared Asia in the next eighteen years.

As a footnote to history, there never has been a "Tanaka Memorial." What the Chinese, and later the Americans, publicized as one apparently was a blueprint for aggression presented by some Japanese officer in Manchuria to one of the Tokyo conferees—and possibly even to Yoshida himself. The memorandum had fallen into the hands of a Chinese or Korean agent and made public. As it happened, the document, known as the "Tanaka Memorial," was prophetic. But so was the policy drafted with the aid of Yoshida.

This was one of the first steps in the career of Yoshida the "moderate." He became Baron Tanaka's vice-minister of foreign affairs, and helped to outline the adventures in China. In subsequent years he did his best to persuade Italy to recognize puppet Manchukuo as a free and independent state. While in England as an ambassador, he discussed with Joachim von Ribbentrop the initial details of the Axis pact. Like the other aged diplomats, he spent the war years brooding in retirement. Like them, he saw the writing on the wall and plotted with Prince Konoye to make secret overtures to the Allied powers.

But fifty years from now, and possibly less, a nationalist Japan will remember Yoshida gratefully as the man who, together with another "moderate," Shidehara, circumvented the will of the alien conqueror, sabotaged his orders for drastic changes in the fabric of old Japan, and fought skillfully and well to preserve the feudal system.

And some American historians at about the same time might raise a curious eyebrow, wondering why and how this champion of feudal Japan was singled out by the American command as the molder of a new democracy. For it is no secret that Yoshida has been the liaison man between the Japanese government and General MacArthur, and that he has devoted admirers in American Headquarters.

This man tonight began the formation of Japan's first "democratic" cabinet.

The Baltimore *Sun* today recalled Cochrane, to manage its new radio station. I feel lost. For Cochrane has been more than a good friend and a brilliant reporter. He was also a teammate, whose interests dovetailed with mine. I worked the Japanese side of the street and he worked Headquarters, and between us we managed to learn much. I could not tell him that, for fear that it would sound pompous, but I felt that his departure would be a serious loss to the new Japanese democracy, for the most effective pressure for reform today comes from reporters, and there are mighty few with Cochrane's good mind and with faith in good, old-fashioned democratic ideals.

May 19, 1946   TOKYO

The political pot is boiling madly. Yoshida is still struggling to form a new cabinet. As fast as he picks his ministers, it is discovered that they are war criminals subject to the purge. Meanwhile, the food rationing machinery has bogged down. In the far north the distribution of food is thirty days behind schedule; in Tokyo, twelve. There are street-corner rallies, parades, mass meetings of protest. On Tuesday, eight hundred people demonstrated before the palace, demanding to know what the emperor was eating. On Friday, there were eight "food demonstrations" in front of rationing stations. Yesterday, twenty. There is a steady stream of marching men past the Diet and the premier's residence.

The climax came today with a "Give Us Rice" mass meeting. By ten o'clock on this bright, warm morning, there were at least 60,000 people at the imperial plaza. They had put three trucks together, and mounted tables on them for the speakers' platform. The chairman was the head of the Transport Workers' Union. But the meeting was actually run by a hard-looking man in corduroy knickers and a sports jacket. This was Katsumi Kikunami, an editorial writer for the *Asahi*, head of the Newspaper Union, and founder of the huge Congress of Industrial Unions. Grimly, he introduced a succession of speakers—union leaders, political workers, and just plain people.

One of these was a housewife of thirty-five, slim and plain looking and obviously undernourished. She came from a ward in which there has been no rice distribution in two weeks. She had a child strapped to her back, and as she denounced the police and the rationing officials, the child's wailing came clear and loud over the loudspeaker.

But most of the speakers talked of politics. They demanded Yoshida's resignation, a Popular Front, a new cabinet including workers and farmers. "We must use the privileges we've gained since the war," cried Suzuki, editor of the *Yomiuri*, "One of them is the right to make revolutionary changes that will produce a democratic government. A one-day general strike will force Yoshida out!"

Tokuda was the last to speak. He wheeled around on the table top, pointed at the palace, and shouted: "We're starving. Is he?" He denounced Yoshida and the war criminals in the Diet, but he saved his sharpest barbs for the emperor. "Last week," he said, "we went to the palace and asked to see the emperor. We were chased away. Is it because the emperor can say nothing but 'Ah, so. Ah, so, Ah, so?'" He mimicked the emperor. The crowd cheered wildly.

When the meeting ended Fromm, Cochrane, and I walked up to the cable which marked the line beyond which no one was allowed. The cable was guarded by one American and one Australian sentry. We were talking to them when a file of six Buddhist monks in bright, loose robes came up to the cable. They lined up, facing the palace, and began, alternately, to beat cymbals and chant. That done, they prostrated themselves on the ground in prayer.

Just as the monks finished, up came three husky youths, halted at attention, bowed reverently towards the palace, and then extended their hands in worship. Their leader told me they were university students who wished to express their devotion to the emperor in this crisis. But, he hastened to assure me, "We're not reactionary. We're with the people."

When the students left, their place was taken by a frail, middle-aged woman with a small, square box such as usually contain the ashes of dead ex-servicemen. She knelt and began to pray. Soon a large crowd formed around her, and crossed into the forbidden territory. The sentries forced the people back with their rifles. We talked to the woman and found out that the box contained not ashes but rice for the emperor, whom, she said, she loved. The more she talked the more excited she became, until she wept without restraint. The palace policemen came up and urged the woman to go away. The emperor, they said, gets enough to eat.

Finally she traipsed off happily. The policemen said she was crazy. On her chest, large as a saucer, was a badge some demonstrant had given her. It said: "Down with the Reactionary Government!"

The demonstrants, meanwhile, had formed a column and headed towards the premier's residence. Cochrane counted 70,000 before he gave up. The procession streamed by the building, singing the usual assortment of songs, plus a new one:

> Put back into our hands the food
> That rightfully belongs to the working man.

They also shouted such slogans as "We need more food to be able to work," and "Give us a people's government," and "Food before the Constitution." The compound was guarded by four jeeploads of American MPs, and the demonstrants made no effort to enter it.

After a while we went back to the plaza, to take a look at the Sakashita palace gate. The bulk of the crowd was gone, but there were small groups scattered on the lawn. At a signal, each group would start at a trot towards the gate, with the usual chant, *wassho, wassho*. As each column came closer, it went into a snake dance, and then another group would start trotting. An American sentry stopped us. We argued until an officer drove up and let us through on the promise that "when those armored cars up there open fire, you get the hell out of there." We said, "You bet," and went on.

The moat at this point is probably thirty feet wide, and a bridge crosses it to the massive gate in the palace wall. The bridge was now a no man's land. The crowd stood or sat at one end, while a force of palace guards, armed with staves, stood in front of the gate. Earlier, the crowd had come up to the gate, and in the melee a policeman was tossed into the moat, and some demonstrants were beaten. A delegation of twelve men had gone in three hours earlier, and the growing crowd was waiting for their return. While waiting, the demonstrants sang, or listened to pep talks by men who spoke from atop a small police kiosk.

Around four one of the delegates came out, and climbed on the booth. Both the emperor and the minister of the imperial household, he said, had refused to see the delegation. It was finally permitted to talk to a secretary, who said he would report to the minister, who would report to the emperor.

"Geez," said the delegate in effect. "This is the first time I've been in the palace, and it's wonderful. Why, the lavatory there is better than the house I live in."

Half an hour later the rest of the delegation came out. It was led by Kikunami, who looked even grimmer than he had earlier in the day. One after another, the delegates climbed atop the kiosk to report their failure, to say they would come back in forty-eight hours, and to detail their discoveries in the palace. It appeared that they had gone through the palace kitchen, and had had a look at the emperor's cooking pots, refrigerators, and menu for tonight.

"What will you have for dinner?" they shouted to the crowd. "How much is there in your larder? Now hear what the emperor and his family will eat tonight. . . . "

They listed the dishes, and the kinds of food which came to the palace from the imperial preserves—fresh milk daily, chickens, pigs, eggs, butter.

"This is what the emperor and his officials eat. Do you think they understand the meaning of the word 'hunger?'"

But the big show of the day was going on elsewhere. After this morning's meeting, a delegation went to the premier's residence to demand that Yoshida give up his job, and that hoarded food be distributed to the people. Yoshida refused to see the group. In an argument with a secretary, someone (it sounded like Tokuda to me) said, "All right, if he won't see us, we'll just sit here until he resigns." The delegation then made itself comfortable for a long stay, while the photographers' bulbs flashed, and reporters scribbled furiously.

The unorthodox "sit-down strike" came close to being the last straw. By late afternoon it had been estimated that 250,000 people in all had demonstrated in Tokyo, and the nerves of the politicians had become frayed. Yoshida's advisers spent most of the day with Hatoyama in his house, discussing, among other things, the tactics for meeting the public pressure.

Around seven in the evening the secretary came out and said to the delegates, "You can go home now. Mr. Yoshida has decided to give up the job."

It is possible that at this moment Yoshida was ready to give up—partly because he was having trouble finding ministers, partly in fear of what was beginning to look like a full-scale, nonviolent revolution. But Tokuda, the sceptic, would take no promises secondhand.

"We'll sit here," he said, "until Yoshida himself tells us he is giving up."

Cochrane and I left at eight o'clock for dinner with Leo Cherne, the New York economist who is in town to work on a new schedule for Japan. Around eleven we had a call that something was happening in the premier's residence. We dashed over. Some of the "sit-downers" were asleep; others were visibly worn out. Tokuda had gone home because of a stomach ache. The group was now led by Suzuki, the tall, graying editor of the *Yomiuri*. He said he did not believe Yoshida's pledge, and intended to remain in the building through the night.

We left at two in the morning.

May 20, 1946   TOKYO

This morning General MacArthur issued a warning to the Japanese people.

"I find it necessary," he said, "to caution the Japanese people that the growing tendency toward mass violence and physical processes of intimidation, under organized leadership, present a grave menace to the future development of Japan.

"While every possible rational freedom of democratic method has been permitted and will be permitted . . . the physical violence which undisciplined elements are now beginning to practice will not be permitted to continue. They constitute a menace not only to orderly government but to the basic purposes and security of the Occupation itself.

"If minor elements of Japanese society are unable to exercise such restraint and self-respect as the situation and conditions require, I shall be forced to take the necessary steps to control and remedy such a deplorable situation. . . . "

The statement had a startling effect. I could actually recall no American move that matched this pronouncement in its repercussions. There was consternation in union headquarters and in the offices of the left-wing parties. In conservative quarters, there was undisguised jubilation.

As soon as word of the statement reached the premier's residence, the "sit-downers" quietly left the building. All demonstrations scheduled for today, and for the rest of the week, have been cancelled. The Japanese press, which thus far has been explaining that the people had no other way to change the government but to go into the streets, hastily backtracked.

The right-wingers in the Social Democratic party, who

were being pushed into the Popular Front by the sight of the marching multitudes, now happily announced they needed time to reconsider the issue, "in the light of the new circumstances." Two left-wing leaders admitted to me privately the fight was lost.

And Yoshida, who may have wavered last night, no longer wavered this noon. He announced that he would have a cabinet ready by tomorrow, and indicated that Twiddledum, or Shidehara, would be in it. As clearly as any of us, Yoshida saw the statement for what it was—a prop for Yoshida.

May 21, 1946   TOKYO

Late last year a colonel told me a curious tale. It dealt with the Recreation and Amusement Association (RAA), the world's biggest white-slave traffic combine.

On September 9, two nights before the First Cavalry Division entered Tokyo, it set up a road block near Chofu, outside of Tokyo. Everyone was jittery. Although everything thus far had gone smoothly, no one knew what the fanatical Japanese soldiery might do when the invaders entered the capital. The GIs were watching every shadow, and jumping at every sound.

Long after nightfall, the GIs heard the sound of an approaching truck. When it was within hailing distance, one of the sentries yelled, "Halt!" The truck stopped, and from it emerged a Japanese man, with a flock of young women. Warily, they walked towards the waiting GIs.

When they came close, the man stopped, bowed respectfully, swept the group behind him with a wide, generous gesture, and said:

"Compliments of the Recreation and Amusement Association!"

It was this tale, and odd bits we picked up here and there, that led Cochrane and me to the offices of the RAA this afternoon. We parked on the Ginza, Tokyo's main street, and walked up a flight of stairs to the main office—big, noisy, crowded with clerks, typists, accountants, and seedy looking hangers-on. In the absence of the president, we were greeted by his "High Adviser," Masanao Kanechika. Kanechika was nattily dressed, handsome, and he spoke excellent English, learned during his long career as a restaurateur in the United States. From unabashed and businesslike Kanechika we got the history of RAA.

"On August 15, 1945," said Kanechika, "the day the emperor announced the end of the war, the Metropolitan Police Board summoned the presidents of the seven major entertainment guilds in Tokyo. These included the restaurant, cabaret, *geisha* and brothel associations. The chief of the Board addressed the group.

"'Gentlemen,' he said, 'the American Army is coming to Japan. We fear that the Americans will molest our women— our wives and daughters and sisters. We need a shock absorber. Moreover, it is desired that the Americans enjoy their stay here, and become our friends. The government, therefore, hereby orders you to form a central association which would cater to the amusement of the Americans.'"

"How about the funds?" someone asked.

"The government will see to it that you do not lack for funds."

Thus, by August 23—before any American had yet set his foot in Japan—the association was set up and in operative condition. It was capitalized at Y.30,000,000 ($2,000,000), lent by the powerful Hypothec Bank. The shares, valued at Y.10,000 each, were acquired by individuals and associations. (Colonel Logie told me some shares were presented, as a mark of esteem and appreciation, to high Japanese officials.)

Next, the permission of a Colonel Wilson, Special Service Officer of the Eighth Army, was obtained to open dancehalls. Together with these came "houses of entertainment." RAA was ready to go places.

By last month, when the Army placed all Tokyo brothels off limits, RAA had become a tremendous going concern. It had

450 employees in the head office; 2,000 taxi-dancers (most, if not all, of whom were prostitutes on the side); and 350 unabashed professionals. In Tokyo alone the RAA operated 33 establishments, including the famous dancehall "Oasis" on the Ginza, which boasted of its own army prophylactic station in a specially erected quonset hut. There were also two hotels and a cabaret at the seaside resort of Atami; a place at the mountain resort of Hakone; and one at Ichikawa, going under the tempting name of "Dreamland." It ran two hospitals for its infected women. It had agents throughout rural Japan, and in the badly bombed cities, seeking likely recruits. There were by now 668 known brothels in Tokyo, with 8,000 women, but RAA was beyond competition. It had the prettiest girls, who bought their clothes on credit from the company. It had men like Kanechika, to sell the cultural aspects of RAA. Finally, it had the undiminished blessings of the Japanese government.

Now Kanechika was complaining, "Why did the army put our places off limits? We have tried to make the stay of the American boys here as pleasant as possible. We wanted them to meet nice Japanese girls . . . "

But Kanechika refused to be pessimistic about the future. "More and more Americans will come to Japan, and some of them will be married, and we will have high class hotels and restaurants for them; and there will be single men. . . . "

May 27, 1946   TOKYO

Although it gave me only three hours of sleep, I forced myself to get up at eight o'clock so that I would not miss Brigadier General Dyke's farewell talk with the Japanese press. I am eager to hear it for two reasons. One is that Dyke, one of the shrewdest of General MacArthur's men, is expected to provide some verbal pyrotechnics. The other is that his statement is regarded as a landmark in the political history of our Occupation.

In this world of military alphabet soup, Dyke's section of

Headquarters is known as "C.I. & E." or Civil Information and Education. It is one of the three most important sections, for its prime concern is with the mind of defeated Japan—with the schools, press, movies, the stage, books, magazines and even the itinerant puppet shows.

Increasingly, this section has been waging war on the Japan Newspaper Union. The sole reason has been politics. Some of the leading members of the union, in their roles as editors or editorial writers for Tokyo's major dailies, have been vigorously attacking the solidly entrenched conservatism. They have been assailing the Shidehara-Yoshida Cabinet for the collapse of rationing, for sabotaging reform, for playing politics while Japan has gone hungry and ragged. They have been baying at the heels of some of the most loathsome war criminals remaining in political power. They have been clamoring for some genuine reform—not in words, but in action. All these attacks have irked Headquarters, which has done its utmost to maintain the present Cabinet in authority. Dyke's talk is one of the counter measures, designed to check the Newspaper Union.

On May 18, Dyke saw General MacArthur and secured his consent to clamp down on the union. In the week which followed, the Japanese publishers were twice told informally by C.I. & E. that they did not "have to stand for any union interference."

Dyke's speech was a masterpiece of the kind of oblique talking with which Headquarters now chooses to exercise its will on the Japanese. Later I reread my notes, and could find very little in them that was truly newsworthy. Yet I remembered that the Japanese at the conference kept gasping through the talk. It was all done by hint and inference—at a time when hints are one of the prime instruments for molding and remolding Japanese policy and behavior.

Dyke's two specific suggestions—both relatively innocuous— were for the creation of a publishers' association and the opening of schools of journalism. But the tense crowd, packed tight into the hot room, was more interested in what seemingly came as frills.

"Freedom of the Press," Dyke said, "is having men designated by publishers decide the editorial policy. It is no more right for the Japanese government, or for the Supreme Command, except in broad policy, than for any other group to dictate editorial policy. Whomever the publisher may designate as the most mature man must establish the policy of a newspaper. . . . The creation of great unions is essential. . . . But if an individual is out of sympathy with the editorial policy of a newspaper, he has the perfect right to resign and go somewhere else."

The crowd broke up in silence. Outside of Radio Tokyo, I saw an editorial writer for one of Japan's great newspapers. "What's my reaction?" he said. "I feel this will further curb our freedom to say what is on our minds. It will also give a new, and bigger club to the old bunch. Those men are not filtering back any more. They are swarming back in mobs."

Dyke's talk shocked many of us. Readers back home, I knew, would find little wrong with the thesis that free speech is the publisher's right to decide his own editorial policy, or that a man who did not like his newspaper's editorial policy, could go peddle his wares somewhere else. But this is the terrible thing about understanding, or misunderstanding, Japan today. The most incredible things are being done to, and in, Japan with the simple explanation that that is the way it is done in the United States.

Japan today is *not* like the United States. She is still an unreformed aggressor nation, in which the agencies and instruments of jingoism remain virtually intact. This for us should still be the season of wrecking, before we can embark on our building projects. Too soon, too many Americans here have forgotten that we did not go to war merely to avenge the sinking of some of our superannuated battleships at Pearl Harbor, but—to a much greater degree—to reshape Japan, so that she would not war again.

Most certainly, one of our objectives should be the creation of a truly democratic press. Not the kind that skillfully parrots the jargon of American democracy. But it must be a people's press, which represents the needs and desires and yearnings of the people—the general contempt for the government of the old-timers, the demand for better rationing or for wages that give a family two square meals a day, the yearning for a change.

Yet the old-timers, or their henchmen, are back in control of the press. The other day, I asked an editor of the *Asahi*, Japan's greatest newspaper, what had happened to the *Asahi* men purged as war criminals.

"Oh, they are upstairs," he said.

"What do you mean 'upstairs?' Haven't you fired them?"

"You can't fire *them*. This is their newspaper. They draw a salary, and they have a separate conference room upstairs."

It was the rebellious *Asahi* workers—organized in a union— who forced the war criminals out of their old jobs. But Dyke's words now mean that these men—by virtue of such concepts as Free Enterprise, and Free Speech, and That's The Way We Do It Back Home—once again can dictate the editorial policies of the *Asahi*, and tell their writers who have advocated reform to go elsewhere with their wild-eyed, radical ideas.

We are trying to bring order and normalcy to Japan, but order and normalcy can be terrible things when they serve to perpetuate the old order.

The most interesting feature of Dyke's speech is that his own departure for home is a symptom of the momentous events taking place here this spring.

Officially, Dyke is retiring to rejoin the National Broadcasting Company as a vice-president. But most of us are convinced that Dyke has been sandbagged out of the army by some of his colleagues, envious of his keen mind and afraid of his seeming readiness to toy with progressive ideas. Dyke is no radical. He is not even a liberal. He is simply readier than most other generals here to accept such things as labor unions and social security as part of the pattern of living. Thus the word has been spread around that Dyke is "a Commie," and one general usually refers to Dyke as "that damned pink."

Dyke's departure coincides roughly with the end of the political honeymoon in Japan. When I arrived in Tokyo, it was an exhilarating experience to talk to some of the younger officers in his section or in the sections dealing with Japan's economy, labor, or government. These were the planners who blueprinted the democratization of Japan. They had written the noble directives giving land to the sharecroppers, purging government of war criminals, assuring the Japanese people of basic human liberties.

One by one the dreamers were eliminated. Some went home because they had grown lonely for their families, or the smells and sounds of a native town. Others left in frustration. Still others were forced out. Their places were taken by "reliable" officers. There was much talk of surrendering the job of governing Japan to civilian experts. But the civilians hired in the United States, to their dismay, have been put under the absolute control of colonels and generals. With the Brass firmly in the saddle, the spirit of reform died. Only the pretty verbiage remained.

The Japanese themselves were quick to grasp the change. The other day, a Japanese publisher told his staff that early in the Occupation he felt the U.S. Army was ready to alter the entire social and political fabric of Japan. "Now," he said, "I have come to see that General MacArthur is interested mainly in fighting communism."

Reluctantly, the Brass accepted the paper directives in last year's Season of Promise. Those were the vague pledges which met the orders from Washington and helped to keep the defeated people happy—at least for a while. But this was now the Season of Performance, and the Brass wanted no radical changes.

Last year's magnificent land reform directive, drafted by two of Dyke's young, bright men is still knocking around the sixth floor of the Dai-Ichi Building. The attitude there is typified by a General Staff officer, who, after a study of the official American blueprint, pronounced his judgment: "This is communism, rank communism."

Another major reform—the dissolution of the *zaibatsu*—is having tough sledding at the hands of the Anti-Trust and Cartels Division, which is supposed to be enforcing it. In what is known generally and bitterly as the "Zaibatsu Preservation Division" the refrain is, "We can't destroy our best allies."

We had issued a series of directives encouraging the unionization of labor, urging the people to take a direct and active interest in their political life, and *even providing specifically for keeping our hands off should the Japanese people ever want to employ force to overthrow the old order*. Yet, when the unions marched out into the streets with posters demanding that the government of old-timers resign, the Labor Division stepped in with the dictum that unions are not allowed to participate in politics. "Just devote yourself to wages and conditions of labor, as our own unions do back home!" But this is not "back home"; this is a country in revolt, which we ourselves have consciously encouraged, so as to sweep Japan clean of feudal ideas and institutions. The men who drafted President Truman's early directives on Japan knew this axiom, but many Americans here do not: the common man, when he takes a militant interest in politics, is the world's best defender of democracy.

But this is not the only reason why the Brass objects to drastic reform. There is an unnatural obsession with what is known here as "the coming war with Russia." Elsewhere—in Washington, or Moscow, or Paris—there is undeniable friction with the Soviets. Envoys exchange acid remarks, notes fly, demarchés warn and threaten. But all this is still the language of diplomacy. Here, today, one lives in an atmosphere of front-line trenches. Increasingly a correspondent's critical news report of this or that activity in Headquarters is greeted with the angry comment:

"We're at war with the Russkys. Whose side are you on?"

With war on Russia supposedly imminent, it becomes imperative to modify reform. We no longer want to purge the guilty, the monopolists, the reactionaries. A purge now would produce social tensions. No general wants tensions at his base of operations. Nor does he want to eliminate the men and groups which would heartily participate in a war with the Soviets. Back in 1919 we found it necessary to send an expeditionary force to Siberia to put out the Japanese invaders. The old dream is not yet dead in Japan. The other day, a conservative member of Parliament told me Siberia would "meet all the needs of a new Japanese democracy." The old-timers would love to try their hand again.

Many of us here are unhappy over what we see. We feel that it is wrong whichever way one looks at it. If the generals are right and we are to fight Russia, we are getting the wrong sort of allies. The social forces awakened by Japan's defeat are too strong to watch placidly the re-emergence of a feudal, militarist, ultranationalist Japan, even under a set of carefully chosen democratic banners. We are merely asking for trouble if we side with the old-timers. But our blunder is even worse if the war does not come—for we are helping to maintain an unreformed, essentially unweakened Japan, which fifteen years from now again will become the cancer of Asia.

SEASON OF PERFORMANCE

A conference of almost all the sections in Headquarters was held four days ago, to formulate a directive purging war criminals from Japan's economy. The meeting was held in Room 506, Forestry Building, a whispering distance from General MacArthur's own office. Like Dyke's talk yesterday, the conference is bound to remain a landmark in the history of the Occupation.

The meeting was heated enough. But even more heat has been generated in angry arguments since. At least half a dozen people have come to me to give me indignant glimpses of the conference. It is easy enough to understand the indignation. It was bad enough that the meeting hesitated to purge the men who subsidized aggression. What is worse is that the conference climaxes the re-emergence of the "Japan-is-our-bulwark" and "Let's-not-kill-off-our-best-allies" school of thought. One of the many corpses left on the conference table was the pledge of the Potsdam Declaration to eliminate "for all time the authority and influence of those who have deceived and misled the people of Japan into embarking on world conquest."

As at last year's conference on the political purge, the conferees promptly divided into two irreconcilable camps. One comprised a solid phalanx of the four Staff sections—G-1 (Personnel), G-2 (Intelligence), G-3 (Plans and Operations), and G-4 (Supplies). They found allies in such unmilitary quarters as the Diplomatic and Civil Communications sections. Ranged on the other side in this unequal contest were scattered representatives from the three departments which actually administer Japan—General Dyke's C.I. & E., General Whitney's Government Section, and General Marquat's Economic and Scientific Section.

The meeting started on a note of accord. Everyone agreed that the Potsdam Declaration indeed prescribed a purge. But on that, agreement ended. One representative of the military camp noted that the Declaration did not say *when* the purge was to be carried out. Another questioned the validity of the Declaration "under the existing circumstances." Max Bishop, State Department officer and Atcheson's right-hand man, underscored this point with, "The Potsdam Declaration is not an inviolate document."

My friend Colonel Creswell was one of the most active spokesmen for the military camp. "If the Potsdam Declaration were to be rewritten now," he said, "without the pressure of public opinion, or passion, or other emotion, it would be quite different." Then, changing from the contemplative to the emphatic approach to the problem: "To hell with the Potsdam Declaration."

Once the line of division between the camps became marked, the military group began to argue that we could not risk taking competent men out of Japan's economy.

"We can't turn the industry over to foremen now," said one officer.

"You issue this directive, and you will throw the entire communications industry into chaos," said J. D. Whittemore, chief of the Civil Communications Section and a vice-president of the Chase National Bank.

Creswell insisted that the prepared memorandum on the purge was "on the premature side"; that General MacArthur should "think over carefully the additional confusion the directive might cause"; and that the purge would "remove all experienced personnel" from industry and finance.

Another colonel, representing G-3, put the problem on a tactical basis: "We don't have enough men in the Occupation force today to risk any chaos by instituting a purge."

Eventually "chaos" was replaced by the "are you sure they are criminals?" argument.

One of the basic flaws in the Potsdam Declaration and similar pronouncements, Creswell said, was their assumption that anyone who made munitions was a militarist. "Look at the political purge we had in January," he said. "Now we find that we have to disqualify from public life people who joined the Imperial Rule Assistance Association (wartime totalitarian party) and similiar organizations merely to exert a restraining influence on them."

The colonel from G-3 came in to say that the directive would "turn the best brains of the country against us." Bishop chimed in with the argument that the directive was not in the interest of the United States ("It might also catch many people who were opposed to militarism").

"Ryozo Asano," said Creswell, "would be affected by this directive, and I happen to know that he should not be." Asano, the "cement king" of Japan, also was one of the major munitions makers and protagonists of overseas expansion. Since surrender he has been Japan's spectacular party-giver for Allied personnel.

Other officers volunteered the names of additional *zaibatsu* men who would have to be purged "unjustly."

But more than any of these arguments, three remarks struck me as a barometer of the new political weather in Japan.

Creswell: "There might be a time when we would want a strong Japan."

Another colonel: "We must not experiment with Japan's economy."

A third: "Look back on our purge of the Japanese Army. What it did was to weaken our own tactical position."

It is not enough that we abandon our high ideas for the reform of Japan's economy, or that we talk frankly of remilitarizing Japan. The point has finally been reached in the minds of some men where even our destruction of the Japanese Army is regarded as an error. Like the British Tory delegates to the conference of the Institute of Pacific Relations seven months before Japan's surrender, the colonels obviously regret the dis-

appearance of the Japanese Army as "a stabilizing element in a time of chaos."

June 3, 1946 TOKYO

Spent several hours with a newspaperman who, by sheer will power, has made himself the most important man in the Japanese labor picture. He is Katsumi Kikunami, an editorial writer for the *Asahi,* who is now organizing a labor federation patterned after the American Congress of Industrial Organizations. Kikunami is forty-two, compact, bushy-haired. He speaks quietly, in slow but beautifully precise English. Despite his calmness, he gives an impression of tremendous tension, as if he were a human spring wound up to the last turn of the knob.

The son of a poor country merchant, Kikunami studied at an American missionary school in Kobe. He has been with the *Asahi* for nineteen years. In 1935–38, he was its correspondent in London, covered the Ethiopian war, and reported the last, unhappy disarmament conference. When the war ended, he organized the union which tossed the *Asahi's* jingoist editors out. Later, he merged the Tokyo newspaper unions into a central Newspaper and Radio Workers' Union. He still sounded a little puzzled by the whole thing. "I've never had any union experience," he said, "and I make the most elementary errors." What saves him is his conviction, inner strength, and courage.

He spoke without bitterness of the American blows to the labor movement, of the Dyke declaration, General MacArthur's statement on demonstrations, the U.S. support of the conservative politicians. "It can be pointed out justly that none of the American statements, on its face, is directed against labor. But the Americans must know that each of these statements is used as a weapon by the Japanese employers. You ought to see what the Japanese publishers are doing with General Dyke's speech. . . . "

He also gave me some of the latest details on the union formed by Red Cross hospital employees. Prince Shimazu, vice-president of the Red Cross, apparently complained to Headquarters. As a result, someone in Headquarters wrote a memorandum exhorting the hospital management not to be influenced by the union, and advising the doctors and nurses who joined the union that "such activity is damaging to your prestige." The management quickly caught on, and fired the doctor who was president of the union.

June 5, 1946   TOKYO

More and more, the Ando case is beginning to sound like an Eric Ambler thriller. The known facts invite fascinating hypotheses, which take one into the realm of high intrigue. This, I discovered today, is as true of rank amateurs like myself as it is of professionals like Captain N, who has been working on the case for three months.

"Look at it this way," he said. "The Dai-An Company is capitalized at Y.100,000. Yet last year it earned Y.500,000,-000. I've looked into its operations. They show the boldness, the imagination—and the cash reserves—that only the *zaibatsu* or the imperial household have displayed in the past.

"Ando owns six contracting firms. He is president of the Tokyo Private Automobile Association, with 8,000 members. He has his men on the gasoline rationing board. He controls companies making car parts and tires. You actually can't own a car in Tokyo without paying a tribute to Ando. He owns a chain of soap works, tugs and lighters, fleets of trucks, engineering plants, and real estate. He will build you an outhouse or a factory; he will lay telegraph lines or highways; he will provide labor for any construction job, however big.

"Ando is a gangster. Yet he is on intimate terms with Prince Takamatsu, the emperor's brother. He is also friendly with cabinet ministers, with black market 'kings' in half a dozen cities, and with a lot of Jap generals. Nine out of every ten of his aides are military men.

"Before the war, the Jap Foreign Office ran a flock of phoney 'cultural' outfits. They are back again, with Ando as one of their angels, Prince Takamatsu their patron, and Kagawa, the holy man, their organizer.

"Ando has at his call any number of Japanese women. But he can also have the services of a dozen Occidentals—White Russians, Germans, Italians, former mistresses of Nazi gauleiters, daughters of emigrés, spies. Many of these work for Headquarters as receptionists, telephone operators, or interpreters. One of them told me she doesn't approve of Ando's methods, but 'owes him a debt.' Another gal, a Russian named Maria, works for Ando on 'special assignments.' In one case I know, Ando paid a Japanese gal Y.10,000 for a week-end in the mountains with an American officer.

"About two months ago, I went to dinner with Ando. I took along a Japanese gal who works for me. In half an hour Ando was offering to put up Y.20,000 to finance her campaign for a Diet seat. Another time Ando told me: 'I know I'm being investigated, but I'm too big for it. I'm used to getting what I want—legally, if possible.'

"Now put all this together, as I have, and start guessing. Ando might be a 'dummy' investor for the imperial family and some of the *zaibatsu* anxious to conceal their wealth. He might be a receiver for the colossal hoards of war supplies the Jap generals hid after the surrender. Or he might be the paymaster for what you might call the General Staff of the Japanese underground."

Captain N invited me to join him the next time he calls on Ando—socially.

June 7, 1946   TOKYO

Heard of a curious byplay involving the long-delayed, much-publicized land reform. After months of bitter argument with the Japanese government, the American farm experts have drafted a model land reform bill, and sent it through "the channels" for approval. The bill has been gathering dust for five weeks now because the Chief of Staff feels it "smacks of communism." But, meanwhile, Atcheson presented the Japanese plan to the Allied Council for study. The plan, though discarded and condemned as a fraud by American experts, came with Atcheson's endorsement: "While the agrarian reform law is not perfect, it marks a great advance. . . . " The experts, who have put an agonizing six months of work into the bill, have not even been informed in advance that the Japanese plan would be presented to the Council. Nor do they understand the purpose behind the move.

The Russian and the British members promptly submitted land reform plans of their own—and the British to a large degree depended on the knowledgeable advice of Headquarters' own experts. While these byplays go on, the landlords continue to prepare for the dark day by distributing their acreage among "dummy" holders. Under the Japanese plan, characteristically, the last word on who is to buy land under the "reform" will remain with the landlord-dominated local committees.

June 8, 1946   TOKYO

Right after lunch Lee Martin, of the Overseas News Agency, Walker, and I picked up Captain N and drove over to Ando's office. Lee, who is a lovely girl and Sally's closest friend, has just arrived from the Philippines and China for a short stay here.

The Dai-An Building is a neat, four-story, narrow structure in the Ginza district. There were a few clerks in the office downstairs, and a few waiting people—some of them men of military bearing. Captain N led us upstairs. On each landing we were scrutinized by young men who made me think of

Grade-B gangster movies. On the third floor, we were met by a small, thin man who said he was "Professor Yoshida, chief of the Foreign Affairs Department."

Ando was waiting for us in the middle of his room on the top floor. He was a stocky, handsome man, with an alert face and graying hair. He wore a well-cut gray suit, and looked like a diplomat on a good-will tour. He said "Good Afternoon," and having apparently exhausted his English vocabulary, led us to comfortable, low armchairs at one end of the room.

The large room was a strange compound of a courtesan's boudoir and a banker's inner sanctum. There was a huge bedroom mirror on one wall, and a life-size painting of a nude on another. Below the nude stood a suit of ancient *samurai* armor. The dominant color was white. The chairs had white slip covers, and the davenport was covered with a white bearskin. In a corner by the door stood a small desk with a battery of telephones. Right above me hung a small, autographed portrait of General MacArthur.

With Yoshida translating, Ando told us of his affection for the United States, and for American correspondents. He named a few for whom, he said, he had done "certain small favors." Our visit, he said, was especially happy because this was the first time he had ever met a woman correspondent.

"We must do something to commemorate this event," Ando said. He talked into a phone. A young woman came in and gave Ando a small black case. Ando opened it, and pulled out a pearl necklace. "This is for you, Mrs. Martin," he said, "to show my appreciation of your visit." Lee started saying she couldn't possibly. She was still protesting when Ando clasped the necklace around her neck, over her army shirt and tie. "Jesus," said the captain. "I bet even he had to pay a couple of hundred bucks for that." The pearls were big and lustrous.

Lee was still protesting when a large, burly man, with a small forehead, cropped hair, and the shoulders of a professional wrestler came in. "This is Mr. Matsuda," said Ando. "He's chief of my General Affairs Department." It was curious to watch the relationships between the men. Ando and Matsuda spoke to each other in terms of intimacy. Both addressed

Yoshida in terms of contemptuous command, and Yoshida looked flustered and unhappy. I remembered an overheard remark that Professor Yoshida would have liked to leave Ando, but dared not.

Ando himself gave me an opportunity to pump him. The most urgent need of the moment, he said, was the establishment of contacts between "the better class Japanese" and Americans. I promptly said I agreed with him, and I thought it was unfortunate that these contacts were not made easier.

"Look at Prince Takamatsu," I said. "I understand that he is a very intelligent man, and I've made every effort to see him. But the Japanese government and the Court insist that I submit my questions in writing. I don't want to interview anyone in writing. I want to talk to them, face to face."

Ando said, "You're right. That's unnecessary. When do you want to see the prince? I'll arrange it for you." I said next Monday, and Ando said I would see the prince then without fail.

"Why don't you all come with me to the Wakatombo Club?" he asked. "Let's celebrate our first meeting, and we can talk there over a snack."

Lee went with Ando in his large, shiny coupe. Walker and I followed in our jeeps. The club was hidden behind a weather-beaten fence. Inside, the yard was neat and graveled, and there were young women standing at the door to welcome us. We took our shoes off, and were led down a maze of corridors into a large room—one of the twenty-two in the house. The floor mats and the wall paper were new, the scroll in the niche beautifully simple, the foot-high lacquered table solid and highly polished.

The waitresses began to glide in and out of the room. Each had a diamond ring, a present from Ando. They brought sweets and a bottle of Guckenheimer whisky, which costs a fortune in this land of raw liquor.

"I always bring my American friends here," said Ando. "I have between two hundred and three hundred of them in Headquarters alone. I feel that working so hard, they need relaxation. . . . " He named some of his guests—a general, a judge, a few well-known officers, a few correspondents, one or two members of the Allied missions in Japan.

"But not all Americans are my friends. There are Communists. Do you know Mr. Conde?" I did know Dave Conde, the very able head of the Motion Picture Division, who has been interested in Ando's efforts to muscle his way into the movie industry. "Mr. Conde is fighting me all the time. I know. I have informants. Have you heard of Colonel ——? [The colonel had just been arrested for black-market operations, as he was leaving for the United States.] The colonel, I think, didn't like me, and look what an unfortunate thing has happened to him. Wouldn't it be too bad if the same thing happened to Mr. Conde? He really should go home."

Matsuda said, "Mr. Ando is fighting communism very hard."

Ando said, "I shall fight communism as long as I live. All I have will be put into this fight. I stand for democracy and the preservation of the imperial system."

Yoshida asked me, "What do *you* think of the imperial system. Don't you think it's a system without parallel in the world, and beneficial to our people?" I agreed readily that it was without parallel.

Ando said, "I'll cooperate with the United States. I'm putting half a billion yen into a chain of movie houses, to show American pictures. I also intend to start a trans-Pacific shipping line. I have big plans."

The women now began to bring in food, fried shrimps so delicate they dissolved in our mouths, thin breaded veal chops, shredded chicken in wine sauce, and for those who liked it, raw fish, pickled radish, octopus, and other Japanese delicacies. Ando listened happily to our compliments.

"I'm self-sufficient," he said. "All you see on the table is my own. The fish comes from my own fishing boats, the meat comes from my cattle, the grain is from my own fields. We bring the food here in my own trucks." I was beginning to see why one official report said Ando spent Y.4,000,000, or $260,000, on entertainment in six weeks.

I had a dinner appointment at six, and I had to bow my-

self out. He and Yoshida walked me down. "Don't forget the appointment with Prince Takamatsu," said Ando. "We'll be friends, no?"

June 10, 1946 TOKYO

In the morning Ando took Lee Martin, Walker, and me to Prince Takamatsu's palace. While Ando was closeted with the prince, we waited in a small reception room and examined the ornate furniture, the antiques, and the fine vegetable garden flanking the two-story pillared building.

Takamatsu bears little resemblance to the emperor. He is surer of his body and better poised, and his face is reasonably alert. Before Japan's surrender, he served in the army, and the various military cliques fought over his adherence, until he tied himself up with one of the extremist groups. We now sat in a circle, with Ando next to the prince, and we asked our questions.

Later we agreed there was nothing noteworthy about the interview, except for an insight into the curious relationship between the prince and the racketeer. The prince parried our political questions with, "I'm not qualified to speak of that," or "I prefer not to talk of politics." He did say that he favored democracy, and that the imperial family shared the hardships of the commoners.

"We even grow our own vegetables," he said, pointing at the garden outside.

But each time that the prince felt himself unequal to a question, Ando came in quickly with the explanation that "His Imperial Highness thinks that . . . " Sometimes he interrupted the prince in the middle of his answer; sometimes he answered our questions before the prince had a chance to open his mouth. This was not a humble subject in the presence of a semidivine member of the imperial family. These were equals, perhaps friends.

As we filed out, Ando lingered behind. We used the time to look at the guest book in the vast lobby. The book contained the names of the highest men in the Army of the Occupation.

June 12, 1946   TOKYO

I was nearly $400 ahead in a lovely game of poker and feeling very smug, when John Rich of International News Service came in and said that two hours earlier he had filed a story on Ando's arrest.

Walker and I promptly got on the phones. Though it was nearly one o'clock in the morning, we roused every agent who we knew had been working on the case, and demanded to know why we were not tipped off. Invariably, the men refused to believe the news, and promised to check.

Having found nothing, we next went to the Metropolitan Police Board to check on the arrests made by the Japanese police through the day. There was no mention of Ando, but an American MP on duty suggested we wait for the sergeant. The sergeant did not come, and at three in the morning we got bored and left. I would like to think that John made a mistake, but he is too careful a reporter to pull a boner like that.

June 13, 1946   TOKYO

Sally left San Francisco today on the S.S. "General Meigs." I feel Christmasy. Japan is a world of ruin and frustration, and Sally will have an awful job of adjustment, but this is preferable to our being apart. The house has been scrubbed and painted, and some of the stench it had acquired in the years of disrepair and pickled radish has been aired out. All that remains to be done is to find some presentable furniture, fill the pit left in the yard when the air raid shelter was torn up, and hire a new team of servants.

My landlord has found for me a gloomy woman who said she had been a cook in the German Embassy. Luter, who has been staying with me, shares my doubts. The other day I suggested that the lunch start with orange juice. The cook looked puzzled. "Instead of soup?" I said yes. She did serve the juice—boiling hot. Another time, after serving the first course, the servants disappeared. I found them planting flowers in the garden. When I remonstrated, the cook explained sullenly: "This is a vacant lot. We *must* plant on it."

Though I share her faith in victory gardens, out she will go in favor of a cook who will devote himself to horticulture at more convenient hours.

John Rich was right. This morning an informant called me up to say Ando was arrested on direct orders from Colonel R. S. Bratton, Military Intelligence. The reason we could find no record of his arrest was that both Ando and Matsuda were not "arrested" but "taken into protective custody." No other investigating agency was let in on the secret. Military Intelligence people are tightmouthed, but after four months of digging into the Ando story I do not have to rely on them for information. Despite the raid, the Dai-An Building was open, and the clerks were doing business. I did not go up.

For weeks Headquarters has been sharpening its axe for use on the *Yomiuri*. The matter is known to have gone up the official channels to General MacArthur himself, and received his blessings.

The *Yomiuri* has admittedly been a thorn in Headquarters' side. While most of the other newspapers have been induced to toe the line, the *Yomiuri* has remained militant. It has helped to get Shidehara out. It has taunted Yoshida. It has kept exposing the unsavory past of the war criminals now in power. It has backed the demonstrations as a democratic instrument of dissent. Occasionally it was shrill. Sometimes it was wrong. But this is a time of strident voices, a time of wrecking and reform. The *Yomiuri* has done more than its share to create a new Japan. What it has had to say, has influenced millions. But even more than that, it influenced other papers, by its own example, to champion reform and democracy.

In doing this, the *Yomiuri* has run afoul of our policy—not the one with which we marched into Japan ten months ago, but the new policy, whose outlines have been taking shape in the past ten weeks. We have now firmly allied ourselves with men and forces on which the *Yomiuri* has been waging war. But the axing is to be done not in the name of the new American policy, but for the sweet sake of "Free Speech." Although the union did sign an agreement last December whereby it shared in the formulation of editorial policy, the agreement, we are now saying, was undemocratic. It impinged on the right of publisher Baba to make the *Yomiuri* policy.

Sometime ago Baba presented his Board of Directors with an ultimatum to fire the six "trouble-makers," led by editor-in-chief Suzuki. The board refused to act. Yesterday, Baba went to see General Baker, Public Relations Officer. Baker, with justice, kept reiterating that he had nothing to do with the direction of the Japanese press. But when Baba stumbled reciting the six names, Baker picked up a slip of paper on his desk, read off the remaining names, and said, "Aren't those the men?"

Baba jubilantly returned to the *Yomiuri*, and according to a man who has been with him through most of the day, informed his staff that Baker had ordered him to fire the six men.

June 14, 1946   KARUIZAWA

This morning Walker, his assistant Haru Matsukata, and I left Tokyo for this mountain resort to look for furniture. We took a trailer along, just in case luck was with me.

It was a pleasant hundred-mile drive. The countryside was brown, and heavy with grain, and there was no look of want on its face. In the tiny, wet patches of paddy, women in baggy pants and conical straw hats tugged at green rice seedlings. In the wheat fields, farmers rubbed stalks tentatively, as farmers do the world over when the harvest is near.

The road picked its way between the fields until it found a village. Then it ran, pockmarked and dusty, between rows of busy little shops filled with the produce of the country—bamboo stools, wooden clogs and buckets, straw mats, cheap kitchen utensils hammered out of discarded oil cans. When the children heard the roar and rattle of our jeep, they rushed out to yell *herro* and *goota-bye*, and waved madly. There was delight in their faces, and none could tell that this technically is still an enemy land, and that this officially is a year of near-famine.

We weaved and circled around mountains until we emerged into the pine country, above a layer of damp, fluffy clouds. This was Karuizawa, the prewar retreat of the diplomats, the millionaires, and the rich demimondaines who could not stand the wilting summer heat of Tokyo; and the wartime refuge of the wealthy or cautious Japanese, and a small army of German and Italian diplomats, advisers, and spies.

We drove up a narrow, tree-lined road, and stopped before a Japanese inn where I had stayed before. The landlady greeted me like a long-lost son. She was small, wrinkled, and very cheerful. We ordered two charcoal braziers for cooking, and went upstairs to our two-room suite. Haru, who owns a house here and knows a lot of people, went out. Walker and I stretched out on the straw mats. The paper panels had been slid open, and I could look down at the old Buddhist temple across the alley, and smell the incense, heavy in the warm air. Little bare-bellied boys were playing baseball in the yard, and they called the play out in English—"strike one," "borr (ball) one."

I sank into nothingness, and the next thing I felt was a firm hand nudging me. A voice unmistakably American said, "Wake up." There were two military policemen, and they wanted us to get out, because the inn was off limits to Allied military personnel. We insisted that we were civilians. The argument was a draw. The MPs promised to take it up with their officer. Around dinnertime, while we were eating our stew of canned corned beef hash and string beans with chopsticks, a young lieutenant came in. He had just had orders from his colonel to let no civilians stay in Japanese inns.

I said, "Look. There's a GI hotel here, but we, as civilians, are not allowed to live there. Yet, as military personnel, we aren't allowed to stay in a Japanese inn. Where do we stay?"

The lieutenant sounded embarrassed. "The colonel," he said, "suggests the Goerder boarding house here. It's quite good." Walker cut in: "Goerder is the former gauleiter here. Wasn't he in Sugamo Prison for a while as a suspected war criminal?" The lieutenant said it might be the same man. Walker and I said we would have nothing to do with Goerder.

We spent the night in Haru's house, still boarded up from the war days. In the calm of the early night, we could hear a boy's thin little voice saying in German:

"Mamma, there are men in that empty house. What are they doing there?"

June 15, 1946   KARUIZAWA

Bought a complete set of beautiful wicker furniture for the living room and porch. With what we already have in the house, and with a couple of borrowed army cots, Sally ought to have enough to start with.

Before leaving for Tokyo, we called on Saburo Kurusu, the "peace envoy" sent to Washington on the eve of the war. I wanted to know if Kurusu was interested in selling his memoirs to the Chicago *Sun* Syndicate. Kurusu, a trim, handsome, confident man, said he was not yet ready to "tell all." His two beautiful daughters came down, and for an hour we talked small talk and pretended none of us was interested in politics. Kurusu told us of Hatoyama, who stayed here during the war. Hatoyama, Kurusu said, took his farming very seriously, and from time to time sent a gift of vegetables to the Kurusus.

"The society ladies here," Kurusu said, "used to complain about Hatoyama. They would say, 'How can you get any fertilizer for your garden, when Hatoyama-san wakes up with the sun, goes out on the cowpath and picks up in a tray all the dung he can find? By the time we get there, the path is all swept clean.'"

June 16, 1946   TOKYO

The head of the Tokyo Chefs' Guild today suggested to Roy that I might be able to hire the British embassy chef who used to be the favorite of Sir Robert L. Craigie, the last prewar ambassador. We drove out to the embassy compound and talked to the chef, whose name is Mogi. In five minutes I had hired a whole crew, including the chef's wife, who will be Sally's personal maid, and a junior maid. With the excellent gardener we already have, we are ready for Sally.

The new servants will spend the next fortnight giving the house a new cleaning. The gardener has already done a good job, terracing and landscaping the garden. The wisteria over the porch has broken out in buds, the flowers are in bloom, and the breeze from the bay mixes the aroma of the flowers with the smell of the incense drifting from a near-by temple. It will be a nice home.

June 23. 1946   TOKYO

Before Prince Konoye took poison six months ago, he wrote a thin memoir in which he detailed, blow by blow, Japan's entry into the war. One of its more apparent objectives was to show Tojo as an arch-villain and a plotter of wars. In contrast, Konoye himself was portrayed as a valiant fighter for peace.

On the basis of an item that came to me today, I am inclined to call the late prince an artful liar.

In September, 1940, *while Konoye was premier*, the Japanese Printing Bureau was ordered by the government to begin printing "Occupation Currency." These were Japanese military banknotes, for use primarily in the South Seas—the Philippines, Burma, Malaya and the Dutch East Indies.

In May, 1941, when Premier Konoye was "fighting for peace," the Printing Bureau began to ship the banknotes to the Bank of Japan for storage.

In November, 1941, just after Tojo succeeded Konoye as premier, a top secret order was issued to the Bank of Japan to turn over the bank notes to the Army disbursing offices.

From these facts just discovered by American investigators, it would appear that there was a continuity of policy, irrespective of whether peace-maker Konoye or villain Tojo was premier. This would also confirm anew that Japan did not go into aggression with her eyes shut. She prepared for it thoroughly and at length, with the army, the government, and Big Business working as a team.

This is an important point. It has a special bearing on the current efforts to show that Tojo and a few of his fellow-conspirators alone should be held guilty as war criminals. Tojo, God knows, is guilty enough. But the sight of all these men, from the emperor and Premier Yoshida on, jumping up and down with righteous indignation and saying, "He done it all by himself," is obscene.

Still more significant is the fact that many Americans have found it useful to swallow the new myth. Some of them—mostly the top-ranking men in Headquarters—realize that if they reject this thesis, they will have to admit that most of the men we maintain in power, including the emperor, should actually be tried as war criminals and hanged by the neck until dead.

The other group—primarily former isolationists—must adhere to the new myth if only to preserve its argument that Franklin Roosevelt "provoked" Japan with such measures as the oil embargo of July, 1941. Think of what happens to this thesis when one discovers that the Japanese were printing military currency for the Philippines fifteen months before the attack on Pearl Harbor.

June 24, 1946 TOKYO

Told today by two distressed Headquarters men that General MacArthur has in effect rejected Professor Edwards' master-blueprint for the destruction of the *zaibatsu*. The rejection, sent to Washington early this month, expressed agreement with most of the Edwards report "in principle," but insisted that a way less painful to Japan's economy could be found.

General MacArthur's critique, my informants said, reflects the feeling in top Headquarters that:

Any drastic steps taken now against the *zaibatsu* would seriously hamper the revival of Japan's economy, thus prolonging the period of social stress;

Any directives aimed at the *zaibatsu* would embarrass the Yoshida cabinet; and

These directives must give the *zaibatsu* a fair deal, and provide for the continuity of the Japanese business tradition.

June 27, 1946 YOKOHAMA

The three of us, Howard Handleman of International News Service, Tom Lambert of the Associated Press, and I, spent most of the day here, waiting for the S.S. "General Meigs"—and our wives. We managed to borrow staff sedans from the army, so that at least on the first day the women will have the comforts of civilization. After that it is back to the jeeps. Late in the afternoon, a colonel took pity on us and invited us to his apartment for drinks. We spent an eternity alternately drinking and chewing on our nails, until a lookout on the roof reported sighting the ship.

At breakneck speed we drove to the wharf, for another interminable wait until the ship slipped into the small inner harbor. Then we shouted and waved as we recognized, or thought we recognized, familiar faces on board, and tried to ask questions which could be asked with greater comfort in another half hour.

By the time we had unloaded all the hand baggage, from hat boxes to skis, it was mercifully dark, and Sally was spared the sight of the miles of ruin between Yokohama and Tokyo. We had been out of touch with each other ever since she left San Francisco, and now we were filling in the gaps of information, and saying the things that people say to each other after a long parting. We drove up the hill to the house, turned into the lighted, graveled driveway, and here was Mogi the chef, in an immaculate white coat, and the two women, in gay kimonos, bowed in welcome. As is only proper in Japan, Sally took her shoes off, and wandered into her new home.

July 2, 1946   TOKYO

For weeks officers at C.I. & E. have been working on a directive making it possible for the common man to criticize the emperor without going to jail for it. The draft made the required rounds until it reached the Chief of the Section. He killed it with the explanation that "this is not a propitious moment." Thus, for the time being, the emperor remains on the law books as an absolute, semidivine monarch.

This is in line with a hush-hush Washington order of which

there is much agitated talk here. The directive was issued to General MacArthur by SWINCC (State, War, and Navy Coordinating Committee) in mid-April, and it is so strikingly different from what we have been saying up to now as to indicate a sharp change in our policy in Japan.

The Washington order runs along these lines:

Although the United States favors ultimately the establishment of a republican form of government in Japan, the Japanese people themselves apparently favor the imperial system. Therefore, General MacArthur is instructed to assist the Japanese people in the development of a constitutional monarchy, and *preservation of the imperial system.*

A direct attack on the imperial system would weaken the democratic elements, and, on the contrary, strengthen the extremists, both Communist and militarist. *The Supreme Commander is, therefore, ordered to assist secretly in popularizing and humanizing the emperor.*

This will not be known to the Japanese people.

I have long known of the efforts of an American general here to persuade the Imperial Household Ministry to change its public relations policy. "You must advertise," he has been telling the Ministry. "Sell the emperor to the people."

And yet, I find the Washington order startling. For almost to the last day of the war, General MacArthur's Psychological Warfare officers were under orders to deal with the emperor as a war criminal. And, the general here notwithstanding, it is difficult to see the United States Army in the role of a public relations counsel to Hirohito, selling this jittery little man to his own people. In the early days of victory, expediency might have dictated the use of Hirohito to secure compliance with our orders. The new order goes far beyond the limits of expediency, into the realm of long-range, high policy which somehow impresses me as thoroughly undemocratic—and to use a contemporary cliché—thoroughly un-American.

Was "invited" today to call on Colonel W. S. Wood, Civil Intelligence Officer, in connection with the Ando case. Wood saw Walker yesterday, and threatened him with court-martial if Walker did not disclose his sources of information. Walker stood his ground. This afternoon, he joined me in the visit.

The colonel was obviously fishing. He wanted to know how much I knew of the involvement of U.S. Army officers in the Ando case, and where I obtained my information. I was prepared to tell the colonel all, except for the names of my informants. Some of them had themselves been Ando's guests at his "club." Others were subordinates of Ando's happy customers. I did not want them punished just because they had talked to me —especially since the army was doing nothing about some of the high-ranking men named by Ando himself.

Eventually the conversation got to the threats of court-martial against correspondents who refused to disclose their source of information. I told Wood I thought any correspondent—including me—would welcome a test. I would not challenge Wood's authority if national security were involved. But the Ando affair is a foul cesspool which had to be cleaned out whether the army is sensitive to exposure or not. Wood did not take me up.

The Ando affair is formally closed. Tried in a U.S. Provost Court, he was found guilty of failing to surrender firearms, of illegally possessing U.S. Post Exchange supplies, and of failing to obey orders to close his "club." The sentence was six months in jail and a fine of $3,300.

The first inkling we had of the trial came in General Baker's handout which took exception to the "sensational news stories which converted this case of disobedience of orders into one alleging involvement of Occupation officers." The handout admitted that "some Allied personnel patronized Ando's third-rate night club and, on occasion, he had distributed to his guests traditional gifts such as Japanese dolls and similar trinkets." But, it added, "a thorough investigation of all sources, including the press . . . failed to reveal the name of any military personnel that had illegal dealings with Ando."

Thus the Ando Affair, which was at the least a symptom of a deep spiritual corrosion in the Army of Occupation, and at the most a hint of a vast and powerful nationalist underground, has been trimmed down to the size of a petty larceny, an amusing tale of a petty racketeer who spent uncounted millions of yen for parties in "a third-rate night club," and for "traditional gifts such as Japanese dolls," so many of which were very live. The incredible ramifications of Ando's interests, from films and communications to the imperial court, have been blandly ignored. Ando was actually put in jail for the possession of a couple of pistols and twenty cartons of cigarettes.

July 11, 1946   TOKYO

Once again the *Yomiuri*, Japan's largest daily, has become a testing ground of our labor policies. This noon, after weeks of jockeying, 750 of its employees went on strike.

Spread over the strike lies the shadow of Major Daniel Imboden, Chief of the Press Division. A few days ago, representatives of Baba, publisher of *Yomiuri*, called on Imboden and discussed the impending strike with him. Whatever it was that Imboden said, Baba immediately summoned members of his staff, one by one, told them Imboden was behind him, and asked them to sign a statement supporting his stand against the union. The Japanese Labor Relations Committee, one of our better efforts in the field of labor, indicated that it did not like the smell of the procedure. Baba then informed it that, "in the opinion of

American authorities," the Labor Code was superseded by the "press code," drafted by Imboden.

Anyway, Baba hired some *gorotsuki,* or professional toughs, and waited for trouble. Walker and I went into the *Yomiuri* building this afternoon, and here were the *gorotsuki* standing guard at the door, and the walls were covered with the posters of both sides. We tried to see Baba, but he was out. We then went to the fourth floor, where the strike committee sat in session in a tiny room. Just outside of the door lay a large straw bag with 120 pounds of rice—a gift to the strikers. Summer is here, and most of the committee members were stripped to the waist and damp with sweat. At the head of the table, with his usual scowl, sat Kikunami, the *Asahi* editorial writer who is now forming the Congress of Industrial Unions.

The atmosphere in the small room changed from minute to minute, as messengers came in to report the latest news. Now it was word from the printing plant, where seven more men decided to join the walkout. The faces smiled, and there were shouts of Good, Good, and the warm air was saturated with confidence. But there was a glum silence when a report was brought in that Baba had called in key *Yomiuri* officials to discuss the formation of a company union.

Major Imboden is having a busy time. The liberal daily, *Minpo,* ran an editorial saying Baba sought to dominate the Newspaper Union. Imboden warned the paper that the comment was "one-sided." Long under pressure from Imboden, the daily is gradually modifying its progressive policy or using doubletalk allowing it to say what it feels needs to be said, and yet escape Imboden's wrath.

The *Jinmin Shimbun* is a Socialist paper, with a circulation of 250,000. One of its editors told me Imboden had warned the paper that it was following a "pro-Communist policy," and gave it until July 13 to change its ways, on fear of suppression. There was much brave talk of free speech and of defying the major. But courage oozed out. Yesterday's edition carried mostly innocuous "literary news." From now on the paper will pretend it is living in a nonpolitical Wonderland.

The *Hokkaido Shimbun*, in Japan's extreme north, has just gone through one of Imboden's famous purges. In all, 59 union members have been fired for being "Communist racketeers." The union, of course, is broken up. Imboden's dark view of the daily does not jibe with the official opinion of Headquarters, which less than a month ago said the daily was "comparatively conservative," and noted its strong editorial attacks on communism. My Japanese friends tell me the paper was one of Japan's most reputable provincial dailies. They think Imboden is simply union busting.

July 17, 1946   TOKYO

The *Yomiuri* strike is over, with the union defeated.

There really never was a fight. While the *Yomiuri* was on strike, other units of the Newspaper Union merely watched the show. So did other unions. And on the *Yomiuri* itself more than half the workers stayed out of the strike. What sympathy they might have had for the strikers, shrank with each reminder by Baba, the publisher, that Headquarters was behind him.

Baba has formed a company union, and yesterday ordered its members to drive the strikers out. Spearheaded by professional toughs, the small army forced its way into the composing room and threw the strikers out. Another force went up to the strike headquarters on the fourth floor, beat up the union people, and drove them out too. Dozens of Japanese policemen on the scene watched the fun, but did not intervene.

When I left the building, a few printers caught up with me. They said they wanted to tell the American people that fear alone impelled them to join the company union, and that their hearts were still with the strikers. An old printer added:

"General MacArthur doesn't know what Baba is doing. Please tell him. Tell him everything."

Left Tokyo by plane this morning for Hiroshima and Nagasaki to do a series of stories on the first anniversary of the atomic bombings. Our first stop was at this British base, near Hiroshima.

Early in the morning we drove out to Hiroshima, a painful two-hour ride over a washboard road. The destruction crept upon us slowly. In a hamlet we saw the first cracked walls. In another we saw a few wrecked houses. After that the signs of destruction multiplied, until we came to an area where nothing was erect, the bricks had been pulverized, and the soil was burned to a rusty brown. Eventually, we reached the river and the building on the bank where the first atomic bomb fell on the morning of August 6, 1945. The building looked like an observatory and it still retained some of its shape, but its walls were shattered, the roof and the ceilings had collapsed, and the metal webbing in the walls hung limply, with bits of plaster still adhering in little clumps. The bridge near by looked as if a powerful hand had pushed it sideways cracking the concrete and bending the metal.

We crossed the bridge and drove to the biggest of the surviving buildings. It was an eight-story department store that now apparently housed many other establishments. Most of the building front was covered with two tremendous, illustrated posters advertising the arrival of normalcy: the moving pictures, *Casablanca* and *Babes on Broadway*. The babes were fleshy and scantily dressed, and they looked like cruel caricatures against the injured building behind them, or the shabby people below.

The City Hall was a large, low, concrete building standing alone in a vast, unpeopled, unhoused stretch. The windows had all been knocked out, and few of them had been replaced. Inside, the plaster had been knocked off, and even now, a year after the explosion, it crunched underfoot. We looked for the mayor but could not find him, and finally talked to his deputy. He told us the population, which was 320,000 before the bomb fell, and then dropped to five or six thousand the week after, was now up to 170,000. Most of them lived outside the town and came into Hiroshima from habit, or memory, or hope.

The Japanese spoke in a low, emotionless voice. "We figure 66,000 people died, and twice as many were hurt. We had 75,000 houses in this town. Two-thirds of them were burned down, and most of the rest collapsed. Back on Mount Hiji . . . " He pointed at a mountain overlooking the city. "Back there, trees a foot thick were snapped. Rice paddies eight miles away withered and died. The heat bleached stone, and etched shadows of objects on the walls. There was a man on a ladder. The atomic rays left the imprint of his body on the wall, but we never did find him. . . . "

The city had drawn a five-year plan of reconstruction. But a year after, the reconstruction was largely confined to clearing the streets. The government, the deputy mayor complained, had done next to nothing. The prefectural authorities were only little better. Only after a prod from the British Command, did they dip into their stocks of Japanese Army lumber to provide 15,000 "prefabricated houses"—a few boards, a few frames, and a blueprint—for Y.3,600 ($233) apiece. They also gave each household Y.1,000, or enough at the prevailing prices for a hundred eggs. Not all in Hiroshima could afford a prefabricated house. Those who could not, scrounged around for rusty sheets of corrugated iron and a few bricks and built themselves a home.

Hiroshima ate poorly. After the bomb came a typhoon and floods which ruined the crops. Supplies from the outside were irregular. The people here feel forgotten, and they daydream of American largesse, to make up for the American-made damage.

"Last month," said the deputy mayor, "we finished a month-long clean-up campaign in one of the city districts. We found a thousand dead. Sometimes people begin to clear the ground to build new homes, and they find bodies, or just several limbs."

We left the City Hall and went out again, into the heat and the strange, unidentifiable odor. A badly battered street car, with the black marks of fire still on it, ran by, with passengers hanging off the platforms. The electric wires have been repaired, but the metal poles which support them were bent and twisted into grotesque shapes, and some of them looked like floor mops, with the old, torn wire hanging off the top. The trees were black and lifeless, and the grass, coming up in small splotches, looked tired.

We walked to the Red Cross Hospital, a white building now badly scarred. The doctor in charge told us that the bulk of "atomic patients" had been released, and only ten remained. But plastic surgeons were still working overtime, grafting fresh skin on faces burned past recognition, and dozens still came in to complain of a strange fatigue.

"Who can tell what it is?" said the doctor thoughtfully. "Perhaps imagination. Perhaps lack of food. Possibly the result of atomic radiation. We know so little."

He recalled the morning of the blast. He was knocked out and hurt, but when people, burned or bleeding, started pouring in, he went into the operating room and worked there in a mess of blood and dust and plaster. He worked all day and night, and prayed for the end of the stream of injured people, but they kept coming. He finally collapsed of weariness, and when he woke up, more patients were waiting for him.

Most of the people, he said, were burned by a heat wave. The next cause of injuries was broken glass, and collapsing buildings and wires. The hospital building itself showed graphically what happened that day. As the bomb exploded, it radiated heat waves which traveled in all directions. The waves were strong enough to blow down wooden structures and bend metal window frames, as they did in the hospital. Everything that could be bent was bent outward from the point of explosion. People whose bodies were not exposed to the heat waves often escaped with minor injuries. Those who were exposed had patterns impressed on their skin where buttons, or window frames, or tree branches interposed themselves between their bodies and the heat. Radioactive sand had blown into wells, and thousands suffered from "atomic diarrhea," and many died.

We talked to a young woman who had been pregnant at the time of the explosion. Her face and hands were burned to a deep red, and her skin was scarred and wrinkled into pink, uneven folds. But she had borne her child, and he lay next to her and gurgled. Safe from the heat wave in her womb, he now looked normal. We told the woman the child was beautiful, and she smiled, as mothers do, in pride and pleasure.

Again we wandered into the streets, and looked for people to talk to, and found few. Here and there a family, with bare hands or with crude tools, was patiently clearing a spot for a foundation. Women fed their infants, or washed rice, or struggled with a charcoal brazier. A small boy cried. An old man was watering a tiny vegetable patch on the edge of a vast rubble-covered lot.

We went back to the jeeps parked in front of the City Hall, and this time there were a few youngsters clustered around them. We asked one if he had been hurt. He said he was out of town, but there were many boys and girls in his class who had been here, and they had scars.

"They look terrible," he said gravely. "We have great pity for them."

We asked him the inevitable question. "What do you think of Americans?" He looked at the other boys, at the rubble, at us. For a child of twelve, he was giving it much thought.

"The Americans are all right," he said. "They are very kind."

August 15, 1946   TOKYO

A year ago today, the emperor's voice, recorded on a wax disc, announced to his people the end of the war.

In vain, on this historic day for Japan, I looked for soul-searching, for penitence, for a sign that the lessons of defeat had been taken to heart. The premier has issued a statement filled with generalities. The press has contented itself with pious phrases. The emperor communed with the spirits of his ancestors in the palace shrine.

But if there is no repentance, there is subservience—made uglier by the smugness with which the victors accept it.

The *Nippon Times*, the mouthpiece of the Foreign Office and the imperial Court, came out with a saccharine editorial: "Even those who welcomed the surrender most ardently could not have realized how great would be the blessings which were to follow. . . . It surpasses the rosiest hopes which the most optimistic ones dared hold a year ago. . . ."

The front page carried General MacArthur's enthusiastic endorsement of the Land Reform Bill, which his Headquarters had rammed down the throat of the unwilling Japanese government. ("It is gratifying that the present government has shown courage and determination. . . .") The page was topped by a large photograph of the general entering his black Cadillac. The caption began simply:

"General Douglas MacArthur, mighty man of war . . ."

This would have been a good day for the Japanese press to begin telling the people the real and complete story of the war and defeat. A year has gone by since surrender, but little of the story has yet been told.

Early in the Occupation, General Dyke's Section made an attempt to tell it in a series of broadcasts and newspaper articles. But the American officers who wrote them did not know all the facts, and, what is worse, they helped to whitewash some of the war criminals who had taken over the government. Some good material on the rise and growth of militarism in Japan has appeared in the *Yomiuri* and other newspapers and magazines. There have been three or four good books. Some excellent information has been dug up by the interrogators of the U.S. Strategic Bombing Survey in interviews with some seven hundred Japanese officials. Finally, some data is beginning to dribble in from the War Crimes trials.

But no one has yet thought of collating this information either for the victors, so that they can understand much of what is happening here today, or for the losers, so that they can prevent the recurrence of what has happened in the past. It may well be that the public, both here and at home, is indifferent. But much of the blame must also fall on the rulers of Japan, who have kept their secrets well. Unlike Germany and Italy, Japan has had few politicans or generals ready to tell all to save their skins or make some money. Nor have there been any archives left waiting for the Americans. The Japanese spent the two weeks between the surrender and our arrival in an orgy of burning the printed and written word.

For eight months now I have been collecting the shreds that escaped destruction. Put together, I have hoped, they would tell me the secret story of Japan's war-making and defeat. But the story I have is still incomplete. All it supplies is a glimpse into the relentless struggle for war, peace, and political survival that went on for four years in the shadow of the throne.

Even to those who know the history of Japanese intrigue, it is an incredible story. Constantly I found it necessary to remind myself that the evidence was unimpeachable. For the story of plot and counterplot unfolded before me was in the best tradition of E. Phillips Oppenheim. Incomplete as they were, my files contained the records of four major conspiracies, four or five murder plots, a few minor intrigues, and at least one attempt at an armed *coup d'état*. Sometimes the conspiracies merged or overlapped, and then there were plots within plots, and it was difficult to draw the borderlines between them.

The most remarkable feature of the secret history was its record of dissension within Japan's ruling clique. Some of its members foresaw the defeat and opposed the war. Others wanted to quit after the initial victories, when the quitting seemed good. Still others wavered and lost heart as the defeats began to multiply. What conspiracies there were were peace conspiracies, and their scope widened as Japan's strength waned. The army alone, with few exceptions, stood resolute. Its prime weapon against the peace plotters was fear. For, as every conspirator knew, it would have been easy for the army to arrange a murder or even a military *coup*, and this knowledge made the plotters timid, and silenced their tongues when a courageous stand was needed.

There was something else worth noting in the plots. They were all confined to the thin upper layer of Japan's society. Except when a few of them were drawn in as handymen, the people of Japan neither took part in the conspiracies nor even knew of them. No liberal ideas ever entered the plotters' minds. They were merely concerned with the preservation of the *status quo ante*, now endangered by defeat. Each group of plotters, in its own way, saw Japan's salvation in the maintenance of monarchy, absolute and feudal. All else could perish, but if the emperor survived defeat, the fabric of old Japan would with time mend itself.

Japan's ruling clique, out of which sprang the conspiracies of the war, was comprised of many elements.

At the moment Tojo and his shabby gang of military fanatics, ambitious hangers-on, and political manipulators were at the helm. Tojo seemed closer to being a dictator than any man in Japan's recent history. He was, at the same time, Premier, Minister of War, Interior and Munitions, head of the totalitarian Imperial Rule Assistance Association, and, for a few months, Chief of General Staff. He controlled the army and the police, the making of bullets and the shaping of minds.

But this picture was only partly true. Tojo governed only at the sufferance of the other ruling groups—Big Business, the navy, the entrenched bureaucrats, and the Elder Statesmen. He was also bound by political rules and conventions that could be traced to feudal days. It was permissible to cause an opponent to be murdered; it was impermissible to make a formal promise to the throne and fail to keep it.

The Elder Statesmen were mostly former premiers or Court officials. Most of them were old, and few of them held official positions. But their power lay in their control of the emperor-symbol. They helped to decide the retirement of one premier, and the choice of another. Superb political puppeteers, they put words in the emperor's mouth and inspired actions in his name, and used both to maintain the kind of Japan they preferred. The Elder Statesmen were not opposed to war. They were opposed to a weakening of monarchy, and of their own position. They were in alliance with Big Business, the bureaucrats and the navy "moderates" not because they abhorred militarism, but because army extremists were wont to engage in gambles in which the element of risk was too great. It is important to remember this, for all that follows was colored by the inter-relations among the elements which composed the ruling group.

I am convinced that the Japanese went into the war with most of the tactical details of aggression worked out beforehand. Their web of espionage extended from Pearl Harbor to Kuibishev. Their puppets were waiting in nearly every land they coveted. Their stocks of strategic materials—in most cases adequate for a two years' war—had been laid.

But together with this attention to minute detail came a most astounding absence of strategic objectives. The Japanese High Command did not know what it wanted, or where it would stop. The war was a gamble, and in a world already at war, military gambles seemed inviting. The army was mired in China, and it thought it could extricate itself by tossing some more chips on the table of history.

It placed its chips on two numbers at once. One went on Indo-China, linked only by the most tenuous bonds to defeated France. Japanese troops here, according to Japanese testimony, were always intended for a strike at Malaya, Burma and the Dutch East Indies. If England surrendered, all this and India as well would fall into Japan's waiting hands.

But in June, 1941, Hitler attacked Russia, and the officers in the Army General Staff in Tokyo began to talk of "missing the Soviet bus." Tremendous reinforcements were poured into Manchuria. Everyone in the War Ministry and General Staff (in a curious parallel to a similar forecast by General George Marshall) gave Russia three months on the outside. The fall of Moscow would be the signal for marching into Siberia. But in another parallel to our own experience with Colonel Philip Faymonville, the Japanese military attaché in Moscow began to file warnings against underestimating Russia's capacity for resistance. By September, 1941, when the German advance into Russia fell behind the time table supplied to Japan, Tokyo began to read the messages from Moscow with greater care.

"The motto, 'Don't miss the Soviet bus,' which prevailed in the General Staff offices two months ago," a Japanese general wrote later, "passed out unnoticed. In its stead, a new one gained fashion. 'Those who conquer the Sunda Islands [in the East Indies], can conquer the world.' "

Thought of war on Russia was abandoned for the moment, and the General Staff devoted itself to expansion southward. So great was the military fear that some sort of an accord might be reached at a proposed mid-Pacific conference of Prince Konoye and President Roosevelt that arrangements had actually been discussed for a general and an admiral accompanying Konoye to commit *hara-kiri* in protest if and when agreement was reached.

Japan's strategic thinking on the coming war was marred by three errors. The first was the curious failure of Japanese Intelligence to estimate the American industrial potential and will to win. The second was the failure to understand the possibilities of air power. The last was the inability to forecast the striking power of American submarines. If nothing else did, these three errors proved Japan's undoing.

There was a rash of minor plots—peace or murder—almost from the first month of the war. They all failed, and they were important only as a symptom.

The first of these minor conspiracies was hatched in the spring of 1942 by Prince Konoye and Prince Naruhiko Higashikuni, until then known mainly as a military figurehead. The plotters wanted to overthrow Tojo's cabinet and make peace overtures to Washington. Japan was then at the height of her success and power, and the two princes felt the best time to bargain was before America re-armed. The plot found few adherents, and even some of these came from the lunatic fringe of the ultranationalist movement. The conspiracy quickly fizzled out. But a hint of it had leaked out, and Tojo put Konoye under surveillance.

Equally futile were the murder plots. Some of them were inspired by General Ishihara who hated Tojo and, anyway, felt that the enemy to attack was Russia and not the United States. Another plot was led by Seigo Nakano, probably the best known of Japan's Fascists. Founder of a reactionary political party and an able spellbinder, Nakano had visited Hitler and Mussolini, and aspired to be the Fuehrer of Japan. But German fascism is not indigenous to Japanese nationalist soil. When Nakano's hopes came to nothing, he organized a plot to kill Tojo. Nakano was seen visiting Prince Konoye's residence, and was arrested shortly afterward. One day the gendarmes took him out of his cell and drove him home. There, they waited until he disembowelled himself. I do not know what means they used to persuade him to commit *hara-kiri*.

It was not until the summer of 1943 that the first major conspiracy of the war began to take shape. This was the "Navy Conspiracy," which ran like a red thread across the secret history of the war. In terms of decisive action, this plot was barren. But it had a profound influence on other conspiracies and on the course of the Pacific conflict.

Before Japan entered the war, the navy estimated its staying capacity at two years of combat. Many factors went into this estimate, but the most important of them was fuel. December 7, 1943, was the navy's deadline for victory, and the admirals agreed that if no decisive victory came by then it was time to start worrying. The admirals began to worry months earlier.

The prime brain behind the "Navy Conspiracy" belonged to Admiral Mitsumasa Yonai, the bulky, whisky drinking leader of the so-called "moderates," who objected to the army's pace of aggression as too precipitous. In September, 1943, Yonai summoned Rear Admiral Sokichi Takagi, of the Navy Headquarters, and ordered him to make a secret study of the course of the war. A gifted research man, Takagi went at his job thoroughly. In the five months that it took him to complete his inquiry, Takagi had considered every factor from shipping losses and morale to the likelihood of large-scale American air raids on Japan.

In February, 1944, Takagi reported orally to Yonai that there was *no possibility of victory, and that a peace treaty should be sought, even at the cost of abandoning China, Korea, and Formosa.*

The "co-ordinator" of most of the plots was Marquis Kido, the shoddy Court politician with Machiavellian ambitions who is now on trial. Kido was his monarch's keeper, and no plot could succeed without his support. Thus, though few plotters trusted him, nearly all had to confide in him. He weaved from one conspiracy to another, listening, watching, saying little, a shadowy and sinister figure.

Like his old patron, Konoye, Kido was a nationalist with sympathy for the military day dreamers. He, too, wanted Japan to spread from the Rockies to the Urals. But this balding, little man, who looked much like an owl, was also an ally of the *zaibatsu*, a confidant of the Elder Statesmen, the emperor's active mind. To Kido, preservation of monarch—of the whole political *status quo*—was far more important than a military victory a continent away. Late in 1943, surreptitious word had come to him from Admiral Keisuke Okada, a well-informed Elder Statesman, that victory was escaping Japan's grasp. Kido did not turn against the army. He did not until the last minute, if one can trust a diary he failed to destroy. But he did join the Elder Statesmen and the admirals in seeking a way out.

Those who wanted peace, and those who felt the war might be lost because of Tojo's incompetence, agreed that Tojo had to go. All they needed was an excuse.

The excuse was provided by the United States. In mid-June, 1944, U.S. forces landed on Saipan, and China-based B-29's began to pound southern Japan. The debacle on Saipan came as a personal blow to Tojo. He had just transferred some crack units from Manchuria to the island, and he had been going around puffed up like a peacock and saying, "Let them take Saipan *now!*"

The American landing yielded a new crop of minor plots. Most of these sought to return to Japan from the field some "strong" general who could challenge Tojo's control. Typical of these intrigues was the effort of Nobusuke Kishi, a member of Tojo's "Kitchen Cabinet," to bring back from Singapore a doddering field marshal who had the advantage of being senior to Tojo in the rigid army hierarchy.

But all these little plots were overshadowed by the second major conspiracy—the so-called "Okada Conspiracy."

This plot was born in the agile mind of the 77-year-old Admiral Okada, who only eight years earlier had had to disguise himself in a woman's kimono to escape from army rebels. Okada's goal was to oust Tojo and form a new cabinet, with himself as premier. Okada started by telling Tojo, at a heated and secret conference of the ruling clique called to hear reports from Saipan, that Tojo was holding too many important posts for the country's good. Tojo, in effect, told Okada to go jump in the lake.

However, on June 23, 1944, more bad news had reached Tokyo. This time it was the defeat of the Japanese Combined Fleet. Feeling much less secure, Tojo decided on a bluff. He called on Kido and announced that he was ready to resign, "if a promising successor is available." Kido remained noncommittal. Tojo then played on the strings of fear which, he well knew, dominated the lives of these men. He let the word pass around that he was prepared to carry out a military *coup d'état* if he was forced out.

Simultaneously, Tojo placed Admiral Okada under surveillance. The old admiral felt he had to act before it was too late. He managed to smuggle a message to Admirals Yonai and Nobumasa Suetsugu. The message offered the Navy porfolio to Yonai; Suetsugu, an old firebrand, would become Chief of Naval Staff. Both accepted. If the conspiracy succeeded, this would be a cabinet of admirals.

Next, Okada confided in Baron Kiichiro Hiranuma, a former premier and one of the most influential Elder Statesmen. It must have been a dramatic meeting, for at one time or another both men had been the quarry of army killers, and they knew the risks inherent in their talk. They agreed that the best stratagem was to get all the Elder Statesmen to sign a memorandum to the emperor, appealing for the dismissal of Tojo. Sometime later, Prince Konoye joined in the conversations. He agreed with the plan.

Kido refused to become involved. "As Lord Keeper of the Privy Seal," he said, "I must remain outside of this. Anyway, I'm afraid Tojo will stage a *coup* if this goes through."

The intrigue consumed nearly three weeks, and the conspirators were not getting anywhere. A blunder by Tojo rescued them. He called on Kido, to announce that he had decided to reorganize his cabinet. He would take in two more admirals, including Yonai.

At Tojo's insistence, Kido reported the impending changes to the emperor. Once the reshuffle was completed and the navy was made happy with patronage, Tojo would be ready to crush the "Okada Conspiracy."

But Tojo reckoned without the wily minds behind the throne. The conspirators met clandestinely with Kido, and found the one fatal flaw in Tojo's plan. Tojo had assured the emperor that Yonai would serve in the renewed cabinet. Suppose Admiral Yonai refused to come in? Would that not be a bad breach of Tojo's promise to the emperor?

Another secret meeting was held. Admiral Yonai, the planner of the First, or "Navy Conspiracy," was present. The authors of the Second, or "Okada Conspiracy" presented the issue to him. He assured them he would go along.

When word of Admiral Yonai's decision reached Tojo, he saw no way out for himself. In a way, he was a victim of a feudal convention. He had made a pledge to the emperor, and could not keep it. Now he could either let loose his young assassins, or resign.

On July 16, 1944, he summoned his ministers and asked for their resignations. But his spies had already discovered the plot of his good friend Kishi to bring the rival field marshal from Singapore, and the knowledge of the betrayal hurt. As the meeting ended, Tojo turned to Kishi and said bitterly:

"You, doublecrosser! You and Kido!"

That night, Tojo packed his papers and moved out of the premier's residence to the War Minister's official home. The next morning, the people of Japan were told officially that the man who had dominated their lives for five years was out.

Now Admiral Okada confidently expected to be the new premier, and perhaps bring the second peace conspiracy to a happy culmination. But he was sorely disappointed. When the Elder Statesmen met with Kido to choose Tojo's successor, Kido turned thumbs down on Okada—or on any other admiral.

"If we pick an admiral," he argued, "the army will take it as an affront. It will stage an armed rebellion, and then all will be lost. The only thing we can do is choose another general."

The admirals and the Elder Statesmen argued in vain. Kido was adamant, as he was adamant three years earlier in forcing through Tojo's selection as premier. The choice now fell on Tojo's rival, General Kuniaki Koiso, known variously as "The Tiger of Korea" and the "Champion Bald-head of Japan." The peace conspirators were not happy, but they were too unsure of themselves to risk a wave of assassinations by army fanatics.

Properly coached by Kido, the emperor instructed the new premier to "reconsider the situation" so as to bring the war to an end. Obtuse Koiso, who has long specialized in continental aggression, did not understand. He promptly issued a call for the last ounce of energy to win the war.

One of Koiso's first acts was to choose Admiral Yonai, one of the peace conspirators, as his Deputy Premier and Navy Minister. Another was to establish the Supreme War Direction Council (SWDC). Consisting of six regular members—the Premier, the Ministers of Foreign Affairs, War and Navy, and the Army and Navy Chiefs of Staff—SWDC became in effect the Inner War Cabinet, with direct access to the emperor. For the first time now the peace-makers, headed by Yonai, and the bitter-enders, led by Koiso, faced each other across a conference table.

But the intrigue went on. Once again, Admiral Yonai picked up the thread of the "Navy Conspiracy." He summoned Rear Admiral Takagi, and ordered him to resume his secret survey. Takagi later told American interrogators that his study included such questions as (1) how to secure the army's consent to end the war; (2) the possible Allied peace terms; (3) public opinion and morale should the government seek peace; and (4) means of reaching the emperor, and working through him to achieve peace.

The plotting admirals began an educational campaign. They started holding briefing sessions on Japan's military position for such people as Marquis Kido, Prince Konoye, Admiral Okada, Matsudaira, former ambassador to London who was now Minister of the Imperial Household, and Baron Hiranuma. Cautious word of the conspiracy was slipped in to the Chief and Vice-Chief of the Naval General Staff. Neither did anything to halt it. An effort was even made to win over the army. Some army men were persuaded that the war was lost, and it was necessary to seek peace. But when these officers approached the new war minister, he balked. Fear and discipline ended the dissidence within the army.

Thus, the peace conspirators were now set squarely against the army, and none of them really dared to do anything for fear of arrest, or assassination, or even a military uprising. The only hope in view seemed to lie in the use of the emperor-symbol. An imperial command to end the war might stop the military fanatics where nothing else could.

Admiral Okada began a series of talks with Kido to see what could be done. Kido began to talk to the emperor. The conspiracy was about to enter a new stage.

Meanwhile, the United States forces kept hacking at Japan's defense perimeter. Guam was retaken in July, 1944. Japanese lines to the raw materials in the south were slashed by U.S. aircraft and submarines. Japanese troops ran short of supplies and ammunition. The Japanese air force was reduced to a shadow of its former size, and it had no more good pilots left. Fuel for both the navy and the air force was running desperately low. Things got to be so bad, Japanese officers testified later, that all over the vast southern front, hundreds of planes were grounded for lack of gasoline.

Washington decided that the time had come for a new big jump toward Japan. The Joint Chiefs of Staffs ordered a landing on Leyte for October 20, 1944.

To the Japanese General Staff, the projected American move was hardly a mystery. For six days early in September, the U.S. Task Force 38 roamed the Philippine waters, in what was obviously a pre-invasion raid. The loss of the Philippines would have been catastrophic to the Japanese war machine, which depended so much on the oil, rubber and the metal ores of Southeast Asia. The Japanese admirals had to make a fateful decision. What it was, was later explained by a General Staff admiral to American interrogators:

"By the time . . . you had begun to land on Leyte, we realized fully that it would be impossible for us to maintain a battle fleet in Japanese waters subjected to bombing. Therefore, we decided to commit our entire fleet to the Leyte campaign . . . with the knowledge that we would lose most of it. But it was worth it if we could prevent conquest of the Philippines. . . ."

Though counseled by desperation, the Japanese move was cannily plotted, and came so near to success that the memory of it must still send a shudder down the spine of many an American admiral. The Leyte battle has been fully described in American documents, but briefly this was its course:

The Japanese split their fleet into three forces. One came from the south, the second in the center, and the third, acting as a decoy, came from the open seas to the north. The decoy worked well, and Task Force 38 dashed north, leaving the beaches and the skies of Leyte unprotected. Meanwhile, the Japanese Center Fleet, slipping through the San Bernardino Strait undetected, came within seventeen miles of our Seventh Fleet and opened an attack. The Seventh Fleet had just caught the Japanese Southern Force in a trap in the narrow Surigao Strait, and very nearly wiped it out. But as a result the fleet was low on fuel and ammunition and in no shape to meet the new challenge. Our escort carriers, shielded only by a thin screen of destroyers, were being picked off by Japanese gunfire. Short of bombs and torpedoes, carrier planes tried dummy runs over the Japanese fleet, in an effort to frighten it off. Three American destroyers were lost in a suicidal attempt to sink the heavier Japanese units. Our difficulties were compounded when swarms of Japanese planes came over for suicidal dives at U.S. ships—the first large-scale *kamikaze* attack.

To many Americans it seemed that night as if the end was near. Two of our escort carriers had been sunk, and the others had been damaged. Our destroyers had either been sunk or were driven off. Nothing now lay between the Japanese fleet and our helpless transports and the troops on the Leyte beaches.

Then, at 9:24 A.M. of October 25, 1944, came one of those providential turns which defy explanation. With victory in his grasp, the commander of the Japanese Center Fleet ordered a retreat. At that moment, Japan irrevocably lost the war. For the next four or five days, *kamikaze* pilots continued to make a nightmare for our navy. But it was too late.

The fiasco at Leyte cost the Japanese most of their fleet. Inevitably, it supplied a new impetus to the peace conspiracy in Tokyo. All through December, 1944, admirals, courtiers, and Elder Statesmen met in secret conferences. What is more important, Kido had prevailed on the emperor to lend an ear to the conspirators.

In February, 1945, one after another, the plotters trekked to the palace to expound their views. They told the emperor defeat was near, and Japan should seek peace at once.

The curtain was now ready to rise on the Third, or "Konoye Conspiracy."

Back on November 24, 1944, the first of the B-29 attacks which finally broke Japan's back was launched from Saipan. This was a high-altitude daylight raid aimed at the aircraft plants in Tokyo. But our reserve of B-29's was still small, and for months attacks could be mounted on an average of only one every five days.

For the people of Japan the turning point of the war came on March 9, 1945. That night, 300 B-29's heavily laden with "fire jelly," were sent over Tokyo. They carried no armament or ammunition, and they flew low.

"The storm of fire," the Tokyo Radio said the next day, "swept whole districts. Only here and there blackened walls of the rare stone building remained standing. . . . After the first incendiaries fell, clouds formed and were lit up from below with a pink light. From them emerged Super-Fortresses, flying uncannily low. . . . The city was bright as at sunrise. . . . That night we thought the whole of Tokyo was reduced to ashes."

That night, according to Japanese figures, 78,000 people died; 270,000 buildings were burned down; and 1,500,000 persons were left homeless. Important munitions plants and dumps were destroyed. The raid, said an official, "caused the morale of the people to sink down to the lowest ebb."

Meanwhile, another blow was being prepared for Japan. This came on April Fool's Day, with a landing on Okinawa. The Japanese met it with a furious counteroffensive by *kamikaze* planes. Although the people back in the United States knew nothing of this, the enemy attacks were so effective and our naval losses so high that for days the U.S. Navy was on the brink of pulling out of the Okinawa waters, leaving our forces ashore without naval protection. But sustained raids on Japanese airfields—and our greater stamina—enabled us to hold out.

Once again the Japanese Navy was facing a dilemma. It let the counsel of despair provide the solution. This is the way Admiral Soemu Toyoda, former Commander-in-Chief of the Navy, put it:

"The fleet situation became very acute early in 1945. . . . Any large-scale operations requiring heavy supplies of fuel became almost out of the question. On April 7-8, 1945, when the battleship Yamato was sent out with a dozen or more destroyers to Okinawa, we questioned whether it had a fifty-fifty chance. Even in assembling this squadron, we had a very difficult time getting the necessary 2,500 tons of fuel oil. But it was felt that even if the squadron did not have a fifty-fifty chance, nothing was to be gained by letting those ships lie idle in home waters. . . . "

With the fleet lost, with the cities in smoking ashes, with

the people aware for the first time that the war was lost—and with Germany dying—a new peace conspiracy came into being.

This time, the chief plotter was Prince Konoye, and most of his handymen were relatively unimportant figures. Konoye's mind, never clear on major issues, was now in a whirl. He had always been close to the army, including its most lunatic segments. Much of his own political philosophy had been colored by contacts with these fanatics. But he was also convinced of the impending disaster, and fearful of its effects on the whole social and political fabric of Japan.

For a time, Konoye apparently toyed with the idea of getting friendly ultranationalists to assassinate the army leaders who opposed peace. He abandoned this project in favor of a shrewder plan. He would get one extremist army camp to war on another. His choice was General Jinzaburo Mazaki, one of the noted figures of Japan's nationalist dementia of the 'thirties. Mazaki had been one of the wire-pullers behind the military rebellion of 1936, and had been arrested. Now he was living in retirement, and nursing his old hatreds for his rivals within the army command.

Konoye's plot was simple. He would get the emperor to name him premier, and he in turn would name Mazaki war minister. Yoshida, a follower of Konoye, would become foreign minister.

Konoye then went to work on a petition to the emperor. He worked on it for a long time, with the aid of two friends. Some knowledge of the plot came to me from one of these two men, an old and pathetic figure nursing his part in history and trying desperately to understand why he was no longer in it.

Konoye spent the night of February 13, 1945, with Yoshida, putting the finishing touches on the plot and on the petition to the throne. The next day Konoye saw the emperor, for the first time in three years. The emperor was cordial. Konoye began with the statement that defeat was inevitable, and apologized for failing to prevent the war.

He then launched into a statement which can best be described as a compound of wild fancy and political acumen.

Konoye's intent was to frighten the emperor, but it is quite possible that he believed much of what he said.

"A defeat," he said, "is a serious stain on our history. However, we can accept it as long as we can maintain our imperial system. Public opinion in America and Britain, on the whole, does not yet demand a fundamental change in that system. What we have to fear, therefore, is not so much a defeat as a Communist revolution which might take place in the event of defeat.

"Conditions, both internal and external, point to the danger of such revolution. In the first place, there has been a notable ascendancy of Soviet Russia. In the light of her recent activities in Europe, we must assume that she has not abandoned the hope of bolshevizing the entire world. . . .

"At home, potentially dangerous factors include the rapid deterioration of living conditions; increase in the voice of labor; rise of pro-Soviet feelings as enmity against America and Britain mounts; attempts by an extremist group in the army to achieve radical changes in internal policies; and disguised activities of the Communists behind both the military and the bureaucrats.

"A majority of younger officers seems to think that the present form of government is compatible with communism. . . . The Communists are influencing them with the theory that, even under communism, Japan can maintain the imperial system.

"I have now come to doubt seriously whether the whole series of events from the Manchurian Incident [in 1931] to the present war has not been what they have purposefully planned. It is a well-known fact that they openly declared the goal of the Manchurian war was to achieve drastic reforms in domestic affairs. . . . Of course, the 'reform' sought by the military may not necessarily be a Communist revolution, but the bureaucrats and civilians (both left and right) who are collaborating with the military definitely intend to bring about such a revolution.

"In the last few months the slogan 'Hundred Million Die Together' has become increasingly louder, seemingly among the right-wing people, but it has its real basis in the activities of the Communists.

"Under such circumstances, the longer we continue the war the greater will be the danger of revolution. We should, therefore, stop the war as soon as possible."

Shown that his throne was in jeopardy, the emperor for the first time displayed acute interest. He demanded to know how the conspiracy of the generals, now proven to be Communists, could be stopped.

Konoye said: "The army must be purged from within. Your Majesty must yourself choose the man to carry out this purge. But it is obvious that such a project requires a man of great strength. Such a man as General Mazaki. He has been accused of complicity in the military *coup* of 1936. An investigation I have made shows that Mazaki has been a victim of an army plot."

Konoye discussed no more details of his conspiracy. He had hoped for more talks with the emperor, who seemed so receptive. And besides, there was a third man at the interview. Right behind the emperor stood Marquis Kido. Konoye no longer trusted his old friend. He hoped to manage a talk with the emperor without Kido.

Konoye's distrust of Kido was not misplaced.

On April 8, 1945, when our troops already held a secure beachhead on Okinawa, Premier Koiso was forced out.

Konoye now expected a call from the palace. But the call did not come. Kido, Admiral Okada, and Baron Hiranuma went to someone else—the seventy-eight-year-old Baron Kantaro Suzuki, a retired admiral, for long a Court official and maker of cabinets, and a clever political manipulator. Suzuki was reluctant. The three callers told him, in appropriately hushed tones, of Konoye's plot to purge the army .

"If you turn the post down, Konoye will get it," they argued. "He will bring in Mazaki, who will carry out a purge. Inevitably, this will produce a bloody incident, the outcome of which no one can foretell."

Suzuki accepted, and heard the emperor's unequivocal

command to "make every effort to bring the war to a conclusion as quickly as possible." But Suzuki was ever mindful of patriotic assassins. While, *sub rosa*, he was seeking surrender, outwardly he was calling for a still greater war effort. Either he or Kido, or both, also went a step beyond words: the army was informed of the Third Conspiracy.

A week later, the army struck. It did not yet dare to seize Konoye. But it arrested Yoshida, and the two men who helped to prepare Konoye's memorial. The questions asked of Yoshida and the others indicated that the army knew every word of what happened at the meeting attended only by the emperor, Konoye—and Kido.

The three arrested men were permitted to leave the gendarmerie headquarters on May 30, 1945. As they obtained their freedom, an army judiciary officer told them:

"There is great opposition in the War Ministry to your release. I am letting you go on my own authority. If you are ever brought to trial, you'll be found guilty."

In less than six months, Yoshida was Foreign Minister, and in less than twelve the premier of Japan. Konoye was dead.

While Konoye was busy with the Third Conspiracy, other plots—all minor—were boiling furiously. Prince Higashikuni, who once wanted to kill all American airmen shot down over Japan, now wanted to get out of the war, and quickly. His plan was to ask China to serve as a peace mediator. If the Allied powers agreed to let bygones be bygones, the prince was ready to have Japan return to her pre-aggression, pre-1931 boundaries. The Cabinet discussed the plan in March, 1945, but apparently did nothing about it. Another plot, which was actually discussed with the Swedish Minister to Tokyo, was to seek Sweden's good offices in ending the war.

But all these plots were overshadowed by the Fourth, or the "Surrender Conspiracy." It was initiated by the new premier, Baron Suzuki, with an order to his chief secretary to make a secret survey of Japan's capacity for continued resistance. The survey was completed in May, 1945, and in its graphs the face of disaster was plain.

The survey showed that in the two major fields—shipping and steel production—Japan now had only a quarter of what she had in 1941. Stocks of coal and industrial salts were running so low that many factories—including those producing munitions—would have to close up. With imports halted, food was also running short. The production of planes had dropped from a high of 2,200 to 1,600, with spare parts, engines, pilots and fuel so scarce as to make all statistics meaningless.

The report was shown to the emperor, and to the members of the Supreme War Direction Council. Germany had just surrendered, and by now even the army knew that Japan would not last much longer. The War Minister who was irreconcilably opposed to surrender, asked for an imperial conference to decide the "fundamental principle of the war."

Simultaneously, and in great secrecy, an international phase of the fourth or "Surrender Conspiracy" was opened. One of the Elder Statesmen was instructed to approach the Soviet ambassador in Tokyo, Yakov Malik, to seek Moscow's intercession with the United States. While these talks were in progress, the Japanese ambassador in Moscow was ordered to prepare a way for the arrival of a special Japanese envoy to "improve relations with Russia" and to seek Soviet good offices in ending the war. Only four of the highest army and navy officials were told of the talks with the Russians, for fear of a *coup d'état* by fanatics if the news spread.

So great was the fear of assassination that even when the Supreme Council met—with its two army members—no one yet talked of surrender.

"Nobody," said a participant, "expressed the view that we should ask for peace. When a large number of people are present it is difficult for any one member to say that we should so entreat."

On June 8, 1945, the imperial conference requested by the War Minister was held, but still no one—not even the emperor —spoke of what was on his mind. Twelve days later the emperor summoned the same six men to another conference, and this time timidly asked them for alternative plans—one for surrender, and the other one for the defense of the Japanese homeland. Yet even this vague expression was important. On returning from the conference, Premier Suzuki told his secretary: "Today the emperor said what everyone has wanted to say but yet was afraid to say."

Sometime during the meeting, the emperor asked Premier Suzuki when a special peace envoy would leave for Moscow. Suzuki did not know. He said he would try to send the emissary before Stalin and Molotov left for the Potsdam Conference.

Russian intercession, however, was running into delays. Soviet Ambassador Malik was ill in Tokyo. The Japanese ambassador in Moscow was instructed anew to approach the Kremlin.

Days and weeks went by, and the dreadful statistics of air raids kept piling up. By mid-June the United States Air Forces marked *all* the large cities of Japan as destroyed, and turned to secondary cities. The air units involved also grew— from 300 to 500 to 800 Superfortresses, dropping 4,000 and 5,000 tons of bombs at a time. The weight of explosives was being translated into political pressure on the Court and the peace-makers.

Prince Konoye had already been selected for the Moscow mission. Unabashed by the failure of his own, the Third Conspiracy, he was now immersed in the Fourth. On July 12, 1945, the emperor invited Konoye to the palace, and ordered him—secretly—*to accept any terms* the Russians mentioned, and to communicate directly with the emperor. Hirohito was obviously impressed by the report of the Japanese ambassador in Moscow that the Russians would convey to the Allies no terms other than an unconditional surrender.

But it was all in vain. The following day, Moscow told the Japanese ambassador that since Stalin and Molotov were about to leave for the Potsdam Conference, no reply to the Japanese overtures could be made until their return. The peace conspirators, who had pinned high hopes on Russian intercession, felt as if everything was lost beyond retrieve.

The Potsdam Declaration was issued on July 26, 1945. It listed as the final Allied terms:

(a) Unconditional surrender, and the removal from authority and influence *"for all time"* of *those who have "deceived and misled the people of Japan into embarking on world conquests"*;

(b) Military occupation of Japan, and disarmament of all Japanese armed forces;

(c) Shearing Japan of all her territorial loot, including Manchuria, Korea, and Formosa;

(d) Stern punishment of war criminals, and the establishment of all human liberties, including freedom of thought, religion, and speech;

(e) Destruction of the war industries, with the promise to Japan of future access to world raw materials and participation in world trade;

(f) Withdrawal of the Allied occupation forces as soon as a "peacefully inclined and responsible" government had been set up "in accordance with the freely expressed will of the Japanese people."

The Supreme War Direction Council met at once, and promptly split into two irreconcilable camps. The trio of peacemakers—Premier Suzuki, Navy Minister Yonai, and Foreign Minister Togo—urged the immediate acceptance of the Allied terms. The two Chiefs of Staffs and the War Minister, although ready to end the war, opposed some of the Potsdam terms. With Japan prostrate, the tragic haggling went on.

The army people talked darkly of making a suicide stand on the beaches of Japan, and some even predicted that the landing could be made so costly for the Americans that they would prefer to soften the peace terms. Japan still had 2,800 serviceable planes, saved up for the last battle, and these were to be thrown at the U.S. invasion fleet in hourly *kamikaze* waves. Fleets of the small two-man submarines, which penetrated into Pearl Harbor in 1941, were hidden in the coves near Tokyo. Swimmers were trained for suicidal one-man attacks on invasion barges.

But time was running short even for suicidal stands. On the morning of August 6, 1945, an American bomber came over the city of Hiroshima and dropped a single bomb.

With communications disrupted, Tokyo could not understand what had happened in Hiroshima. Many believed it had been another large-scale raid. But the ignorance did not last. President Truman announced that Hiroshima had been destroyed by an atomic bomb, and a special committee of Japanese scientists rushed to the city confirmed the report. The following morning, Premier Suzuki and Foreign Minister Togo repaired to the palace, and told the emperor the acceptance of the Potsdam terms could not wait.

But more harsh blows were yet to come.

On August 8, 1945, Russia declared war on Japan, and Soviet troops crossed into Manchuria. The government was strangely unprepared for the news. Suzuki later told American interrogators that he was at a loss as to his next step. He considered one of three alternatives: resignation as premier, declaration of war on Russia, or acceptance of the Potsdam terms.

But still Japan had not endured her full measure. On August 9 an atomic bomb fell on Nagasaki and wiped out half the city. An American airman, shot down in another raid, assured the Japanese that the third A-bomb would fall on Tokyo within the next few days. The plotters were now working against time. If they delayed surrender, the capital, the government, perhaps the emperor would be destroyed. Suzuki rushed to the palace for an interview of desperation with the monarch. There could be only one decision: acceptance of the Allied terms.

An emergency meeting of the six-man War Council was called at the palace. But after two hours of heated argument, the peace plotters and the military group remained deadlocked. The peace-makers urged surrender, with the single proviso that the emperor's legal position not be altered. The opponents were ready to surrender, but with these strings attached:

(a) Japan not be occupied by Allied troops;

(b) Japan disarm and demobilize her own forces, and punish her own war criminals; and

(c) Monarchy be left untouched, and no Allied plebiscite on the form of government be permitted.

The meeting broke up for a day of feverish political maneuvers. But close to midnight of that day, the six members of the Council returned to the palace to have their differences resolved by the emperor. The meeting opened with the reading of the Potsdam terms. Foreign Minister Togo then spoke up, urging their immediate, unconditional acceptance.

By three o'clock in the morning of August 10, 1945, the deadlock was not yet broken. Then this historic exchange took place:

Suzuki (rising): "We've discussed this question for a long time without reaching any conclusion. The situation is urgent, and any delay in coming to a decision should not be tolerated. I, therefore, propose to ask His Imperial Majesty for his own views. His wishes should settle the issue, and the government should follow them."

Emperor: "I agree with the opinion expressed by the foreign minister. . . . My ancestors and I have always wished to put forward the nation's welfare and world peace as our prime concern. To continue the war now means that cruelty and bloodshed will still continue in the world and the Japanese nation will suffer severe damage. So, to stop the war is the only way to save the nation from destruction and to restore peace in the world. Looking back at what our military headquarters have done, it is apparent that their performance has fallen far short of the plans expressed. I don't think this discrepancy can be corrected in the future. . . . "

Suzuki: "The imperial decision has been expressed. This should be the conclusion of the conference."

But the peace-makers soon discovered that even the emperor's intercession, so subtly prepared by his advisor Kido, was not enough.

Right after the members of the War Council left the emperor, the full Cabinet was called in session. It heard Premier Suzuki's version of what had happened at the palace and approved unanimously a decision to accept the Potsdam terms—

provided the emperor's position remained unchanged. At seven o'clock in the morning of August 10, 1945, the decision was handed to the Swiss for delivery to Washington.

The American reply—firm and noncommittal—was heard over the San Francisco radio in the early morning hours of August 12, and the official reply arrived a day later.

In the afternoon of August 13, the War Council and the Cabinet met once again to study the American reply, and a rift became obvious at once. Thirteen ministers voted for acceptance, three were opposed. The deadlocked meeting was recessed.

One of the three bitter-enders later testified: "On the question of the emperor's position, the American reply stated that the powers of the emperor and the Japanese government would be subject to the authority of the Supreme Allied Commander. The main point had to do with the emperor's position since it was the conviction of the Japanese people that the emperor was a living god above whom there could be no earthly being. It was feared that the Japanese people would not readily accept the wording of the reply which placed the emperor in a subordinate position. . . . So it was suggested that we query the Allied governments as to whether it would be possible to have the Supreme Commander's orders go directly to the Japanese government, and those orders passed on by the Cabinet to the emperor who . . . would carry out the work connected with the termination of the war."

That night the chiefs of the Army and Navy General Staffs reaffirmed their opposition to unconditional surrender. They spent the entire night with Foreign Minister Togo, demanding that he seek a "more exact" Allied answer on the emperor's position. Togo refused to do so.

An old man who was beginning to feel that the world was crashing down on him, Suzuki proceeded to the palace early on the 14th and appealed to the emperor to call another emergency meeting. The emperor himself was becoming intensely worried. The meeting opened at 10:00 A.M., and once again the War Minister and the two Chiefs of Staffs voiced their opposition to the American reply. They demanded a clearer answer from Washington.

Looking at the bitter-enders, so that there could be no mistake, the emperor said: "It seems to me that there is no other opinion to support your stand. I shall explain mine. I hope all of you will agree. *The American answer seems acceptable to me.*"

The War Minister wept.

The emperor instructed Premier Suzuki to draft an imperial rescript ending the war, and it was agreed that the emperor would broadcast the decision to the people the noon of August 15th.

Japan had lost the war, but to the last moment, the men behind the throne—both the peace-makers and their military opponents—strove to maintain the position of the emperor unaltered. For nearly seventy-five years, he had been the pillar of Japan's feudal political structure and society. If they could manage to retain this symbol without too many changes, he would help them to carry Japan through defeat with her image unaltered, and their own position secure.

And all this while, the common people—the people who had lost their families and their homes in the raids; the people who did not eat enough and worked too hard; the people who could not talk freely for fear of secret police; the people who bore the whole terrible burden of feudalism on their shoulders—the common people knew nothing of what went on behind the throne.

The "Surrender Conspiracy" had succeeded, and now the time had come for the counterplot.

On the evening of the 14th, engineers of the Japan Broadcasting Corporation arrived at the palace to make a recording of the emperor's message to the people. The emperor was very nervous, and it took two hours to make a short record. The disc was then turned over to Kido, who locked it up in a vault in the Imperial Household Ministry.

But the peace-makers reckoned without the army. Word of

the "great betrayal" of the army by the emperor's "corrupt advisers" spread into the barracks. Quickly, a group of lieutenant colonels and majors in Tokyo organized a counterplot to seize the government and demand of the emperor that the war continue. By nightfall, in the pitch darkness of a city blackened out for air raids, thousands of restless and vengeful younger officers and soldiers left their barracks to hunt for the "traitors" and to try to stop the next day's broadcast. Strong bands of armed men burned to the ground the mansions of the two leading conspirators—Premier Suzuki and Baron Hiranuma. Kido himself returned home, to find his house occupied by soldiers. They did not recognize him, and he was not allowed to enter. Gratefully he fled back to the palace. A few younger officers shot the chief of the Imperial Guards Division after he refused to join in the military counterplot.

The Imperial Guards, who had joined the rebels, began to search the grounds for Kido and the Minister of the Imperial Household. Both escaped recognition by the soldiery brushing past them, and eventually hid themselves in the secret air raid shelter beneath the palace. Late at night, more rebellious infantrymen and a detachment of artillery entered the palace grounds. They helped to break down doors and tear holes in walls, in the hunt for the men-behind-the-throne. They seized the emperor's aide de camp and other Court officials, but none of the key men was in sight. The emperor himself, having made up his mind to surrender, apparently slept soundly through this night of chaos.

At three-thiry in the morning of August 15, the rebels took over Radio Tokyo, a huge black-painted cement structure a quarter of a mile from the palace. They tried to broadcast, but there was a raid alert on, and as a matter of routine the Army Command refused to put them on the air. Indecisively, the rebels milled in the lobby until daybreak, when the gendarmes arrived and took over the building. The Tokyo radio then went on the air and announced that the emperor would broadcast at noon.

Also at sunrise, General Seiji Tanaka, Chief of the Eastern Army, drove into the palace grounds. He demanded that the rebel troops leave at once, and insisted that their leaders atone for their "insult to the emperor" by committing *hara-kiri*. Lacking competent and centralized direction, the *coup* disintegrated. There were quarrels among the leaders, and a great amount of indecision.

Within two hours the rebels had been cleared from the palace grounds. Five of the leaders then knelt on the yellow gravel of the imperial plaza, and facing the palace disembowelled themselves and died in pools of blood.

Discovering the soldiers gone, Kido and the Minister of the Imperial Household emerged from their hiding place and rushed to the emperor—whom they were presumably to guard with their lives—to congratulate him on his safe deliverance.

Sometime that day, the War Minister killed himself. A few days later, General Tanaka, who single-handedly broke up the *coup*, also committed *hara-kiri*.

With the radio station now under a strong guard of gendarmes, the fateful record was taken to the studios from its hiding place. At noon, the nation switched its radios on. What everyone was expecting was yet another call for resistance unto death.

Instead, they heard: "We command all our people forthwith to cease hostilities, to lay down their arms and faithfully to carry out all the provisions. . . . "

Mrs. Kato told me she wept when she heard the emperor's "low and sorrowful" voice. A twenty-year-old youth who now works at the War Crimes trials said he saw many people weep when the emperor spoke, but that he himself was happy. He was in the army, in a unit chosen for a suicidal stand on the beaches of Chiba Prefecture, where the Japanese Command, quite correctly, expected one of the major American landings.

"I was out on a pass that day," he said, "and heard the broadcast in a small shop. I was glad. I didn't want to die. And our food was poor and morale low. I returned to the camp, and the officers told us the war was over. Many of them cried like children."

The people now knew, and the slaughter was ended. The men who ruled Japan would now turn to two tasks, the immediate job of destroying all evidence of war crime, and the long-range task of protecting old Japan against the buffeting of American orders and the ideas generated by the defeat. The peace plotters would now start on a new conspiracy.

August 16, 1946

An unbearably hot, still, depressing day. The latest typhoon, nicknamed Lilly, is nearing Japan, and even the foliage seems to be waiting fearfully. On the Ginza, the street vendors have covered their stalls with canvas and straw mats. They squat in the shade, and perspire, and fan themselves. But there are few customers, except at stands selling flavored ice shavings.

Went to Kyoritsu Hall, the shabby auditorium where Japan's postwar leftism speaks its mind, to watch the inaugural convention of the Congress of Industrial Unions. Shaped in the image of the American CIO, CIU has been six months aborning. Today it claims 1,600,000 members, to make it Japan's biggest labor organization. It is also the most militant.

The CIU comes into being in the shadow of official disfavor. Headquarters has clearly indicated its belief that CIU is Communist-dominated. Just as clearly, General MacArthur's blessings have gone to CIU's conservative rival, the Japan Federation of Labor. CIU's prime sin apparently is its insistence on going into politics. Ted Cohen, the diminutive head of the Labor Division who has never been a labor union man, wants CIU to stick closely to the simple formula of "wage-hour-working conditions."

"How can labor keep out of politics?" Kikunami, in whose mind CIU was born and who is slated to become its first president, asked me. "The government of Yoshida is a *zaibatsu* government, hostile to labor. If we hadn't been watchful, it would have put us back where we were five years ago, under the Japanese Army. When we go into politics, we're fighting for our lives."

CIU's member-unions came close to keeping Yoshida out of power in April, only to see him saved by General Mac-Arthur's ban on demonstrations.

The lobby of Kyoritsu Hall was filled with Counter Intelligence agents and Military Policemen. Beyond them, the dark, airless hall was packed with sweating men. The first thing that struck me about the hall was the absence of tobacco smoke. With the daily ration at three cigarettes, men treasure their moments of smoking.

The large, bare stage was decorated with banners, exhorting the workers to fight for the forty-hour week, oppose mass dismissals, and battle against the "remnants of militarism and nationalism." Behind a long table sat the dozen odd union men who helped to organize the Congress. They were strangely of a pattern—tall, lean men, with the faces of intellectuals. As each of them took his seat, he introduced himself to the audience and bowed low in traditional Japan style. The speakers, too, bowed low before and after their addresses. It added an odd Oriental touch to this thoroughly Western gathering.

I was mainly interested in the keynote speech, delivered by the head of the Chemical Workers' Union. He was a hard-looking, slender man, with a clear purpose: to disassociate CIU from the Communists, without forfeiting the right to political militancy.

"Some think," he said, "that under the Occupation the labor movement should not be militant. But we've been given the democratic right to organize, and there's no reason why we shouldn't use it. Our job is not to promote violence but to organize labor, and to teach each worker to tell an enemy from a friend. The government and the capitalists declare that since Japan is now suffering from the consequences of defeat, all internal differences must be forgotten, and labor disputes be put off. But when have the capitalists welcomed disputes?

"A strong labor movement cannot be handed to us on a platter. It's something that the workers themselves must struggle for. . . . Labor leaders who are afraid to resort to violence in the struggle for workers' rights are cowards. . . . "

Then came the all-important issue of communism:

"The present campaign against the Communists is just the same as the tactics used by the Japanese Fascists and militarists during the war. It's scarcely in accord with freedom of belief accorded in a democracy. . . .

"But if you, Communists, thinks that CIU is your own, you're mistaken. The CIU belongs to no one but the workers themselves. We, in CIU, don't care if our members, as individuals, belong to the Communist or any other party. But CIU—as an organization—belongs to no party. . . . "

Despite the formal disavowal, the Communists—and Russia—remained solidly in the background. Some of CIU's key unions are led by known Communists, and thousands among the workers represented in this hall were party members or sympathizers. In the lobby, youths busily peddled the *Akahata (Red Flag)*, the official party organ. On a counter, one could pick a large selection of Communist magazines, books and pamphlets.

Still more significant was the Russian influence. The word "Russian" is used advisedly. For though much of the material on display was Bolshevist, even more was Slav Russian. About the counter hung portraits of the Communist trinity—Stalin, Lenin, and Karl Marx. Dozens of the books were translations of Stalin's works. One of the Japanese magazines, showing a buxom Russian peasant woman, even carried its name in Russian—*Russkaya Kultura*. It was plainly a propaganda magazine.

But for each image of Stalin I found one of Count Leo Tolstoy and three of Maxim Gorky. And there were literally scores of translated works of these two authors, plus Chekhov, Gogol, and Turgenyev. It may well be that Russian propagandists were responsible for publishing these translations. But if they were, they were capitalizing not on the world revolution but on the traditional Japanese interest in Russian literature.

I remembered going through a large book store on the Ginza ten or twelve years ago, and being amazed by the number and variety of books by Russian writers. I remembered talking to Japanese intellectuals, and discovering that they were conversant with all the trends and schools in Russian belles-lettres. Eventually, the Japanese military swept the bookshelves bare of Russian literature. But the interest was never killed. With Japan's surrender, it was revived and magnified.

I do not know if the Soviet embassy is responsible for any of the translations pouring into the market. With its large staff here, it could certainly include a number of cultural attachés. But whether it is or not, it certainly reaps the benefits. A Japanese admirer of Gorky will find *Russkaya Kultura* of interest. And a reader of that magazine—especially if he is unhappy over his rice ration, or his government, or even the U.S. army "fraternization"— will find a ready solace in enthusiastic articles on the Soviet system.

In Japan, as elsewhere, the middle ground has shrunk, and the extremes have gained strength. When a Japanese does not like the Yoshida government, which we support, he has few places to go to but the Communist camp. When he dislikes us, he turns his face westward, to Russia. The Soviet officials to whom I have talked do not conceal their intense interest in Japan. But they deny meddling in Japanese politics. What they seem to think is that by backing the conservatives, we are alienating the working people and the intellectuals. In this mental picture, *we* are the best recruiting agents for the Japanese Communist party and the Soviet Union. The Russians do not have to work very hard. They feel time is on their side.

August 17, 1946   TOKYO

Joe Fromm and I went to see W. MacMahon Ball, British Commonwealth's representative on the Allied Council, whom many of us regard as one of the most brilliant thinkers in official Tokyo. Ball has been having a difficult time on the Council, for while Britain's policies have paralleled ours, he can never forget that he also represents the Australian government whose views on Japan at the moment often differ from ours. Moreover, he adheres to the unpopular belief that slapping the Russians down, with or without provocation, is a dangerous parlor game.

We sat in Ball's large office and argued on the subject of experts.

"Our difficulty," Ball was saying, "does not lie in a scarcity of experts. It lies in the fact that it's simply useless to bring any factual information before the Council, for it's immediately pounced on as an affront to the Supreme Commander. I've stopped bringing up any facts because it always provokes George [Atcheson] into attacking me.

"I'll give you an example of the low regard in which the Council is held. Back in June, George presented the old Japanese land reform bill to us with a request for our advice. He told us it was a matter of extreme urgency. We worked on it very hard, and drew up a model program. It was presented to the Council, and the Russian and Chinese delegates concurred with us.

"Five days ago, quite by accident, we heard that the Japanese government had prepared a new land bill of its own. We promptly asked the American secretariat to send us a copy, to see if any of our recommendations had been incorporated. We kept calling every hour, but without success. Yesterday morning, I read in the *Nippon Times* where General MacArthur had issued a message complimenting the Japanese government on its 'courage and determination.'

"At eleven yesterday morning, the new Japanese draft was finally delivered to us."

This, both Joe and I knew, was not an isolated instance of a deliberate slight to the Council in general and to Ball in particular. Both General MacArthur and Atcheson are irritated by Ball. They feel that he should be a faithful and unquestioning ally in the Council. They resent his air of independence, and his occasional acid comments on some of the more extravagant claims issued by Headquarters. Atcheson is also irked by Ball's urbanity, and his sharp wit.

When the Council first met, Ball invited Atcheson to tea and assured Atcheson that he, Ball, had "the greatest possible affection" for the United States. At great length Ball recited the reasons, from his wife's relatives in America to his own education on American scholarships, Rockefeller and Carnegie. At the moment, he added, the foreign policies of the British Empire and the United States coincided.

"There is no reason," Ball said, "why we shouldn't work very closely together. If I ever say anything at the Council that I shouldn't, just kick me under the table, and later tell me where I was wrong."

At the Council sessions which followed, Atcheson treated Ball with a demonstrable hostility. Finally Ball called up Atcheson and said, "What's all this about? Couldn't we figure out some way in which we could work more harmoniously?" Atcheson's reply, I understand, was unfriendly.

I suspect that, like most of us here, Ball thinks that the Council is useless, and even worse, for it merely supplies another arena for international friction. I have heard that at least three months ago, Ball recommended the dissolution of the Council to his government. What is happening in the Council is often quite beyond its power to control. It was established to give international advice to General MacArthur at a time when our relations with Russia are so strained that no Russian advice is likely to be accepted, and when General MacArthur regards any hint of criticism of Japan's plodding progress as a personal slur.

A newly arrived Russian correspondent yesterday gave me a clipping from the Moscow *Pravda*, in which Atcheson was described as "a twentieth century anachronism." The article added that "the difference between Atcheson and Ball is the difference between the seventeenth and twentieth centuries."

I showed the clipping to Ball, and jokingly suggested it might have been one of the reasons for the friction between him and Atcheson. Ball laughed.

"Maybe. George himself sent me a translation of this story the other day."

Japan is a carpetbagger's dream. It is not easy to get in, but once that is over, a businessman with imagination, boldness and an American uniform is limited only by the sky. The prize is one of the richest in history, and representatives of some of America's industrial and financial mammoths are on hand, scheming, conniving, pulling wires. Theoretically, a businessman in a U.S. Army uniform is his country's servant, and he is enjoined from contact with his firm. In practice, no one cares.

The overall design is clear. The latter-day carpetbagger is after control of Japan's economy. He is buying his way into the *zaibatsu.* He is using his official position to try and force some utilities, now nationalized, back into private hands. The carpetbaggers concentrate in the lobby of the Dai-Ichi Hotel, where they talk the international language of cartels. Exclusive agency. Price agreement. Loans. Monopoly. The men cajole and exhort. Their stock in trade is the promise of credits and dividends. But the *zaibatsu,* who have ruled the economy of Japan for generations, have not yet quite made up their minds. A few of them want credits. Others resist American encroachment. The carpetbaggers are busy.

The other night, Sally and I had dinner with two oil men, on loan to the U.S. Army. The men did not deny they were in touch with their firms. With open-eyed candor, both told us that "naturally" their companies were paying them the difference between army pay and their civilian salaries, and that, "you know, we have to look forward to representing our companies here when peace is signed." The dinner was especially piquant because one of the men had already made a deal with the Japanese oil interests. Now the other man, obstinately but without success, was trying to discover the nature of the deal.

Another item. In collaboration with the Chicago *Sun's* bureau in Washington, I have just helped to expose the activities of Peter Magagna, a silk adviser to Headquarters. A small, profane, violent man, Magagna flew into Tokyo in February.

Before he found it desirable to leave, he—in the opinion of many qualified officials—had come close to winning control of Japan's silk industry. Magagna's weapons were spunk, a letter and a cable. The letter was from the State Department, and it described him as an adviser to General MacArthur. The cable was from the Pennsylvania congressman Daniel Flood, and it said, in more or less these words: "Keep up the good fight. I'll back you to the limit." Apart from being a powerful congressman, Flood was also Magagna's private attorney in Washington. Magagna used the letter on the Japanese, the cable on Headquarters.

Unlike the other businessmen, Magagna preferred the vehement approach. He knew how to get to the press, and he knew what made a headline. He charged incompetence and worse. He shouted things that were only whispered until now. He attacked General MacArthur's closest aides, the War Department, Secretary of War Robert P. Patterson—anyone who seemed to stand between him and the silk industry.

To give Magagna credit, he gave Headquarters a worse case of jitters than almost any other individual or issue since Japan's surrender. Fearful of what a hostile congressman could do to General MacArthur's requests for appropriations, the men in Headquarters cajoled and humored Magagna, and took his insults with a smile. They did nothing even when Magagna had two members of an Australian Trade Mission thrown out of a silk testing station.

The press, which did some probing of its own, seemingly succeeded where the generals feared to act. Magagna left for Pennsylvania before his job was done. Congressman Flood girded himself for the election, in which adverse publicity might mean the difference between defeat and victory.*

In the files of the Japanese Finance Ministry, waiting for the eyes of any enterprising newspaperman, there are three letters written in behalf of Ando, the racketeer, by M. Bergher, Chief Film Officer of Central Motion Picture Exchange in Headquarters. The letters, dated May 27, 1946, are exhibits in

* He was defeated.

Hollywood's fight to win control of the Japanese market, to the exclusion of all other movie makers, including Japan's own.

The first letter "asked" the Finance Ministry to lend Ando the Y.20,000,000 ($1,333,000) he needed to capitalize a new firm, which would exhibit American films in Japan. The second letter "asked" the Japanese government to release to Ando 50,000 tons of duralumin he said he needed for the construction of "several hundred" movie houses. The third letter certified the readiness of the Exchange to supply Ando with enough Hollywood films to run fifty-two weeks a year.

The letters were filled with such pious phrases as, "We are thoroughly convinced that Mr. Ando's endeavor is directed to further better understanding . . . of the American ideals. . . . " Thinking of Hollywood, and its relation to American ideals, reminded me of a movie they recently ran here before packed houses. It dealt with the adventures of Arsene Lupin, the larcenist, and it provoked a minor wave of housebreaking in Tokyo. When the clumsier burglars were caught, they explained:

"I wanted to be like Arsene Lupin."

The latest instance of carpetbagging—"The Case of Mr. X"—was brought to my attention today. "Mr. X" is one of the highest economic officials in Headquarters. Before the war, he headed the Japan branch of a major American concern.

Recently, an American investigator going through the files of the Nissan Trust, a great munitions combine, came across copies of letters sent to "Mr. X" by the president of Nissan. The letters dealt with the Nissan's plans to gain control of the light car and truck field in Japan.

One of the letters informed "Mr. X" that Nissan had decided to contact the Detroit automobile company he recommended. Another letter included a copy of a contract sent to the Detroit firm. Since Japanese companies are not permitted to correspond with American concerns, it could be assumed that "Mr. X" had forwarded the contract to Detroit. The purpose of the entire arrangement apparently was to exclude Ford,

Chevrolet, and Chrysler companies from the Japanese market.

The investigator at first did not realize the import of what he had read. Later he decided the documents were worth copying, and asked for permission to borrow the folder. After he left the Nissan office, the officer discovered that the correspondence with "Mr. X" had been replaced with statistics on nuts and bolts.

Later in the day, the investigator returned to the office, and demanded to see the folder. He was told by the Japanese clerks that the correspondence was "secret" and "doesn't concern you." An argument developed, and the president of Nissan appeared on the scene. He explained that he had long been "Mr. X's" friend, and the correspondence was purely personal.

He was backed up by an Occidental, who said he was William Gorham, a director of Nissan, and demanded to know the officer's name, rank, serial number, the commanding officer's name, and whether General Marquat knew of this request for the correspondence.

Gorham is a San Franciscan who came to Japan twenty-nine years ago and worked for Nissan through the years of war. "The letters," he said, "are merely arrangements which 'Mr. X' made with a Nissan in behalf of the Detroit firm. They are personal, and they are none of your business. They are now locked in the president's safe. If you want them, go and get an order from General Marquat."

The investigator had to retire from the scene. He has submitted a report, but no action has been taken on it. The two noteworthy features of the case are that, technically, we are still at war with Japan, and that "Mr. X", as a War Department employee, can have no interests other than those of the U.S. Government.

September 10, 1946   TOKYO

In the evening, Sally, Dave Conde, former chief of the Moving Picture Division in Headquarters and now a reporter for Reuters, and I drove to the suburbs to look for Akira Iwasaki.

No kin to the *zaibatsu* Iwasakis, Akira until last month was a producer of documentary films for the Nichiei Studios. He has produced two pictures, *The Tragedy of Japan and A Year of Occupation.* The former, made up of old newsreels, showed the emperor, bankers, and politicians urging Japan on to war. It was boycotted by the three big exhibitors. The second film was held up by U.S. Army censors, because it showed labor demonstrations, Premier Yoshida in secret talks with old-time political manipulators, and the *zaibatsu* still doing business.

With its pictures making no money, Nichiei went bankrupt, and Ando the racketeer tried to buy it out. Iwasaki blocked the deal, but was warned to "look out." Eventually Iwasaki negotiated the sale of the studio to a big movie concern and resigned.

We left the last bright lights of Tokyo behind, and then darkness was around us. It was warm and humid, and rain was in the air. We drove on until we came to a tiny police booth, with a dim red light over the door. The policeman was talking to two youngsters. We asked for directions, and the youngsters volunteered to guide us. We turned off the main road into a maze of lanes that seemed to have no end. At last we reached an alley just wide enough for the jeep. Far ahead of us was a two-story Japanese house with a single light in a room upstairs.

"That's it," said one of the boys.

We drove towards the house, with the rumble of the jeep funneled and magnified by the walls confining the lane. The light blinked and went out. It was as if the sound of the jeep had reached out and extinguished it.

We stopped before the house, and I turned the headlights off. It was dark, and the silence in the house was wary and frightened. Conde began to hammer on the door. There was no answer. The two youngsters shouted. The house remained still. Yet we had seen the light go out, and we knew there were people inside.

"Dave," I said, "talk to them. They know your voice."

"Iwasaki-san, Iwasaki-san," shouted Dave, "this is Conde. Open up. We're friends."

A window upstairs slid open, and a dark face looked down. I flashed my light on Conde. Dave said, "You've got visitors."

The window closed, and again there was silence. Then there was a metallic click, and the front door opened. In it, in the light of our flashlights, stood a tall, slim figure in a kimono.

"Please come in," Iwasaki said in English.

We took off our shoes and sat on the straw mats in the living room. The electric light over the low round table cast dark shadows. Iwasaki's wife, a handsome woman with the face of a suffering madonna, was kneeling by the door. Iwasaki knelt by the table. His dark, steady eyes were watching ours. Over his face, starting just under the hairline, crossing the left eyebrow and eyelids, and ending below the cheekbone, was a wide, dark, ugly scar.

"Bad?" we asked.

"The eye is safe," said Iwasaki.

"Does it hurt?"

"Not too much, except for the headaches. I have them all the time."

We sat around the table, drank tea, and talked of the life of Iwasaki, a progressive Japanese in a new democratic Japan.

"I'm forty-four," said Iwasaki. "I have two little children. I studied at the Tokyo Imperial University; specialized in German literature. Before the war I made a living as an essayist and a literary critic. I liked to argue on literary trends, and I even belonged to a small philosophy club—just a few professors, writers, and students.

"In 1939, two years after the China Incident broke out, every member of the club was arrested. The charge was violation of the Peace Preservation Law. Under that law, they could put you in prison for wrong thoughts never uttered. I was kept in various police station cells for eight months. Then I was put in Sugamo, where the war criminals are being held now.

"I was lucky. In Sugamo they let my wife bring me books in German and English. Books like these. . . . " He pointed to book cases behind him. There were rows of books by Arthur Schnitzler, John Dos Passos, Pearl Buck, Carl van Vechten, Vladimir Tretyakov, and Leo Tolstoy.

"I learned English and read Dos Passos' trilogy. When I understood a passage, I was happy. Dos Passos is my favorite author. I was in prison, but my mind and my spirit were free.

"After eight months I was tried. The court sentenced me to three years' imprisonment, but suspended the sentence. I was forbidden to do any more writing. We lived by selling what we owned. When the war ended, most of my library was gone. Then I got a job with Nichiei Studios, and began to work on documentaries.

"I thought: here was my country which went into a war, not knowing why, and which lost the war, still not knowing why. Here was the Potsdam Declaration, and few people knew of it. I thought: why don't I produce pictures showing my people what kind of men and forces got us into the war. The military. The emperor. The *zaibatsu*. The venal press.

"When the movie was ready, I thought again: why don't I put together a lot of newsreel shots, showing what has happened to us, and to the war criminals, since surrender. Tojo and a few other generals in jail. The emperor still free. The men of the *zaibatsu* still pulling the wires.

"The American censors stopped it. I asked them why. They said it was orders from General Willoughby. Then my friends told me the picture was shown secretly at Premier Yoshida's residence, and there were some American guests from Military Intelligence Section, and Yoshida asked them to ban the picture.

"Meanwhile, Ando tried to buy Nichiei. He came to the studios and promised gifts to all the workers if the sale went through. He also talked of instituting morning worship for the emperor once he bought Nichiei. I tried to stop the sale.

"One night two weeks ago someone knocked on my door. I thought it was someone from the studios. I opened the door. There was a youngster standing there. He asked me: 'Are you Iwasaki-san from the Nichiei Studios?' I said yes. He stepped aside, and another youngster came forward and struck me. Then they fled.

"I felt stunned, but I thought I was merely hit. My forehead ached. I touched it, and saw that my hand was covered with blood. I realized then that I had been cut with a razor. A doctor put stitches on my forehead. He thinks I shall have to have an operation. The police made a routine investigation but found nothing.

"The two boys were professional killers, no mistake about that. They didn't want to kill me. Just cut me enough to give me a warning."

"What will you do now, Iwasaki-san?"

"I don't know," he said quietly. "I get unsigned letters. They say, 'This was just a warning,' or 'You're a Communist because you attack the emperor.' My wife is afraid for me and the children. She doesn't let them out to play with other children. The magazines don't want to buy my articles. They say they can't antagonize Ando. And Ando himself will be out of jail soon. At night we sit and listen to the sounds outside, and wait. We've been thinking of getting out of Tokyo and hiding in some village. . . . "

We had heard that the family did not dare even to go shopping. We brought some powdered milk for the children. His wife thanked us, with moist, frightened eyes. They both walked us into the dark street.

"It was good of you to come," he said. "We see so few people."

I started the engine, and both of them went in. Quickly, quietly, like shadows. The door lock clicked, and the lights went out. The house was dark again.

September 26, 1946   ISOHARA VILLAGE,
                                                        IBARAGI PREFECTURE

Ten days ago, though it seems an eternity, we left Tokyo for a tour of this prefecture. We started in two jeeps, loaded with food, gasoline, blankets and five passengers—Sally,

Joe Fromm, Roy, and I, and our guide, Chikosaburo Hayami, a poet, dancer, wrestler, a former agent in China, and an adviser to the Cabinet. We were primarily interested in the land problem and in the nationalist underground, and for the first five days we put ourselves in Hayami's able hands. He managed our itinerary, and set up a succession of interviews with landlords, members of parliament, town mayors, and rural officials.

For most of this time, our headquarters was a landlord's mansion atop a hill. We lived in a sumptuous suite that opened on its own garden, with gnome trees, flowers in bloom, and a brass crane, spewing a fountain of water out of its beak. Prince Higashikuni, once premier, had lived in these rooms, and they were known in town as "the prince's suite."

Men came to this house to talk to us, and from it we drove out to neighboring villages and towns to talk to other men. Once we spent a morning with a young landowner, whose living room was furnished with a couch covered with leopard skins. He sat there, a pale and effeminate man, and talked of the fleshpots of Tokyo. His uncle ran the estate. On another day we were rowed to an island in the center of a large lake, and talked to the officials. News and ideas had trouble getting across the water, and the island seemed removed from life elsewhere in Japan, and from this century. A small, tight band which ran the island before and during the war still ran it without opposition. We sat in a shabby and crowded office of the Agricultural Association, and these men talked blandly of the negative features of the Occupation—the land reform, the growth of communism, and the decline of public respect for the officials. They had heard that the emperor had renounced his divinity, and they had heard vaguely of the new Constitution, but it did not seem to matter: "Our relation to the emperor will not change."

This was the landowner's country, a corner of unreformed and feudal Japan. Hayami had said nothing, but his purpose was clear. He was showing us the landlord in his native habitat. The landlord dominated the economy and the government. He was the spider weaving a web which included the town mayors and the money lenders, the county officials, the village cops, and all the men who ran the all-important Agricultural Associations. No sharecropper by himself could break through its web, and it smothered every effort to form a strong Farmers' Union.

The men we saw were enemies of land reform. Slyly they talked to us of the many tricky ways in which the law could be circumvented, and they forecast its failure. The land reform law by itself could not destroy this system. By hook or crook, the landlords would continue to control much of the land. By using their wealth adroitly, they would continue to dominate rural economy. Through intrigue, or bribery, or superior education, or wealth, or social prestige, they would continue to run the machinery of government.

Land reform could succeed only if it were part of a deeper and wider reform program, which would recognize the intimate relation of rural economy to the nation's politics, industry, education, and thought patterns. No such recognition was yet in sight, and the landlords seemed unworried.

Physically it has been a tough trip. The rough roads had shaken the jeep bolts loose. They were even harder on us. Sally discovered a huge, red blister on her back where she sat leaning against a can of gasoline. Now her back hurts, and she has to sit stiffly, on the edge of the seat. It has drizzled almost ceaselessly, and we seem never to be able to dry ourselves, and all of us have colds. On the fifth day, a loose kidney stone sent Joe hurrying back to Tokyo. Hayami left us in Central Ibaragi, and after that Sally, Roy, and I were on our own. We stayed in small village inns, with their inevitable bugs and drafts, and we ate one hot meal a day, lunching usually on cheese, hardtack, and chlorinated water.

Yet, the trip was so exciting, and so much fresh material seemed to wait ahead, that we were loath to turn back. We had brought letters of introduction from Nissho ("Sun-chosen") Inouye, one of the three great political terrorists of Japan, and as we penetrated the "nationalist belt" near the city of Mito, we put them to good use. Mito has been wiped out in the air raids, and to be close to the patriotic killers, we lived in a bordello in a neighboring town. The place was busy, and at night from our porch we watched Mito officials make merry in the banquet hall, and take the girls in relays to a back room. Sally made friends with the *madame*, who was an officer's widow and a very charming woman, and from her we learned much of the way people thought and lived in this corner of Japan. ("At one time, so many killers came from this district that no one on the outside would marry our girls.")

We drove on northward, and close to the northern edge of the prefecture one day, the three of us trudged warily six hundred feet underground into an old mine. We squatted in a small circle at an intersection of tunnels, and talked to sweating miners, who wore nothing but loincloths and sweatbands. Without passion, the men told us of their wages, on which no one could raise a family; the poor rations of food and clothes; and the bloody battles their union was waging against the company police. They had heard of the fights the American miners had with the owners, and of a man named John L. Lewis, and they wanted us to tell them more. From time to time, wagons loaded with coal rolled by, and then we pressed ourselves against the sweating walls and watched in apprehension the rotten mine timbers.

In an inn, at a village called Hokota, the county administrator and the police chief called to pay their respects. The sharecroppers here have a militant union, and there had been two mass raids on the police station. The police fled, and the sharecroppers briefly held the station, but there was no violence and no damage. The first time, the sharecroppers wanted an end to evictions by landlords; the second, the arrest of village officials whom they accused of malfeasance.

The police chief was a small, fat, youngish man. He was shrewd and lucid, and he completely overshadowed his companion. I asked him to name the achievements of the Occupation, and he listed these: the ploughing up of the Hokota army airfield, the collection of arms, and the re-establishment of the Farmers' Union. But once he met my curiosity, he wanted me to tell him if the Americans ever resorted to violence against the established authority. I told him of a little fracas they had in

Tennessee a few weeks ago, when ex-servicemen, after some gunplay, ousted the unpopular town machine, and set up a more progressive administration. Both men said, hm, thoughtfully, and then became silent.

At this point, Sally turned on our portable radio, and here was Anthony Eden's ominous analysis of the critical relations with Russia. Roy translated the highlights of the speech, and I asked the chief what he thought of the possibility of a war between the United States and Russia. He said simply, "The Japanese people have had enough of wars."

Another afternoon, we sat in the living room of a farm union organizer—a neat and shabby room, with books piled high against the rear wall and the front wall panels removed—and talked to a group of tenants. Unlike other farmers we had met, these did not think well of land reform. They thought only one man in five would buy land. Reform, they said, had been tried before, but in the years of depression the land invariably reverted to the landowners, because the sharecroppers found channels of credit blocked to them.

"Look at it this way," one of the young sharecroppers said. "Under the new law, I can rent an acre of land for Y.80. What I raise on it, under the prevailing prices, would bring me Y.1,000 in the black market. I make a fair profit. But if I buy the land, I have to pay the annual installment, plus the taxes, plus the possibility that the landlords, one way or another, will throw me off. They've always had friends in the government. Maybe, after you Americans leave, they will again."

The men were worried about the growing nationalist movement. Returning soldiers, they said, had taken over the influential Young Men's Associations. What was worse, small bands of ex-servicemen were forming "collective farms" on land bought for them by well-known Fascists. Not far away, they said, there was one such farm, with thirty young, sturdy war veterans, who were receiving paramilitary training and an education patterned closely after the curriculum of the famous "Farmers for Manchuria" schools.

The following morning, at an inn in a neighboring village, a muscular youth of eighteen sauntered down the porch to our room, and watched me type. I gave him a cigarette and asked him if he belonged to the Young Men's Association. He said he did. Until recently the local group was headed by ex-officers, but the U.S. Counter Intelligence ordered them to resign, and now they were acting as "advisers" and "lecturers."

He told us a bit about himself. At the age of fifteen, he joined the air force and later became a *kamikaze* pilot. On the day of surrender he was actually up in the air, headed for our fleet north of here, when the emperor's surrender broadcast came over his radio. "I was very downcast," he said, "but it was the emperor's orders, and there was no choice. Some of my friends talked of refusing to surrender, but we dissuaded them."

A plane flew high overhead, and he leaned out and watched it. Roy asked him if there was any talk of a United States-Soviet war, and the youth said, yes. "I want to join the American air force and fight Russia. The Americans to us are like superior beings to animals. We want to learn from them. There's much talk that the war will come soon, and we'll be recruited by the United States Army." We wanted to know if he was training himself for his future military career, and he said, "No, we have no military training, but we take calisthenics at the Young Men's Association, and we also go to the post office here and study the Morse code." We waited.

"When I see a plane in the sky," he finally said, "I want very badly to fly again."

We arrived here, at Isohara, after dark. The inn, called "The Mountain-Ocean Hotel," had been recommended to us as superb. We found it somewhat less than that. We had no complaints about the beauty. Our suite was right over the breakwater, and the sea waves, smashing against it, sent a foamy spray into our windows. But the straw mats were old and crawling with bugs, and the paper-panel doors have been shredded to strips. A band of women brought in our charcoal braziers, sat on the floor, and proceeded to stare at Sally. They explained they had seen no white women in ten years.

They left us only when a delegation from the Isohara Farmers' Union came calling. The four men were middle-aged and self-conscious. They were the union officers—the president, who was a landlord, and three sharecroppers, one of whom, a gray-haired man with oversized glasses, was also a district organizer for the Social Democrats. We exchanged polite remarks while Sally cooked, and the men courteously kept their eyes off the food. Then we ate our dinner, and they ate canned fruit cocktail, and commented in delight on its sweetness. No sugar rations had been distributed here in four years.

After dinner we talked, and it was good to discover that here at least men gave the feudal landlord system a spirited battle. There was always misery at Isohara, they said, and the incentive to rebel was always there. What was lacking was the opportunity, and Japan's defeat provided that. ("Premier Yoshida," they said, "claims credit for the land reform. We know it was General MacArthur and the Americans who gave it to us.")

Five months ago, twenty-five men got together and decided to do something to stop the swindling of the sharecroppers by the officials collecting rice for the government. The officials set arbitrary quotas and kept part of the crop for themselves. The union won its battle, and then began to extend its activities. Right now it was fighting evictions.

Fertile land is scarce here, and the competition among the sharecroppers to rent it is severe. The landlords take advantage of it, and raise the rents up to 50, 60 and more per cent of the annual crop. The union president, who owned seven acres, said proudly he charged only a third of the crop for the two and a half acres he rented out.

"Our country is in a crisis," he said, "and it isn't right to own more land than a man needs to live decently. I'm ready to sell most of my land."

He was an earnest man who, I thought, felt himself a bit out of place among the sharecroppers, and he tried hard to show that he was a good man.

The three sharecroppers each rented less than an acre, and to make ends meet they worked at a saw mill and a coal mine. They thought the Land Reform Law did not go far enough, "but even this is so much better than anything we could hope for." Two of the three said they would buy land. The third thought he would not; the land would inevitably revert to the landlords; you could not beat them.

Two months ago, the Farmers' Union put up its own candidate for the village headman. The opposition threw its support behind a former officer of the Ex-Servicemen's Association. The opposition was woven of many strands—the landlords and the shopkeepers, the defunct but still powerful Manhood Society of the Fascist Imperial Rule Assistance Association, a "community" group that succeeded it, and the Young Men's Association, headed by an ex-officer and son of the saw mill owner. The opposition candidate won out. "But," they said, "we made new friends, and we know now who the enemies are. Our next job now is to organize the young sharecroppers."

From their village problems we turned to the problems of the world. They said they thought there would be no armed clash between us and Russia. "There's much talk of war in our village," they said gloomily. "Our people don't want war. But if the disaster comes, we feel we must take up arms to defend the United States, which is our friend."

We had by now talked for four hours, and unsubtly I told the men that it was midnight, and we had been up, traveling and talking, since six o'clock this morning. They said sympathetically, "You must be tired," and also, "Can we ask you a question?" We were squatting around a low table, with a small electric bulb just over our heads, and in its dim light I saw four pairs of intent eyes watching me. They had more than one question. They had been cut off from the world for a decade, and now they wanted to know if there were men like them in the world without, and how these men were meeting their problems.

Do you have sharecroppers in America? they asked, and, How much rent do they pay? and, What party do they belong to? Do the American farmers have crop insurance? Do they have State aid, and cheap credit, and expert technical guidance? How about erosion, and fertilizer, and farm equipment? Was it true that President Roosevelt had been a friend of the sharecroppers?

These were questions out of their own experience, and it was important to them to have the answers. I was genuinely ashamed of the inadequacy of my knowledge. I tried to remember what I knew, and I tried to put it in terms they could understand. I told them of the share croppers in the south; I told them of the Dust Bowl, and of how thousands of American farmers found themselves forced to leave their ruined farms and travel to other corners of America to seek new land, and how other states sometimes shut their gates in men's faces, or maltreated them as they would unwelcome strangers. Then I told them of what the American people, in the Roosevelt 'thirties, did for the farmers in stress. I told them of crop insurance and rural electrification, of cheap federal credit and other federal aid, I told them of reforestation, and of the Tennessee Valley Authority.

I was talking slowly, in the simplest words, and as I told these men of what America had done in a crisis, I took a new pride in my country, in its inner strength, its vastness, and its ability to meet a harsh test. Sometimes it blundered badly; sometimes it allowed itself to be led by false leaders. But these faults were overshadowed by its greatness.

The men said, "America is a wonderful country," and "It would be good to try that in Japan." And one said simply, "We've just started. Give us time."

Around two in the morning, we walked them to the front door and watched them light the miners' lamps on their bicycles. They said, "Thank you for telling us what was done in America. It means much to us here," and then we watched them vanish in the mist. We went back to our rooms, and though we were tired, we felt so moved by the encounter we could not go to sleep. We sat around the same table and thought, and wrote out our notes.

Got up early, with last night's talk still heavy on my mind. I thought I alone had felt the impact so strongly. But Roy started talking about it, and then Sally showed me an entry in her diary. It said, in part:

"When we stopped questioning the men, I moved to a far corner and leaned against the wall. The four men sat facing Mark across the table. Roy sat a little to the back, just out of the circle of light. They wanted to know how their kind of people lived in America, and Mark talked to them of the TVA, crop insurance, and federal aid. They sat there, as if listening to a divination—not moving, and not even blinking. Their faces bore a rapt, almost saintly expression. I don't think they breathed often while Mark talked. Mark has given them a dream which they will not forget and of which they will tell others."

September 29, 1946   MITO, IBARAGI PREFECTURE

We have spent the last two days with a man named Takeuchi, who is to Ibaragi what the DuPonts are to Delaware. He owns bus lines and railroads, steel works and rice land. I think that he also owns most of the Ibaragi prefectural legislature. We had a letter to Takeuchi from Nissho Inouye, the spy, priest and arch-terrorist. Twenty years ago or more, Takeuchi built a temple near here and put Inouye in it, to preach his curious doctrine of militant Buddhism and ultra-nationalism. Young villagers and military men climbed up the hill to the temple to hear Inouye talk of the need for cleansing the political impurities with blood, and later met with him in an abandoned railway car to plot assassinations. Still later, Inouye went to Tokyo, to hatch a series of murder plots, for which he and his followers eventually paid with long terms in prison.

It was not by accident that political terrorism sprang up

here, for Mito has always been the cradle of extreme nationalism, and *Mito Gaku*, or the Mito school of Nationalist thought, had left an inerasable shadow on Japanese history. As Inouye's killers were released from prison, they drifted back to this friendly patch of Japan, to work, to rethink the doctrine of political terrorism, and perhaps to plot anew. And Takeuchi, who was Inouye's financial angel before the war, still remained his friend and patron, and still kept in touch with Inouye's band.

Yesterday morning, we met Takeuchi—a small, thin, old man who looks like a tired shopkeeper. He told us he had just had a letter from Inouye about us, and peremptorily he announced that he was taking us to hot springs he owns a hundred odd miles to the north. Our curiosity was his ally, and we finally gave in and let him drive us north in his limousine. Takeuchi's crony, the mayor of Mito, came along.

We drove into a small valley with two large hotels. ("I own both of them, to prevent competition.") A score of servants waited for us outside, and escorted us to a corner suite overlooking a steaming river. A pool fed by a hot spring was assigned to us, and after we had bathed, the limousine drove us up a mountainside to Takeuchi's "farmhouse." It was an old, old house which he had bodily moved from another prefecture, and around which he had built a shell of beauty so exquisite neither Sally nor I have ever seen anything to match it. The house was sparsely furnished, with artistic economy. Each item was functional, and yet each excited admiration. The floor was made of hardwood planks, and the wall of windows opened on a vista of blinking lights. In the middle of the room there was a pit, with a fire burning in it, and over it, suspended on an old farmhouse crane, was an ancient brass pot. The stools around it were early Japanese, and shining with age and care. We drank tea around the pit, and then moved to a small Japanese banquet room for a tea ceremony, combined with a concert on old Japanese instruments. Then came two separate feasts, fish and meat, cooked by two sets of white-capped chefs, who broiled the food on charcoal braziers set before the table.

All through the dinner, we kept probing for information on Inouye, and each time Takeuchi parried the question with a toast. After dinner, when he had had a great deal to drink, he rose and began to dance. His were not the smooth and slow movements of a typical Japanese dancer. This was a warrior's dance, violent and jerky. We were the enemy, and he lunged in our direction and slashed the air with an invisible sword. The long kimono was in the way, and he picked up the bottom ends and opened them, exposing his spindly legs in long white woolen drawers. The sight was grotesque, but it was never funny. This was an angry dance, done in premeditation and filled with meaning.

As abruptly as he began, he now returned to his seat on the floor, filled his cup and offered us a toast. His face was red and unfriendly.

"You Americans talk of democracy," he said. "We don't understand your brand of democracy. It doesn't suit us. Does it mean that the workers get a voice in the management of an industry? Do you have that in the United States? Does it mean that the workers can take over factories, as they have done in Japan? Does it mean that the unions can strike in such a crisis as we have now? Does it mean that men can criticize the emperor?"

His voice was sharp and high and angry. He spoke in long stretches, and even while Roy was still translating, Takeuchi would begin anew. He was getting out of hand, and I was beginning to get worried. Both of us, I knew, would lose face irreparably if I had to restrain him. When a pause came, I thanked him for the gracious reception, and Sally and I retreated to the hotel. Before we left, Takeuchi said, "I'll come for breakfast, and we'll talk about Inouye."

This morning a servant woke us up at five, and I went down to the pool to wash and shave. When I returned, I found the room full. The servants had brought in tiny lacquered tables and placed them in a circle, and now Takeuchi, the mayor of Mito, Sally, and Roy sat waiting for me. Sally, who likes to drink her morning coffee undisturbed, looked intensely unhappy. Each table had a quart of beer, and Takeuchi's table also had a bottle of whisky.

Takeuchi said he was ready to talk of Inouye as soon as we had drunk a toast. The maids poured beer in our glasses, and Takeuchi and the mayor added a slug of whisky to theirs. Takeuchi laughed: "A friendship cocktail—American whisky, Japanese beer." More toasts followed. Inouye was not mentioned again.

I tried anew in the car, when we started back for Mito. Takeuchi said: "When Inouye wrote to me that a close friend of his was coming this way, I made every effort to make this friend's stay here comfortable. But if you desire information, you must go to Inouye himself."

We were silent for a good half hour. Then abruptly Takeuchi began to insist that we go to a historical museum which he had endowed. The museum was close to Inouye's old temple, and I took it that it glorified Japan's past. "You won't understand Inouye, you won't understand *Mito Gaku*, you won't understand what we think and feel until you come with me, and let me explain to you what there is in the museum."

We could not go. We had an appointment with another arch-terrorist, Kosaburo Tachibana. "Tachibana," he snorted. "What's Tachibana compared to Inouye? Listen to Tachibana's words, but don't believe them. He's not sincere."

We lapsed back into an angry silence, and our parting was somewhat less than cordial. All we did find out was that Inouye and his band had had a recent rendezvous in Takeuchi's hotel, "for rest."

Three great Japanese plotters of patriotic murder are alive today—Inouye, Tachibana, and Shumei Okawa, who slapped Tojo on the head at the war crimes trial. All three, in their past, were far more than mere killers. They were philosophers of extreme nationalism, men who did no killing themselves, but whose ideas fired young fanatics into patriotic mayhem. All three agreed that Japan had a political system divinely willed, and matched by no other system. All three felt that corruption had set in, and they wanted to fight it through a coalition of farmers and military fanatics. All three believed in force, and in the name of this solution they plotted the murder of moderate statemen, generals and financiers. But though all three agreed on all this, they detested and mistrusted each other.

The contact between the bands was maintained by special liaison men, and we were now headed for the seashore, where a liaison man named Watabiki, a former navy lieutenant and a follower of Inouye, was waiting for us. We had already had two extremely long sessions with Watabiki, and we knew that he had served a long jail term for trying to murder a statesman. We also knew that Watabiki was a fierce and proud man, who would resent our arrival two hours late.

"Let's tell him we had a flat tire," Sally said.

I agreed it was a good idea. In five minutes, we did have a flat tire. We left it to be repaired in a village garage, and drove on. A few hundred yards this side of Watabiki's house another tire went flat, and we rolled up on a wheel rim. Watabiki listened to our apologies with dignity. "My brother is a chemist," he said. "He'll help you to patch up your tube."

Watabiki's brother was grim, burly and highly competent. But still it took the four of us an hour to remove the inner tube and patch it up. In the course of this hour, we learned that Watabiki and his brother were now distilling salt out of sea water, and that the brother had sat in jail for five years. Very calmly, he explained that he had made dynamite for murder plotters, and got caught at it.

The tube was fixed, but we had no pump. Watabiki said, "I know where I can get one." He got on his bicycle and went off. Fifteen minutes later he returned with a pump, and in another half hour the tire was hard enough to get us to the nearest town. I offered to take the pump back to its owner and asked, "What's his name?"

Watabiki said: "His name is Osawa. He used to be known as Hishinuma. He killed Premier Inukai."

We went on to Tachibana's, and I thought that nowhere in the world could it be possible for a stranger to have a flat fixed by a dynamite maker, pumped with a pump that belonged to a killer, and then be guided by another assassin to a meeting with an arch-plotter of political murder. This is truly a fantastic land.

Tachibana lives on his farm outside of Mito. There is a large and busy yard, and two houses, one an enormous structure with a thatched roof, and the other a smaller house in which Tachibana resides.

Though we were six hours late for our appointment, Tachibana showed no displeasure. He looks like a thin version of Rasputin I once saw on a Russian postcard—stiff, sparse black hair which seemingly has never been cut, long whiskers, a wispy beard and crooked teeth. He wore an untidy black kimono over a polka-dot kimono over white woolen underwear. His eyes were hard and bright, and when he smiled the subject was not necessarily amusing.

We all sat in his study—a large and shabby room, with one wall stacked with books. The straw mats on the floor were tattered, the paper in the door panels was torn, and all through the interview there was a sound of gnawing right over our heads. When Tachibana saw that Sally was uneasy, he reassured her: "*Nezumi!* A rat!"

There were at first six of us: Sally, Roy, and I; Watabiki and Tachibana, and his sister, a homely, middle-aged woman with a warm expression on her face. We later found out she had been a well-known concert pianist. Soon after the interview began, a very dark, tall man came in, and Tachibana introduced him laconically as, "Uno, a friend." Uno wore a black frockcoat, which made him look professorial.

Tachibana is a fluent speaker. He constantly interspersed his Japanese with such Occidental expressions as "absolutism," "Nihilism," "William the Conqueror," and "narodniki," for the Russian Populists. He also quoted freely from Fraser's *Golden Bough*, Tolstoy, Hegael, Walt Whitman, and others. The entire conversation was a weird mixture of Japanese feudal philosophy and Western liberalism.

"*Mito Gaku* is a Japanese type of democracy," said Tachibana. "It teaches that the Japanese people and history cannot be considered apart from the emperor. The whole nation is a family, and the emperor is its head. The Communists are screaming now that unless the emperor is removed, Japan will remain a feudal country. They don't understand the emperor's true essence. It was only after the usurpers were overthrown eighty years ago, and Emperor Meiji came to power, that feudalism came to an end. And it was through Emperor Meiji that the teachings of *Mito Gaku* became the basis of our philosophy."

The emperors, Tachibana said, liberated the rural folk. The final emancipation came with the American-written Land Reform Law, "which's exactly what I've been preaching for twenty years."

"The only trouble," he said, "is that the farmers have been oppressed for centuries, and they don't yet understand the nature of the reform. What they need is an instrument of political power. A political party—like the Farmers' Party of Ibaragi Prefecture."

"I haven't heard of it," I said. "Who are its leaders?"

Uno edged forward and smiled. Tachibana stuck his finger at Uno: "He! He's the president." In the last election, they said, the party ran three candidates, one of whom won 25,000 votes, or 5,000 votes short of the number that would have elected him to the Diet. The party seemingly drew its members from among poor farmers, and its cash from the landlords.

I said, "If Mr. Uno is president, am I right in assuming that Mr. Tachibana is the adviser?" They both thought it very funny. Uno said, "Mr. Tachibana isn't allowed to hold political posts under the purge directive. Therefore, I'm the president, and he's the adviser."

I told them I thought the directive did not apply to local politics. Both of them then went into a long and spirited discussion. Finally Uno said, "We'll check on what you say. If it's true that the purge directive doesn't apply, then Mr. Tachibana will become president, and I'll be the adviser." We all laughed. It was a good joke.

"I am a Socialist," said Tachibana, "yet, instead of joining up with the Socialists, I joined with the younger officers.

You may wonder why. The reason is simple. The Socialists and the Communists come from the cities. Most of the younger officers, on the other hand, came from the villages, and they were deeply concerned about the rural distress.

"You must also know the truth about the emperors. The Japanese emperors descend from a line of Sun goddesses, who are agricultural gods. The bonds between the emperor and the farmers are, therefore, very close.

"I'm now fifty-three. At the age of twenty, I first realized that farmers must take political action. Though I was a farmer myself, I began to study. First, I was interested in the Germans —Kant and Hegel. Then I read most of William James and Bergson. I also studied Tolstoy, who exerted a great influence on my ideas.

"After years of thinking, I opened a school in that house over there. . . . " He pointed at the big house in the yard. "It was called Native Land-Loving School, and in the beginning it had twenty-five students. Twelve of them later took part in the May 15th Incident. . . . "

Calmly, he told us of the "May 15th Incident"—a *coup d'état* attempted by the Big Three of patriotic terrorism, Priest Inouye, Okawa, and Tachibana. Okawa supplied the funds, Inouye supplied the murderers. Tachibana's young followers were to blow up the Tokyo power stations and some *zaibatsu* banks. On the appointed day in 1932, they tossed their Navy handgrenades, but so clumsily that little damage was done. Tachibana stood trial, at which he delivered blistering accusations against "corrupt" society. He spent eight years in prison.

We said goodbye to him, and in the darkness, I went over to the big house, to see if it was true that it was now occupied by Tachibana's relatives. The hut was enormous, and in the dim light I saw a number of people there. They were all young men. For all I knew, they might well have been Tachibana's cousins.

We drove back, across the ruined city of Mito, and Watabiki, the killer, broke his silence just twice. The first time he asked me if I had seen the old scroll in the room. It had been drawn by the last of the military usurpers, and it extolled the happiness of men in a peaceful world:

A turtle
Enjoys itself
By the peaceful pond.

We were silent again, and he said: "You know, this Farmers' Party of Tachibana's. Actually, it's being run neither by Tachibana nor Uno. Its real boss is Tachibana's son-in-law, Hanawa. He has also been purged, but he works unofficially."

We dropped Watabiki off at his small, dark house on the seacoast and said goodbye. He wheeled about and walked across a narrow stretch of rocky shore, a small, straight, compact figure in clothes that were three sizes too big for him, but did not detract from his dignity or strength.

We drove back to the bordello, and I watched Sally, tired and beaten by her severe cold, start cooking on a charcoal brazier. It was raining again, and the room was cold and dark. "To hell with it," I said. "Let's go back to Tokyo tonight." Sally agreed. She was worn out, but she had not wanted to say anything because she thought it might spoil an exciting trip for me. We packed in half an hour, said goodbye to the *madame*, and drove off. We reached Tokyo six hours later.

September 30, 1946   TOKYO

In our absence, the Chinese Mission here called a press conference, at which it attacked "vested interests" for denying China the silk cocoons she wants from Japan. This was the first time the Chinese had kicked over their traces, and they did it with considerable vigor: "The same interests which before the war exported scrap iron into Japan. . . . "

I am told that when General Marquat rushed to General MacArthur with the news of the Chinese statement, MacArthur said irritably: "What do *they* want? They've forgotten they're in debt to us." I am also informed that it was

General MacArthur himself who turned down the Chinese application.

General MacArthur's reason was given to me by one of his silk advisers: "It just doesn't make much sense to build up the Chinese silk industry when you're trying to help Japan."

What no one except the Chinese cares to recall is that China had a lusty silk industry in 1937, when the Japanese Army came in, and tore it out by the roots. The Japanese silk industry liked competition no better then than it does now.

October 4, 1946   TOKYO

The *Yomiuri* is back in the news.

After four months of desperate maneuvering, Kikunami's Newspaper and Radio Workers Union went on strike today. Ostensibly it is seeking to force Baba, the publisher, to comply with the order of the Labor Arbitration Board to rehire the thirty-one men he fired in July. But no simple explanations ever apply to the *Yomiuri*. The union wants more than justice for thirty-one men. It is fighting for its own life.

With the help of General Baker and Major Imboden, the Japanese publishers are gradually destroying the union. Baba has set up a company union on his paper. Imboden has helped to break up the union on a daily in Japan's north. Now he has been moving in on the two great newspaper chains, the *Asahi* and the *Mainichi*. The union knows that it will be crippled if Imboden succeeds.

But even that is too simple an explanation. Neither Baker nor Imboden is an important man. Both are merely instruments of a policy which must inevitably destroy the progressive press in Japan. There is no longer any question of communism. Baker and Imboden are now after the moderates who find fault with the "new democracy" and its Japanese sponsors.

This time the Newspaper Union is better prepared than it was in July. It is not fighting alone. The newspaper strike will be a part of what labor calls "The October Offensive."

Instead of calling a general strike, which might be banned by Headquarters, the unions will walk out in succession, each with a demand for a living wage. The second in the strike line are the coal miners. The third are the electrical workers.

Special care is being taken to give Headquarters no cause to break the strike. The printers will continue to set the army newspaper. The striking radiomen will stay on the job in the army stations. The Japanese papers will cease publication, but will issue special editions carrying the texts of any new American directives and reports of the War Crimes trail.

Correspondents were told of the strike at a press conference called by the union. Two of them, noted for their antilabor views, very deftly tried to catch the union spokesman in an anti-American statement. The bait they dangled before him was a visit paid by Major Imboden to the *Asahi* plant. It seems that the good major said nothing; he just looked stern. But as soon as he left, the management started a rumor that Headquarters was planning to take over the plant, if the union went on strike.

The spokesman chose his words with care. "I've heard that Major Imboden visited the *Asahi*, but I don't like to say anything about it. Whatever we do, is done to protect the workers' rights. It's also done with full respect for the Occupation policies. . . . A state of uncertainty has prevailed in the *Asahi* since the major's visit. What worries us is not the suffering, but the solidarity of labor. Ours is a young union, and there are great outside pressures at work."

Later, in the gutted power plant which serves as strike headquarters, we found out what some of the outside pressures are. The plant is a two-story blackened shell. The strikers have strung out a few dim lights in it, built a ramshackle stairway, and put in old tables and benches. Now a "financial committee" was at work in a corner. In another, a committee was considering the problem of getting rice for the pickets. Artists were drawing posters, a mimeographing machine was turning out leaflets, messengers were rushing in and out. In the center sat the "Strike Direction Committee."

Fromm, Costello, and I came in just as a message arrived from a daily in southern Japan. After the workers voted to strike, the message said, a U.S. Army sergeant came to the plant and announced that no strike would be allowed.

We were still there when two agitated delegates arrived from an interview with an American officer in the Radio Division of Headquarters. He had told them bluntly, they said, that if the radio workers struck, he would throw them in jail.

"These are Headquarters orders. If you disobey, you'll suffer the consequences."

Such decisions are not easy to make. There was a ring of men around us now, dark and silent. They waited for the committee's ruling. Work elsewhere ceased, and more people came up. The members put their heads together, and whispered. Finally the chairman spoke up:

"We shall not in any way interfere with U.S. Army broadcasts. All we want is to exercise our legal right to strike, given to us by General MacArthur. The radio strike will begin as scheduled."

Imboden's tour of the *Asahi* was a shrewd move, for the only axiom of this strike is, "As the *Asahi* goes, so goes the press." All the tremendous power that is seeking to break the strike—Headquarters, the Yoshida Cabinet, the publishers—has now been concentrated on the *Asahi*, on the large auditorium on the top floor, where the workers have been closeted for nearly twenty-four hours in an effort to make up their minds. They had once decided to join the strike, but the fearful among them asked for a new debate.

At midnight, word came that the *Asahi* might reverse itself, and pull out of the strike. Hugh Deane, of the Allied Labor News, and I went to the *Asahi* building. We came into the closely packed hall just as a delegation of *Yomiuri* strikers was pleading passionately for support. The sentiment in that room was a tangible element, and we could see it sway this way and that as one speaker followed another. The last speaker put in words what was hidden deep in their minds:

"General MacArthur is opposed to strikes. He would not

hestitate to close up the *Asahi* if we strike. You saw Major Imboden. . . . "

When the decision not to strike was finally announced, there was a period of silence. And the only sounds that were audible in the room were the sobs of men—both the victors and the losers. For even the men who opposed the strike said fear was their only counsel.

October 5, 1946   TOKYO

This morning the five million radios of Japan went silent. Despite the *Asahi's* decision last night, the radio workers decided to strike. The official heat is now on the *Mainichi*, whose workers have voted to walk out. A Japanese editor told me the *Mainichi* management was in conference with General Baker—presumably to map out strategy.

I went to the Labor Division of Headquarters to find out its stand on the strike. I found only a group of disheartened, frustrated men. Our policy in Japan has been based on the premise that a strong labor movement is the best guardian of democracy. The Labor Division was given the job of nursing the unions to strength. But back last spring, the Labor Division discovered that strong labor was anathema to many powerful men in Headquarters. While the Labor Division was talking in pious phrases to Japanese union leaders, Counter Intelligence agents were breaking up labor demonstrations, Imboden had begun his campaign of union-busting, General Baker had entered the picture. Men big and small, from sergeants in remote detachments to General Willoughby, have begun to remake the U.S. labor policy for Japan. From time to time, the Labor Division tried to assert its interest in the subject. It was quickly slapped on the wrist. Its chief, Cohen, a young man with a pathological fear of being labelled red (though Lord knows he is not), was no match for his tough military opponents. At this point, not even Japanese labor pays much attention to the Labor Division. It has learned at a bitter cost where the real power lies in Headquarters.

"We had orders to stay out of this mess," an officer said. "We also had orders not to talk to correspondents. Go away."

Thus, while Japanese labor fights its greatest battle in history, and Imboden and Baker are engaged in what is known as "housebreaking the labor movement," the Labor Division is hiding in a neutral corner.

At noon, for the fourth time, the *Asahi* workers decided to reconsider their decision. They filed back into the auditorium, and began the argument anew. At this point the strike score stood: 40 newspapers throughout Japan for the strike, 3 against, 13 sitting on the fence. But the *Asahi* remains the heart of the movement. As long as it is working, there is no real strike. If the heart stops, other newspapers will shut their plants. The radio workers are thus fighting it out on their own. The government today threatened to set up an emergency transmitter, but discovered it could get no one to operate it. Baba, the *Yomiuri* publisher, meanwhile announced that he would start a campaign for a chain of company unions in the newspapers of Japan.

In the afternoon, the Japanese police threw cordons around every newspaper plant in Tokyo. Employees were allowed to leave the buildings, but not to re-enter. This meant that the mass meetings in half a dozen newspapers were isolated from each other. The central strike committee countered with loudspeakers mounted on trucks. The loudspeakers cruised in front of the *Asahi*, and roared pleas to the workers to join the strike. Shortly after noon, American Military Police broke up one rally of radio workers, while the Japanese police dispersed another.

Later, a procession of sympathetic unions marched by the *Yomiuri* building. It sang lustily, and waved posters denouncing Baba, the Yoshida Cabinet, and the so-called "depression firings." The *Yomiuri* doors were locked. The plant guards stood in the upper-story windows, and yelled insults and challenges.

The whole crew of correspondents was covering the parade. To all of us, whether we sympathized with Baba or the strikers, this shabby building was the testing ground of our policy for Japan. Everyone of us knew of the secret moves being made by American officers to break up the strike. But we all wondered if these moves could be translated into positive action.

We got our answer. Sally and I were sitting in our jeep catty-corner from the *Yomiuri* building. A military policeman came up and asked my business. I pointed at the "Chicago *Sun*," painted in foot-high letters on the jeep. He took down my name and the jeep number. He said, "Move on." I told him I would stay put and cover the procession. That ended the conversation.

But, meanwhile, in front of the *Yomiuri*, a hundred Japanese policemen and a unit of American MPs had gone into action. The procession was orderly. Then suddenly armed men were upon it, pushing the demonstrants, seizing the posters, breaking up the parade. The marchers did not resist. But as fast as one group was broken up, another one reformed its ranks somewhere else. Their own marshals kept them in line. The men and women fell into new ranks, and sang, and waved flags.

In the middle of it, Captain William Riley, who led the force of MPs, ordered American correspondents off the sidewalk. When Costello, whose leg bothered him, lagged behind, Riley threatened him with arrest. Costello, who is an extremely calm and competent individual, told the captain to go ahead and arrest him. Margaret Parton then pitched in:

"Yes, go ahead! And me too!"

Riley thought better of it.

At eight at night, the *Asahi* workers, for the third time, re-affirmed their decision to stay out of the strike. But this time, bitterness had broken through the walls of self-restraint. Few men now hid their resentment against the American policy. One after another, they rose to cry out their support for the strike, and to protest against a policy that filled them with fear.

"If I were allowed to talk of the Allied policy toward labor and the press," said a young *Asahi* reporter, "I could speak for three hours. There's much talk of a 'free press.' But how about the censorship which forbids us to criticize our own government?

"Headquarters gives us freedom to print all we like, but expects us to print only propaganda. Now it's trying to break up the *Asahi* and the *Mainichi*. Three months ago, Headquarters warned the *Yomiuri* of its 'inaccuracy.' After that the *Yomiuri* was destroyed. Now the *Asahi* is warned, and Major Imboden attacks us for publishing a story that has already been passed by the American censors."

After the meeting, men filed out of the building weeping. There was no need to tell the crowd waiting outside what had happened. The sobs told the story. I went down to the strike headquarters in the power plant. There were a few score men and women there, but the militant spirit was gone. The strikers are learning some bitter lessons. One of their leaders was discovered to be a government agent provocateur, who has been in constant touch with one of Yoshida's secretaries. I talked to Kikunami in a corner. He was utterly worn out. "The printers were with us," he said, "but the white-collar people were frightened. They need more education before they learn to stand up for their rights."

I was with Kikunami when the word came that the *Mainichi*, in a double-reverse, had again decided to strike. But few in this dark, gloomy barn were cheered. The *Mainichi* unit will reverse itself again when it learns of the *Asahi* vote.

October 8, 1946 TOKYO

The newspaper strike has fizzled out. There is a split within the Newspaper Union and the Congress of Industrial Unions, both headed by Kikunami. The *Asahi* union is breaking up, and Kikunami is to be ousted. The emboldened Yoshida government has given orders to the police to "go all out." Some Japanese officials have already met to chart an antiunion campaign. A union officer today described the past two days to me as "the darkest since surrender."

The trouble began yesterday morning. Some strikers tried to prevent the distribution of the printed *Mainichi* and *Yomiuri* papers. They threw a ring around the bundles of newspapers and locked their arms. The management summoned the police. Eight strikers were arrested, and the strike headquarters in an adjoining building was closed up.

In the afternoon the police ordered the strikers out of Radio Tokyo. About fifty men and women walked out, in ranks and singing. As they reached the sidewalk, the police were upon them. The leader of the group, a young man in a dark suit and glasses, was hit on the head with a night stick. When he turned around, dazed, the policeman struck him in the face. A woman who protested was hit in the mouth with a night stick. The ejected strikers were chased across the street, beaten with batons, kicked and slapped.

But the police made a tactical error. The place was in full view of the correspondents in their newsroom. Handleman of I.N.S. and Fromm halted the policeman who struck the young man and asked his name. The policeman produced his card and seemed pleased with the whole affair. While they were talking, the victim ran up. His shirt was torn. He was shouting:

"You can't do this to us. We have democracy in Japan."

Handleman led the policeman inside to the Japanese captain in command. After listening to the policeman's explanation, the captain gave his verdict:

"Mistake!"

But having tasted the old delight of breaking up a crowd, the Japanese police got into the habit. This afternoon, four thousand people met on the Imperial Plaza in a "Sweet Potato Rally." The meeting was called to protest the spoilage of hundreds of tons of potatoes at the railroad stations because of an official mix-up.

After the meeting, six hundred demonstrants marched to the Metropolitan Police Board. As they massed before the huge, red brick building, a flying wedge of a hundred policemen came out and charged into the crowd. Thirteen paraders were seriously injured. The demonstration was broken up.

As splinters of it drifted away, a group of twenty men and women went to the headquarters of the striking radiomen. They said, "We want you to fight to final victory." A woman, who said she was hit on the head, kept pointing at her mussed hair as if it was a badge of honor. Ordinarily, this might have been funny. But this time none of us thought the scene comic. It was an episode charged with drama, and involving little people who took their democratic rights seriously. Were they not assured by the new laws of their right to strike, to bargain collectively, to voice their grievances?

A young Japanese who says he is a relative of Premier Yoshida was at the club tonight, as a guest of an Australian correspondent. The latter describes his guest as "that young man with an Oxford accent and a homosexual giggle." We were talking of the police violence, and the young man with the giggle said, with that lovely, high-pitched accent of his:

"You know, old fellow, you can't blame these chaps for breaking up the demonstrations. They haven't had so much fun since Japan's surrender."

After dinner, Margaret Parton and I were working on our stories in the dining room. By accident, we discovered we had written similar leads: "Two hours after the Diet passed the new Constitution, officially labelled as democratic, Japanese police today brutally broke up a demonstration of striking radio workers. . . . "

For today should be a great day for Japan—the formal inauguration of a democratic state, based on respect for man's rights, a state in which no heads are cracked for protesting against the wastage of food in a year of hunger, a state in which the laws are put on the books to be enforced by the government, and not sabotaged. It was perhaps symbolic of the great, publicity-made mirage which is the Japanese democracy that the sounds heard on this day were not the cheers of a happy people but the groans of men assaulted by the police.

Later, a large group of us got into a heated discussion of the labor picture, with more than one correspondent recalling the Washington "hunger march" that General MacArthur helped to break up back in '32. Before long, five of us—Margaret, Walker, Costello, Fromm, and I—were drafting a letter to the general requesting a group interview. The letter was simple enough: we pointed out that the actions of some officers in Headquarters in recent weeks have indicated a change in the avowed U.S. labor policy in Japan, and we respectfully requested an opportunity to obtain what information we could.

Personally, I am puzzled. If the strike *is* political, it certainly comes under the provisions of that wise statement of policy sent to General MacArthur thirteen months ago by the Departments of State, War, and Navy. The general was expressly ordered to "permit and favor" changes in the form of government, *even if this involved the use of force by the Japanese people*. Yoshida is so generally detested that even Headquarters is aware of it. Yet, all popular efforts to unseat Yoshida are deliberately, if furtively, broken up. I am convinced that had Headquarters stayed out of the newspaper strike, Yoshida would have been forced out.

But if the strike is *not* political, then, in the light of our own professed labor policy in Japan, we should not have interfered, nor should we have allowed the Japanese police to interfere with a legitimate demand for better wages. For even Headquarters' own statistics show that no man can live on the Y.500 ($33) a month permitted him by law.

Considered either way, it is a tragic blunder of policy. Our avowed goal is to create defenders of democracy in Japan, so that when we pack up and go home, democracy can survive the offensive of the Old Guard. Among the prime defenders of democracy we have listed labor. Yet every time labor becomes restless, we try to beat it down and smear it with red paint. The Americans who do it are men puny in their concept of democracy and their view of our objectives in Japan. The only result they achieve is to split the labor movement into two camps, neither of which we seemingly want in Japan. One camp is packed with the timid non-reds who want to stay out of trouble today as they will want to stay out of trouble when the Japanese nationalists openly take power. And the other camp is the red camp, into which our policy is driving embittered men, to whom we promised hope and strength and instead have given police batons and a government of old-timers.

October 9, 1946   TOKYO

Two months after the Japanese were ordered to write a land reform law, the obscene haggle continues. Only on the matter of the *zaibatsu* has the Japanese resistance been more skillful or obstinate. The Old Guard has shown a genius for sabotage that leaves our officers gasping in amazement.

The Japanese have been using what is known here as "go-chase-your-tail" technique. They send a draft to Colonel Schenck's Natural Resources Section for approval. The Americans find it full of loopholes, and toss it back for redrafting. The Japanese make the desired changes but open up clever loopholes somewhere else. It was not until mid-August that General MacArthur found a bill that met with his approval.

Recently, experts in General Whitney's Government Section took a long look at the approved bill, and found it full of holes. The biggest was the fact that the success of the law depended on local committees, dominated by landlords. The Americans talked to the Japanese about it. The Japanese shrugged their shoulders. There was nothing they could do about it, they said, "because General MacArthur has already approved the bill."

Five days ago, Colonel Kades, General Whitney's deputy, met with Colonel Schenck to see what could be done about some safeguards. Schenck, who is not too happy about General

Whitney's poaching on his preserves, said he also could do nothing:

"The bill is a sacred trust from General MacArthur."

October 10, 1946   TOKYO

One of the major tragedies of our Occupation is that we have chosen small minds for one of the biggest jobs in our history. There are luminous exceptions. But too many men in too many sections are woefully unequal to the problems with which they must cope. Some of the blunders are merely funny. But there are errors of judgment which can be measured only in terms of vast human suffering, economic dislocation, and spiritual vacuum. What is even worse than mere incompetence is the fact that many Americans do not understand the essence of democracy, which they have come to teach.

Typical are the two American comments on an ordinance removing the imperial princes from the public trough. The ordinance was pushed through by some able officers in General Marquat's Finance Division. Before the day was gone, two indignant telephone calls were received in the division.

The first was from a general in command of a Section. "What do you mean by this outrageous business?" he demanded. "Do you realize that it will compel the princes to go to work?"

The other call was from a colonel close to General MacArthur: "This ordinance puts the princes on the same basis as any other people. You can't do that! They're royalty. Why, now they can be sued like other people."

The division's retort, quick and much bolder than could be expected: "We thought that's what democracy is all about."

I got to thinking on this topic today after reading excerpts from a personal memo written by Major Imboden and now being circulated at the Press Club. What struck me as significant was not Imboden's attack on the concept of war guilt, or on the unions (which, after all, we are pledged to encourage), or on the Labor Division in Headquarters. I was primarily interested in the memo as a statement of political faith from a man to whom we had granted the power to give Japan a truly democratic press.

"The concept of the 'reorganization' [of the Japanese press]," Imboden said, "was predicated upon the belief that the Japanese themselves would do the job and get rid of war editors and owners. . . . Personal freedom has always dominated my make-up, and, as I see it, a newspaper's social and economic system predicated upon war guilt threatens in Japan to destroy free speech. . . .

"The development of the Japanese industrial society has been accompanied by standardizing pressures through unions, that are subtly enslaving in their effect. . . .

"In the case of Baba, there appears to be a Japanese who values personal freedom. I recommend earnestly that we secure permission to assist Baba in his present troubles. . . . There is no one to whom Baba can go. He is entirely on his own, for the Labor Division apparently is interested only in union labor and its right to strike, whether justly or unjustly. . . . "

But Imboden is only a tool, a minor figure in the elaborate Army super-government which runs Japan. The policies and the high strategy are made by about a dozen men around General MacArthur, a group variously known as the Inner Circle and the Bataan Boys. Incompetence here is relatively rare. Most of the men are shrewd, hard working, and ruthless. What sins are found here are the typical sins of military minds, dedicated to the ideas of order and discipline, accustomed to the use of force as the answer to difficult problems, and—with exceptions—unendowed with the talent of statesmanship. There are in the Inner Circle men who had been civilians before the war. They, too, through the process of assimilation, have acquired the military mind.

At the moment, the top men of the Inner Circle are Major General P. J. Mueller, Chief of Staff, and Generals Marquat,

Willoughby, and Whitney. There are a few colonels close to General MacArthur's ear, and they wield great influence, but it is upon this quartet that General MacArthur depends for counsel.

General Marquat once ran an automobile page on a West Coast daily, and still likes to remind listeners that he is a newspaperman. During the war he became chief of General MacArthur's antiaircraft artillery. This is why men, mindful of his past qualifications, could not quite understand why he was appointed Chief of the Economic and Scientific Section, and thus granted powers roughly combining those of the U.S. Secretaries of Treasury, Commerce and Labor, Director of the Budget, and Chairman of the Federal Reserve System. It was then that official Tokyo originated the cruel, and totally unjustified, quip of "MacArthur's worst mistake." General MacArthur made no mistake in selecting Marquat for the post. He wanted a loyal military man at the head of the mass of suspicious civilian experts in a key section, and he picked Marquat. The latter candidly admitted his inadequacies and readily took the advice of his experts. He carried with him, to the most crucial financial conferences, a leather cavalry whip, with which he marked the emphases. He floundered in a sea of technical detail. He made a mess of his brief chairmanship of the Allied Council by behaving like a drill sergeant. But he fulfilled the mission assigned to him by General MacArthur. And he remained the most likable of the men of the Inner Circle. He did not pretend to be what he so obviously could not be, and he had a rough sense of humor.

Willoughby and Whitney were different. Their minds were quick and complex. They had sharply defined ideas on the kind of Japan they wanted to see, and they fought hard to sway General MacArthur to their way of thinking. If there are gradations in extreme conservatism, Whitney was more liberal than Willoughby. Both were dedicated to the defeat of Russia and communism, but they differed on the method. Willoughby believes in suppression, in drastic surgery. Whitney feels that a small measure of reform might win more allies than the use of night sticks. Each hates the other.

Four weeks ago, Willoughby made a speech before the Stanford Club here which well mirrored his political philosophy. As reported to me by an American listener, Willoughby said:

> The Japanese Army has been a first-rate army. It fought well. It is accused of having committed atrocities. But this is understandable when an army has its back to the wall.
>
> We have just dealt with the German police state. We shall take care of the new police states that have now emerged in Europe.
>
> I know many of you are worried over the possibility of new conflicts flaring up on Japanese soil. I want you to know that when such a conflict comes, we shall be shoulder to shoulder with you. I also want you to know that you have many friends in Headquarters.

Even more significant than the speech itself were the circumstances in which it was made. The general spoke before a gathering of some twenty-five Japanese and four or five Americans. The Japanese, among whom the *zaibatsu* were well represented, were highly pleased. One of them later asked me to find out if Willoughby spoke for General MacArthur, and if Japan is to be our ally in the coming war with Russia. ("You force me not to speak privately before any group," Willoughby said to me petulantly when I questioned him. "I honestly don't remember what I said. There was a small group of Japanese. Completely unimportant people. You know, a group of shabby gentility.")

The common denominator for the men of the Inner Circle is devotion to the Chief. Those who lack the full measure of loyalty have long been dropped by the wayside. It is this devotion, to a degree, that impels many of them to fight each other for the privilege of being closest to the Chief. Many of them ganged up on General Dyke when he seemed to be doing too well. General Baker, who, as Public Relations Officer, is always with General MacArthur, and yet is not one of his major political advisers, is openly critical of some of his rivals. Baker may not realize it, but some of his irritable *bon mots* about his fellow-generals have become part of the Press Club lore.

Possibly as a result of this rivalry, the composition of the Inner Circle fluctuates. In the first six weeks of the Occupation two top men in Headquarters were Colonel Sydney F. Mashbir and Brigadier General Bonner Fellers. One of General MacArthur's key Intelligence officers through the war, Mashbir was constantly by the Chief's side. But he made some awkward statements, the correspondents pounced on them, and since adverse publicity is one of the cardinal sins in this theater, Mashbir quickly vanished from the scene. Fellers lasted a little longer, but he also could not survive his feuds.

If anyone among the Bataan Boys could be described as a political analyst and philosopher, Fellers came closest to it. I do not know exactly how much influence Fellers had on General MacArthur's patterns of thought, but I am constantly startled to find the reflection of Fellers' ideas in the general's pronouncements. Until recently, when (he told me) General MacArthur ordered him "to keep my mouth shut," Fellers had spoken readily on almost any political topic. Thus a substantial file has accumulated on his political and social philosophy.

Fellers, for instance, is convinced that President Roosevelt forced the United States into the war, and that there never should have been a war with Germany. "Emperor Hirohito," he told a correspondent, "is no more a war criminal than Roosevelt. As a matter of fact, if you examine the record closely. . . . "

The Soviet influence, Fellers holds, is expanding, and may even reach the English Channel. In other words, the Russians are "closing in on the white races, which are looking to Britain for leadership. The Slav is coming in with communism, and the Anglo-Saxon is the one to save the West."

If the United States pulled out of Europe, he asks, "Will the countries from which the white races came perish?" And his own answer is not unexpected: "It's almost worth another war" to save "the cradle of the white race."

Fellers has been vigorously opposed to peacetime compulsory military service as unnecessary, and accused "New Deal

bureaucrats and war mongers" of using it as a means to perpetuate themselves in power. The Navy, Fellers believes, is obsolete.

"The atomic bomb did that," he has said. "In the next war
the Navy will be carrying freight.

Not unnaturally, because their own destiny was welded to
his, the Bataan Boys have been urging General MacArthur on
to a wider stage. One of the choicest Inner Circle secrets,
whispered about but never as yet published, is the story of how
General MacArthur might have missed the climax to his career,
the occupation of Japan.

In the last stages of the battle for Europe in 1944, the general's advisers began to feel that his time had come to move to
a larger stage. It was felt that the transfer of men and supplies
to the Pacific theater would take many months. These would
be months of enforced and unwelcome obscurity for the
general.

Instead of waiting, the advisers felt, the general should seek
wider responsibilities elsewhere. They wanted to see him as
U.S. spokesman in liberated Europe, an impregnable rock
against foreign intrigue, a match for a Churchill or a Stalin.
Enthralled by this vision, the advisers urged General Mac-
Arthur to announce that he had brought his mission to a successful end with the recapture of Corregidor and Bataan, and
proclaim his availability for a new assignment.

General MacArthur did not take the advice. Perhaps he
felt that his mission would not be complete until he entered
Tokyo. Possibly he was not certain that once he gave up the
job in the Pacific, jealous Washington would give him a top
assignment elsewhere. But it is interesting to speculate on what
would have happened had he been chosen to speak for us in
Europe.

Would he have followed the political precedents he set in
the Allied Council here? Would our relations in Europe have
degenerated to the shameful squabbles exhibited every other
Wednesday, like dirty linen, in the Council chambers? Would
he have backed the Yoshidas and Shideharas of the West?
Would his generals have considered Europe as a battleground

for the coming war with Russia, or would they have seen it as a continent of a score of nations, each with its pride, its needs, its yearning for peace, and its own way of life and foreign policy?

But the men who wanted the general to speak for the United States in Europe saw even that assignment as a stepping stone to the biggest job of all—the presidency of the United States. For though few Americans have known it, the Inner Circle has functioned for years as a tight political machine with a "favorite son" and with intimate bonds with the solid, conservative, isolationist core of the Republican party.

In this union, the key role has belonged to Fellers, a friend of Herbert Hoover and General R. E. Wood, Chairman of the Board of Directors of Sears, Roebuck and former head of America First. Another important figure in Headquarters has been J. Woodall Greene, now with the Civil Information and Education Section. Greene is a retired millionaire, a former Republican National Committeeman, and a friend of Colonel Robert McCormick, of the Chicago *Tribune*. During the war, Greene requested duty with General MacArthur in Australia. According to shop talk in Headquarters, one of Greene's tasks was to sound out General MacArthur on running in the presidential elections.

In 1944 some of General MacArthur's aides met in a secret conference in Brisbane to discuss the general's chances in the election. Among those present were Philip LaFollette, then on General MacArthur's staff, and General Willoughby, himself an ardent Republican. The decision, of course, was against entering the election. It was realized that President Roosevelt was a tough man to beat. General MacArthur also wanted to complete his mission in the Pacific.

But the men around General MacArthur are now looking to the next election. The general's chances, they feel, are better than ever before. He is not only a military hero. He is also an administrator, who in a year has transformed an aggressor nation into a democracy.

"Mac is not a young man any more," a colonel told a few of

us a week ago. "His mind is still quick and sharp. But his body can't last much longer. He has been following a pretty rigorous schedule. At sixty-six, you can't do too much of that sort of thing very long. When he is tired, he shows his age. He knows this is the last election he can enter, or influence. We all think he'll make a try at one or the other."

October 12, 1946

In a cold, hard rain went to Hibiya Park to watch a strike rally. Fifty thousand people had been expected, but only a couple of thousand showed up, and now they hid under umbrellas and sought inadequate shelter under trees undressed by autumn. The meeting was originally scheduled for the Imperial Plaza. At the last minute, the police said the emperor was to cross the plaza, and they did not want any crowds around, and threatened to break up the rally if it were not moved.

The speakers, soaking wet and grim, stood on a truck. Among them was Kikunami, hard and defiant and unwilling to concede defeat in the press strike. ("Only the first skirmish has been lost," he told me last night.) It is hard to believe that this man is essentially a scholar, with no union experience. He has made bad errors of judgment in the past few weeks. He has been over-emotional, and unable to delegate authority. But he is learning, as the whole Japanese labor movement is learning, and if constant frustration does not drive him to extremes, he may yet be a great labor leader. As it is, he already belongs to the history of this turbulent era.

Now the speakers talked to the coal miners, fifty thousand of whom have just walked out in the far north, and of the electrical workers who will strike in three days. It will be an unorthodox strike, in which power will be supplied as usual, but no one will come around to collect the money.

The speeches were brave, and so were the resolutions. Among the latter were demands for the end of police repression, a wage tied to the soaring living costs, and the perennial one on the settlement of the *Yomiuri* dispute. Later, a delegation led by Kikunami tried to see Premier Yoshida. He was having lunch and would see no one.

October 14, 1946 TOKYO

Leaving for Korea tomorrow, with Charlotte Ebener, of *Newsweek*, and Foster Hailey, of the New York *Times*. A sudden hitch developed three days ago, when Brigadier General A. P. Fox summoned me to the Office of the Deputy Chief of Staff, announced that he was sitting as a court-martial officer, and demanded that I reveal the names of my informants for a recent article. The story was a belated report on that fantastic conference in May when a group of colonels objected to purging war criminals from Japan's big business. Headquarters apparently was far less perturbed by what the colonels had to say than by the fact that one of them had talked to a reporter.

I was told that I could inform no one—not even my editor —of the summons, and that I was not entitled to legal counsel. General Fox also told me I could not leave Tokyo. I refused to answer any questions without guidance from the *Sun*, and promptly filed a long report to Chicago. The next morning, the *Sun* notified me it had taken action with the War Department. And yesterday morning thirteen correspondents, led by Russell Brines of the Associated Press, and Crane of the New York *Times*, filed into General Baker's office, and demanded an explanation. The right to protect one's sources of information is one of the basic elements of a free press, and no correspondent is willing to make any concessions on it. Ten minutes after the group left Baker's presence, General Fox telephoned me to tell me I would "no longer be required in this investigation."

KOREA

The trip from Tokyo, in an old army transport, was uncomfortable and uneventful. I slept most of the way and did not wake up until the plane started coming down to a landing. The airport was buzzing with activity—bombers and transports warming up, fighters taxiing all over the place, trucks, jeeps, bulldozers at work. It was a regular army base with little civilian nonsense about it.

A young lieutenant gave us a lift to Seoul in a sedan. We drove along a wide dirt road, and watched the face of poverty—the straw-and-mud huts sagging at the corners; the bare yards; the lean mongrels lying in the sun; the men with enormous loads of straw and branches on their backs; and the women with jars and bundles finely balanced on their heads. Charlotte and I agreed that, in contrast, China looked well-to-do.

The lieutenant spoke of the Koreans with contempt. He said they were dirty and treacherous. We were watching a flight of fighter planes cavorting over villages to the west. The planes dived in a mock attack, re-formed in the sky, and then dived on a new target.

"Psychological warfare," the lieutenant said. "That's the only way to show these gooks we won't stand for any monkey business."

Major Buel A. Williamson, the red faced, stout Public Relations Officer to Lieutenant General John R. Hodge, our commander for Korea, made a stab at affability. He made me think of a real estate agent, appraising visitors to his office to see if he would earn a commission. His face fell when I said I did not want to see General Hodge until I had had a chance to look around and understand the picture a little better. Briskly, Williamson made us fill out a long questionnaire, and assigned us to billets.

Hailey and I were put in a room in the Chosun Hotel, a colonels' billet known hereabouts as "Frozen Chosun." Charlotte was sent to a women's billet. The Chosun is a weird compound of a mid-Western, small-town hotel, an army barrack, and a Korean roadside inn. It is large and shabby, filled with the smell of garlic, and serviced by Korean bellhops who understand nothing of what you are saying, but smile hopefully. Both Foster and I went to sleep.

We woke up in time for dinner. Charlotte was already waiting downstairs with two local correspondents, Stanley Rich of the United Press and Roy Roberts of the Associated Press. Both are nice, keen boys, and while we ate our dinner, they gave us a general survey of the situation.

The biggest story, they agreed, is the bloody riots which have been sweeping the countryside in our zone. General Hodge has called them "disgraceful agitated riots." There is apparently some reason to think, however, that the economic distress and the universal hatred for the Korean police, which we have taken over from the Japanese, have had something to do with the uprisings. No Americans have yet been attacked, but at least sixty Korean cops have been killed.

Later Charlotte told us of her billet. She was put in a room with a woman who violently objected to Charlotte, on the ground that the room was reserved for CAF 9's. (CAF is a civilian salary rating, going up to 15). Charlotte explained that under army regulations, she was CAF 14. The woman promptly called her darling, told her they had had no water in the house for eight days because the Russians had stolen a turbine on the Yalu River, in North Korea, and warned Charlotte against the Korean servants. They steal everything in sight, she said, to support their relatives who had fled from the Red Terror in the Soviet zone.

"When things come to such a pass," the woman said, "they have to be resolved one way or another. Even if it means war—now!"

Spent the day making rounds of the XXIV Corps, the Military Government, and the Joint U.S.-Soviet Commission. Discovered, with some surprise, that orders had been sent down the chain of command to give me no information.

Two of the men I met especially interested me. One was Lieutenant Leonard Bertsch, the rotund and bespectacled political adviser to General Hodge. A doctor of philosophy from Holy Cross and a lawyer from the Harvard Law School, Bertsch, I suspect, fancies himself as a sort of "American Century" Machiavelli. His primary concern is Korean politicians, and he is saturated with their lore. Bertsch's current assignments in intrigue are two: he is trying to split the Korean Communist party, and he is promoting a coalition of moderates of both the right and the left. Bertsch is a delightful talker, one reason being that he remembers, and quotes, every *bon mot* he has ever uttered.

The other man was Dr. Arthur Bunce, a Treasury official on loan to the State Department on loan to General Hodge, with the personal rank of Minister. Bunce spent six years setting up rural YMCA's in North Korea, and he speaks a fluent Korean. The difference between Bertsch and Bunce is vast. Bertsch is immersed in political scheming to the exclusion of all else. Bunce considers Korean problems in terms of social and economic forces. He is the first man I have met here who speaks with genuine affection of the Koreans. He is also the first to lay emphasis on social reform, and not on the Soviet menace.

There is an atmosphere of violence, intrigue, and uncertainty about this place. Seoul may not look it, but it talks and acts like an armed camp on the eve of an insurrection. It is hard to analyze this impression, for it is compounded of things both seen and intangible. Such things as the submachine gun next to my jeep driver, news of yet another uprising, or an officer's lament, "I've got six more months to go. The Russkys will be here before then."

I find that fear of communism, rather than a desire to reform or rehabilitate, forms the solid base of our policy for Korea. I am told that when we came here on September 7 of last year, we found that a progressive Korean government had been formed thirteen hours earlier. Bertsch and many others feel that, with all its defects, the government—known as the People's Republic—could have been converted into a staunch and useful ally. Instead, we branded the People's Republic red, and wasted two precious months driving it underground.

This was more than a functional conflict between our own Military Government and a native government with roots in the resistance movement. Their very ideas were different. The Koreans thought of themselves as a nation liberated. To this day we appear uncertain whether we had come to liberate or to occupy. The Koreans wanted to be rid of the collaborators. We not only kept the collaborators in office (for we were understaffed), but also we actually began our "liberation" by ordering the hated Japanese governor general, his officials, and his police to stay on the job as if nothing had happened. The People's Republic wanted social reform. The Americans vetoed any drastic social or economic changes.

But, having suppressed the People's Republic, we turned to the other extreme. We imported an aged rightist by the name of Syngman Rhee all the way from Washington, and made him and other rightists our counselors, and the bearers of our hope. Rhee, Bertsch assured me, is not a Fascist. "He is two centuries before fascism—a pure Bourbon." Yet Rhee was allowed, and even encouraged, to build up a political machine. Rhee's followers took key posts in our Military Government, from police chiefs to county masters. They also set up a network of mass organizations, from women's clubs to terrorist bands.

Rhee's was a one-track mind: he wanted independence for Korea. But he saw an independent Korea as a feudal land, with himself at the head. He spoke for every Korean when he demanded that the country, now split along the 38th parallel into a Soviet and a U.S. zone, be reunited. But he spoke for no one but the landlords when he opposed land reform, social security, or civil freedoms.

Like many other politicians in East Asia with whom we have allied ourselves, Rhee did not fight Japanese collaborators; he embraced them. They hated the same things he hated, and they saw in him the promise of continued well-being. And since we —General Hodge and the Military Government—depended on Rhee and trusted him, and since we were terribly short handed, we condoned a government by collaborators.

"The Koreans in the Military Government," one official told me today, "represent a conspiracy of insufferable corruption. People we now use to govern Korea are rightists who happily did Japan's dirty work. There are now men in the Korean police force who actually were decorated by the Japanese for their cruelty and efficacy in suppressing Korean nationalism."

We did, I was told, issue a stern order for the purge of collaborators. This was mistranslated so skillfully by our Korean interpreters in the Military Government that when the hour of purge came, it was discovered that in all of our zone the order could be applied to only one official.

I was also told this: One day early last spring, it dawned on our policy-makers on the Potomac that our Korean allies—and our own blunders—were losing us Korean good will at a catastrophic rate. If on September 7, 1945, our men landing in Korea were greeted with hosannas, now a Military Government poll of public opinion showed that the Koreans in our zone preferred the Japanese to us.

Thus our command here was ordered to sever its bonds with the extreme right. Instead, every effort was to be made to form a coalition of moderates, both left and right, who would and could give the Koreans a measure of reform.

The job was delegated to Bertsch, and he cast about for a conservative who could head the coalition. Bertsch's choice fell on Kimm Kiu Sic, the U.S.-educated moderate rightist who knew the language of reform, and could even clothe it in fine Elizabethan English. To win over the leftists, Bertsch persuaded the great leader of the wrecked People's Republic, the silver-haired, silver-tongued Lyuh Woon Heung, to enter the coalition as co-chairman. The first meeting of Lyuh and Kimm took place in Bertsch's own house on June 14, 1946.

Although Bertsch sounded confident, there seemed to be two oversized flies in his ointment. One is the feud between General Hodge and Major General Archer Lerch, Military Governor. Lerch's men told me Bertsch was "an upstart," with whom "it's impossible to work." The other fly is the inability of the military here to readjust their minds to the new policy. Directive or no directive, they feel that only a "strong man," like Rhee, can stop communism. Bertsch's plan may remain a scrap of paper unless the military, in and out of the Military Government, agree to carry it out.

Late at night talked Roy Roberts into going for a walk. The streets were still crowded, and there was much more electric light than one sees in Tokyo. We walked down to Bun Chong, the main shopping street. The shops were closed, and women peddlers, in their brightly colored little jackets and long white skirts, were hurrying home with their bundles balanced on their heads. What amazed me was the number of drunk Koreans and GIs. I saw an American arguing with a Korean. The soldier was holding the Korean by the lapels of his coat and shouting, "I'll show you, you goddamned gook!" The Korean did not seem to be frightened. Roy stepped in and said to the soldier, "Go easy, boy." Then the GI's companions, who were watching from the sidelines, came up and pulled him away. Roy said such incidents are frequent and generate much resentment against the Americans.

At night there was some scattered gunfire outside our wall, and we could see some Korean policemen running down the street with pistols on the ready.

After lunch Charlotte and I went to see Bertsch in his office in Duk Soo Palace, where the U.S.-Soviet Joint Commission holds its sessions. When Bertsch came in, a little late, he began to search for a lost button, some missing papers, and a mislaid corps insignia. At the same time he conducted a conversation with five different people, making little sense but being very witty. Finally, over the protests of his secretary, whom he called Blossom ("Every woman under seventy is Blossom to me."), we took Bertsch up to the roof.

Bertsch's topic for today was the Communist party. He said it lost some strength as a result of police repression and the party's approval of Allied trusteeship for Korea, but he thought it still had some 18,000 members in our zone and at least 100,000 active sympathizers.

Like some other officers I have talked to, Bertsch felt that one of the secrets of Communist strength lay in our own mistakes. "If a free election were held today," he said, "the Communists would get 20 per cent of the votes in our zone, and five in the Russian zone. The people here would be voting not *for* the reds, but *against* us."

The Korean Communist party, Bertsch said, was formally organized in 1922, and admitted into the Comintern in 1926. After that, the party disintegrated into a flock of rival "clubs" —"Tuesday," "The Northwest M-L" (for Marx-Lenin), and "Seoul." In 1937, there was a reorganization, and, as Bertsch put it, "The Seoul Club was anointed as the bearer of the true word."

Sometime this year Bertsch obtained the membership lists of the old factions, and had gone to work trying to split them apart. He sounded well pleased with his handiwork, but from another source I have heard that there had been only one defection from the Communist party. A small clique of Communists called on Syngman Rhee, and asked for his blessings and cash. If they join up with Rhee, these "converts" will be of little use to Bertsch's coalition.

In the morning Bertsch took Charlotte and me to see Kimm Kiu Sic, the man he had chosen for head of the new moderate coalition. On the way, Bertsch told us that Kimm came of "the standard poor but respectable parentage," studied at Roanoke, Virginia, and taught English literature to the Chinese. Bertsch went to special pains to tell us that U.S. Army doctors had found Kimm to have "a satisfactory life expectancy." I did not grasp the point until much later, when Bertsch, with bitterness, told us of a State Department official here, who, at a banquet, referred to Kimm as "Mr. Kimm Kiu Sickly." Since Kimm is, in fact, no athlete, the pun achieved some irritating fame.

Far in the outskirts, we drove up a steep hill, and stopped before a lovely Japanese-style house, guarded by a Korean policeman and an American MP. Japan-fashion, we removed our shoes, and were taken to a spacious sun room. There were three men already in the room—a Colonel Shaw, Chief of the Labor Division in the Military Government; a natty, young Korean named Moon; and Kimm himself.

Kimm struck me as a grotesque figure. He is very short, and tremendous around the waist. He was wearing a beautiful gray gown, which made him look feminine, and American zippered felt slippers. His lap was covered with a rug. As we came in, he was filling a two-foot-long reed pipe with a tiny brass head with tobacco out of a GI pouch. Once he began to talk, I was charmed by his cultured and smooth flowing speech.

While Kimm talked to Moon, Bertsch was explaining the significance of the conference. This appeared to be another of his Machiavellian shenanigans. The Korean Federation of Labor had been driven deep underground after last month's strikes, but it still remained a powerful force. Moon, the Federation's only officer still at large, was now being wooed into supporting Bertsch's coalition. Moon, I thought, looked uncomfortable.

When Kimm turned to us, he quickly established his own position. He was a moderate rightist. He favored State control of the major industries, farm reform, and social insurance. From this vantage point he proceeded to attack both the right and the left, reserving his sharpest barbs for Rhee. He felt that the United States and Russia blocked the creation of a democracy in Korea by splitting her in two. He thought the rightists were losing popular support by bickering. He believed the leftists, "pre-occupied with sabotage," were missing a golden chance to sweep the country in the election scheduled for the end of this month.

Later, Kimm told us a bit about his father, who had served at the court of the Korean kings. Kimm himself was born in 1881, spent much of his childhood with American missionaries, and at the age of sixteen was taken to the United States by a rich uncle. After seven years of study, he returned to Korea only to go into exile in 1913. He tried to start a secret officers' training camp in Mongolia, but gave it up when the funds promised by the Korean underground failed to arrive. After that Kimm went into business, selling hides in Mongolia, Bibles in North China, and power engines in Shanghai.

Kimm's interest in a Korean revolution seemed sporadic. From time to time, he went abroad to plead Korea's case. But most of the time he was either a merchant or a teacher, including a stretch at the ultraconservative Central Political Institute of the Kuomintang. In 1942 he was appointed Minister of Information of the so-called "Korean Provisional Government" in Chungking, which barely stayed alive on a Kuomintang subsidy. By November 1945, when a U.S. Army plane took him to Korea as "a private citizen," he was vice-premier of the government-in-exile.

Over lunch, Bertsch talked excitedly of the greatness which destiny held in store for Kimm. I had the impression that, perhaps subconsciously, Bertsch was trying to make up for the drive and excitement that were so conspicuously lacking in Kimm. There is a strange relationship between the two men. Bertsch talks as if he were a disciple of Kimm the prophet. Yet, now and then, the schemer in Bertsch wakes up, and then Bertsch is a political puppeteer. What is happening, I think, is that each man is using the other for his own ends. Kimm is shrewd and ambitious, and he hopes Bertsch may help to make him president of the Korean Republic. Bertsch, apart from the delight of playing god, may also be considering the possibility of becoming an adviser to the Korean Government, headed by his friend Kimm.

In the afternoon, Charlotte, Foster, and I went calling on Syngman Rhee.

Like Kimm and most of the other self-respecting politicians, Rhee lives in a building put at his disposal by a Korean multimillionaire. An armed policeman opened the gate for us, and we waited in a large compound filled with other armed men, until word came down from the hill. Then we walked up the steep, well-kept path, and halfway up the hill Syngman Rhee met us. He had thought that Bertsch was with us, and sounded disappointed when we said he was not.

In the small western-style living room, whose main decoration was a huge multi-colored pagoda, we had a chance to look Rhee over. He is a thin man, with sparse white hair, pale lips and almost no eyebrows. His eyes are concealed behind thin slits of eyelids, so that most of the time he looks as if he is asleep. (Charlotte, in an irreverent aside, whispered, "Doesn't the old boy look like a mummy?") But Rhee was not asleep. His mind was alert and busy, and his words were vigorous.

He sat erect in his chair and threw bait out, to see what we would bite. He attacked General Hodge, the Communists, and the famous Moscow decision of 1945, which proclaimed a U.S.-Soviet trusteeship for Korea. When he found out we had seen Kimm, he damned him with praise. He alternately praised and attacked the Military Government, and referred bitingly to U.S. Army corruption.

I was trying to understand what makes Rhee what he is. He has been away from his native land for thirty-five out of his seventy-three years, and when he returned he spoke what was described to me as "a Hawaiian brand of pidgin Korean." Yet he is a political boss without peer in Asia, except perhaps for Chiang Kai-shek. With what must be a sixth sense, he has mastered the complexities of Korean politics, and he plays the game ruthlessly, skillfully, and to his own advantage.

He had long been a legend and a symbol in Korea, and he has made the legend pay. There is much talk of the "assessments" his agents collect throughout our zone. I was told of a Women's Patriotic Convention in Pusan, at which 1,500 delegates were "assessed" Y.200 each in honor of the great man's visit to the city.

Much like the Japanese and the Germans, Rhee talks in terms of a "Great Korea" and the "Korean Folk." His main political instrument is the *Han Kook* (or Korean Folk) Democratic party, an organization of landlords and rich collaborationists.

Rhee has a Master's degree from Harvard and a Doctor's from Princeton. Yet his English is labored, and he puts sentences together with an effort. I wondered by what inner strength he had impressed his ideas on General Hodge and men of the Military Government. Listening to Rhee, I thought he was a sinister and dangerous man, an anachronism who had strayed into this age to use the clichés and machinery of democracy for unscrupulous and undemocratic ends. I have been in Korea only seventy-two hours, and it may well be that my impressions are wrong. But I have begun to think that it is not Hodge who is the most important man in the U.S. zone, but this old, pale man with half-closed eyes.

Rhee was now in the middle of a passage on Hodge:

"When General Hodge landed here, a Japanese general saw him and told him to stay away from the terrible Koreans. Then I heard that when five hundred people came to welcome General Hodge, the Korean police fired on them and killed five men. General Hodge has also said that the Koreans and the Japanese are the same breed of cats. It was unfortunate that Hodge got his information from a Japanese general. . . ."

The door opened, and an Occidental woman came in with a small silver pot. This was Rhee's Viennese wife, who had been his secretary before he married her. She was described to me as "Rhee's greatest liability, because she thinks he is the greatest man in Korea, and he agrees with her." I had expected a fat old ogre. This woman was slim, handsome, and poised.

She made small talk, and poured a white liquid out of the pot. This was *so ju*, or burning wine.

"This is almost my first anniversary here," said Rhee. "I arrived in Seoul on October 16 of last year. You could call this an anniversary celebration."

We took a sip of *so ju* and choked and gasped as it burned our throats. Mrs. Rhee talked of servant problems and the high cost of living.

"Last March," said Rhee, "I went south, and told immense crowds: 'We're trying to save our country from a sell-out. The best thing is to tell every Communist to change his heart. Those who oppose us, let them go home, to their fatherland.' This created a tremendous stir in the south.

"Last May, General Hodge asked me to cooperate with the new coalition. But I couldn't change my stand. So I said I'd stay silent. I've now kept silent for five months, even though the program of the [Bertsch] coalition is contrary to the principles of democracy. The men of the coalition, for instance, want to confiscate all land and redistribute it among the sharecroppers. I say land reform must be left to the Provisional Government, when we have one."

I told Rhee I was planning to go south. He produced three large calling cards, and on them wrote notes of introduction. They were to the governors of three provinces.

"All these are my friends," he said. "They'll get *good* information for you."

Dr. Bunce was waiting in the crowded bar of the Chosun Hotel when we got back. He is a charming, mild-mannered man, with a ready store of anecdotes and a tremendous background in world—and Korean—rural economics. Over the dinner, he expressed his conviction that the best way to meet the challenge of communism is through social reform. He is very pleased with the new turn of policy here, and with the coalition. If a progressive regime could be established in Seoul, he said, the Communist administration in the Soviet zone would willy-nilly have to come to terms with it.

Once again Major Williamson said he was unable to get a jeep for us, and once again we were sitting disconsolately in the Chosun lobby when a Korean delegation came in to see Foster, in the apparent belief that he was publisher of the New York *Times*. They wanted to know if we were in Foster's entourage, and when I said no, their faces fell. They rose just as fast when they discovered we met Rhee yesterday. The delegation, two men and a woman, came in behalf of one of Rhee's numerous political satellites, the Representative Democratic Council, which, local wits told me, was so called because it was neither representative nor democratic.

The delegation was led by a fat and voluble man with a shining Phi Beta Kappa key. He said, "I am Pak, Brown '05, you must've heard of me," and to make him happy I said yes, indeed I had. With him was a shabby looking man who once studied at the University of Iowa, and a Mrs. Kim San, who said she represented the Women's Patriotic Association and the Women's Nationalist party, both of the Rhee camp.

The trio talked of the subversive Communists and the treacherous nationalists, who once worked with Rhee but were now forming their own little cliques. It soon appeared that there were wheels within wheels in Rhee's machine. All three readily agreed that the banker who had given his house to Kimm Kiu Sic was enjoying wealth "generally regarded as ill-gotten." But there was disagreement when it came to the multi-millionaire who had given his house to Rhee.

Brown '05 said, "He's a *nouveau riche,* an economic upstart. Why, he made his fortune in the last six or seven years, as a Jap contractor."

His male companion agreed: "The man is wallowing in wealth."

But Mrs. Kim San dissented. "No," she said sharply. "He's a patriot. He also has a very fine mind."

The men beat a hasty retreat, and Mrs. Kim San proceeded to tell us the story of her grandfather, whose land in North Korea once yielded 20,000 bushels, but the Communists had now taken this land away and given it to his tenants, and all he was allowed to keep was land producing 200 bushels a year.

At this point, Foster showed up, and Charlotte and I fled. Behind us, we could hear the rich baritone: "I'm Pak, Brown '05, you must've heard of me. . . ."

After lunch, Charlotte, Foster, and I wandered over to a Korean newspaper office and looked up a man named Muk. He was an English speaking editor, recommended to us as both impartial and well informed. We had already met some Korean rightists, and Bertsch was lining up more of them for us. Now we wanted Muk to get us interviews with labor and farm union people, and with some leftist politicians.

"That will be difficult," said Muk. "They've gone underground."

We said, "You don't understand. We aren't looking for Communists. We just want people left of center."

"They're underground or in jail."

Muk explained that since the railroad strike, three weeks ago, the Korean police had arrested many scores of leftist leaders, closed up leftist newspapers, raided union offices, and handed over the headquarters of the Korean Federation of Labor to a rightist group (which, we later learned, was controlled by Rhee).

We kept pressing, and Muk, after consulting some reporters, finally said he would try to find Ho Hun, one of the five leaders of the defunct People's Republic. Bertsch had already told us that he was trying to win Ho Hun's support for the coalition. The army still could find no jeep for us, and so we walked across the sprawling city, down dusty roads and filthy alleyways, until we reached a two-story building. Muk went in, and returned in five minutes to tell us that Ho Hun was upstairs, in a conference of leftist groups called to form a united leftist front to oppose Bertsch's rightist coalition.

We went upstairs to a huge, bare, ugly room with dirty white walls. There were two long tables. At one a dozen people sat in conference. At the other two men waited for us.

Ho Hun is a handsome, graying man of sixty, with a smiling face. His hands were trembling. The other man had a stern face and a tremendous neck and shoulders. He said he was Kim Yak San, War Minister in the defunct government-in-exile in Chungking and now head of the Korean National Revolutionary party. I gathered that he had moved leftward since his Chungking days. Both men talked readily, but occasionally one of them would go over to the other table to join in the discussion there.

In the three hours that we were with him, Ho Hun said two things of especial interest. One was his spirited defense of trusteeship.

"Korea," he said, "has been under Japanese domination for so long that she has to prepare herself for independence. But during this period she must also be secure. Therefore, it's desirable to have a trusteeship—but not under one power. We have had too much trouble in the past dealing with single nations, China, Russia, and Japan. . . . The trouble with the U.S. Military Government is that it doesn't understand the situation, and makes blunders. One of these is the inability to see that most of the Korean leftists are nationalists and not Communists. Yet, all of them are being oppressed alike."

The second item dealt with the current wave of arrests.

"On the morning of September 30," Ho Hun said, "I heard 500 or 600 shots outside of my house. This was the beginning of the raids, carried out jointly by the police and Rhee's terrorists. They concentrated on the railroad union, but they also raided other union offices, beat up people, wrecked the furniture, and took the places over.

"In all, 3,000 people were arrested here, and of these 1,700 were kept in jail. Today 1,400 remain imprisoned. The morning the raids started, I went to General Lerch. I said, 'Did you order the arrests and the shooting down of the people, or are the police doing it on their own?' Lerch didn't answer."

He pulled a piece of paper out of a pocket. "For six months I've been trying to get a house to live in. There were 60,000 Japanese homes distributed to Koreans by the Military Government, but I can get nothing. I have an authorization, but I still can't get the house. Korean rightists in the Military Government say, 'You're a Communist. You've lots of counterfeit money. You can buy anything.'

"Now I'm told that if I support the coalition, I'll be able to get a house. It's such tactics that alienate the Korean people."

Kim Yak San now returned from the other table, and Ho Hun left us. Kim talked softly, and his gentleness looked odd beside his powerful hands, or the tale of violence he told us. "Ho Hun is a lawyer," he said. "I'm a professional revolutionary." As a youth, he fled to China, studied in Chiang Kai-shek's Whampoa Military Academy, and then served as an officer in the great Chinese Northern Expedition in 1926-27. Ever since he has been in the Korean underground, in Shanghai, Manchuria, and North Korea. By the time the war ended, he said, he had 3,000 guerrillas under him.

The only other guerilla force, he said, was Communist-led and based in Manchuria. It made two major raids on North Korea, in 1935-36 and again in 1940, attacking Japanese installations. It totalled about 3,000 men. The Communists also had a small, tight, and active underground within Korea. It was led by Pak Heun Yung, who is now top leader of the Communist party in our zone, and has gone into hiding. Pak had served three jail terms for anti-Japanese activity by the time he was twenty-five. In 1926, while in prison, he feigned insanity and managed to escape. He fled to Russia and spent three years at the Lenin University in Moscow. In 1929, he returned to Korea and was arrested the minute he landed. On release from prison in 1936, he became a worker in a brick factory and an underground leader.

Ho Hun now returned to us, and the two men began to fire loaded questions at us. Can we have a democratic election, they said, when thousands of leftists are in jail? Can we have an election when labor unions are barred from politics, and the police terror is at its height? Can the coalition of Kimm Kiu Sic and Lyuh Woon Heung be taken seriously when Lyuh Woon Heung's entire People's Party is in jail or hiding? Can the Military Government expect cooperation from the Koreans when even such a meeting as that—they pointed at the other table—could be raided at any minute?

We did not answer. All we wanted to know was if the two men could arrange a meeting for us with some leftist labor or farmer leader. Very firmly, both said no, because any man leaving his hiding place would be arrested on sight. We kept insisting, and finally it was agreed that a special guide would lead us to some hideout tomorrow.

October 20, 1946 SEOUL

Our difficulties continue. Yesterday we had drinks with an officer from Military Government, and invited him to have lunch with us today. This morning he sent word down he would not come, for he had been seen with us yesterday and severely reprimanded.

Although there are several jeeps assigned to Williamson's office, they seem to be available only when we go to "approved" interviews. Today, finally, I demanded to see Hodge at once so that I could register a formal protest. Williamson then backed down and said he would have a jeep for us this afternoon.

After lunch Charlotte, Foster, and I picked up Muk, our interpreter, and went off to our rendezvous with a leftist. Somehow everything went wrong, and at the end of an hour we were still looking for our special guide. Foster, who had another appointment, left us. We kept making stops, while Muk, with a conspiratorial expression which we felt was overdone, went into buildings to investigate.

Eventually he emerged from a four-story office building, and beckoned to us. We walked to the top floor, passed through a small door cut in a wooden partition and guarded by a middle-aged man, walked through another office, and found ourselves in a small room, with a man sitting behind a desk. We recognized him instantly. He was Moon, the labor leader to whom Bertsch introduced us at Kimm Kiu Sic's house.

Moon still looked very dapper and diffident, and I did not particularly like him. He told us the story of the Korean Federation of Labor, which for thirteen years had been an underground organization fighting the Japanese, and which a month ago had 270,000 members in our zone. Now, once again, it has been driven underground. Moon also talked of Rhee's Labor Association, and of how factory owners and Military Government officials ordered workers to become its members. This, Moon said, plus the low wages and short rice rations, provoked last month's disastrous strikes.

Thus far the interview had not been particularly exciting, and Charlotte was openly bored. Moon spoke in a low monotone, and much of what he said—especially about the rightist terrorism—cried for substantiation.

"The worst of the terrorist bands," Moon was saying, "is Rhee's Great Korea Young Men's Association. It works with the police. Together, they . . . "

We were sitting around a small, round table. To my right was a door which, I assumed, led to a corridor. Now, in the middle of Moon's sentence, there was a terrific crash, and the door came open, sagging on its hinges. I looked quickly but saw nothing. Then slowly a bayoneted rifle appeared in the doorway, and began to make a swing in our direction.

In a few moments, a sturdy young Korean in civilian clothes came out cautiously and aimed a pistol at us. Next to him, a uniformed policeman materialized behind the bayonet. The two men walked into the room, and behind them came a band of young men, of the type one meets in tough Chicago or New York neighborhoods.

The man with the pistol walked over to Moon and placed him under arrest.

To me, the whole scene was unreal. It is true I was warned by Ho Hun yesterday that this would happen. But Moon was no subversive. Bertsch himself told us Moon was a moderate, and when we first met Moon, he was being chaperoned by an

American colonel. Things like that simply could not happen in the American zone. It must be, I reasoned, one of those unauthorized raids of which we had heard so much.

I asked the man with the pistol for his credentials. He took out a card showing that he was a Detective Sergeant Kim Ho Ik, Korean National Police. I asked him if he had a warrant. He said yes, there was a warrant. Moon was being arrested on General Hodge's orders, for leading the railroad strike. Unfortunately, the warrant had been left at the police station. I said I would stay around until the warrant was produced.

Sergeant Kim sent a youth out, and we all settled down to wait. From time to time, the sergeant slapped Moon on the back and laughed. Moon remained noncommittal. Charlotte suggested that she go out, contact General Hodge, and find out if he had issued an order for Moon's arrest. We arranged that if I was not there on her return, she would proceed to the main police station.

After about fifteen minutes of waiting, the sergeant lost patience. He began to shout that I was interfering in the arrest, and who was I, and what was I doing there anyway. Through Muk, I explained that I was a reporter; that his band broke in claiming it had a warrant, which it seemingly did not have; and that I had no intention of interfering in anything the sergeant wanted to do. I would merely tag along, and report all I saw. I also told him to lower his voice.

Sergeant Kim then ordered Moon to stand up, and we all filed out of the room. On the landing just outside, I saw thirteen kneeling, frightened men, guarded by four of the youths in civilian clothes. The sergeant arrested one of the thirteen, and told the rest to go. We walked downstairs, and I waited in the doorway with Moon and the sergeant.

It was a long wait, and soon my attention was drawn by the youngsters. They had all gone into the street and were pushing people out of the way. One of them pushed an old man resting a huge load on his back against a tree, and the man fell. The boy was about sixteen, and he was as hard as they come. I went out with Muk and asked the youngster if he was a detective.

"No," he said, "I'm a member of the Great Korea Young Men's Association."

"What are you doing here?"

"We're helping the police to catch leftists."

"How many of you are there here?"

"Eight—"

An older youth ran up to the youngster and ordered him not to talk to me. At this point, a car drove up, and the sergeant got in and began to talk earnestly to a stout, middle-aged man in a police uniform. Later, I found out this was Chang, chief of the Seoul Police. After a few minutes, Moon was put in the back of the car, with Chief Chang. I asked Chang's permission to come along, and he nodded at a seat next to him. Muk sat in front.

We drove up to the main police station and walked in, past armed sentries and a roomful of youngsters engaged in horseplay. Moon was taken upstairs, and Muk and I followed him.

Sergeant Kim sulked in a corner. After a while Moon told me that back in August he had gone to the town of Taegu, was arrested as a vagrant, and was released on September 24 on Colonel Shaw's orders. He returned to Seoul, and was promptly set upon by a band of young terrorists, who beat him up so badly that he was hospitalized until five days ago.

Moon told me he was thirty-six, was first jailed by the Japanese at the age of eighteen, and had spent eight years in prisons and ten years in underground union work.

"Until two hours ago," he said in a matter-of-fact voice, "I was the only officer of the Labor Federation still at large. Both our president and vice-president are in hiding."

Muk told me Moon is a leading moderate in the labor movement, and has often been used by the U.S. Army to settle labor disputes. He also said that Moon had decided not to join Bertsch's coalition. "Kimm Kiu Sic is a good man," Moon explained, "but he doesn't know what the common people want, and the common people don't know what he stands for."

A policeman asked Muk and me to go to Chief Chang's office. We found Chang sitting in a corner, with his hands folded placidly over his stomach. An American officer came up to me, and said he was Major F. E. Richardson, chief of the Police Division of the Military Government for Seoul. He said he had been ordered by General Hodge to investigate the incident. Richardson was very affable, and told me he had been an investment banker in Chicago. While I was telling him of the incident, another uniformed American came in and introduced himself as "Whittaker, Counter Intelligence."

After I finished, Richardson said smoothly, "Have you lived in the Orient before?" and when I nodded, he said, "Well, you know then that the police don't operate our way. They are cruel and undemocratic." This discussion went on for some time, with me saying that I thought we could expect the police in our zone, and under the direction of such men as the major himself, to obey some of the Military Government directives, and Richardson saying that we could not expect much progress overnight.

"And anyway," I said, "I'm a little puzzled by the use of members of a private terrorist band in a police arrest."

Richardson said he had never heard of the Great Korea Young Men's Association. "Have you?" he asked Chief Chang. Chang said he had not. "Are you sure you're not mistaken?" Richardson said to me. "You don't speak Korean."

At my insistence, Sergeant Kim and Moon were brought into the room. Richardson said to the sergeant: "Mr. Gayn charges that you've been using some private hoodlums to make this arrest. You know that if this is true, you'll be severely punished. Is it true?"

Sergeant Kim said it was not true; I was certainly mistaken. He said he had seen no young men in the room. Later he recalled seeing some, but insisted they must have been passersby. When I suggested that no passersby were likely behind locked doors on the fourth floor of an office building, Kim guessed they might have been Communists.

Richardson said to me: "You must've made a mistake." Sergeant Kim decided to go on the offensive. Pointing at me, he said I had interfered with the arrest and ordered him out of the room. I was still wondering how to cope with that one, when Muk, my wonderful, quiet, courageous Muk, spoke up. "Major," he said, "I was translating for Mr. Gayn. Not once did he say anything of the sort to the sergeant."

At this point Whittaker came to life. "What's your name?" he asked Muk. "Where do you work?" He then proceeded to question Muk on his position, his relation to me, and his work for any other correspondents. While they were talking, a policeman brought a folded note for me. It was from Charlotte, and it said: "Sit tight. Talked to Hodge who says he will investigate. Don't go away until Big Brass investigates." In another five minutes, a policeman told me I had visitors. I went out, and saw Charlotte and Foster.

Charlotte told me hurriedly that Foster had telephoned Hodge, who said he knew nothing of the arrest; Dr. Bunce, who said, "Lord, more of their stupidity;" and Colonel Shaw, who said in exasperation, "But I've just gotten Moon out of jail. I guess I'll have to get him out again."

Whittaker now wanted to know if I had interfered with the arrest, and both Charlotte and Muk had the answer. I, in turn, wanted to know about the Great Korea Young Men's Association, and everyone, Richardson, Whittaker, Chief Chang, and Sergeant Kim, was denying knowledge of it.

A memory that was turning in the back of my mind now came closer, and I caught it. I said: "O.K., Major, this has been going on long enough. How much would you bet me I could find you a room full of the Great Korea boys right in this building?" Then, for fear that someone would send a word of warning out, I rushed downstairs to the room where I saw the young men at horseplay. Behind me came the whole group.

The first person I saw downstairs was the youngster to whom I talked after he had pushed an old man. I headed for him and he began to run down the basement steps. I caught him and brought him before Richardson.

"Here's one. Ask him if he's a cop. Ask him what he's doing in a police station."

Richardson asked him. The boy said he was a member of

the Great Korea Association, assigned for duty to this station. I asked him who gave him his orders, and he said they came from his "leaders," who were in the other room. I went in, spotted some more boys who were in on the arrest, and dragged them out. It was becoming very embarrassing.

"Did you know of this?" Richardson asked Chief Chang. Chang shook his head vigorously. Richardson said to me. "An honest arrest has been made. But a mistake has also been made in using these young men. I didn't know of this. But I'll instruct Chief Chang not to use such help in the future." He thought briefly. "I'll recommend that a special board sit to decide on the sergeant's negligence."

I asked him what he intended to do about the thirty or forty youths in the room, and Whittaker said he would "investigate." He had three of the "leaders" brought out. They were small, compact men of about twenty-five, in well-cut Western clothes and trim overcoats. They looked like a Hollywood idea of underworld killers, and I wondered if they got their inspiration in movie houses. "Come on," Whittaker said curtly, and marched out with the three men.

Richardson offered Charlotte and me a lift to the Chosun. In the jeep he told us there had been some trouble up north, in a town called Kaesong, just this side of the 38th Parallel. Early this morning bands of twenty to thirty armed men each, raided ten police boxes, killed a Korean police officer and a detective.

"In some troubled areas," Richardson said, "the police were shorthanded, and so the Military Government gave them authority to recruit sons of well-known shopkeepers to patrol the streets and help the police. You know, act as a stabilizing influence."

As for Moon, Richardson said he was arrested on charges of involvement in the recent railway strike. I did not remind the major that Moon had spent the last two months either in jail or in a hospital.

This morning had an appointment with Muk to see some Korean professors. When Muk did not show up, I asked an American friend to check. He learned that Muk was visited by an agent of Counter Intelligence, told that General Hodge did not want him to work for correspondents, and ordered to leave town. Muk left at once.

Heard that the press conferences given by Military Government officers for Korean newspapermen are worth attending, for the Koreans ask sharp questions on current problems. Asked an officer in the Military Government to arrange a visit for me tomorrow.

He put his arm around my shoulders, said he hoped I would not mind his frankness, and told me I could not attend. When I asked why, he explained:

"General Brown will be there to answer questions tomorrow."

"I don't mind."

"No, you don't understand. You haven't been introduced to General Brown yet, and it wouldn't be protocol for you to come to his press conference until you are."

I said, "Oh, is that all? I'll come fifteen minutes earlier, and you introduce me."

"You still don't understand," he said. "I can't introduce you to General Brown until you've met General Lerch."

"All right," I said, "I'll come an hour earlier, and you introduce me to both Lerch and Brown."

"No, no," he said patiently. "I can't introduce you to Lerch because you haven't yet met General Hodge. You know, everyone here's talking about it. It isn't right. You must follow the rules, you know."

I promptly walked over to Major Williamson's office and asked for an interview with General Hodge.

In the afternoon the three of us were taken to a former Japanese textile plant, now being operated by the U.S. Military Government. We had been trying to get to the port of Inchon, where, we were told, we would find more typical sweatshop conditions, but Major Williamson could find no jeep for us. The plant we saw was obviously a show place for visiting firemen. But even as a show place it was instructive. Of its 1,300 employes, nearly 900 were little girls. They all said they were fourteen, but they were either lying to keep their jobs, or they were so undernourished they looked no older than nine. We walked past the endless rows of looms and the endless lines of little, pale-faced children, and our guide, an American officer, was telling us of the great strides in industrial rehabilitation being made under the management of the Military Government.

As we were leaving, I took one of the workers aside and asked him if there was a labor union at the plant. The Korean manager, handpicked by the Military Government, hurried back to us. "I can answer all your questions," he said. "Union? Yes, we have a union." It was, as I expected, Syngman Rhee's Great Korea Laborers' Association. "We used to have the Federation of Labor, but they were a bunch of trouble makers. We threw them out, and the Great Korea Association came in."

Saw General Hodge. The conservation was "off the record," and I could write no story on it. All I could say was that he dwelled on the difficulties, human, political, and economic, facing the United States in South Korea. Hodge is a handsome soldier, with an alert face and a long jaw. From time to time the conversation lagged, and at such points I raised myself in my chair and said, "Well, general, it was . . . " But each time he resumed talking. When I finally left him, I realized what had happened. It was an hour to the minute since I went in. Apparently, there was an hour assigned to me on the calendar, and the general was being punctual.

Later Charlotte and I paid a formal call on General Lerch, the Military Governor. He opened the interview by saying, "You know, I'm peeved at you." I thought he was joking, but he was not. He was in deadly earnest. "I'm very peeved at you. You've been here a week, and you haven't thought it necessary to call on me. There's such a thing as military protocol. When you arrive in town, you must call on the commanding officers."

Lerch talked of Korea's scarcities, and of the supplies ordered in the United States but not yet received. He impressed both Charlotte and me more favorably than Hodge had. This morning we heard more details of the feud between Hodge and Lerch. Theoretically, Lerch, as Military Governor, should be the most important man in South Korea, and Hodge should devote himself solely to the command of the tactical troops. But Hodge is a lieutenant general and Lerch is only a major general, and Hodge keeps butting into political and economic problems which lie within Lerch's province.

I was told, however, that Lerch is just as opposed to reform as Hodge, and just as friendly to the Korean rightists. One of the officers we talked to told us of entering Lerch's office just as another American visitor was leaving.

"See that man?" Lerch said. "He comes here from Tokyo, and tells me there are too many little children working in factories, and we must change this and change that. I told him, 'As long as I am Military Governor, we change nothing.'"

Moon was released this afternoon, after a perfunctory examination.

At night Charlotte and I packed for our trip north, to the 38th Parallel. We're going to do our best to cross the line into the Russian zone.

October 22, 1946   PAKCHON

Early in the morning, Charlotte, a Captain G. of Military Intelligence, an Army driver, and I started north. Just ahead of us was another jeep with a Nisei lieutenant. The countryside is restless and military men prefer to travel in groups. The two drivers kept their carbines close at hand, and the officers wore automatics in shoulder holsters. Quite suddenly we came to a cleft in a mountain, and the bustle of Seoul was left behind. At once the road became bad, and we began to bounce wildly, gritting our teeth and bobbing our heads like toys with springs where necks should be. The jeep ahead of us sent back a thick cloud of fine yellow, choking dust.

By all accepted standards, the road from Seoul north is the world's worst. For centuries an ox cart route, it has now become a scarred and rutted ribbon of dirt, winding across rice paddies. Most of the bridges were washed away in last year's great flood, and no effort has been made to restore them. ("Why should we make the Russian advance any easier?" an officer asked me later in the day.)

We drove at a steady thirty miles an hour, slowing down only in the villages. As we roared by, the women in their bright red and yellow and green silk dresses, and old men in their invariable white gowns and tiny black straw hats perched on top of their heads scattered into the bushes. At the first river the bridge was down, and the ford made a wide detour across an uneven, pebbly bottom. We splashed across, bumping in and out of holes and taking in water. A few feet away, a middle-aged man carried an old man, with a white beard and the incongruous hat, piggy-back. The younger man had carefully rolled up his trousers, but it did not really matter for the water was well up to his hips. Neither man looked at us. Only a few miles further, an ox blocked our passage. When we honked, the ox came closer, lowered its head, and tried to gore the radiator. Both the radiator and the beast were rescued by a flock of farmers.

The harvest time was over, and the road was now hemmed with straw mats, covered with rice, garlic, and red pepper out to dry in the sun. The whole countryside was dotted with these patches of red and white, and occasionally there was a crunching sound as our wheels went over a protruding mat. *Kimchee*, with which every Korean spices his rice, seems to consist predominantly of garlic and red pepper, and its aroma hovered over each village.

Captain G. is a silent, sullen man of twenty-nine. He glumly evaded our questions on the peasant riots. But the signs of unrest were difficult to conceal. In nearly every village, we ran through a patrol of Korean policemen, with their Japanese fur coats and carbines. Occasionally, around a turn, there was a road block, with half a dozen policemen questioning and searching the rare traveler. And once, some twenty miles out of Seoul, we waited patiently until a U.S. Army tank, standing guard at a bridge, slowly crawled to one side to let us through.

Beyond Mungson, on a ridge high above a broad river, we turned off the road into a U.S. Army camp. It consisted of about twenty quonset huts set on a bare mountainside. Even an amateur could see that a few field guns set here would command the river and its approaches for many miles. The men in the camp looked grimy and preoccupied. It is no more than forty miles from here to the Soviet outposts on the 38th, and war is on every mind. "No." said an officer, "I'm not bringing my wife out. I'd hate to have her caught here."

Far below the camp, on a small, narrow beach, a Korean policeman waited for a ferry coming across from the other bank. The current was strong, and the crew pushed hard on the single oar. The ferry—an oversized, badly leaking junk—ran onto the beach. From it a heavily loaded truck rolled ashore. The policeman halted the vehicle, and ordered the men out. He examined their passes, patted their sides and legs for concealed weapons, looked through their wallets.

Captain G. explained: "He's looking for Communist spies." Later we rode the ferry, and Captain G. talked shop with the Nisei lieutenant. Both agreed that the Korean policemen were something terrific. "I saw a truck hit a kid on a bicycle," the lieutenant said. "So a cop comes up, and instead of giving hell to the truck driver, begins to belt the kid on the head, first one side, then the other."

"Oh, that's nothing," said the captain. "The other day, the cops caught some guy with Y.40,000 and asked him where he got it. He said he had sold his property and was now going to Seoul. So they made him kneel and started asking him questions.

Every time he'd open his mouth to answer, they would kick him in the groin. They sure beat hell out of him before he admitted he was a Communist.

At Kaesong, which five centuries ago was the capital of Korea, we waited for the other jeep which we had somehow left behind. As soon as our jeep stopped, the entire street, as far as the eye could see, came to life with hundreds of children rushing toward us. They clustered around the jeep, fingered our clothes, hopefully pulled and tugged at everything that might come off. Occasionally the captain bellowed, and the kids backed off, but not for long. Not far from us, as a sort of huge island in the middle of the street intersection, stood an ancient, moss-coated tower. It was now circled with barbed wire, and we noticed that many of the supporting posts were fresh. We knew already that two days ago Kaesong had an uprising, that its jails were packed, and that some three hundred of the more important "leftists" had been shipped to Seoul. The police stations were heavily guarded by uniformed policemen and by tough youngsters in civilian clothes, much like the boys I met in Seoul two days ago.

The second jeep did not show up, and we decided to move on. We were now running along the 38th Parallel. Somewhere between Kaesong and Pakchon, we met another jeep. It halted to unload a slight, blond captain, with a pistol strapped across his chest. The two captains walked back out of hearing and had a conference. Then the newcomer, a Captain K., said, "See you tonight," hopped into his jeep, and roared off in a cloud of dust.

We arrived in Pakchon, tired and filthy and much after the dinner hour. We rolled into the compound of what was once a Japanese hotel, and was now the billet and headquarters of Company Fox. The company commander, a trim, compact captain, met us with exemplary courtesy. We splashed some water on our faces, drank up our host's last remaining liquor, and then addressed ourselves to a steak dinner. There a strange atmosphere in the place, as if everyone was watching us. Questions on what was happening in Pakchon or along the border were ignored. We stuttered along until we hit on two safe subjects: the University of Wisconsin, of which Charlotte is a graduate, and the hot springs which feed the hotel baths.

Later that night, six or eight officers and I went down to a typical Japanese bath pool, filled with steaming sulphurous water. The army's vaunted efficiency is sorely missing in Korea, and the billet—among so many other things—lacked electric light bulbs. We undressed and washed in the dim light of two flashlights. Someone said, "I wish I were back home, in California." Another young, wistful voice joined in: "Me, for Iowa." One voice after another called the roll call of states represented in this shallow Japanese pool, in a Korean no man's land, a few miles away from the nearest Soviet outpost. After the bath, we stumbled up the dark stairs. Captain G., who, I suddenly realized, had not left me alone since we left Seoul, slept on the other cot in the room. There were some panes missing in the window, and a cold wind blew in. Around midnight I was awakened by the sound of shots very close by. The captain also woke up, and I asked him what the shots could be. He said he had not heard any.

October 23, 1946   RUSSIAN ZONE IN NORTH KOREA

After it was agreed at Yalta to divide Korea in two along the 38th Parallel, someone unhappily remembered Onjin. A peninsula on the western edge of Korea, Onjin—or most of it, anyway—lies on our side of the 38th. Unfortunately, the only way to enter Onjin by land is through the Soviet zone. Thus, by agreement, American supply convoys were allowed to cross the dividing parallel, make a 23-mile run inside the Soviet zone, and then re-enter the U.S. zone at Onjin. After a brief stay the convoy has to retrace its route the same day.

Our convoy started forming very early in the morning, while the sun was still down. We shivered in the penetrating chill and dashed down to the pool, to wash and shave in its hot water. Our group had grown, and the little Captain K. whom we met on the road was now with us. We learned that he is S-2, or Regimental Intelligence Officer, and guessed that he was watching us. We all had tall mounds of hot cakes and enormous soup bowls filled with coffee. Then we pulled on all the warm clothes we had and got into the jeeps.

The convoy had four jeeps and a truck with oil drums. We started early, for there was a long, hard run along the 38th before we got to the Soviet border gate. Once again we bumped and bounced, choked in the heavy dust, and shivered in the cold. We passed through the town of Yonan, where there had been a bloody uprising the previous week. We also passed through many villages, where the road blocks were busy and each police station resembled a fort.

Then we reached a belt devoid of villages and travelers. We skirted a hill and came to a sudden halt before a GI with a submachinegun pointed at us. The man looked trim, tough, and competent. Across the road from him were a couple of quonset huts and a few incurious GIs. Even Charlotte, who is young and good looking, aroused no visible interest. This was U.S. Outpost No. 7.

The quonset huts were bare, neat, and very cold. The mess hall was a tent, with the flaps open and the wind whistling over the rough table and benches. We squatted in the sun and talked to a GI. "No," he said, "this place is not too cheerful. I wouldn't want to get stuck here very long. As it is, we're supposed to stay here only two weeks, and I've already been here three. It's too damn lonely. and nothing to do. And them Russkys sitting up there." He pointed his thumb at the hill behind him.

At 9:45 A.M. we got back into the jeeps and drove a few hundred yards to the border gate. The gate was a wooden bar suspended over the road. Just behind it was a small sentry box and a Russian soldier with a rifle. He wore a thin shirt which had long lost its original white, and his trousers had a big patch of a different color. It was hard to tell his age, for he had the peasant's ageless face.

At ten, a Red Army truck drove up to the gate. It was a

Studebaker, filled with officers and men. Three or four of the officers approached us. They looked neat, and each wore a string of tinkling medals. One of the officers, an extraordinarily handsome youth with a fat briefcase, saluted and engaged us in conversation. He talked first in Russian, then in German. Our officers responded in English and French. A common ground was found briefly in Korean and Lettish. The American officer, who spoke a little Lettish, explained his family had come from Latvia. "America," said the Russian sententiously, "is an interesting country. It has peoples of many races and nationalities," We readily agreed. After a while the conversation floundered. We stood and smiled at each other, and the Russian said to his neighbor: "Many new faces today." Then he nodded decisively, and said, "Well, let's go." The sentry raised the gate, and we entered the Soviet zone.

The instructions to the U.S. convoys are specific. The vehicles are to follow a definite route, they must not stop, and they are to average twenty-five miles an hour. We had heard that on the previous Wednesday one of the jeeps turned off at the wrong road, and the Russians in the escorting truck promptly fired a shot overhead. The errant driver quickly backed out and took another turn. Some weeks earlier, another jeep managed to break its axle on the road. The Russians quickly transferred its occupants to another vehicle, and when the convoy returned four hours later, the jeep had been repaired —with the Red Army's compliments.

A few miles beyond the border we passed by an airfield, with a swarm of Russian Yak pursuit planes warming up. At the gate to the field, a large group of Red Army officers and men watched us with smiles. Behind them, on the guard house, there was a large sign in Russian: "Soldier, keep your secrets. The enemy is watchful." Next to the field there was a cluster of shabby buildings that must have once been occupied by the Japanese garrison. Now they were tenanted by Russians, there were flowers in the windows, fresh laundry flapped in the wind, and children played in the bare yard under the eyes of young, breasty Russian women. Another half-mile, and we reached a huge wooden arch, decorated with flags and portraits of Joseph Stalin and Kim Il Sun, the ranking leader of North Korea. Kim is a youngish looking man of about thirty-five, with stubby hair, a determined chin, and, reportedly, the assumed name of a famous guerrilla said to be dead.

We were now in Kaijo, one of Korea's few large cities. We soon realized that we were in a sign-painter's paradise, for nearly every lamp post, every fence and building was decorated. Sometimes it was merely a brief slogan, or the crossed hammer and sickle. Sometimes it was a string of twenty-one stars, for the twenty-one points of Kim's program of national reconstruction. Sometimes it was a portrait of Kim. But we also passed by a two-story building nearly hidden behind the portraits of four Red Army marshals who had fought against Japan. And here and there we saw intricate—and excellently done—political drawings. Some showed a farmer turning in his rice at a state collection point. Some showed the same farmer stomping vigorously on snakes with unmistakable capitalist heads. Some portrayed Kim talking to children, or the trinity of farmers, workers, and Red Army men, or a group of Asiatics. All through the town there were hundreds of colored posters, urging the populace to vote in the forthcoming local election, or appealing to women to assume their responsibilities as citizens. The posters gave the city a gay, carnival air.

We rolled down the road and made a sharp turn into the main street. A Korean traffic policeman let us through, but halted the jeep behind us. Within a few seconds the Russian truck appeared on the scene, the Russian officer bounced out and impatiently waved the convoy on. The policeman sheepishly stepped back.

The streets of Kaijo were packed with shoppers, vendors, children, farmers come to market with their produce, students milling in front of their schools, ox carts, bicycles, and an occasional horse-drawn cart of the Red Army. Here and there a Russian soldier ambled by, as often as not with a Russian woman by his side. There were a few policemen and militiamen, but there was no display of police force. As our jeep went by, children cheered and shouted in Russian, "Americansky."

Some thrust out their fingers in a "V for Victory," and one dissident tot stuck out his little finger in the common Asiatic expression of contempt.

The shops seemed to be well stocked and well patronized. In one store we spotted smudged portraits of Stalin, Roosevelt, and Churchill, and above them the three Allied flags, including the Stars and Stripes. There were several Red Army PX's, one of them displaying children's garments in its window, and two others labelled "The Red Army's Vegetable and Provision Store." They looked small and rundown; were they American, they would, beyond the shadow of a doubt, have led to some passionate Congressional oratory.

It took half an hour or more to cross the town. Then our jeeps passed the last flag-bedecked arch, and once again we were in a world of dust, terraced fields running up hillsides, and tiny villages, with their red pepper, garlic, peasant carts with huge wooden wheels, and bolts of brightly colored silk laid out on display along the main street.

In an hour we completed the run through the Soviet zone and approached the exit gate, to the Onjin Peninsula. The Red Army truck, lost in the dust for most of the way, caught up with us. We stopped by the gate and watched the two Russian guards—lean men in thin, dirty shirts. One of them was probably near forty, the other looked no more than sixteen. Both were probably billeted in a Korean school near by—an ugly box decorated with a huge banner in Russian: "Let's Not Allow the Arsonists of a New War to Disrupt the Peace We Have Won. Let's Maintain Our New Peace."

Though the road was no better, we picked up speed. In ten minutes we reached a cluster of neat houses and quonset huts. This was U.S. Outpost No. 4—a couple of officers, a handful of men, a few trucks, and an overpowering feeling of impending crisis, in which a Russian tide would sweep over the helpless Americans. The commanding officer, a young lieutenant, took us to his house across the road. There were a few Korean laborers, busily hammering and sawing. "Those goddamned gooks," said someone, "they just pretend they are working." The Koreans were fixing up the living room—a bright room with a small fireplace and a bar with two tall stools. We washed and went to the mess hall for lunch. There were two middle-aged engineers eating with us. They talked of weather and of dust, but said nothing of themselves. Later we saw them testing field phones.

After lunch we walked uphill to the quonset huts and stretched out in the sun. Next to me was a young, pink-cheeked, alert lieutenant, who, we soon found out, is the Military Governor of the county. We struck up a conversation, and he talked readily of the smuggling junks, intercepted on their way from North to South Korea; of a Patriotic Youth Association, being formed by the U.S. Army's interpreter here; of rice, fertilizer, and prices; and of taking a bunch of policemen to the mainland a few days earlier, to break up a riot. "We went in," he said, "and found the city completely empty. The police stations were a mess. The cops had fled. The townsfolk were hiding. We took over the stations, and then started. . . ."

He was in the middle of a sentence, when one of the Military Intelligence people with us—a very young corporal—came up to the lieutenant, tapped him on the shoulder, and said: "Sir, could I speak to you for a second?" They walked behind the quonset hut, and when the lieutenant returned, his face was flushed, and he talked no more. We took pity on him, and asked no questions.

Instead, we watched a painfully blue sky for the plane which we could hear but not see. "Must be the Russkys," said a sergeant, and cranked the handle of the field phone.

We tried to talk to some of the other men, but two Military Intelligence men broke up every conversation. They were not offensive, but very obvious. We were glad when the time came for the return trip. Again we waited by the border gate, until the Russian truck arrived. Then we rolled back, through the villages, through Kaijo, and past the Russian airport. In another hour we were back at the first border gate, and the Russian officer smiled broadly and said, "Well, I guess we'll see you in another week." Everyone saluted formally, the gate was raised, and in another minute we were back at Outpost No. 7.

It was late afternoon when we returned to the hotel, and the air was cold. Our teeth beat a tattoo, and our bodies were numb when we climbed out of the jeeps. We thawed out in the pool, had dinner, and then gathered in the commanding officer's room, which he had gallantly surrendered to Charlotte.

The previous night I had talked to the commanding officer of writing an article on him and his unit, and we had agreed that he would try to remember the landmarks, the anecdotes, and the human touches. Now he smiled apologetically and said he could remember nothing. It was plain that, although he wanted to see his name in print, he would not talk.

This went on for half an hour, until Charlotte exploded. "Look, fellows," she said, "this is getting to be silly. Remember? We're American correspondents. I've been in Manchuria with the Russians, and in North China with the Chinese Reds, and in Chungking with the Kuomintang, but I've never been treated like this. You're watching us all the time, and you make a secret of things which have no business being secret. Like rice collection. . . . "

I was sitting in the corner and writing in a notebook. I set down the answers. "In this country," said one captain, "everything is secret." Then Captain K. came in with a longer, more passionate reply. He was about to go home to Minnesota, become a dentist, perhaps be married and raise American children.

"We like correspondents to visit us," he said, "but not for news. The army is doing a competent job, and it doesn't want any interference. The American people are too dumb to understand what's going on here. We can't wait until they wake up to our problems. The army will tell the people what they ought to know. I am not the only one who feels this way. I happen to know that this also represents the views of my regimental and divisional commanders."

He went on and on in a high-pitched, angry voice. He denounced the press for misreporting, and wanted to know why we thought our reporting would be any better. He called the U.S. Congress "a farce," and insisted the army had to make its own policy in Korea, for there was no time to wait for decisions in Washington. He snorted as he spoke of the meddling, ignorant, inconsiderate American people. We all felt very uncomfortable, and gradually the group broke up.

We went to bed early. I climbed into the sleeping bag and read a magazine condensation of *The Hucksters* by the light of a flashlight, and thought of the unreal people in the unreal city a world away. The cold wind still blew through the missing window panes, and with it came the shreds of a monotonous Korean tune, sung by a man. The hot spring gurgled near by. Dogs barked. Then all was silent.

October 24, 1946   PAKCHON-KAESONG

Left Pakchon after a substantial breakfast, topped by a real stateside MacIntosh apple which made me homesick. We took off in a convoy of three jeeps, with Captain K. leading. I take it that he will keep an eye on us until we leave his territory.

We made the twenty-three miles to Kaesong in thirty-six minutes, which must be some sort of a record for this kind of road. At Kaesong, we spent the morning talking to Japanese repatriates, returning home from Manchuria and North Korea by way of our zone. Most of the Japanese looked amazingly neat and fit, considering the trials behind them.

We questioned four Japanese—including the wife of a Japanese brigadier general—on the conditions in the Soviet zone. Captain K. supplied the interpreter, a Nisei Intelligence officer. The Japanese said that the Russian troops behaved badly in the early months of the occupation, but that discipline was restored with the arrival of Soviet Military Police.

One of the Japanese, a teacher who on the side ran an orchard yielding an income of Y.400,000 a year ($26,000 at the current exchange rate), complained that the Communists had redistributed all the land. "Men who used to work for me now have my orchard."

From the outset, we began to run into difficulties with the interpreter, who insisted on censoring both the questions and the answers. I wanted to know if it was true, as Seoul rumor had it, that the Soviet garrison in the capital of North Korea was being reduced. "This I will not translate," said the interpreter.

The same thing happened when Charlotte wanted to know if the Japanese had seen any Chinese Communist troops in North Korea. It happened again when I asked for a physical description of Kim Il Sun, the Communist leader. I blew up.

"We must've seen a thousand portraits of Kim Il Sun across the line yesterday," I said, "and his appearance cannot be a secret to us. A picture of Kim Il Sun must be in the files of every large American newspaper. What's going on? What is it that the Japanese can know, and the American correspondents cannot?"

Captain K. turned red, and told the interpreter to translate the question. The Japanese said Kim Il Sun looked about thirty-five years of age, was about five and a half feet tall, always wore civilian clothes, and was an impressive speaker.

From the camp we drove to the city to see Major John Stein, Military Governor for the province, who was noted for his excellent administrative record, a magnificent moustache, and a loaded pistol with which he seldom parted. At the city hall Captain K. asked us to wait in the reception room, and went ahead into Stein's office. He returned ten minutes later and said the major was waiting for us.

Stein did have a magnificent moustache and a pistol in a shoulder holster. I assumed it was loaded. A huge man with bushy hair, he towered behind a writing desk meant for a Japanese executive.

"Come in, come in," he boomed. "Pull up the chairs and put your feet on the table."

We sat down and asked him if he could tell us the story of rice collection in his province.

"You ought to get that in Seoul."

"Could you then tell us the mechanics of rice collection?"

"You can get that in Seoul too."

Charlotte asked him if any preparations were being made for the election, now a week off.

"I never talk to the Korean press," said Stein. "I won't talk to the American press."

"O.K., Major," I said. "Let's call this a social visit. We just dropped in to pay our respects. Thanks very much for seeing us." He rose and said goodbye, and we went out into the outer office to wait for Captain G., our guide from Seoul, who had the keys to our jeep. Captain K. came out and said the major did not want us in the building. We got into Captain K.'s jeep and drove to his office atop a hill. The captain took us into his own bare room, pulled two clippings from his desk—one from *Time*, the other from the Chicago *Tribune*—and began to denounce the press.

"Goddamned lies," he said, "all lies. I can't tell you how much harm they've done here. Did you write this one?" He waved the *Tribune* clipping before me.

Charlotte said mildly, "Captain, he works for the *Sun*, not the *Tribune*."

"Oh," said the captain, "well, it doesn't matter. All the papers are alike. There's a war on here, and the goddamned reporters are meddling in our work. . . . "

Captain G. finally arrived, and we drove the hundred miles back to Seoul in silence.

October 25, 1946   SEOUL

In the morning Charlotte and I went to the National Police Division of the Military Government to try and get a picture of the unrest sweeping our zone. We were taken to an enclosure, where copies of American police reports were being kept. There was a huge wall map, with little labels showing the trouble spots. The labels were grouped in three clusters: one near the 38th Parallel, in the areas we visited; another in a city called Taegu, in the heart of our zone; and the third in the extreme south, around the city of Pusan.

For the next two hours we scribbled feverishly. What we had before us, in the form of laconic two- and three-line reports, was the face of a revolution. It was a face covered with blood, and contorted with pain and agony. As most revolutions, this one was based on deep distress—on a hunger for land, food and justice.

It was a full-scale revolution, which must have involved hundreds of thousands, if not millions of people. In Taegu alone a third of the 150,000 inhabitants took part in the uprising. It was here that the fuse of the revolution was set off last month. The railroad workers went on strike, followed by the phone and metal, textile and electric workers. As each strike was suppressed by the police, another one took its place. Students went out into the streets to demonstrate, and then the whole city was aflame.

From the city, the revolution spread into the countryside and was taken over by the sharecroppers. The farmers refused to surrender their rice to the police. They attacked the homes of the landlords, and then the police stations. They tore off jail doors to release arrested sharecroppers, they burned the records, and stole the weapons.

Arrayed against the revolution were the police, the rightist organizations, and the U.S. Army. In one town after another, right-wing leaders offered their aid to our local commanders, or actively participated in the mass roundups of suspects. As for us, we did far more than just transport the Korean police to the trouble areas, or supply arms, or maintain preventive patrols. Our troops—come here as liberators—had fired on crowds, conducted mass arrests, combed the hills for suspects, and organized posses of Korean rightists, constabulary and police for mass raids.

It was amazing to recall again that despite our active involvement, no harm had come to a single American. To me it was a remarkable stroke of luck or an indication of stern discipline in the ranks of the rebels. The revolutionists wanted no trouble with us. They were merely settling their scores with the men and forces which oppressed them under our rule, as they did under the Japanese. By today, about 75 policemen have been killed, and 200 to 300 were missing.

This was the face of the revolution:

September 26: two men killed in strike at ———.

September 28: two cases of dynamite stolen at ———. Railroad, phone and metal workers on strike at ———.

October 1: Communications workers on strike at ———. Clerks operate street cars in Pusan. Stores and schools on strike in Seoul. Thirty leaders of streetcar strike arrested. Demonstrations in Seoul. A food demonstration at Taegu. One civilian killed, six policemen injured. Four hundred policemen disperse demonstration.

October 2: Fifty thousand rioters at Taegu seize all police stations. Jail broken into. Homes of policemen raided. U.S. troops in control with tanks. Thirty-eight policemen dead. Post office burned down at ———. County government buildings and former Japanese houses destroyed at ———. Five thousand demand food in front of a county office at ———. Uprisings spread through province of ———. U.S. troops on patrol trying to arrest all leaders and agitators. Korean police reinforcements reach Taegu.

October 4: In the early morning, U.S. troops retake police stations at ———. Colonel Gundy, U.S. Army, with 150 troops, made 15 arrests, recovered 40 weapons, rescued all but 37 policemen at ———.

October 7: At night, 500 attack police station at ———. Police fought from half-destroyed buildings until rebels fled. At Taejon, right-wing leaders pledge support to U.S. commander. In Pusan, half a squad of U.S. troops assigned to each police station. Number of arrests: 254. Several thousands attack city hall at ———. Rioters dispersed by police and U.S. troops; 7 rioters killed, 8 injured. Student plot discovered, 13 leaders arrested. U.S. troops and Korean police repulse mob with machineguns at ———. Number of agitators arrested: 18 . . . 25 . . . 17 . . . 7 . . . 8 . . .

October 8: Mob of 200, mostly women, demand more rice at ———. Three hundred men being surrounded in hills north of ———. U.S. troops dispatched.

October 10: Report from Taegu—"Have borrowed gymnasium, cell block, and office space from Taegu prison to relieve pressure on police jails. Capacity of 1,200 prisoners held there while being investigated."

October 11: Leftists set fire to right-wing homes near Pusan. From Taegu: *"Do not believe it safe to withdraw reinforcements until after coming election."*

October 12: A Korean police lieutenant and five policemen, investigating unlawful meeting, accidentally shot and killed a labor leader at ———.

October 14: Detachments of fifty men each sent to ——— to comb hills for suspects, and to show force to villages. Hundred men held for investigation, hundred escaped to hills.

October 20: A democratic leader killed in Kaesong (where we saw Major Stein yesterday). Fifty-four leftists arrested. Jail full, and now using school as arrests continue. District station at Yonan captured by rebels; 64 rifles stolen. Rebels seize police station at Pakchon (where we stayed two nights), but station retaken by U. S. troops. Arrested: 11 at Pakchon, 100 at ———, 117 at ———, 150 at ———, 43 at ———, 23 at ———, 13 at ———, 20 at ———. Three hundred and fifteen prisoners being moved from Kaesong to Seoul. "Choy Chang Ki attacked a police station, and then committed suicide. . . . "

We kept making notes, and a worried colonel hovered over us. From time to time, he disappeared into the office of the American chief of the Police Division, Colonel William Maglin. We had already heard of Maglin. He is a son of a New York City police captain, a West Pointer, Commandant of a Provost Marshal school at Fort Custer. A professional policeman, he has served in the French, Italian, and Mexican police. The worried colonel came to us and said Maglin wanted to see us. We found half a dozen American officers in Maglin's office. They sat in two neat ranks, and stared at us. We took the two chairs facing Maglin. He is a tall, square-shouldered, handsome man in his forties.

Maglin told us of the steps taken to democratize the Korean police. Swords, he said, have been replaced with clubs. A bar with the word "Service" has been placed above the police badge. Policemen have been told to abstain from political activity. The police have been barred from keeping people in jail without charges for more than forty-eight hours, though this could be raised to a maximum of ten days by using the "vagrancy" charge.

"You must remember," said Maglin, "that when we took over last year, 12,000 out of the 20,000 men in the police force were Japanese. What we did, after sending the Japs home, was to push the Koreans up, and then build up the force by incorporating all the young men who had been helping the police. In this manner, we have brought up the police strength from 20,000 to 25,000 men.

"Many people question the wisdom of keeping men trained by the Japanese. But many men are born policemen. We felt that if they did a good job for the Japanese, they would do a good job for us. It would be unfair to drive men trained by the Japanese out of the force."

October 26, 1946   SEOUL

Charlotte and I told Major Williamson we wanted to go south, to Taegu and Pusan. He said we could not because there were no accommodations for correspondents. During the argument, we discovered that General Baker's office in Tokyo had pulled a fast one on us. I applied for permission to spend thirty days in Korea. Charlotte wanted to stay a fortnight. Someone cagily predated our travel orders, so that by the time we arrived here, my time had been reduced to fifteen days, and Charlotte's to ten. Now Williamson agreed to give me a ten-day extension, but told Charlotte she would have to leave Korea in a few days. Since we expected to spend at least two weeks in the south, we obviously did not have enough time.

I told Williamson that unless I had my permission this afternoon I would file two messages to the *Sun*. One would be an article describing army censorship methods here. The other one would be a request to my editor to file a formal protest with the War Department.

In the afternoon Williamson informed us that General Hodge had granted us permission to go south, but that Charlotte would have to leave Korea as soon as she returned to Seoul.

Had lunch with Bertsch. He talked of the coming election to the Interim Legislative Assembly, which in effect will be the Korean Government for our zone. The Assembly will have 90 members, of whom 45 will be elected. The rest will be appointed by General Hodge, on Bertsch's recommendation.

The elections, Bertsch said, had already begun in many areas, a bit ahead of schedule, and he intended to seek their annulment. "The fact is," he said, "that the people know nothing of the elections, and the thing might prove embarrassing to us in the end." (We later checked with Military Government, and discovered that they did not know the elections had already begun, and were still waiting for orders to publicize it to the Korean people.)

Bertsch also said he has come to doubt that the left will win. "By the very nature of the election," he said, "the forty-five elected men will be old and reactionary. It will remain for the forty-five appointed men to be the solvent." Bertsch said he knew Rhee would get many of his henchmen elected, but the system of appointed seats would give Kimm Kiu Sic the balance of power.

As we left the Chosun Hotel, a colonel approached Bertsch with a radiant smile. "Say," he said, "I understand you're recommending men for the Interim Legislature."

"Yes."

"Well, I know a wonderful guy. His name is Rah, and he is the president of the Horse Racing Association. He wants very much to serve in the Legislature. You'll do me a great personal favor if you meet him."

"O.K.," said Bertsch. "Send him to me with your card. I'll talk to him."

"I believe in the inevitability, and necessity, of conflict with Russia," said Bertsch, as we were walking down the street, "just as the conflict with Germany was inevitable and necessary. We should proceed in two phases: atomic preparedness and democratic reform in the occupied countries."

We are leaving for Pusan by air the day after tomorrow.

October 28, 1946 PUSAN

By the time we got to the airdrome, we found our transport filled to capacity with unscheduled, but high-priority Korean politicians. A colonel with whom I had played poker at the "Frozen Chosun" then put Charlotte and me on a small, rickety plane carrying a U.S.O. company to Pusan. It was fiercely cold, and poor Charlotte, who promptly went to sleep, and who had nothing over her thin uniform but a light, bright, unmilitary red coat, kept whimpering through the trip.

Why the single, sand-coated strip at Pusan is called an airfield is a mystery. There was only one seemingly unused quonset hut, and not even a phone. The transport that brought us in took one quick look at the place, and took off again. We picked a ride to Pusan with a colonel, who had a jeep waiting for him. Pusan, we found, is a shabbier version of Seoul. It is a city of 350,000 people, rutted streets, rundown stores, and buses made out of old automobile chassis drawn by apathetic horses. It is a sad, sad place, filled with dust.

I registered at the U.S. Army's Railway Hotel. Later we went to the Public Relations Office to look for a Captain Hooper who was supposed to take care of us here. The captain was out, and we proceeded to the Military Government to talk to Lieutenant Colonel H. O. Benton, Deputy Military Governor. We learned that there were 1,300 political prisoners in the province, that rice shortages loomed large in the riots, and that the Military Government made every effort to operate through the Koreans themselves. "You know, this is their country."

note

On the way out, we asked a major, sitting importantly behind a desk, the name of the Korean provincial governor. The major could not remember it.

Now we went back to the Public Relations Office to see if Captain Hooper was back. We met him in the entrance, and his smile was distinctly below zero. He told us that he had just returned from the airfield, where he had gone with two other officers to meet us. When the scheduled transport arrived we naturally were not aboard. Since then the three officers had been scouring the town for us. Hooper was very anxious to learn where we had been, and with whom. He insisted on escorting us to the Railway Hotel, where, inevitably, we found the other two officers waiting for us. One of them was Lieutenant James of Military Intelligence; the other a Captain Davies, a company commander assigned to us "for security."

Our first hours together were quite strained, for we resented being under surveillance, and the officers were angry because we managed to get away from them. Eventually, Davies' wife, an extraordinarily pretty girl, arrived, and we had a silent dinner together. After dinner, Davies took Charlotte to her billet, and James remained with me. It was six o'clock in the evening, there were no books or newspapers in sight, and James and I found few subjects of common interest. We had a couple of drinks, and he suggested going to a movie. It was a very poor whodunnit, and when we left the theater I said so.

"It stinks," said James tersely. "I saw it last night."

After breakfast Charlotte and I, with our two escorts, went back to Military Government. This time we had a chance to observe the machinegun nest over the arched driveway, the Korean policemen who examined the papers of all Koreans entering the compound, the floors worn so badly even the boards under the linoleum showed grooves, and the numerous helpful signs in English: "Care for Fire" and "Way in Meeting Hall," with an arrow pointing towards the auditorium.

We spent most of the morning with Chief of the Home Affairs Division for this province, C. V. Bergstrom. He is an easy-going, good-looking man of about forty who had served for ten years in the city government of Milwaukee, and intends to enter politics there when his term here is ended.

The election procedure, Bergstrom explained, was decided by the Military Government's Advisory Council, whose members were nominated by the Korean governor. The governor, I recalled, was the "friend" to whom Rhee gave me a letter. The procedure was complex. In the first-level election, already held, family heads in each village chose two representatives to the county meetings, being held today. Each county meeting would pick two delegates to go to a provincial meeting.

"You know," said Bergstrom, "strategically, this is the proper time for the rightists to hold the elections. All the leftists are either in jail or in the hills."

We arranged to go this afternoon to the neighboring county seat of Tongnae to watch the election.

Our escorts, who sat in on all our interviews, including the one with the Military Governor himself, were with us at lunch. Davies was telling us about his first day in Korea. He had landed at Inchon, and was ordered to proceed with his unit to a town on the southwest coast. The trains, of course, were packed, and many Koreans rode the roofs. They kept throwing refuse down, and some of it came in through the open windows. The exasperated GIs finally sprayed the ceilings with tommygun fire.

"You should've seen those guys slide off."

Tongnae is a fair-sized, undistinguished town of one-story buildings, a gray brick private bank, a busy market, and the inevitable dust. We drove up to the county office, and met the County Master—a slim, handsome and altogether very impressive Korean. He was wearing a well-cut Chesterfield overcoat, in which he looked more like a diplomat than a rural administrator.

The election was already in progress, and we walked to a temple-like building where it was being held. A large blackboard carried the names of the seventeen voters present who would choose two of their number to go to the provincial election in Pusan. The board gave the men's professions—six farmers, five village headmen, two landlords, a sake brewer, a fire department chief, a monk, and an organizer for Syngman Rhee's *Han Kook* Democratic party. ("He used to be no good before," the county master said of the last man, "but he has now changed his mind.")

We were especially interested in the farmers, and we asked the County Master to find one for us.

The man was small and round-faced, about forty-six, and wearing Western clothes. At once we discovered that though he listed himself as a farmer, he was also the headman of his village. He owned some land, which he rented out to sharecroppers. "I belong to no party," he added, "but I lean to the right."

We asked him about the riots. "We had none in my village," he said proudly. "As soon as I heard of riots in other villages, I organized a vigilante unit, armed it with clubs, and had it patrol the village. I control the village, and there were no disturbances."

We were not satisfied with the man. We wanted a real, down-to-earth peasant, who knew the feel of the soil in his fingers and got up before the sun to plough his field. We went into the temple, and began to look for another farmer. There were three tables—one with four official witnesses, another with two official watchers, and a third with two detectives. We found that one of the official watchers was both a farmer and a candidate for election, and we took him out.

He too was a curious specimen. He owned only two and a half acres of land, but he rented two-thirds of it out to three sharecroppers. The man looked well-to-do, and it was obvious it was not farming that gave him his look of affluence.

"Father," he said laconically. "My father is a landlord. Thirty-six acres."

We waited.

"I also hold some offices. I'm president of the Farm Credit Association, president of the Deep Sea Fisheries Association, and president of the Association to Suppress Disturbances."

There had been no riots in his village, because the police arrested eight men and they confessed plotting an uprising. He then formed his Association to Suppress Disturbances, with about a hundred and fifty members—"mainly elderly people." Until recently, the two most important organizations in his area were the Farmers' Union and the Youth Alliance, but now they were inactive, and their leaders were in jail or in hiding.

We asked him who in his opinion was Korea's outstanding man. "Syngman Rhee," he said without hesitation.

We talked to yet another "farmer," an old man in a black silk gown. He told us he owned no land and declined to go into any details. Instead, he told us of a riot in his village, where the Farmers' Union demanded a redistribution of land. The unpleasantness ended with the arrest of "three or four hundred people." The old man then encouraged the remaining citizenry —the substantial folk—to form a vigilante unit.

"The Military Government," he said shrilly, "shouldn't be so lenient with these trouble-makers."

We had had enough of these fraudulent farmers. Now we talked to the County Master. The Farmers' Union, he said, used to be very important, and nearly all of the 20,000 sharecroppers in the county belonged to it. "However," he said, "it made a lot of rash promises: land reform, clean government and such, and it couldn't keep them, and it gradually lost support. Now it's inactive, and its leaders are in jail."

Word came in that the voting was over, and we all went to the temple. The police chief was standing by the ballot box and surveying the scene with a hard eye. The two detectives were now reinforced by two uniformed policemen. Benches were brought in, and about fifty people trooped in and sat down. The County Master took a key out of an envelope and opened the box. Then he removed the ballots one by one, and read the two names written on each. A clerk wrote the names on a blackboard.

The organizer for Rhee's party won with seven votes. There was a tie, with six votes each, between the president of the Association for the Suppression of Disturbances and the old "farmer," to whom we talked. At once, the old man was proclaimed winner. Bergstrom asked the reason for the choice, and the County Master said, "He's the older of the two."

After dinner I decided to see if I could lose my escorts. I pleaded a headache and went up to my room. An hour later, when I came down, the boys were gone. In the lobby I saw a Military Government officer whom I had met earlier. I told him about the election we witnessed, and he shook his head.

"This is quite an election," he said. "First, they let Syngman Rhee's boys decide the procedure. Second, to make sure nothing slips up, they hold the election in a series of four levels, so that the undesirables might be eliminated. Third, they let only family heads, or heads of ten families, vote.

"They put all the possible opposition in jail, or drive it into the hills. Then they leave us nine days to announce and explain the election to the illiterate farmers. You can't beat the machine. It includes everybody in power, from the village cop and the landlord to the provincial governor.

"The machine is the same we found when we got here. For our purposes it's an ideal setup. It's organized military fashion. All you have to do is push the button, and somewhere some cop begins skull cracking. They've been learning the business under the Japs for thirty-five years. Why should anyone expect them to unlearn all they know now?

"Most of our junior officers are sick of being partners with this gang. All they want is to get word of what's going on here to the people back home. Maybe they can do something to stop this crooked show."

October 30, 1946   PUSAN

Went to see Major Atkinson, Chief of the Police Division. He said he had an appointment elsewhere and could not talk to us. We said it was all right; we would talk to the Korean police officers. Atkinson hesitated, but finally agreed. We started with the deputy chief, a small, stocky man, holding on tight to his police cap. Atkinson apparently forgot about his appointment. He stayed, and kept making surreptitious gestures to the deputy and his interpreter. Finally, he called a clerk out of the room, and a few minutes later the clerk returned and said something softly to the deputy chief.

But by that time we had learned that there were 3,450 policemen in this province; that most of the Korean policemen hired after the U.S. Army arrived here had served in the Japanese Army; and that nearly all the high Korean police officers had been trained by the Japanese. The deputy chief had spent all his adult life in the Japanese police force, the chief spent twenty-two of his thirty-eight years under the Japanese; the chief of detectives was also Japanese-trained.

Now Atkinson took over. The new policemen, he said, were trained in law, history, and culture, and although the Koreans are not as sharp witted as the Chinese, they have the merit of sincerity.

The riots, he said, had been organized by "agitators imported from north of the 38th Parallel." They stumped the country, demanding high wages for the workers and land for the sharecroppers. In the past six months, there had been only three complaints of police brutality. They were investigated, and found to be untrue.

He refused to tell us how many people had been arrested in

· 399 ·

the province, how many were presently in jail, or how many outside agitators had been apprehended. "I couldn't tell you for fear of making a mistake."

We talked to the Korean governor, to whom I had a letter from Rhee. A little man with a puzzled expression on his face, he told us that he had started as a teacher, next became manager of the Tongnae Bank (which we saw yesterday), and became governor nine months ago. We told him we wanted to visit a village, and specified the things which interested us. He looked more puzzled than ever, but finally suggested the village of Waya, on the other side of Tongnae. The village has a land-lord named Oh who owns 7,500 acres, and it has had a riot. We are going with Dr. Hahn, a Korean graduate of the Chicago and Princeton Theological Seminaries and Bergstrom's interpreter. I am beginning to think that Dr. Hahn is a very important man, for both the Korean governor and the American Military Governor defer to him.

We spent the afternoon in the Agriculture Department, headed by a Major Fowler. The major, a stout, loud-voiced professional soldier, has been in Korea a month and spent the war years running an army camp in Texas. I wonder what in his background qualified him for the crucial job of collecting rice in a hungry and restless Korean province.

The major knew little, and we finally prevailed on him to bring out his Korean associates. They told us the province was short on rice and on the essential commodities needed by the farmer. The hungry, they said, do not consider American wheat, which they are now getting, as a substitute for rice. The black market is rampant, with the price of rice ten times the official rate.

Midway a Captain Price, who is in charge of rice collection under Fowler, came in. He was a young man—not more than thirty—good looking and alert. He has been in this province for a year.

"Last year," he said, "someone in Seoul blundered and proclaimed an open market in rice. By the time they woke up and instituted rationing, it was already too late. The rice had vanished and there was hunger. We collected only a fifth of what we should have.

"Our relations with the farmers are not so good. The Japanese took rice out of this country, but at least they brought in grain from Manchuria. Now the farmers give up rice to feed the townfolk, and get nothing in exchange. The farmer is worried, and he has transferred his hate from the Japanese to us.

"When we came here, we found the Korean People's Republic in control. This was in violation of our orders to let the Jap officials stay on in their jobs. So we broke it up. I feel that the People's Republic, the Farmers' Union and such are no longer a problem. What happens is that the old men organize their people, arm them with clubs, and protect installations. This is very gratifying to us.

"Three weeks ago I was sent to a county where they had some riots. I fired the County Master and the police chief, organized a posse and raided some houses, raided the headquarters of the Farmers' Union, and helped to get Syngman Rhee's *Han Kook* Democratic Party going."

We asked him if anything was being done about land reform.

"Land reform?" he said brightly. "That's not important. Remember that the present system is the system they're used to."

October 31, 1946   PUSAN

The provincial election was being held today, and the building was crowded with policemen. While we waited for the session to start, we talked to Military Government officers about the Korean Advisory Council, chosen so as "to reflect public opinion of all the people." Because the American Military Governor depends so much on it, it has become more than an advisory body. It nominates all Korean officials, and recommends the dismissal of those it does not like.

Of the Council's 23 members, we were told, 20 are professed rightists. Its president is the provincial boss of Syngman Rhee's *Han Kook* Democratic Party. We learned, without surprise, that the man had been a Japanese collaborator.

While we waited, we picked at random an elector and questioned him. He was a mill owner and a landlord, with seventy sharecropper families. When we asked him about the Farmers' Union, he perked up.

"I've had much trouble with the union," he said. "All my tenants belonged to it. They demanded that the land be redistributed, and the Farmers' Union be represented in the elections. We had to break it up."

There were about a hundred and fifty people sitting in the auditorium. Policemen at the door examined the credentials of the new arrivals. The Korean governor, unshaven and looking very old, sat near the ballot box. The show was obviously being run by his deputy, who looked much like a cop in plain clothes. Dr. Hahn was translating for Colonel Gillette, the Military Governor.

"This is a historic occasion," said Gillette. "There've been elections before. But this is the first one pointed toward a democracy. Your very presence here indicates you're representatives of the people. We've had very few reports of dishonestly or intimidation. I've also had reports of great public interest. You're truly intelligent and able. . . . "

A Korean rose and said he wanted to make a comment. There was some confusion at the table. "We can't have electioneering here," said Gillette. "You can ask a question." The Korean deputy governor, tapping the face of his watch impatiently, said something sharply. The man sat down. No one else rose to speak.

"I think he's an anarchist," explained my neighbor. The audience, he said, consisted mainly of county officials and Military Government personnel.

There were seven men to be elected to go to Seoul—one

representative-at-large and six others. The name of the representative-at-large was announced, and there was applause.

"What's his name?"

"Kim Chul Soo."

This was the president of the Advisory Council, head of Syngman Rhee's party, a former Japanese collaborator.

I sat in an office, and could not help hearing a conversation at my desk. A high American officer was approached by a U.S. Army captain and the Korean governor's secretary. The problem was patronage.

"I've had to remove the County Master in my district," said the captain.

"He was a leftist," said the secretary. "He wasn't firm."

"We can't decide whom to appoint in his place," said the captain.

There was a long pause.

"How about appointing the county's candidate who failed to be elected today," said the high officer. "He's a rightist, isn't he?"

November 1, 1946   WAYA VILLAGE, CHULMA COUNTY

On our way to the village, we stopped at Tongnae to pick up a guide. Dr. Hahn told me he knew the town well; he had worked at the bank for ten years.

We followed the highway for a few miles, turned off into a rutted country road, and finally got on a country path. The only traffic we saw was men with heavy loads on their backs, and ox carts with their tremendous iron-bound wheels. Twice we forded rivers, bouncing hard on the boulders. After that we climbed up to a high plateau. It was a beautiful scene—a wide, sparkling river below, the rugged Chulma mountains, and on every side of us the carefully terraced paddies that were no more than ledges crawling up the steep mountainsides.

Waya was a narrow village, hemmed in between a mountain and a river. Above it, dominating it, lay the magnificent mansion and family mausoleum of landlord Oh, who himself had gone to the safety of Tongnae. We drove the length of the village, until we came to the one-story, whitewashed building of the county government.

The County Master was a tall, lean man of about fifty, in a white robe and a white silk suit under it. He had close-cropped white hair, and a growth of bristle on his chin. We talked to him in the small back room, and the happy shouts of hundreds of children massed around our jeeps came in from without, and at times drowned our conversation.

Waya has 570 people, four out of every five of them sharecroppers. In all, 3900 people in sharecropper families live on 1,350 acres of rented land. The biggest landlord is Oh, who has 75 sharecroppers in this county alone. The current price of land runs at about $1,300 an acre, and there are few sales.

The County Master himself was a farmer, cultivating four acres, some of which was rented. He was elected to his post by the seventy heads of family groups in the county. He also got as high as the county-level in the election to the Interim Legislature.

Up to this point we were getting the information we wanted. James mumbled that he was hungry and walked out. We obviously were not discussing any dangerous subjects. But the atmosphere changed as soon as we asked the County Master about the Farmers' Union and the Youth Alliance. He became uncertain and evasive. Union leaders, he said, sometimes came to see him, but "they never talked like Communists." He had never heard of any "imported agitators." The union, he thought, was primarily engaged in protecting sharecroppers from landlords who might try to evict them or raise the rent.

One morning three weeks ago, he said, the police station here was raided by forty or fifty young men, most of them from this village. They had no weapons, and there was no violence. The three policemen did not resist. The young men occupied the station for an hour, and then left. Later, Major Atkinson arrested about twenty men. All were sharecroppers.

· 404 ·

Since then, all the officers of the Farmers' Union and the Youth Alliance have either been arrested, or have escaped. Only their wives and young children remained.

We asked him to name a member of the Farmers' Union, or just a sharecropper, to whom we could talk. The only two names he would give us were those of former headmen. "You don't want to talk to any sharecroppers," he kept repeating. "The people here are so ignorant, you'll learn nothing."

He followed us when we walked out of the office. In the yard, he took Dr. Hahn aside and whispered to him earnestly. I asked Hahn what the County Master wanted.

"He asked me to talk to the Military Government people, and get the Youth Alliance members out of jail. He said they weren't Communists. They were just young boys who followed the lead of others."

Hahn paused. "I think," he said, "that the reason he didn't want to give you the names of Farmers' Union people was because he's a leftist himself. He doesn't trust Americans."

When we got to the jeeps, James and the GI driver had just finished eating. They picked up the paper and the empty cans, and tossed them into a ditch. There was a great rush of children, screaming and yelling and trampling on each other. Then the pile unfolded itself, and there was a little boy, crying bitterly. His hand was covered with blood. I saw only a nick, and gave him some candy as consolation. However, blood kept flowing over his hand and finally I pried his fingers open, and saw that he had a deep gash on the inside of his thumb, probably cut with an open can. Davies bandaged the finger tenderly with his handkerchief, and volunteered to take him to the school, which had a first-aid kit. The County Master said in a hostile voice, "I'll take care of him," and led the boy off.

The police station was a tall, airy room, with windows on three sides, and a jail cell on the fourth. The cell was three feet wide and six long, and had no window. There were three young policemen in the room, one rifle, and, scattered here and there, inspirational posters reading, "Service" and "Order."

The chief was a man of about twenty-six, with alert eyes and a jaw much wider than his forehead. He seemed nervous, and kept buttoning and unbuttoning his coat. He told us he had been a policeman for five years under the Japanese.

His story of the troubled night differed from that of the County Master. He said five hundred rioters had surrounded the station, and the three policemen within gave up quickly. The crowd then listened to speeches attacking the system of rice collection. There was no violence. The crowd left some youngsters behind to guard the station, and went on towards Tongnae, taking the policemen along. The latter were dropped off at a vacant house, and discovering that no one was guarding them, walked out, and sent a warning to Tongnae.

Major Atkinson was summoned, and a force was dispatched to the village. The police met the marchers on a country path that night, and opened fire. Four of the marchers were killed, the rest fled. By the following noon, Major Atkinson had arrested 45 men—20 of them in Waya village. All of the arrested men were from this county.

"We're now checking on every man in this village to find out if he had been active in the Farmers' Union."

I remembered Colonel Maglin's assurance that the blacklists had been strictly banned. "It must be hard," I said, "to keep an eye on the subversive elements. Do you have any idea who they are?"

"Oh, certainly," the chief said. He slipped a sheet of paper across to me. There were six names on it. "One of them is already in jail," he said. "The others are in hiding. These are the men we regard as unreliable."

Back in Tongnae, we headed straight for the police station and asked to see the jail. The chief, small, flabby and middle-aged, readily agreed. He led us to a wing, into a small, dark enclosure filled with a warm, animal stench. When our eyes grew accustomed to the dim light, we saw before us—separated only by bars—a cell, about 10 feet by 16, with men sitting in rows on the floor. There were 31 men in that cell. In the next cell there were 33, and two men had to stand up because there was no place for them to squat. There were four cells altogether, two with 33 inmates each, two with 31. The chief said the men had been there for twenty-one days.

We stood in front of the cell and listened to the chief's complaint. "I sent a report of our investigation to Major Atkinson seventeen days ago, but he hasn't replied. I tried to borrow a cell in the Pusan jail. They, too, don't answer. These four cells were meant for 30 people. I have 128. Daily I send appeals to the Military Government to move these men. Nothing happens."

The men in the cells listened with impassive faces. A few smiled a crooked smile. We were all Americans, the same kind and in the same uniform that Major Atkinson wore the night he came to Waya village.

We walked back to the chief's room, and he said the food was running a bit low. The bulk of the prisoners were sharecroppers. I asked the chief how many imported agitators there were. He shook his head vigorously, "None."

"What would happen," I said, "if you caught a common criminal? You know, not a sharecropper."

"Unless it's a serious crime, we can't take care of him," the chief said. He thought a moment. "Even if it is a serious crime, I don't know where I'd put him. There's no place."

The chief said he had served nineteen years in the Japanese police force. Never had he been so busy.

From the jail we went calling on Oh, the landlord. He lived in a maze of compounds, fronting on a narrow lane. Right in front of the gate there was a dead rat. We studied it until Dr. Hahn returned with Oh. The latter was a small, old man with a long and scraggly moustache. He was wearing white silk.

He led us into an inner compound, with a small guest house. Now the sliding wall panels had been pushed open, exposing the clean rooms, with paintings on the closet doors and oiled parchment on the floor. There were two younger men, who helped to answer our questions.

The conversation lagged, and Hahn told us Oh had been his friend ever since the bank days, twenty years ago, when

Hahn worked in the bank and Oh was one of the stockholders. I recalled that the Korean provincial governor had also worked at the bank.

Oh confirmed that he had about 7,500 acres of land, but complained bitterly and lengthily that he was getting so little rice from it, "it isn't even enough for the beggars who come to my doors." He said he was selling his land bit by bit, "if the price is right. I have a big family. Sixteen people."

In Pusan, at dinner, we told some officers of our visit to the jail. They recounted their own experiences.

"Sometime ago," an officer said, "the Korean police got shorthanded, and our troops were assigned to guard the police stations. I spent two days at a station, and I saw an eyeful. I saw cops crack men's shins against sharp-edged wooden blocks. I saw cops put burning wooden slivers under men's nails. I saw more men than I care to remember get the water treatment. They just kept pouring water into a guy's mouth through a tube until he damned near drowned. I saw cops beat a man across the shoulders with a metal rod, and then hang him on a metal hook under his shoulder blades.

"I finally couldn't take it. I went to my commanding officer and said, 'Sir, we've got to stop this. Our soldiers are now guarding the police station, and this is giving us a black eye.' The officer said he agreed with me, but there was nothing he could do. He had orders not to interfere in Korean 'administrative detail.'

"Well, I just went back to my station, and told the sons of bitches to stop the tortures at once. Boy, was I happy when they pulled us out the next day!"

November 2, 1946   PUSAN

In the morning, talked to Colonel Gillette, the Military Governor. He is a shrewd man, high above the run of military administrators. But he too had the blind spots common to the military. He never mentioned the words "land reform" and though he saw clearly some of the abuses which led to the riots, he still blamed the latter on "outside agitators."

He spoke at length of the tremendous educational work being done by the Military Government. He also noted some of the handicaps, one of them being the Hollywood movies available for showing here. "They're mostly gangster pictures," he said, "and the Koreans are beginning to think of us as men with two guns." Somehow, there was a small stock of French movies in Korea, and the people much preferred them to the Hollywood product.

"You mustn't think too harshly of us here," he said as we left him. "I used to run a CCC camp in Louisiana when Huey Long was in power, and some of the things I saw there would make Koreans look like amateurs."

I did not comment, but I have little patience with this argument. Whenever any shortcoming becomes so glaring as to require comment, it is pointed out that things are not ideal back home—corruption, strikes, race riots. With equal justice, this argument could be used to condone all that happened in Hitler's Germany.

Outside of Gillette's office we ran into a major who is in charge of the educational work in the province. He was a harassed-looking, middle-aged man. We told him we were leaving Pusan tonight. He said he was sorry we did not have a chance to see some of the great work being done by his department.

"I tell you what," he said. "You got a few hours. Why don't you visit some school here. I've been a physical education instructor for thirty years, and I tell you, I've never seen boys do better gymnastics."

I told my escorts that I had to pack, and went up to my room. Pretty soon there was a tap on the door, and a man came in. He was an American civilian attached to the army. "I heard there was a correspondent around," he said, "and I've been waiting for you to get back to your room. I want to talk to you privately."

He was a mild, low-voiced man who spoke unemotionally of the things that troubled him. There were two of them—the low morale of the troops and the poor supply service. He has been here a year.

"Some congressmen went through here," he said. "They heard that the PX stores were bare of supplies, and they raised holy hell. The next thing you knew, the supplies appeared in some of the bigger towns. But in the smaller places, today, fourteen months after we landed here, we still lack cigarettes, beer, tooth paste, and electric light bulbs. Most of the military men I've met are lousy administrators. There are all kinds of alibis —no ships and stuff. There are plenty of ships that come here to pick up the boys going home. There's no reason why they can't send supplies here aboard the ships.

"The lack of supplies only makes it harder for us to deal with the problem of morale. This is not the disciplined war army. This is a peacetime army of boys of eighteen and twenty, who have had only eight weeks of basic training before they came here. Except in the big towns, nothing is being done to keep up their morale. No radios, few movies, little athletic equipment.

"Even window shopping is discouraged. In Chinhai entire areas are off limits to GIs. You can drive through in a jeep, but the moment you get off, an MP will pick you up. Association with Koreans is frowned on. You may have a Korean friend, but you can't take him for a ride in your jeep, or even invite him to your billet. The boys never get a chance to meet the Koreans and learn something about them, and pretty soon the Koreans are 'goddamned gooks,' and you try to see how close you can drive to a gook to scare him to death without touching him. You ought to write this up. A lot of guys here would be grateful to you. Newspapermen never get here, and we sort of feel lost."

An hour before train time, Charlotte and I went to Bergstrom's house to say goodbye. We had just finished our first drink when a tall, balding American in a civilian suit and a loud tie came in. This was Mr. Flaherty, the Military Government's legal officer. Flaherty, we learned, was a Boston lawyer, served in Korea as a major, and on demobilization decided to stay on. He said he had land in Massachusetts, but he loved Korea, and would just as soon go to Tongnae and settle down there.

After that the conversation followed its carefree way.

We said, "We've visited the Tongnae jail, and it was jammed."

"They're jammed everywhere."

We said something about the Tongnae riot.

"There's been no riot in Tongnae."

"What do you mean no riot, Mr. Flaherty? Why are all those people in jail?"

He said, with a happy grin. "Oh, we just put them in on a charge of conspiracy. We can jail anyone on that charge. Hell, I've just come back from the riot country. The cops would bring a man before me and say he is a rioter. I'd say, 'How do you know?' They'd say, 'He has just confessed, in the back room.' Well, it's easy to get a confession the way the Korean cops work."

We told Flaherty of our visit with Oh the landlord. "I know the guy well," he said. "I've been his guest many a time. Have you visited his place in Waya village? It's a real palace. They serve you delicious food on gold plate or on solid silver. And if Oh likes you, he'll bring out some choice liquor that he brought with him from France fifteen years ago."

From Oh, the conversation naturally shifted to land reform. Charlotte said that once the reform bill passes, Oh might have to sell his land to the State for redistribution among his sharecroppers.

For the first time, Flaherty showed agitation. "That's impossible. You can't take a man's property away from him. I know what I'd do if you tried to take my land in Massachusetts away from me."

After a ride on the Pusan-Seoul Express—which is shabby, jerky, unbelievably overcrowded, and evil smelling— we got to Taegu. We were met by Lieutenant Lewis, adjutant to Colonel Potts, the regimental commander. Lewis was a portly young man with a steel helmet, and a pistol strapped to his leg. His martial appearance impressed us until we learned that Taegu was quiet, and Lewis himself has been here only eight weeks. He spoke to us with a politeness that somehow bordered on insult.

Charlotte was put up in a Red Cross billet. I was put up with a Major Arne Stenslie of Devil's Lake, North Dakota. I was now so accustomed to the constant surveillance that, on a hunch, I asked the major how long he had been with Regimental Intelligence. He answered promptly, "Two months."

Picked up Charlotte after breakfast. She told me that last night, at dinner, she asked the other girls if they were in town during last month's riots. There was a stony silence. Charlotte tried a few more questions, but there was no answer. At midnight, after she had gone to bed, one of the girls came in and said: "Honey, please don't think that we're rude, or that we don't like you. It's just that we had orders not to talk to you about the riots."

Later we met Lieutenant Hitchcock, Public Information Officer for the Military Government here. He is a young and pleasant fellow, interested in the work he is doing. He brought us our first news of the election in this province: of the seven successful candidates, six are Syngman Rhee's followers, and the seventh is "some sort of a neutral."

"You know," said Hitchcock, "the results amaze me. I

thought that since most of the people here are sharecroppers, the leftists would run away with the election. Instead, the rightists won, and the leftists got nothing."

The courts, he said, are working overtime trying the rioters. The Military Commission which deals with major crimes is still on its first case. But most of the work is done by the U.S. Army Provost Courts, in which the judge is at the same time the counsel for defense and the prosecuting attorney. My ideas on justice are pretty orthodox, and this combination somehow frightens me.

Every defendant, Hitchcock said, had been advised that he could have an American defense counsel. But the sharecroppers' reaction has been as expected. "Very few men have asked for counsel, and you can't assign one to each defendant. There are too many of them."

In the afternoon, Charlotte, Hitchcock and I drove fifteen miles out of Taegu, stopped in a hamlet, and walked into the first yard. There was a man sitting in front of his hut. Our interpreter told the man we were newspapermen, and could we talk to him, please.

The hut, windowless as most of the Korean country houses are, was made of yellow mud. It was set in a small yard, no more than thirty feet long. The highway, laid atop a dam, towered over the yard and the hut. The man was dressed in a ragged white jacket, under which he wore a thick vest. He was peeling an apple, and watching the road through the bamboo fence.

We started talking to him, and pretty soon other people started coming in. Before we knew it, there were eleven men squatting on the ground around us, and twenty or thirty kids, and more men and women sitting on the road behind the fence. The village meeting was on.

The place—the hamlet of Yenho in Kosan county—was poverty-ridden. Of its seventy families, sixty were sharecroppers. The men in the yard averaged just over an acre per family. They agreed that half an acre was needed for each mouth. The man with the apple had five children and only an acre of land.

and that was not enough. To keep alive, he worked for other farmers. I asked them if they would buy land if the government gave them credit and cut the price, which in this area ran upward of $1,600 an acre. They all laughed. "No matter how low the price," said one, "I couldn't buy it."

Under the Japanese, they said, they could borrow money from the Rural Credit Association at 24 per cent a year. But now the Japanese were gone, and the only source of credit was the local landlords, who charged up to 60 per cent, when they wanted to lend money. This village was so poor few men in it were able to get a loan.

The land belonged to men who lived in Taegu. The biggest landlord was a man named Soh. They called the names of their landlords out, and most of them said Soh. Then we came to what seemed to me to be the high light of the day. I said, "You pay your landlord a third of the crop in rent?"

There were immediate protests. "No, we pay half the yield." I said, "There must be some mistake. Don't you know of the Military Government order limiting all land rents to one-third?" They said, no, there were some rumors of that, but is certainly was not true in this village. Nor in the next one, a voice said on the road. Nor in the next county, said someone else.

The man with the apple explained, "We take all our rice to the Military Government. The Korean clerks give us credit for half the value, and credit the landlord with the other half."

There could be no clearer proof of the alliance between the Korean personnel of Military Government and the landlords. And I thought it significant that it was in this general area that the worst riots had taken place.

We now talked of the election. The man with the apple thought most of the family heads had voted. Two men next to me said this was the first they had heard of the election. Hitchcock said indignantly to them: "That's impossible. I sent out the election posters myself. You must've seen them." The men admitted they could not read. I remembered then a passing remark I heard in Seoul that 80 per cent of Korean farmers were illiterate. I asked the people around me how many of them could read and write. Two or three said they could; the others could not.

I said, "How then did you write in the names of your candidates in the election?"

"Others wrote the names in for us."

"Was the headman one of the men who helped you?"

"Yes, he helped everyone."

"Was he himself elected?"

They all caught on. They laughed and said, "Yes."

But Hitchcock's mind was still on the posters. That was his job—telling people of the election—and he wanted to know what had slipped up. We drove back to the office which the headman shared with a barber. There, on the barbershop wall, were two large posters. "See," said Hitchcock, "what did I tell you?"

The barber was outside. We asked him when the posters were put up. "I helped to put them up myself," he said. "That was the evening before the election."

November 4, 1946   TAEGU

The Military Commission was sitting in a large, airy, and fairly clean room. The five judges—a colonel, two majors, and two captains—sat on a high dais, with the flag and an iron stove behind them. In the center of the room stood the witness chair. The two defendants sat with their counsel on the judges' right. There were nine benches for the public, but these were occupied only by us and the wives of the defendants. Later I was told that "anyone can come in here and see the trial, provided they're solid, reputable people. We don't want any mobs here."

One of the defendants was an alert, handsome man of forty named Hwang. He lived in Manchuria until 1942, when he returned to Taegu, and owned first a liquor store and then a

· 415 ·

fruit stall. The prosecution said he was one of the minor ring-leaders of the riot.

The other man was named Chang, and by profession he was a brothel owner. Chang was tall, slim and about fifty-five. In his Korean trousers tied at the ankles and a Western coat worn directly over his undershirt, Chang looked sloppy.

Both were accused of murdering a recently retired police captain.

As the witnesses followed each other on the stand, it became clear that the brothel owner had had an old grudge against the police captain. When the Japanese surrendered, the brothel owner's brother moved into a Japanese house. Sometime later, the police ordered him out and assigned the house to the police captain. Now, when the riots began, the brothel owner went to the police captain and told him to get out of the house by nightfall.

Then a crowd of sixty or seventy men, allegedly led by Hwang, swept through the alley, and the brothel owner guided it into the police captain's yard. The captain hid himself, and the crowd contented itself with wrecking the furniture. The brothel owner was shouting jubilantly, "We've got the house back," and, to the crowd, "Please don't damage the house."

A woman found the police captain in his hiding place, and the crowd began to beat him. His wife, a small, old woman, threw herself over him in an effort to save him, but she was pulled off, and the police captain was dragged into the street and beaten to death. Then an American tank appeared in the lane, and the rioters threw the body into a Buddhist temple, and dispersed.

The defendants had a Korean lawyer, who, with his each word, helped to hang them. His questions were stupid, his witnesses evasive. One witness, who was meant to clear Hwang of all guilt, looked terrified by the scene. He kept saying, "Had I known I would be a witness, I would've looked around, but I'm just a carpenter." His failure to testify, I thought, condemned Hwang. The damage was compounded by the tragically poor interpreting.

After recess we went to a Provost Court, a bleak and dusty room where a lone American officer—a lieutenant colonel—was trying a ragged young Korean. There were only four people in the room—the judge, the defendant, an interpreter, and a Korean policeman with a rifle.

Just as we sat down on the dirty bench, the judge pronounced his verdict: one year at hard labor. The boy tugged at his long, unkempt hair and said, "This is a very harsh sentence." Then he began to cry, saying that he was not a rioter, and that his old father depended on him for a livelihood. The colonel said he knew all that, and would put in a recommendation for leniency in the court report to the provincial Military Governor.

The guard took the young Korean away. The interpreter left. There were only the three of us in the room. Charlotte and I sat on the bench and looked at the colonel. After a while he began to speak. First he told us of the case: the boy and four men had heard that the head of the rationing board had concealed seventeen bags of rice for police use. They talked it over, and decided to get the man to surrender the hoard. They had lured him out into the street, and were talking to him when the police appeared. The four men fled; the boy was caught.

The colonel said: "I realize that this is a very light sentence, and in other provost courts in this building he would have gotten five years. But I think a year is enough."

We walked to the colonel and stood facing him. "This is a bad job," he said. "I don't like any part of it. We sort of get assigned to it between jobs. Anybody who passes through and has no definite assignment gets a job on a provost court. I don't like the idea of having to decide what a young man is to do with his time for the next year or two. We're just infantry officers, not legal people. I try to treat these people leniently. But some officers just give them five years as a rule. I'm soft hearted. I guess it takes a little longer to get callous."

He paused again. "There're still three thousand cases to be tried in this town alone," he said. "In so many of them people just pay off old grudges, and you can't tell where the grudge ends and the evidence begins."

We stopped at the Provost Court office, which channels the cases to the judges. There was a crowd of happy officers there, headed by the major in charge. They told us that up to this morning one hundred ten cases have been tried in the provost courts in town, and an unknown number by the six courts operating elsewhere in the province. The major thought the dock would be cleared in thirty days.

The others cried, "Want to bet?"

The Army's Criminal Investigation Department, the major said, could not investigate the cases fast enough, and it became necessary to admit Korean police testimony.

"The Korean cops," the major said, "still function under the Jap rules of evidence. You have to have a confession. How you get it doesn't matter. We see these jokers brought in all beat up, with lacerations. Each has made a confession. We finally had to try indoctrinating the Korean cops, and now many prisoners are set loose."

"We still get funny ones," said a captain. "The other day they brought in a guy who confessed murdering a cop. Quite by accident, we discovered that the murdered cop was still walking his beat."

I found that some 6,500 people had been arrested in Taegu—not one of them an "outside agitator." I also learned that the police chief had to be fired for "softness" during the riots, and the new chief was made of a harder mettle. He had served in the Japanese police force for ten years. He was teamed up with a Captain Tyree, U.S. Army, who, we were given to understand, was no softie himself.

Before we left, the major invited us to attend another trial later in the day. Although no case had been scheduled, he said he would arrange a trial for us.

"Come a little later," he said, "and see our justice function. Quasi-justice, I guess you can call it."

In the evening, two officers who had taken an active part in suppressing the Taegu uprising told us its tragic story.

One day about five weeks ago two schools had a football game, followed by a fight. The police came to restore order, and after they were done, a student was dead. This provoked resentment, and student groups met clandestinely to plan protests.

Meanwhile, a railroad strike was in progress in the Taegu railway shops. On the night of October 1, with the permission of the Military Government, some 4,000 workers gathered in front of the railroad station in support of the walkout. One of our informants who was on patrol duty in the area said the meeting was orderly.

The meeting was to disperse at 10:00 P.M. Long before the deadline, police units began to move up. "The Korean cops," said the other officer "were trigger-happy that night. They were shooting all over the place. When they got through dispersing the crowd, there was a dead man."

There were shots through the night, and in schools and factories meetings of indignation were in progress. With daylight, the town was out in the streets. "It was the craziest thing you ever saw," said the first officer. "Everyone was out— workers, students, farmers from the countryside, school kids marching in long columns. They all marched toward the police station, and then most of them just squatted in the street and waited. I walked through and nobody even gave me a dirty look."

The students brought a body, which they said was the body of the student killed by the police, and laid it before the police station. Then they submitted two demands to the frightened police chief: disarm the police, and release the political prisoners. The chief accepted the first demand, but said he could do nothing about the second without the permission of the U.S. Army. By this time, the policemen were climbing over the wall into the adjoining American compound, and were being sent back because "we didn't want to take sides in this mess."

In the late morning, the crowd poured into the station, destroyed the files, and released a hundred prisoners. Little other damage was done. The rioters remained in control of the building for an hour. During this hour, meetings were bubbling up all over the town, with the workers and the farmers reciting stories of police brutality.

Around noon, a U.S. Army major ordered the crowd surrounding the police station to disperse by 3:00 P.M. Before the deadline, army tanks and armored trucks began to patrol the streets. The enormous crowd broke up slowly. But as each splinter drifted away, it swept over other police stations and the homes of policemen. Many policemen were beaten to death and their relatives injured.

That night American patrols began to find policemen's bodies in the dark streets or vacant lots. Seven bodies, two still alive, were found in a park. All had been mutilated. A few had been castrated. Injured policemen sent to the city hospital received no help. "We soon discovered," one of the two officers said, "that the leading Korean doctors were in cahoots with the rebels. We put them in the clink too."

Order returned to Taegu on the third day. On that day, 1,100 police reinforcements arrived in town, and the policemen who had gone into hiding returned to duty. "Every grudge that any cop ever had against anyone was now being paid off." One truckload of prisoners after another began to roll toward the jail. When this was filled, schools and offices were taken over. Among the arrested were teachers, and lawyers, farm and labor leaders, and all prominent members of the People's Party, whose leader, Lyuh Woon Heung, was even then advertised as a co-chairman of Bertsch's moderate coalition.

From Taegu, violence spilled over into the countryside. The farmers were rougher on home soil than they were in Taegu. Cruelty was more extreme, and sometimes county offices as well as the police stations were attacked. In some places American patrols made tentative pokes, and hastily retired. At these points, the committees of sharecroppers governed for many days. From this province, the wildfire of revolution spread to other provinces. For a time the uprising in South Korea appeared to be a match for some of history's great peasant revolutions. By today, it appears to have been crushed.

After dinner there was a reception for a visiting general, and all the officers had gone upstairs. I begged off, saying I had to put my notes in order and pack. I was typing when there was a gentle tap on the door, and a young captain came in. He wanted to know if he could read in my room. I said yes. He sat down and pulled *The Nation* magazine out of his pocket. He did it with such a conspiratorial air that I said: "That's dangerous stuff you're carrying around with you." He said eagerly, "I have to hide it. If anybody sees it, I'll get hell. A friend of mine wrote a letter to *Stars and Stripes,* complaining about the chow. They're investigating him now."

He read and I typed. After a while he said, "Are you having much trouble getting information?" I told him it was not too bad.

"You know," he said, "the day before your arrival, some of the officers here got orders not to talk to you because your papers (The Chicago *Sun* and *Newsweek*) 'have not demonstrably proven their patriotism.' But it's always the same. A correspondent from the New York *Herald Tribune* came here right after the riots. They kept telling him they had no spare jeeps for him and finally gave him a small plane. But you can't cover the riots from that. Then all the men in the office were ordered to give him nothing outside of the official releases. A friend of mine didn't know of the order, and gave the guy some dope. They bawled hell out of him."

We left Taegu by train at 11:00 P.M.

November 5, 1946   SEOUL

At noon Charlotte and I went to the Public Relations Office for our mail. Major Williamson was affable. "Going back to Tokyo tomorrow, Charlotte?" Charlotte said she was staying for another day or two for some interviews we had arranged. Williamson turned red. "You can't stay here. I told General Hodge you're leaving. You must leave."

For a moment Charlotte looked as if she was going to burst into tears. "Look, Major," she said. "I don't understand any of this. I'm an American reporter. This is the American zone. What's the idea of running me out?"

Williamson said: "For one thing, we don't have quarters here. The families of the officers are arriving, and we've no place to put them up."

"That's a lot of bunk, Major," said Charlotte. "The billet I'm in now is practically empty, and the families are not due for weeks. I assure you I'll be out before they arrive. All I want is to interview some of these Koreans."

"You've got to leave," Williamson said firmly. "Tomorrow. There's nothing to argue about."

Our next chat was with the Korean head of the Bureau of Contacts in the U.S. Military Government. He was ordered to get interviews for us with Korean leaders whom we had not met yet. Above all, we wanted to see Kim Koo, the patriotic assassin and head of the defunct government-in-exile in Chungking, and Lyuh Woon Heung, head of the People's Party and co-chairman of Bertsch's coalition.

"I'll get you an interview with Mr. Kim Koo," said the Contact Man.

"We also want to meet Mr. Lyuh."

"Apart from Kim Koo, I'll also get an interview for you with Mr. Syngman Rhee."

"We've met Mr. Rhee already. We want to meet Mr. Lyuh."

"Look," he said. "You want to talk to gentlemen. Mr. Rhee is a gentleman. Mr. Kim Koo is a gentleman. Mr. Kimm Kiu Sic is all right. But Mr. Lyuh is a Communist, a gangster. You don't want to see him."

"Don't you worry about that," I said patiently. "We've met the gentlemen. We now want to meet the gangsters. You just get us an appointment with Mr. Lyuh."

The Contact Man shrugged his shoulders. "I don't even know where to find him. But I'll get you an interview with Mr. Kim Koo."

I wanted to talk again to Ho Hun, the left-wing leader whom I saw on my fourth day in Korea. I mentioned it to an American in Military Government. He said: "I doubt if Ho Hun will want to see you today. A few days ago he finally came out openly against the coalition. He was picked up by the cops, beaten up, and then released with the explanation that it was a case of 'mistaken identity.' He's in no mood to talk to Americans."

There are few problems more pressing in our zone than the police excesses. So sharp has become the public criticism that Military Government has found it necessary to set up a special American-Korean Commission to consider corrective steps. I looked up the list of the members and experts and picked out a name. I went to the man and asked for information. He agreed to give it to me, on the understanding that I would not use his name.

"Let me give you a typical example of what's happening," he said. "In a village not far from here, sixty-two men were arrested on the charge of plotting to attack a police station. Among them was a doctor. The other day, the doctor's relatives finally got to an influential American officer and persuaded him to drive out to the jail and check the reports of brutal treatment. He did. He found the doctor dead of torture. Another man died later, with his face smashed to a pulp. The third had his back broken. A report was turned in to General Hodge. He said: 'This is the way police have traditionally operated in the Orient. What can we do?'

"One reason for the brutality is that the bulk of the police have been steeped in Japanese practices. The Commission has been given these statistics which help to explain what's wrong with the police. Of the one hundred forty police officers with the rank of captain, more than one hundred ten have served with the Jap police. In Seoul, every one of the ten precinct police chiefs is Japanese-trained. So are eight of the ten provincial chiefs in our zone.

"Our army has been concerned solely with the maintenance of order. It took over the Japanese police machinery, without understanding this important psychological fact: under the Japs, the really dirty police work was done by Korean underlings, and this is why the Korean people hated the Korean cops worse than they hated the Jap bosses for whom these cops worked."

The ten American military governors in our zone are meeting here with General Lerch to discuss the election results. Lerch, I am told, is highly pleased with the outcome of the election. He told a meeting, in approximately these words: "We've been ordered by directives from Washington to play along with the moderate groups. The elections, resulting in an overwhelming victory for the right, show that Washington was wrong."

In the evening Charlotte and I drove out to the Rhees for dinner. Once again we passed through the screening board of policemen at the gate, and walked up the hill to the brightly lit house on top.

Rhee seemed happier than he was the first time we met him. I told him I saw his men win the election in two provinces. He said simply, as if he was a feudal sovereign speaking of his domain: "My people are with me."

There were three other guests—an aide to General Hodge, his woman friend, and a small, middle-aged, silent Korean whom I did not identify until later. The American officer talked to Rhee in terms of familiarity and friendship, and I wondered of the propriety of General Hodge's aide visiting the man whom General Hodge—at least on paper—had been ordered to shun.

It was right in the middle of a mouthful of hot cabbage-and-pepper *kimchee*, with which the Koreans spice their food, that I realized who the silent Korean guest was. This was Kim Sung Soo, Rhee's financial angel, Korea's fourth richest man, a great landlord, an educator, and one of the most powerful bosses of the *Han Kook* Democratic party. Kim has been described to me as a political Dr. Jekyll and Mr. Hyde. He is a university president, has helped numerous youths to get an education, and believes he is a model citizen. On the other hand, he is accused by many Military Government officers of having been a collaborator before Japan's surrender, and of having urged young Koreans drafted into the Japanese Army to "die for your fatherland." Kim sees no need for drastic reform, resolutely opposes it, and because of his tremendous influence can do much to block it. Kim is one of the powerful figures behind Syngman Rhee, and much of what Rhee champions was born in Kim's mind.

November 6, 1946   SEOUL

At noon Charlotte went to the Air Transport Command and discovered that she could not get passage until she had taken a whole series of shots, including one for cholera. By the time she got through with the shots, no seats remained on tomorrow's plane for Tokyo. When Williamson found out she was not leaving, his face turned purple, and he started stuttering. "What will I tell General Hodge now?" He ended by going over to ATC himself to check on Charlotte's story. I told Williamson I would take off for Tokyo the day after tomorrow.

In the afternoon we again called on Kimm Kiu Sic. He was still swathed in his gown, felt slippers, and robe, but he was a different man. There were force and anger in his voice as he talked of the election. He said he had just sent a letter to General Hodge, suggesting that the results be annulled, wholly or in part, or the coalition be permitted to name all the ninety members of the Interim Legislature, instead of only forty-five. He called the election fraudulent, said he agreed with his co-chairman Lyuh that no fair election could be held as long as all the leftist leaders were in jail, and revealed that two months ago he had urged General Lerch to establish special safeguards for a fair election. His plea was ignored.

Syngman Rhee's men won forty of the forty-five seats. Kim Koo, another extreme rightist, whom we are seeing tomorrow, took three seats. Lyuh Woon Heung, co-chairman of the coalition, managed to get two, on an isolated island. ("The governor there is an honest man.") Kimm won nothing.

Now Kimm was spelling out for us the story of this, Korea's first "democratic" election. In many provinces, the decision on who was eligible to vote was left to local headmen. In hundreds of villages, the election consisted of a friendly chat between the headman and a selected list of family heads. (Headman: "We're having an election. Do you want to vote for me?") In hundreds of cases, the village and county heads dispatched servants to the prospective voters, asking for the loan of their name seals, which were then stamped on ballots filled in by the officials. No adequate notice of elections was given, and in many cases the date was left to the discretion of local officials. In dozens of instances, men who questioned the validity of the election were jailed on the charge of sedition. Although the Military Government expressly called for a secret election, countless thousands of illiterate voters had their ballots filled in by helpful headmen, who by the oddest coincidence were among those elected. Though the Military Government specified that all persons over eighteen years of age were entitled to vote, in practice only family heads were allowed to vote.

"In Kangwan Province," Kimm said, "the entire election was conducted not by the authorities, but by Syngman Rhee's party. Naturally, all the three elected men were his henchmen. All three were notorious Japanese collaborators.

"In Seoul, the morning of the election, the city hall entrance was covered with the posters of Syngman Rhee's party. All the three elected men are its members. Two of the three are known collaborators. In Taegu, which you've just visited, one of the elected men is a known collaborator. In Pusan, the head of Syngman Rhee's party was elected. He is a collaborator.

"I know that the American military governors attended the provincial elections, and then reported to General Lerch that they had seen no undemocratic practices. As a matter of fact, they didn't. It wasn't necessary to be undemocratic on the provincial level, when all the dirty work had already been done on the village and county levels."

Here, as in Japan, carpetbagging supplies one of the less savory aspects of the Occupation. One well-placed officer told me he knew of "at least one hundred and fifty cases" of Americans who "came to do good and remained to do well." This may be just a figure of speech, but I am flabbergasted by the open and unashamed talk of business ventures by army officers. A lieutenant in the Honta Building, where General Hodge has his office, told me that once he is out of the army, he will remain here "to look after my interests." It developed that these included a million-dollar glass factory whose purchase in behalf of Korean investors he is already negotiating in Detroit—in contravention of all military regulations. ("I keep sending home a couple of hundred bucks a week—as 'poker winnings.' Christ, I don't play that kind of poker.") Charlotte went to a dance the other night, and four majors at her table openly boasted of their business deals.

But all of these seem unimaginative beside the story of a high Military Government officer who visited a Korean museum, examined its treasures, calmly said, "They're nice. Pack 'em up," and then shipped most of the collection back home to the United States. The army allowed him to go home, but stopped the last eighteen cases before they left Korea. My informants said they did not know why the officer was not prosecuted, unless it was the reluctance of Generals MacArthur and Hodge to have a scandal comparable to the malodorous scandals in the European theater.

In my room tonight, I had a long session with an American high in the Seoul hierarchy. I had met him here casually, but we had close mutual friends and we trusted each other. To both of us, I suspected, the talk gave an opportunity for soul-searching. He wanted to know how much I had learned on my visit, and I wanted to match my impressions against his.

"I've been here since October of last year," the visitor said. "I know that right up to last spring we had no policy for Korea.

It's hard to believe that, but it's true. The best proof is a statement of policy sent by General Hodge to Brigadier General Charles Harris, deputy Military Governor, one week before we landed here. You ought to get a copy. Hodge said that Korea, as part of the Japanese empire, was our enemy and therefore subject to the terms of surrender. He said our troops would land in Korea to see that these terms were obeyed. He said that, at least in the beginning, it would be necessary to operate through the Jap administration. He said that during this period we would recognize the Japs as the lawful government of Korea. He admitted it was likely that the Koreans had hopes of freedom and independence. But he said that, as far as he knew, no Allied policy on this had been formulated. Therefore, Hodge enjoined Harris to make no promises to the Koreans but to stress prompt and willing compliance with the surrender terms.

"I know of no excuse for the statement. It betrayed lack of instructions from Washington. It showed, to me anyway, that General Hodge had not read the Cairo Declaration, in which Britain, China, and we said that Korea would be 'free and independent.' It set the tone for the whole mess that followed. We were not an army of liberation. We had come to occupy, to see that the Koreans obeyed the terms of surrender. From the first day, we've behaved as enemies of the Korean people.

"Last spring Washington finally came through with a policy of moderation. But you must've found out that we honor it here only in the breach. To this day our allies are boys like Rhee, to whom moderation is anathema.

"You can say what you will of the Russians. You can justly call the People's Committees in North Korea a puppet regime. But the fact is that the Russians, from the outset, knew precisely what their policy was, they let the People's Committees do the job of governing, and they allowed the Koreans themselves to introduce reforms and wipe out collaborators. . . . "

We were now on the subject of our relations with Russia, a world-wide problem that was especially acute in Korea. In Germany the issue was obfuscated by the presence of other Allied powers and other problems. Here the problem was clear cut.

We faced Russia across an imaginary line on the map, and each of us controlled a chunk of a country in which we could practice what we said we believed in.

In this picture, I agreed with my visitor, the press should have played a major role. Yet, in this world ruled by the military, the press was an unwanted intruder. I was an American reporter who believed in what are generally known as American ideals. Economic democracy. Democratic politics. Free speech and assembly. Government by law. It may be, as the extreme leftists insist, that few of these concepts remain in our American structure, and a man who believes in them is a fool and a dreamer. On the other hand, it may be, as the conservatives assert, that the man who finds fault with American policy or personnel is a dangerous radical.

I did not think I was either a radical or a dreamer. I was a reporter, who had found, with shame and anguish, that under our flag—and often with our active encouragement—there had come into being a police state so savage in its suppression of man's elemental liberties that it was difficult to find a parallel for it. I had found in our zone only the shallow verbiage of democracy, and none of its practices. I had found administrative and political ineptness, and an alliance with the darkest reaction. I recalled Captain K., and his declaration that the army wanted no interference from the American people. I thought of Colonel Maglin, and his belief that "if the policeman did a good job for the Japanese, he will do a good job for us." I thought of my interpreter, Muk, hounded out of Seoul because he helped me to get at the facts; of Major Atkinson, who delayed action while men rotted in a dank police cell; of the officers who felt that Korea needed no reform; and of other officers who engaged in the practice of shadowing American correspondents.

Did an American reporter suppress this dark story because it would reflect on his country? Or would he serve his people better if he reported the blunders and the misdeeds? Was there a way of telling this shocking story without being attacked as a dreamer, or much worse?

The reporting was made doubly difficult because this was not a time of normalcy, and normal standards seemingly did not

· 429 ·

apply. Ordinarily, the foul mess in our zone would have been cleaned up as soon as the people back home learned the truth. But now the basis of our policy in Korea—or anywhere else—was fear of Russia, and many things that should not have happened were committed in the name of that fear.

Here was Hodge, an American general entrusted with the task of preparing Korea for statehood. His language should have been the language of reform. He had a busy Public Relations Office equipped to pass his decisions and his wisdom on to Korea and the world. Yet, day after dreary day, we had marched into the Public Relations Office to receive the announcement of yet another "intercepted Communist document," purporting to show the Communists did not like us, and Russia was prepared to sabotage the reforms we sponsored. But neither the Korean nor Russian Communists could wreck any bold and genuine reforms—if we had them. The real story of Korea was not the Communist dislike for us. The story was that we had had an opportunity to bring freedom and democracy to a people, and we had muffled our chance—partly because our policy was based on fear, and partly because we were represented here by the wrong people.

Korea is a problem for a diplomat and a reformer. We have handed its solution to a soldier, untrained in the devices of diplomacy and distrustful of social reform. What Hodge sees in Korea is primarily a military problem—the problem of a sudden and overwhelming Russian attack on our small and mal-equipped army. For the problem of Korea Hodge sees only a military man's solutions. A basic element in these is discipline. To Hodge and to his men, the peasant riots are not an outward expression of a deep-seated malady for which remedies have to be found. The riots are an act of extreme indiscipline, and only severe punishment can set things right again.

Both Russia and we made gestures at settling the Korean problem jointly. It is difficult to assess true merits in the feverish atmosphere of Seoul, but it would seem that neither side tried very hard. To the Russians this is a problem in security. Their Maritime Province adjoins Korea, and they are determined to have a friendly neighbor.

Thus, the Russians have been obdurate in insisting that the Joint Commission consult only supporters of Allied trusteeship for Korea, though a Korean could be a true liberal and yet oppose continued alien supervision. General Chistiakov, the Soviet counterpart of General Hodge, was described to me by a Russian in Tokyo as "a typical military man, no different from any of yours." I heard Dr. Bunce tell a Red Cross forum that he got along well with his Russian opposite number in a discussion of common economic problems—until the Russian suddenly reversed his stand, presumably on orders from Moscow. But in condemning the Russians, it is useful to think of our own attitude were we to learn that an unfriendly foreign power was establishing itself in Mexico or Canada.

There is also no evidence that we have been any more anxious than the Russians to reach an agreement. As our chief delegate we chose Major General Albert E. Brown, who is known to feel that war with Russia is not far away. His conduct has been colored by this belief. My visitor told me that Brown said, when it was suggested that a certain measure be discussed with the Koreans: "There's no need for discussing things with these fellows. Just tell them what we want done."

And if the Russians were mulish in refusing to consult Koreans opposed to trusteeship, we were equally mulish in insisting on consulting *all* the Korean groups. For, with the jails in our zone filled to the rafters, the word *all* can mean only the wide assortment of groups controlled by Syngman Rhee. Our union with this old man has led us to fight his cause in the Joint U.S.-Soviet Commission.

We discussed these facts of our relations with Russia, my nocturnal visitor and I, and we agreed that our policy was doubly wrong if we accepted the premise of an imminent war. For if one of the arts of war is the making of friends, we have followed a course which has won for us only a small band of allies and alienated the vast bulk of the Korean people. The Military Government's polls of public opinion are an inaccurate instrument. But they have the virtue of consistency, for they show the graph of the Korean dislike for us rising steadily. If war comes, our generals will be in an untenable position, for apart from the enemy rolling down from the north, they will have to reckon with native hostility in the rear. A program of reform alone could have made friends for us. To this day such a program is not even in blueprint form.

If we accept the generals' idea of a great ideological conflict with Russia, we have to confront the dynamic ideas of communism with our own vital concepts. But the tragic fact is that there are no ideas in our armory here. For vital ideas we have substituted an alliance with Korean groups, whose philosophy and methods have nothing in common with the philosophy and methods that we publicly espouse. And when this paucity of ideas was exposed by Korean popular unrest, we tried to conceal the bankruptcy of a policy with democratic clichés and talk of the red menace.

The men in command here neither have a constructive program of action nor are they willing to accept one. I am told that when Dr. Bunce and his State Department mission arrived in Korea last January, they were whisked from the air port directly to General Lerch's office, where approximately the following exchange took place:

note 2

"Lerch: "You're not welcome here. We don't need any advice."

Bunce: "General, we don't accept your ultimatum."

Lerch (retreating): "What I mean is that you'll be part of our organization, and we'll call on you when needed."

Bunce: "General, I repeat, we don't accept your ultimatum. My staff and I will consider it, and will let you know our decision tomorrow."

Bunce and his mission stayed, and made a brave try at concealing their frustration. In discussing land reform with Charlotte, Hailey, and me, Bunce said he had drafted a reform plan providing for the redistribution of land formerly held by the Japanese. Bunce felt that although his plan was limited in scope (since it covered only Japanese holdings), it was superior in many provisions to the land reform law enforced in the Russian zone.

What Bunce did not tell us was that Military Government,

from General Lerch down to the Korean interpreters, was opposed to any land reform. Thus a neat device was employed to kill what was called "Bunce's Folly." A public opinion poll was conducted by the Military Government, and it allegedly showed that *the sharecroppers did not want land now, but were anxious to wait for a future Korean Government to give it to them*. On the basis of this poll, the Bunce Plan was discarded. This was probably the end of the only major reform drafted by an American in the past fourteen months.

November 7, 1946   SEOUL

Charlotte and I received our Travel Orders and seat reservations for Tokyo for tomorrow. Williamson is sulking.

In the morning, guided by the Contact Man, we went calling on Kim Koo, one of the world's distinguished political assassins and a major figure in the Korean rightist camp. We were halted at the gate, examined by a crew of armed policemen and young men with pistols, and then escorted suspiciously to the pseudo-Grecian mansion in the back of an elaborate rock garden. Something had gone amiss, Kim Koo was away at a meeting, and a messenger was dispatched to fetch him.

We sat in the large, ornate, and cold reception room, and talked to a succession of slick young men and women, many of them speaking fluent English, and some of them known to me as among the sharpest political intriguers in Korea. These were a few of the small and politically ambitious band which thinks for Kim Koo and makes him utter the words it wants.

I recalled the story of a press conference at which Kim Koo, the irreconcilable enemy of Japan and of Korean collaborators, was asked what he would do with the latter. With characteristic bluntness, Kim Koo said:

"Practically everyone in Korea is a collaborator. They all ought to be in jail."

A young adviser doubling in brass as an interpreter did not even blink. "Mr. Kim Koo says," he translated, "that it's a problem to be studied carefully."

Now I am told Kim Koo has begun to make compromises, and this mansion, put at his disposal by the "mining king" of Korea, is presumably one of them. But Kim Koo and Syngman Rhee differ in one major respect. While Rhee speaks for the collaborationists and landlords—for the "haves" of the extreme right—Kim Koo speaks for the rightist "have-nots" who refused to play along with the Japanese, spent decades in exile, and came back only to discover that the collaborators were still in control. There is little love lost between the two camps, though from time to time they work in alliance. Syngman Rhee's men hint that Kim Koo is a Chinese stooge. Kim Koo's men delight in listing the records of the collaborators working with Rhee.

A car rolled to a stop in front of the building, and the slick young men rushed out. They returned escorting a large, dark-haired man in a silk robe. Kim Koo gave us a surprisingly weak handshake, and settled down on a divan. He looked much younger than his seventy-two years, but his hands trembled. His palms were baby pink.

He brushed off our questions on political issues, saying that he would answer them if we gave him time to think. He was ready to talk of his life, beginning with his childhood in a family "of the poorest peasant stock, so poor that I had no schooling until I was eleven." Kim Koo began his revolutionary work at the age of eighteen, in a peasant revolt against the noblemen, and in 1896 switched to fighting the Japanese. By 1919 he had served three jail terms for three historic murders. ("In the last of them I wasn't even involved.")

In 1919 he fled to Shanghai, and was made "Chief of Counter Intelligence" of the Provisional Korean Government. Terrorism became his profession. The climax came in 1932, when he organized the bombing of a group of Japanese dignitaries in Shanghai. Admiral Nomura, who was Japanese ambassador to Washington on the eve of the attack on Pearl Harbor, lost an eye. Shigemitsu, who signed Japan's surrender on the U.S.S.

"Missouri," lost a leg. This bombing, as Bertsch put it, "thrust Kim Koo into the political big league." By 1941 he was president of the government-in-exile.

At this point we heard the unmistakable sound of a marching military unit. I looked out. A score of young men in civilian clothes, with white armbands, was marching past the house with military precision. I asked Kim Koo who the young men were, and he said, "A youth organization," and when I pressed, he said he knew nothing about it.

Later Kim Koo walked us out, and we saw the young men posted behind trees and rocks. Some men were watching us; others were scanning the fence. We said goodbye to Kim Koo, and walked over to the nearest youth. I had an interpreter translate the armband. It said simply: "Youth Organization." This, obviously, was Kim Koo's private army, like Syngman Rhee's Great Korea Democratic Young Men's Association.

We drove out, the gates slammed behind us, and the Contact Man said, "Mr. Kim Koo is a real gentleman, isn't he?"

In the afternoon, the Contact Man took us to another "gentleman"—General Lee Bum Suk, head of Korean National Youth, Inc., and a rising star in the rightist constellation. We kept hearing his name all over the U.S. zone, and some Americans insisted that we see General Lee before we leave Korea.

We found him in the large, two-story headquarters of Korean National Youth—a building assigned to it by the Military Government. There were U.S. Army trucks and jeeps in the yard, a few American soldiers upstairs, typing, and a flock of the tough young Koreans which had now become a familiar sight to me. General Lee was waiting for us in his small office.

Lee was slim and muscular, and his thin, hooked nose and a thin moustache gave him a strangely predatory look. Had he lived in California, he would have inevitably ended as an Oriental pirate in a Hollywood technicolor production. His career, as he unfolded it for us with much fist-waving, matched his looks. Born in a noble family, he left Korea for China at the age of fifteen. He entered a military academy under an assumed name, and on graduation went to Manchuria for some extracurricular anti-Japanese terrorism. After that his career was spectacular. He said he served as commander of a Soviet Russian International Cavalry Brigade; a colonel on the staff of a famous Chinese general fighting the Japanese in Manchuria; an inmate for eight months in a Siberian camp for Chinese troops who escaped from Manchuria; head of a Korean military academy set up by Chiang Kai-shek: a miltary adviser to a Chinese warlord, and the principal negotiator with the Japanese, who thought all along he was a Chinese; an associate of Tai Li, the dreaded chief of China's Secret Service; and, for a year, an agent of our own O.S.S. He was flown into Korea four days after Japan's surrender with an O.S.S. team of twelve Americans and five Koreans.

"Korea today," he said, "is like Germany in 1919. There are ideological clashes, national discord, economic distress. National salvation lies in a united youth. It's our purpose to open schools for leaders. We shall teach them obedience to orders, ability to be practical, good morals—much like General Chiang Kai-shek's New Life Movement.

"Fortunately, General Hodge and General Lerch understand the importance of the program, and they've assigned Lieutenant Colonel Ernest Voss, of the Internal Security Department, to help us. General Lerch has given us Y.5,000,000 ($333,000) for the first six months of our work.

"We expect to open our School for Leaders this month, and graduate two hundred youths every thirty days. The trainees will then go into the country and set up branches of Korean National Youth, Inc. The applicants will have to be highly recommended by well-known patriots of good quality. To fulfill their duty, they'll also have to be absolutely healthy. Our purpose is to unify and purify the young men so that they can become leaders."

He talked on, and gradually I began to think that I was listening to a description not of a Korean democratic organization but one of Hitler's infamous "Leadership Schools." The words were the same—the nation, destiny, discipline, endurance; the strange choice of teachers and subjects; the avowed kinship with other rightist strong-arm bands. And then the inspiration became clear.

Lee was telling us of the proposed curriculum: history, ethics (taught by himself), politics. "Also," he said, "methods of combating strikes. And history of *Hitler Jugend*." One of Lee's right-hand men, it appeared, had been an enthusiastic member of *Hitler Jugend* in Germany for three years.

We were distracted by the appearance of an American officer in an adjoining office. He was talking on the phone. He wanted trucks. He had another printing order. He thought it was about time to have that building ready. . . .

"That's Colonel Voss," said General Lee. "A very good man."

Colonel Voss opened the door and stepped in. We said hello. "You don't have to talk to me," said Voss. "My ideals and thoughts are the same as General Lee's. He's a great man."

Lee stuffed two pamphlets in our hands. "You must read these," he said. "They'll tell you of my work and hopes." I picked a sentence out of one of them. It was: "A strong leader who will put behind him all personal ambitions and work for the good of Korea is the need of the hour." The companion brochure met squarely the problem of finding such a leader: "For the past thirty years, Lee Bum Suk has sacrificed all his time, energy, and all else in his life to his country. Despite physical pain, he has never been agitated, nor has he ever lost his iron will and ideas. He is awaiting the orders of his thirty million compatriots. If the nation desires him as a soldier . . . "

The interview supplied a fitting climax to a fantastic visit. This topped it all—a Korean "School for Leaders," teaching the history of *Hitler Jugend*, operating on a subsidy from the American Military Government, and assisted by a colonel of the U.S. Army.

In the evening, we made discreet inquiries. "Oh, you finally found the 'Korean balilla,'" said one officer. "We've been wondering how long it'd take you. And have you met Voss? He calls his little hooligans 'boy scouts.'"

Another officer told us about the help General Lee has been receiving from the U.S. Army. The Army Engineers are building barracks for Korean National Youth in Pusan and Seoul. They are supplying American bulldozers for unspecified uses by General Lee. At the American taxpayers' expense they are doing a vast amount of printing for Lee, much of it political.

"The Korean National Youth," he said, "is probably the most profitable enterprise in Korea. There are all kinds of donations from people who are afraid they'd be denounced as Jap collaborators if they didn't pay off. No one is quite sure who is behind Lee. He may be a political buccaneer, striking out on his own. But there is much talk of close contacts between him and Syngman Rhee. Lee is known to be planning to take over the National Assembly Independence Urge Youth Association, which includes eighteen of Rhee's youth bands. For the time being, Lee is trying to work quietly. But mark my words: he's going to be a big-time operator in another year—with our help.

"It's simple to dismiss his, or Rhee's, bands, as neighborhood gangs. This thing has gotten to be too big to be dismissed lightly. These boys have become the Storm Troopers of Korea. The Military Government has permitted the development of an integrated, large-scale movement much like Hitler's. And probably for the same purpose."

Tonight we also heard the story of Private Peevey and his waterless paddy.

It seems that when the 38th Parallel was accepted as the dividing line between the United States and Soviet zones, it cut off a 70,000-acre Japanese farm from its reservoirs. We received the paddies; the Russians got the water. Private Peevey, who was placed in charge of the farm, soon discovered that rice needed water, and what there was of it was in the Soviet zone.

Thus it was that the relevant department of the Military Government here became increasingly aware of Private Peevey and his problem. There were few days when a plea for help was not received from Peevey. What he wanted was some sort of an understanding with the Russians so that he could have water for his fields. As days passed, and his rice stalks wilted, the messages became more urgent.

But a paddy, however large, could only be a small part of the broad problem of U.S.-Soviet relations. As long as the broad problem remained unsolved, Peevey could not have his water. So from time to time Seoul wired back comforting messages to Peevey, telling him that no local understanding was possible at the time, urging him to get along as best he could, and advising him, for Lord's sake, to keep his shirt on.

One day Peevey's messages stopped coming. Immersed in its own problems, the Military Government wondered mildly about Peevey for a week or so, and then proceeded to forget all about him and his paddies.

Not so long ago Peevey was ordered home after his appointed term of duty, and on his way to the embarkation point he stopped in Seoul, and called on the Military Government. "Peevey?" they said, "Peevey? Oh, wait a second, aren't you the chap that was up there at Onjin, near the 38th?"

"Yes, sir," said Peevey, "that was me."

"Well, well," they said, "didn't you have some trouble with water or something? Whatever became of that?"

"Well, sir," said Private Peevey, "I had no water, and I just had to have some. It was an awful lot of rice going to waste, and the Russkys had all the water. So I made a treaty with them. I—"

"What?" said the colonel in command. "A treaty with the Russians? You're kidding?"

"No, sir, I'm not kidding. I told the Russians that if they gave me water I would give them 10,000 bags of rice at harvest time. So they gave me all the water I needed. . . . "

"Christ, man," the colonel said. "That's impossible. You know what you've done? You're going to be court-martialed for this. *I* am going to be court-martialed. You had no right to enter into any negotiations with the Russians. You've exceeded your authority. Gaddamn it, you had no authority of *any* sort, Private Peevey!"

"Don't you worry none, sir," said Peevey. "I did sign a

treaty with the Russians, and I did get the water. But I never meant to give them any rice."

One week after Private Peevey left Onjin without having delivered the promised rice, a force of North Korean constabulary crossed the 38th Parallel with trucks and drove up to the rice storehouses at the farm. While trying to open the gates, they were challenged by some South Korean policemen and local officials. In the ensuing battle, four of the South Koreans were killed. The North Koreans piled their trucks high with rice and drove back across the line.

November 8, 1946   EN ROUTE TO TOKYO

We left Seoul for the airport at six in the morning. By the time we checked in our Travel Orders, the sun had come out, and it was crisply cold. A Red Cross truck was dispensing coffee and doughnuts, and there was a long line of waiting men, stamping their feet and slapping their bodies to keep warm. We drank coffee, and watched two small transport planes filling in with Korean policemen, with Japanese carbines and fur-lined coats. One plane took off, and the other taxied in in its place. I walked up and asked a crew member where the planes were going.

He said, "About 150 miles to the west. I hear some gooks have barricaded themselves in a farmhouse, and these boys are going to take it. We'll keep taxiing them all through the day."

Hours passed. Something had happened to our plane, and more unscheduled, but high-priority, passengers kept arriving. We had more coffee, read old magazines, and talked to the other waiting men. One of them was a Military Government officer going home after nearly four years of service. "If we don't take off today," he said, "I'll go back to my room, and blow my brains out. I've come to feel I couldn't stand another day here."

We did take off around noon, in a four-engined transport. "Jesus," said the officer, "I thought the day would never come." His face kept breaking into a smile, and he knew it looked silly and tried to frown it off his face. After a while we started talking about Korea, and he calmed down. He has spent a year here and traveled widely.

"The solution of our differences with Russia is one of the dominant needs in Korea," he said. "If there's no solution, both the Russians and we will continue to keep our troops here and foster rival regimes. I seriously wonder if it isn't too late already. In the past few weeks I've talked to many Korean leaders, who for a year have been shouting their heads off, demanding our withdrawal. Now they're subdued. There're two new words in their vocabulary: Civil War. Now they want us and the Russians to stay on a while longer, for they think that our department will throw Korea into chaos and bloodshed.

"But it solves nothing for us to stay here any longer, for both in the north and the south the middle groups have been eliminated, and only the extremes remain. It's idle to hope that they won't jump at each other's throat at the first chance, next year or five years from now. Neither the men nor their ideas are compatible."

I myself had heard the words Civil War on more than one tongue, and I knew that the fear was real and growing. Probably without expecting or wanting it, Russia and we have hurt Korea far more than Japan did. For while the Japanese bled Korea, and made her an unhealthy adjunct to Japan's economy, they kept her as a unit. When Japan fell, Korea was a whole, ready to become an independent state. Then the two liberating powers moved in, split the country asunder, the industrial north from the agricultural south, snapped the railroads at the 38th Parallel, did their best to seal off the border, and then proceeded to foster political systems to their liking.

Now, fourteen months after liberation, the 38th has become a real frontier between two worlds. The moderate groups which shared authority in the Soviet zone in the first four or six months have been swallowed by the Communists. In our zone, the moderates have been wiped out or reduced to impotence, and the extremists like Rhee are in virtual control.

On both sides of the new frontier, feverish preparations are being made for the coming armed conflict. The Communists in the north are said to be training a militia of 150,000 men. On our side, there is a steadily expanding police force, a constabulary and a coast guard whose numbers are difficult to learn, and the tens of thousands of young men enrolled in the private armies of Syngman Rhee, Kim Koo, General Lee Bum Suk, all the way down to the local strong-arm bands organized by U.S. Army interpreters.

As important as the political dislocation is the economic crisis. Korea survived under the Japanese because it was an integral part of the Japanese economy, in which Manchuria was also a part. Now the whole elaborate system has fallen apart, and Korea herself has been split in two. The Soviet north hungers for the rice produced in our zone. What few industries we have in the south depend on the north for such items as coal. This means that as long as the 38th Parallel remains a frontier, South Korea must continue to be a drain on the American taxpayer.

These two problems, one political, the other economic, would tax the resources of a much abler man than Hodge. So would the uncertain policy directives from Washington, the desperate lack of trained American and Korean personnel, the arrival of Korean refugees from China, Manchuria, and Japan by the hundreds of thousands, the ingrained hostility of the Koreans to alien soldiery, and the sharecropper's reluctance to give up the rice to feed the cities.

But the crux of our failure, it is obvious, lies not in the complexity of the problems facing us, but in our failure to act constructively. It is probably true that our differences with Russia cannot be settled in Korea alone, but only as part of a word-wide settlement. But in our own zone there are urgent problems which should have been met, and have instead been ignored. Had constructive action been taken, our position in Korea would have been firmer, and it would not have been necessary to fly Japanese-trained policemen in American-piloted planes to suppress yet another Korean farmer uprising.

We were flying high now, and below us, through a hole in the clouds, we could see the coastline of Korea, a rugged brown mass of land holding back a gray sea. "Goodbye, Korea," said my neighbor, "and am I happy to be leaving!" I, too, was glad. It has been the blackest, the most depressing story I have ever covered. As an American I was ashamed of the facts that I kept digging up, of the ineptness of the men who spoke for my country, of the concerted effort to prevent the American people from learning what was happening in Korea.

But I was proud of the fact that, despite all the restrictions and precautions, in every town and village I visited there had always been Americans who had faith in the power of the press and its role in a democracy, and who tempted punishment by giving us information. Among the things I learned in Korea was the fact that censorship—especially when it is aimed at concealing official blunders—will not work well or long with Americans. And I was as happy with this discovery as I was with the fact that I was able to get some of the story of Korea.

November 14, 1946   TOKYO

Looking through the Allied Council minutes for the month of my absence, found this astounding exchange:

Atcheson: "I often wonder at the continued allegations and charges made against the Japanese authorities. . . . They seem never in this Council to receive credit for the good work they do. . . . When a job is well done, I think that they merit some credit. I think, for example, that the Japanese Government, in carrying out the purge directive, accomplished its task in a very admirable manner on the whole. . . . I would say that the Occupation authorities . . . have obtained ready and willing Japanese cooperation. In fact, the time has come when *Japanese aims have become virtually identical with Allied aims. . . .*"

Ball: "Mr. Chairman, I would like to go on record as saying that I would not . . . be able to identify myself with your expressions of cordiality and confidence toward the present Japanese Government."

Atcheson: "I don't think, Mr. Ball, that you'll find on the record that I've made any expression of cordiality or confidence in the present government. I make a plea for recognition of merit where merit exists."

Ball: "I should only be very glad, indeed, to join with you in any recognition of merit where merit exists."

Atcheson: "[Do you] imply that no merit exists in connection with the conduct of the elections or other activities of the Japanese government?"

Ball: "I think I have noticed in the last few months that when any member of this Council has raised questions which might possibly be construed as a criticism of the Japanese Government, that the U.S. member has been very quick and eager to defend the work of the Japanese Government. All I want to say is that I shouldn't wish to identify myself with the attitude that you have expressed until or unless I have received much fuller evidence about the actual course of affairs in Japan today."

Atcheson: "I shall continue to bespeak recognition of merit where merit exists. . . . An example in point is the question of the Demobilization Board which we discussed at the last meeting. I'm told by officers wholly competent to know who have observed the work from a professional point of view, that the Demobilization Board has done a magnificent job. I don't see why we shouldn't be willing to recognize merit. . . . "

Like Ball, I find it a bit difficult to swallow any identification of our aims with those of the Yoshida government. One reason is the mass of information I have on that very same Demobilization Board whose work pleases George.

It is true that the Japanese armed forces have been demobilized quickly and efficiently. Actually it was to the advantage of the Japanese Treasury to return the soldiery to civilian pursuits. But the breaking up of the war machine has been a deceptive process. While the soldiers had gone home, the planners have stayed behind.

It is my conviction that the two Demobilization Boards are miniature General Staffs, which from the day of Japan's surrender have been planning her military rebirth.

The best proof I have lies in the identity of the men who staff the two Boards. Here, for instance, is the War Data Department of the Army Demobilization Board:

Lieutenant General Miyazaki, former Chief of Operations, Army General Staff;

Major General Joichiro Sanada, another former Chief of Operations, Army General Staff;

Colonel Takushiro Hattori, Tojo's former secretary and, on the outbreak of the war, Chief of the First (Operations) Section, Operations Department, General Staff;

Colonel Kazuo Horiba, for three years Chief of the Second (War Direction) Section, Operations Department, General Staff; later served with the Total War Research Board;

Colonel Nishiura, former Chief, Military Affairs Section in War Ministry, and a General Staff officer;

Colonel Sadao Akamatsu, Tojo's former secretary.

The rest of the staff of the War Data Department consist primarily of Operations and Military Intelligence officers from the General Staff. The department does little work relating to demobilization. The bulk of its activities seems to be centered on a study of the lessons of the war; a critique of Japanese strategy and tactics in the various campaigns; an investigation of war damage, and means of reducing it in future wars; and an analysis of the international situation.

But the Demobilization Boards are not the only military organs in existence. There is, for instance, the notorious and little-known "Arisue Organization," formed by Lieutenant General Seizo Arisue, a key member of Tojo's "kitchen cabinet," and until the last days of the war Chief of Military Intelligence, General Staff.

Arisue set up his organization on Japan's surrender, in anticipation of U.S. requests for military information. But according to my Japanese informants, the real bait that Arisue dangled before the U.S. Army Intelligence was the data on the Soviet military preparations and defenses, gathered by his agents in preparation for a possible Russo-Japanese war.

The "Arisue Organization" was staffed primarily with officers from Military Intelligence, General Staff. Arisue's right-hand man, for instance, was Major General Yatsuji Nagai, former Chief, Planning Section, Military Intelligence. The organization regards its work as completed, but though dormant it remains intact. There are reports, which I have been unable to confirm, that the entire former Russian Section of Military Intelligence has been assigned to Hokkaido, the point closest to Russia, in the guise of a regional Demobilization Office.

Only wishful thinkers can ignore the menacing parallel between these functioning organizations of Operations and Intelligence experts, and the German General Staff, which put the lessons of the First World War to such good use in reviving the Reichswehr.

The machinery is there; the experienced officers have been kept together; the lessons of yesterday's defeat are being studied. Now the men are waiting for the day, surely not too far away, when Japan is permitted "a small army for self-defense."

General MacArthur has not yet answered our five-week-old request for an interview to discuss the new labor policy in Japan.

November 18, 1946   TOKYO

Received a letter from the Chicago *Sun*, recalling me home and announcing what is in effect a dissolution of its foreign service.

The letter was less of a shock than it might have been. For many months, I have watched other newspapers pull their correspondents out of Japan. On my return from Korea, I had also decided to ask the *Sun* to reassign me to another country next year. And yet the news produced a hollow feeling, a sense of loss.

Tonight heard the story of a *Yomiuri* printer, and the role some American newspapermen played in his life.

The printer, Kenkichi Yahagi, was sent to Osaka to win support for the *Yomiuri* strikers. After one of the meetings, three men reported to Counter Intelligence that Yahagi had said that the United States was colonizing Japan. Yahagi was arrested, tried by a Provost Court, and sentenced a few days ago to four years in prison and a fine of Y.60,000 ($4,000). Yahagi earns $60 a month and has a large family. Since he obviously could not meet the fine, the American judge added five years to the sentence.

A number of us learned of the case, and checked with the Government Section. Word of our interest was sent up to Colonel Kades, General Whitney, and eventually General MacArthur. A letter was immediately dispatched to Osaka from General MacArthur's office. It said, in effect:

"There is an impression here that Yahagi's remarks were directed more against the Japanese government than the United States. You are urged, therefore, to reduce the sentence to a year and a day. . . . "

A year and a day is also a harsh sentences, when one remembers all the subversive utterances, misdeeds and violations of orders by high Japanese officials, led by Yoshida himself. But to Yahagi, this is a difference between a year of his life and nine. Chalk up another good deed for the press.*

---

* Compare Yahagi's case with that of a newspaperman named Sumi. Some months ago, Major Imboden made one of his celebrated "purge visits" to a Japanese daily in the north. Soon after his departure, the publisher's representative named Sumi addressed the assembled staff. Sumi attacked Imboden's predecessor in the Press Division as "a Russian Jew" and a "Communist." He also said, presumably on the basis of information obtained from an American source, that General MacArthur was shipping out all the "Communist civilians" in Headquarters and replacing them with trusted army officers such as Imboden. When I called Imboden's attention to the speech, he drafted a fiery message north—in more or less these words: "Sumi should be reminded that he cannot criticize American officers. . . . "

In the evening Sally and I went to a party given by the counsel of the war criminals now on trial. The dinner was held at the famous Gajoen Restaurant, and by the time we got there, the yard was already filled with sedans and jeeps. There must have been a hundred guests there, both American and Japanese, and we figured the party must have cost a minimum of Y.100,000, or $6,600 at the nominal rate of exchange.

We sat on the floor, before foot-high tables loaded with shrimps, fish, chicken and large dishes of pickled radish, which my neighbors enjoyed audibly. Somewhere in the middle of dinner the keynote speaker rose and delivered an address, whose most interesting sentence was, "The Japanese have always been a peace-loving nation." We found the statement especially quaint because it was made by Dr. Somei Uzawa, chief defense counsel, who a decade earlier defended, with ultranationalist fervor, a colonel who had assassinated a "moderate" general. Now Dr. Uzawa prefers to boast less of that trial than of his own one-day arrest back in 1938. Some of us who were in Japan before the war agreed that we could close our eyes and have no difficulty imagining ourselves in prewar Japan. The same faces, the same speeches, the same tone of exuberant good will to all men.

After the dinner, Sally, who was the only Occidental woman present, made the mistake of asking the *geisha* to do *Tokyo Ondo,* our favorite song and dance, and the women promptly got the men up, formed a sort of rhumba line, and proceeded to dance up and down the room. Soon the party degenerated into an orgy of giggling, hugging, and cheering.

We were watching the show when a trim-looking Japanese came up and gave me his card, testifying that he was Chikao Fujisawa, Director of Research, Institute of Multilateral International Relations. After that the conversation took a curious turn. Fujisawa said he had spent many years in China, running "a cultural affairs institute," and had just been repatriated. Quite without prompting, he said:

"You know, I'm a famous reactionary, and I've been purged.

I admit that. I admit that I've collaborated very closely with the Japanese military until about three years ago, when I decided they didn't follow the correct policy in China."

Now he was counsel to one of the more notorious of the war criminals on trial. "I feel," he said, "that the Japanese military have made many mistakes. But the core is sound. That's the point I always try to develop. Take for instance our monarchy. It's a sound institution. Don't you think so?"

I asked him if he was doing anything else besides his court work, and he said, matter-of-factly, that he was on the faculty of the U.S. Army university here, teaching Oriental philosophy. "I have about thirty Americans in each of my two weekly classes," he said. "Some of the officers I invite to my home, where we can discuss various topics at leisure. I should like very much to have you and your wife come to my place. There're so many things we can discuss. Especially the question of the emperor."

I said I would try. The fact that professors purged by the Japanese as war criminals are hired by the U.S. Army to indoctrinate Americans fascinates me.

November 22, 1946   TOKYO

Dixie Tighe, of the New York *Post,* is back from Seoul. She stayed there less than 48 hours. On arrival in Seoul she asked for permission to go to the island where the leftists won their only two seats in the election. Dixie was interested not as much in the politics as in the fact that the island is reputed to be ruled by Amazons. The women are pearl divers, and being the rice winners, they call the tune. Major Williamson, according to Dixie, gave her the permission readily. The next morning, in some agitation, he reversed himself. One word led to another, and Dixie announced that she had had enough of Korea, of General Hodge and of Major Williamson. She drove out to the field, and simply got into the first Tokyo-bound plane. It happened to be General Lerch's personal plane. Dixie complained to him bitterly and he assured her it was all a mistake and invited her to return in a week. Dixie said that while she was debating whether to go again or not, General Hodge barred women correspondents from the theater.

Gordon Walker, after hearing all these stories, is anxious to revisit Korea, but it has been intimated to him that if he did, he might be court-martialled on the thoroughly fraudulent charge that he and a correspondent for the Associated Press, on a visit a year ago, incited Koreans to disobey orders from the Military Government.

November 24, 1946

Last night had dinner with a member of General MacArthur's Inner Circle. Once again, I was struck by the difficulty of discussing the general without passion. It is curious to see how he inspires only the extreme—whether among his critics or his admirers.

Much of the reaction is emotional. It could not be otherwise, with this most picturesque of all living Americans. Even his enemies admit his boldness and imagination, his rich and varied nature, and his sense of history. But even his supporters concede that he is an egotist and an actor, a man intolerant of criticism and unable to admit failure, a man eager to be regarded as a great hero and a great administrator in the textbooks of three nations—his own, Japan, and the Philippines.

For an outsider it is not easy to assess the general's philosophy, for he has the disconcerting custom of fitting his speech to the occasion. He may assail Russia with a crusader's fire in one interview, and urge peace with the Soviets in another. He may call for a progressive Japan and champion state socialism. The next hour, he may talk acidly of the "parlor pinks" sent to him from Washington as advisers, and denounce their efforts to "socialize" Japan.

But the puzzle is for the outsiders only. The Inner Circle

knows pretty well what goes on in the general's mind. Partly it has helped to mold his ideas. Wholly it shares them. Now my guest, with fervor and sympathy, outlined for me the general's thought patterns.

General MacArthur, he said, feels that the war with Japan should not have come when it did. The conflict was precipitated by "President Roosevelt's ultimatum" to Japan on November 26, 1941. The "ultimatum" was an error, for we did not have the force to back it up. Nor did it leave the Japanese militarists any alternative but to strike when they seemed to have an edge in armed strength.

The Philippines, the general insists, would not have been lost had Washington answered his pleas for help. Moreover, the Pacific theater—and not Europe—should have had the first call on men and supplies. The battle for Europe should have been fought in the skies, until Japan was beaten. Instead of being divided between the two oceans, the U.S. Navy should have been kept in the Pacific to guard General MacArthur's lines of supply. President Roosevelt, in the general's opinion, succumbed to British pressure when he agreed to detach a portion of the navy for duty in the Atlantic.

From what my guest had to say I gathered that the general distrusts our wartime allies—Britain, Russia, and China. The general feels we defeated Japan singlehanded. He resents—and resists—what he sees as the efforts of these three nations to cash in on American sacrifices.

Britain, in General MacArthur's eyes, is a perennial opponent. He believes that the British are trying to re-establish their eminence in the Orient, and he is not inclined to help them. This, my guest said, was why the general refused to allow the British to station more than a battalion of troops in Tokyo, instead of the division they had in mind.

But though he dislikes the British, it is the Russians whom the general sees as our prime enemy. Japan to him is, above all, an air base from which our bombers could range all of Siberia. He maintains that it would be senseless to fight the Soviets on land, for an American army would be bogged down in the vastness of Russia as hopelessly as was Hitler's.

As a geopolitician, the general feels we have lost the land mass of Eurasia—whether to communism, fascism, or the British brand of neo-imperialism. There is no spot in Eurasia which we can reach ahead of the Red Army. Therefore, all aid is wasted. But, together with the members of his Inner Circle, he shares General Fellers' conviction that the conflict between the "Mongol-Slav hordes of the East and the civilized peoples of the West" will be resolved on a battlefield.

General MacArthur firmly believes that Japan has replaced China as the pivot of our policy for Asia. He believes the Chinese Nationalist administration to be incompetent and shot through with corruption. He fears that if we identify ourselves with it, we may "lose face" throughout Asia. But if he firmly believed in nonintervention in China before, he has gradually been coming over to the view that military force should—and could—be employed to halt the spread of Chinese Communism.

The general regards the recent war in Europe as a futile effort, since it merely substituted new conflicts for old ones. The conquest of Japan, therefore, was the only positive gain of World War II. This victory has given us an opportunity to solidify our strategic position, with Japan as our new springboard and the Philippines as the rear base.

The next world war, he believes, will be fought in the skies. He often cites his own experience in defeating Japan without ever contacting the main body of the Japanese Army. He denies any major share in victory to the U.S. Navy. (As a corollary to these views, my guest said, the general is opposed to universal military training, in the belief that large land armies are outmoded.)

General MacArthur wants to see all the important Pacific bases remain under our control. He would have the army run the larger islands, such as Okinawa, and the navy operate the smaller bases, such as those on Guam and Iwo.

On the spiritual side, finally, the general would like to see Japan become a Christian nation. Such a conversion, he believes, would weld Japan to the West and make her a peace-loving nation.

All of us have been puzzled lately by the reluctance of Headquarters to issue substantive directives to the Japanese. Now the cat is out of the bag. The reason is General Mac-Arthur's determination to freeze out the Allied Council. Normally, the directives have to go to the Council for reference and discussion. Thus, Headquarters has devised a new technique. Major General L. J. Whitlock, Deputy Chief of Staff, summons Japanese officials before him, *reads* the directive to them, and then orders them to comply with it. Since no written order has been handed to the Japanese, nothing has to be shown to the Allied Council.

The Japanese are canny politicians, and they are making the most of the feuds within and without Headquarters. A bystander like me can only marvel at the extent of their knowledge, and the shrewdness with which they hoodwink Headquarters.

The other day the U.S. Army got hold of a letter mailed by the Yokohama Specie Bank's head office here to its branch in Osaka. The letter dealt with the hottest current issue—the latest purge of war criminals. The letter said that the purge was championed by "three American Jews" in General Whitney's Government Section, but that other groups in Headquarters—General Marquat's Section, Major Imboden's Press Division, and General Whitney's own Local Government Division—are fighting the purge on the ground that it would eliminate the men with whom they have been cooperating.

On the basis of this information, the letter said, Premier Yoshida has decided to resist the American demand for a purge. Instead, he will demand that a formal directive be issued ordering him to institute the purge. To issue such a directive, the letter explained, Headquarters would have to call a staff conference, at which the American foes of the purge might stand a good chance of killing the proposal.

The letter further explained that Premier Yoshida feels it is essential to prevent the purge, as it would affect members of his government, and the conservative political machines.

To me, as to the other Americans who have heard of the letter, it is a shocking indication of the thoroughness with which the Japanese have scouted Headquarters. It would almost appear as if the Japanese have a central Intelligence organization, pooling all the bits of information coming in from spies, friends and business contacts. It is also an indication of the shrewd manner in which Premier Yoshida is sabotaging all legislation which would change the face of Japan.

The most curious feature of the letter was its remark about the "three American Jews." Actually, the three leading advocates of the purge have not been Jews, but they have been so described by one of General Whitney's important aides. How did that remark get to the Yokohama Specie Bank?

The favorite Japanese official refrain this week is: "If local officials are purged, rice collection will be disorganized. If financiers are purged, recovery will be delayed."

Many Americans appear to agree with this view. General Baker gave a party for several correspondents last night, and expounded his view that the new purge was a mistake because it robbed Japan of her best brains, and, moreover, lowered our own prestige, for we are discarding these people after "using" them for a year.

The general, I feel, is aggrieved prematurely: the boys will do all right. The Japanese papers are full of reports on how local bosses and officials are circumventing the purge order by filling all vacancies with their henchmen who are not subject to expulsion. I remember that the political purge directive nearly a year ago was greeted with the same cries of Alas, Alack and Revolution. Yet, there are probably a good hundred men and women in the current Diet who could never survive an honest inquiry into their records.

Sally gave a big Thanksgiving party tonight. Mogi, our chef, had never heard of stuffing a turkey, and Sally arrived in the kitchen just in time to save three fat turkeys from being dismembered. "The British ambassador," Mogi explained, "Never put anything in *his* turkey!"

Among the thirty-five guests were General Derevyanko and his political adviser, Anyurov. Derevyanko thought Thanksgiving was a wonderful idea. "Anyurov told me," he said, "that it is a festival held by American farmers to celebrate a good harvest." I thought it was as good an explanation as any.

Somewhere between our sixth and eighth drink, I commented on the latest clash between Derevyanko and Atcheson at the Allied Council. Anyurov looked surprised. "What clash?" With this as the starting point, Anyurov developed the thesis that the main conflict in the Council was between us and Britain, and Russia was merely acting as a mediator, trying to avert the conflict from developing into an international crisis.

I had heard the thesis before, but somehow it startled me when applied to the Allied Council. The thesis, based on pure Marxism, was that wars are fought primarily for markets. Since Russia coveted none, there were no basic conditions for a conflict with the United States. On the other hand, American capital was trying to move into the markets once dominated by Britain, and a clash was inescapable. Under this thesis, all talk of U.S.-Soviet differences was a smoke screen thrown by American capitalists to disguise their infiltration into the British sphere of influence.

I was willing to agree that idle talk of war, especially of the kind done in this Headquarters, could do nothing but harm. One of General Whitney's subordinates has actually toured much of Japan, giving "indoctrination" talks to GIs on "the coming war" with Russia, and on our need of Japan as a base. Nor could I disagree that in this theater, Britain's legitimate trade interests were getting an awful pushing around. But I also knew that Ball's instructions had been to support U.S.

policies, and what clashes there have been between Ball and Atcheson have been mainly personal.

The big conflict here, as elsewhere in the world, was between Russia and us. The conflict deepened as our military here increasingly thought and talked of Japan as a springboard in the coming test of arms. The Russians, on the other hand, have ranged their big verbal guns on our failure to democratize Japan. Thus, the Allied Council had become an arena in which we and the Russians struggled for the mind of Japan. We wooed Japan's old-timers with our spirited defense of their record. The Russians harped on our failure to implement our paper directives; on continued Japanese sabotage of reform plans; and on the resurrection of militant Japanese nationalism.

To many of us it often seemed as if General MacArthur was seeking, above all, to have a friendly Japanese government, while the Russians sought friends among the people. And just as often, watching the sharp exchanges between Atcheson and Derevyanko, we were distressed to find the American position so unsound. For instead of making empty claims or backing up the Japanese government which deserved no backing, we should have been able to point proudly to a record of genuine reform. Even among the most devout followers of General MacArthur, we now find a readiness to admit that somewhere, somehow we have missed our chance in Japan.

But listening to Anyurov, I thought it did the Russians no good to protest that the conflict so plain to the naked eye was not a conflict at all but mediation. Any policy based on that assumption would produce blunders to match any we have pulled ourselves.

Long after midnight, politics forgotten, the party turned to singing. Soon a contest was on in the center of the room. Sally, Margaret Parton, and Charlotte were matching Derevyanko, Anyurov, and Oscar Kurganov, a correspondent for the *Izvestia*, an American song for a Russian one. Both teams were coached impartially by Eric Ward, an adviser to Ball.

A few days ago, I asked my friend, Chikosaburo Hayami, the Cabinet adviser, what had happened to the men who once held high posts in *Tokko*, or Thought Control police. He smiled his usual vague smile and said he would find out. This morning he called up to ask if he could come to lunch "with a friend who knows a great deal about *Tokko*."

He came in with a small, trim man of about fifty, whom he introduced as "Shigenori Hata, chief of the Fourth Section of the Investigation Bureau in the Home Ministry."

He paused for effect. "Mr. Hata is a former *Tokko* official."

At first Mr. Hata was cautious. He drank pineapple juice instead of whisky, and he answered in monosyllables. But Hayami has a way of getting his friends to talk to me. By the time we sat at the table for lunch, Hata had begun to talk.

During the war—between 1941 and 1944—Hata served as Chief of the Thought Control Division in the Tokyo Metropolitan Police Board. He had about sixty men directly under him, and his main job was hunting for Communists. When the Tojo Cabinet fell, Hata was promoted to prefectural police chief, first in Kagawa and then in Shiga.

I asked him the question that was on many minds during the war: "Had there been an antimilitarist underground in Japan after Pearl Harbor?"

Hata said that only the Communists had been active. While he was in Tokyo, he said, he arrested between two hundred and three hundred of them a year. By the time he left for Kagawa, the number of Communists still at large had dwindled down to "twenty or thirty, with about a thousand sympathizers." These men were organized in tiny "cells" of four or five men each, and since agitation for higher pay was forbidden, the Communists engaged either in agitation for "better working conditions" or in petty sabotage.

"There were small fires," he said, "or something went wrong with the machinery, or ammunition was found to be defective. But all this was on a small scale, and it was difficult to find the culprits."

Over coffee, Hata told us the story of *Tokko* and its successful efforts to retain power after Japan's surrender.

"Before the war," he said, "*Tokko* was a hand-picked force.
To recruit it, the Home Ministry combed the field for bright
men. They were farmed out to other government departments.
Membership in *Tokko* won for us special honors and privileges.
A governor, for instance, could dismiss his section chiefs at
will. But he could do nothing to a *Tokko* man serving under
him, for *Tokko* people were appointed from Tokyo.

"Take the year I went into *Tokko,* for instance. There
were fifty-eight of us that year, all lawyers. We all came into
the Home Ministry at one time and were given special training. Then the Ministry scattered us. We served through the
years of the China Incident, the Great Far Eastern War, and
the early days of the Occupation. We knew the purge directive
was coming out in October, 1945, and we resigned beforehand.

"Today most of us are back in important posts. Some are
in the Ministry of Education. Others are in the Ministry of
Welfare. These include the chief of the Labor Division. Still
others are in the Ministry of Commerce. Several, including the
chief of the Wood and Charcoal Section, are in the Ministry
of Forestry and Agriculture."

The list grew. It was not amusing that the man in charge
of charcoal rationing was a *Tokko* man: charcoal is a Japanese
housewife's only fuel for warmth or cooking, and it is a po-
tent instrument of political pressure. It was even less funny
that the man who watches over the growth of democratic labor
unions is a man who once helped to destroy them.

"Two prefectural governors," said Hata, "are *Tokko* alumni.
Two or three *Tokko* men who served in Korea through the
war have now come back to key positions in the Home Ministry.
Minor *Tokko* officials, who had served in the provinces, have
now been pulled back to Tokyo, to fill subordinate government jobs."

"Early this year," Hata said, "while he was still head of
the Liberal party, Mr. Hatoyama started organizing an anti-
Communist League. It was doing nicely when Mr. Hatoyama
was purged as a war criminal. For a while there was a hiatus.

But now the Japanese Federation of Labor is making ready to launch a major anti-Communist campaign. The Federation is run by right-wing Social Democrats. They hope the campaign will help them to ge rid of Communist competition.

"In general, the anti-Communist campaigns are significant. If a powerful ultranationalist movement reappears in this country it will begin as an anti-Communist crusade. That's inevitable. But right now there's no integrated ultranationalist movement yet. Just numerous small groups of ex-servicemen and former nationalists who gather secretly in private homes and discuss the next step. They are in difficulty. In the past, the nationalists got their money from the army and from blackmail of Big Business. All this has now stopped. What's worse, there is a philosophical vacuum. Most of the men who once shaped nationalist thought are dead. Thus, the nationalist movement is still in ferment. It has a will; it has little money and no philosophy."

I asked Hata which government organs now kept an eye on the leftists—the Communists. the labor movement, the farm unions.

"The job is divided," he said. "The Welfare Ministry, the Home Ministry, the Metropolitan Police Board." He thought a moment. "It was much better before," he said wistfully. "Then, everything was in our hands."

A little sharply, I said: "There are reports of a new purge. Aren't you afraid you might be purged too?"

"I don't think so," said Hata. "After all, my section has been set up at the request of your army."

November 29, 1946   TOKYO

Told the servants that we are leaving Japan, and that we had found jobs for them. Kimiko, the junior maid of whom we are especially fond, was the first to break down and cry. Then Mogi, the chef, went to the kitchen and had a good cry with his wife. Then Sally came into the study to tell me of the emotional crisis in the household—and, incidentally, to exhibit her own red eyes.

Just before dinner I went into the living room, and here was Sally playing Japanese music on the piano, and Kimiko singing. The Japanese folk songs are lovely, and they sounded especially well tonight, with the large room dim, the candles flickering on the mantle, and the canary trilling in time with the music. It is American *gemutlichkeit* in Japan, and it is as incongruous as it is pleasant. We are eager to move on, but it will be painful to leave all this.

Ran into Nozaka today. He said he has just returned from a tour of speech-making in the British zone, in the south of this island. Just before one of the meetings, a British major came in, saw the red flag on the stage, and ordered it replaced with the Rising Sun flag. The Communists objected, explaining that this was the military flag under which Japan's aggression was carried on, but the major was adamant. "When I came in and saw the flag," Nozaka said in his usual quiet voice, "I was very surprised."

Nozaka's speech dealt with the new Constitution, but in a few minutes the major stepped up, and said, "You can't talk about that." After the meeting, when the Communists protested and explained that the Japanese democratic Constitution was meant to be discussed widely, the British had the good grace to admit the major was in error.

My friend, Hayami, the soldier-of-fortune and adviser to the Cabinet, came to lunch. He brought with him a precious parting gift—two roughly made clay cups of exquisite beauty and workmanship. He told me my departure was a blow to him.

"For many years," he said "I've been close to politics, but I always gave more thought to its mechanics than to its substance. Then came the defeat, and I started thinking. When things started reverting to the old ways which brought us to this disaster, I began to lose hope. But I met Tsuru, and he made things clear for me. Then I ran into you, and you've given me hope that perhaps the Americans would understand what's happening here. This is why I tried to show you the kind of Japan you mightn't have seen otherwise. Now you're going away, and I feel very sad."

I share his sadness. He and Shigeto Tsuru have, each in his own way, been among my best mentors in Japan. Tsuru is a brilliant Harvard-trained economist, a source of facts and keen analysis. Hayami is a rough native product, with a thorough knowledge of the inner workings of Japanese politics and mind. Our two-week trip to Ibaragi, for instance, was born of a chat Sally and I had with him and Tsuru one September night. I wanted to know if there was a solid base in the villages for the rebirth of ultranationalism. Hayami refused to answer. He said, "Why don't you come with me, to my prefecture, and see for yourself? I'll help you."

We went, and he carefully set up for us members of parliament, landlords, mayors, heads of the landlord-dominated Agricultural Associations, sharecroppers, and officers of the tenant-dominated Farmers' Union. He never commented, though at times he bore down hard on the men who evaded my questions. When we got through, I had the answer: new and progressive forces have arisen in the Japanese countryside, but they are no match for the forces of old Japan and for the re-emerging tide of nationalism. Some day not too far ahead, I thought, Japan will again turn to militant expansionism, and it will have some of its roots in the restless, nationalist countryside.

December 2, 1946   TOKYO

This is a wet and chilly day. Sally is nursing a bad cold. The radiators are icy, and travel in a jeep is thoroughly unpleasant. Yet there is something fascinating about Tokyo in a December rain: the dark figures appearing out of the bluish dusk, the reflection of the lights on the wet pavement, the sound of the wooden clogs striking melodically against the concrete, the radiance of the neon lights fighting the rain, the shadows cast by the ruins, the crowds, wet and silent, trudging home after work.

Tokyo constantly amazes me. It was a year ago that the Ginza was nothing but a succession of brick skeletons, spaced apart by lots filled with rubble. Now the department stores have been repaired, and shops have been erected in the empty lots. The shops are jerry-built, but their fronts are neat and ingenious, and the display windows carry wares that startle me. The big industries may stand idle, but the artisans are busy, and the families once well-to-do but now pinched by the $33-a-month limit on bank withdrawals, are beginning to part with their treasures.

Yesterday Sally and I spent most of the day in a department store. One of the displays included items for the tea ceremony—tea pots, clay cups, scrolls, lacquered buckets. We were sorely tempted to buy, but were stopped by the prices, ranging from $100 for a scroll to $1,000 for a screen. But our resistance crumbled when we saw an exhibition of modern art. We bought the first painting we saw—a series of three narrow scrolls showing an old monk.

Later, in a dark corner, we saw a stack of rough clay plates —gray, with a red character burned deep into the center. We bought all of them. The manager came up and wanted to know *why* we bought them. Then he told us that the plates were made by one of the three great potters of modern Japan. The Japanese do not want to buy modern china, and the Americans have not discovered it yet, and for lack of customers the ware has been relegated to an obscure corner.

All this leads me to think of how hard it is to destroy a city, or a people, or art. Tokyo was an unbelievable mess a year ago. I remember how depressed I felt for months, watching the people trying to recover from the shock. Then, suddenly, the construction began. I have been watching a mountain of rubble along one side of the Ginza. As new lots were cleared and more buildings were erected, the mountain rose. But it was also pushed back, to make room for new construction. They have now pushed it all the way to the canal, where it towers three and four times the height of my jeep. By next year, they will have to load it on barges and take it out, for there is no more space to push it into.

But the sad thing is that while the merchants can pay $15,000 for building a flimsy shop, the wage earner cannot afford a home. The other day, the City of Tokyo put up for sale a bunch of new, government-sponsored houses. Thousands stood in line through the night. The morning came, and the price of the houses were announced: $3,000. With salaries limited to $33 a month, few people can afford a home at that price. The incident was splashed all over the newspapers, and did not do the Yoshida Government, already heartily detested, any good.

One of the curious features of the situation is the obstinacy with which Headquarters continues to back up the Government. I yet have to meet a Japanese worker, farmer, or shopkeeper who speaks well of Yoshida. When I ask the Japanese their opinion of him, they want to know in return why Headquarters is supporting him. And it is difficult to find the answer, unless it be Headquarters' determination to maintain a "safe" government. The generals and colonels, who detest some of the reforms they have been ordered to enforce, happily condone the failure of reform. And Yoshida is so certain of American support that he openly flaunts General MacArthur's wishes and directives.

This whole process known as "the democratization of Japan" is amazing: Headquarters' claims of progress, so extravagant that Yoshida himself would not dare to issue them; the open violation of democratic concepts; and the slow, steady, uninterrupted growth of nationalism and reaction.

Hessel Tiltman, the careful and experienced correspondent for the London *Daily Herald*, spent the entire morning today taking notes on a new history textbook. The book was turned out by a special committee of "Japanese liberals" at the Education Ministry, and approved by Lieutenant Colonel D. R. Nugent, who has succeeded General Dyke as head of C. I. & E.

The books deals with Japan's history, starting about 1,300 years after the Sun Goddess and ending with the present efforts of "the people and the government to rebuild the nation." The C. I. & E. primly inserted "democratic" before "nation."

The book takes no sides, it is neither for nor against war and aggression. It reads like a police blotter: "Japanese fliers attacked Pearl Harbor, which is in Hawaii, and then war was declared on the United States and Britain." This is a far cry from "the infamy that will live in history." Of the decade of aggression which ended with the attack on Pearl Harbor, the book mentions only the rape of Manchuria, and that with a factual error and not a word of reproach for the makers of war. There is no mention of the steady gobbling up of North China, or of the seizure of Indo-China. When it deals with Japan's war on China in 1937, the book says: "The Japanese government made repeated efforts at negotiation, but when these failed, war with the Chinese began."

Will such history books teach children democracy? Will they deter ultranationalism? Is it the purpose of the Education Ministry to conceal from the children the ugly story of aggression, and the defeat to which it led? Is it not our intent to tell the whole story to the Japanese people?

When Hessel mentioned the paucity of the information supplied by the book, the officer said, "You know, it's intended only to supply the skeleton. The teachers will fill in the gaps." Since of Japan's 400,000 teachers, once screened by the militarists for loyalty, less than 700 have thus far been purged, or have resigned on their own, one can easily imagine the kind of gap-filling the children of Japan will get.

Japan today is a pathetic and ugly picture. The great economic crisis is still ahead, and neither the government nor Headquarters is doing anything constructive to avert it. The currency in circulation has soared to 70 billions, or more than it was last March when it became necessary to freeze bank deposits. The increase in industrial production is almost imperceptible, and the industrialists find it more profitable to speculate in raw materials than to convert them into manufactured goods.

The farmers, unable to get the things they need, are refusing to surrender their quotas of rice to the government. They hold back a substantial portion for sale in the black market. The labor unrest continues. It is computed that a family in Tokyo needs $150 a month to stay alive. Under the currency regulations, it is illegal for anyone to earn even half that much. Thus, labor has no recourse but to strike. The railway workers have just announced that they are "in a state of struggle" with the government. The teachers have filed a long series of demands. The people are engaged in a desperate race with the soaring price index, and they are losing out.

Meanwhile, the Yoshida Government hauls out its blackest paint, to make the picture even darker than it is in the hope of getting more help from the generous Uncle Sam, and winning greater concessions at the peace conference. General MacArthur's eagerness to leave a perfect record for history is no secret to the Japanese, and they play on it with relentless skill.

"If we don't get enough food," they say, "there'll be riots. How will that look in the United States press?" Or, "If we don't get enough cotton, we won't be able to rebuild our peacetime industries, and we'll remain bankrupt. How will that look?"

And so they keep getting their wheat and their cotton and, sooner or later, their credits. There can be no objections to Japan's economic revival. Unless there is a revival, Japan must remain a country wracked by strife, and a handicap to the rehabilitation of Asia. But there can be justifiable, and vigorous, objections to using the American taxpayers' money to rebuild Japan for her old masters.

Sally and I will leave Japan after the monster "Down With Yoshida" demonstration scheduled for December 18. This is to be a Social Democratic bid for political power. But the Social Democrats are in a quandary. They know that to overthrow Yoshida they must have mass support. Yet, they live in deadly fear of the Communists and the Congress of Industrial Unions, and they have actually just launched an anti-Communist campaign.

The whole Social Democratic position is curious. I know that a number of political thinkers in Headquarters are beginning to feel that the Social Democrats are a much safer bet than Yoshida himself. Headquarters knows that the top level of the party, with a few exceptions, is loaded with war criminals—not with conservative nationalists like Yoshida and Hatoyama, but with intelligent and aggressive National Socialists, who before and during the war were on intimate terms with the young army fanatics. Yet Headquarters is willing to forget that. There is a growing feeling that Japan, in her current distress, cannot be content with conservative solutions, but must go a bit to the left. The socialist right wingers supply an ideal answer. They speak the language of social reform and their strength lies in labor unions, but they will not want to destroy the basic structure of old Japan, nor will they make friends with Russia or the native Communists.

The best indication of Headquarters' feelings is its refusal to press for a thorough purge of the Social Democrats. Nor is Yoshida, who controls the purge machinery, trying hard. He is now seeking to arrange a compromise with the right-wingers under which he will give them a few seats in his Cabinet.

Most of the Japanese I have talked to, have little love for the war criminals in the Social Democratic party. But they are eager to see the party come to power. One reason is that the party has some of Japan's best and most progressive brains. Some day these men might make their way to the top. Another reason: anything is better than the team of Yoshida and Shidehara.

The current story on Shidehara, the great democrat and reformer, shows why people feel the way they do. Shidehara, who is close to senility but refuses to admit it, held a press conference today to complain that he had been misquoted. It seems that after inspecting some coal mines in the south, he said there was no need for raising the wages of underground miners. The statement was quoted critically in the Diet.

Shidehara's explanation: it was all "humorous." He said he had gone to the mouth of a pit, and later, at lunch, told his friends jokingly: "The pit I visited was unexpectedly spacious and well ventilated. If that's what is known as a coal pit, I wouldn't mind working there myself, if I were younger. And in that case I wouldn't mind working for the wage the miners get."

The misquotation, he said, was "most embarrassing" to him. "As a matter of fact, I know nothing about the wage problem." This is from the deputy premier of Japan, and the head of one of its major parties.

December 8, 1946   TOKYO

Dinner at the house with two of the Communist "Big Three"—Nozaka and Shiga. Tokuda, who was also to come, is ill in bed. Among other guests, Helen and Bill Costello and Joe Fromm.

Both the Japanese were in fine mettle. They told us a number of anecdotes, boasted of growing Communist strength, and expounded the Communist program.

"I've just returned from Takasaki," said Shiga. "On the train, I talked to students. They all criticized the Americans. In the beginning, they said, the American soldiers were good men. It may be that they came out of combat with ideas of democracy which they wanted to show to the Japanese. But the new men are bad. They are rough, and they don't care about what's going on in Japan."

Both also criticized the Pauley Reparations Plan. "If it's carried out," said Nozaka, "It'll put Japan back to 1900. It will certainly retard the industrialization which Japan needs to survive. We Communists believe in developing a socialized industry—high precision machinery, electrical and chemical industries, mechanization of farms, development of coal by-products.

But having criticized the United States, they also listed her achievements in Japan. "The new Constitution," said Nozaka, "has had a deep effect on the nation. It has reduced the emperor's powers. The various reforms have dealt a blow to the feudal forces. The blow is not fatal, but it's heavy. If the

Occupation forces remain here another five years, the progressive forces will be strong enough to block the efforts of the Old Guard to seize power."

Japan, both men insisted, is turning to the left. The anti-Communist statements by General MacArthur and Atcheson last spring arrested the growth of the Communist party for three months, but it was resumed by August. The party now, Nozaka said, has 40,000 members, and the circulation of its official newspaper is in excess of 300,000. "Our influence in the unions is so great," Shiga said, "that the government constantly asks us to use our good offices to halt strikes."

One of the great problems now, the two men said, is the growing gap between the cities and the country. "The cities," Nozaka said, "are progressive. The countryside is laggard. It is possible, under certain conditions, that the villages will become bases of fascism. This is why we Communists are now turning our attention to the farm country."

Later in the evening we came to the prophecies. I asked the two men what they thought would happen in Japan in ten years. Both answered readily, and cheerfully.

Shiga: "I'll get life imprisonment."

Nozaka: "One thing I'm sure of is that I'll be dead."

What the two men did not tell us was the story of the various schisms within the Communist party. The fissures, though not fatal, affect the party's policy and tactics. One of the divergences is between the "veterans" and the "newcomers." Until recently, the tendency has been to judge a man's merit by the number of years he has spent in jail. Tokuda and Shiga are undisputed leaders because of their ability. But a factor in their favor is that they have spent a third of their adult lives in prison for Communist activity. Many a lesser party man will start a conversation by proferring his badge of honor: "I've served three years. . . . " And some, when they wish to slight a person, say, "Oh, he has spent only six months. . . . "

Only a small fraction of the party's membership consists of "veterans." The bulk of members is fresh blood, mostly workers. But there is a wide marginal belt, in which one can find the most divergent elements, including many young *kamikaze* pilots who only eighteen months ago were ready to lay down their lives for the emperor. So far, the "veterans" have held firmly to leadership. The party's Central Committee, for instance, is an appointive, rather than an elected body, and it consists almost exclusively of "veterans."

But there are not enough "veterans" to go around, and the party's urgent need for organizers compels it to assign important tasks to the "newcomers." Thus, the "veterans" are under constant pressure from below to share leadership and admit "newcomers" to the party hierarchy.

Nozaka's arrival has provided another, and possibly a more important, difference. The "veterans," such as Tokuda, have been isolated behind prison bars for many years. However good their liaison with the outside, their impressions of the world have been secondhand. Inevitably, they have based their strategy for today on the experience of the late 'twenties and early 'thirties.

Nozaka, on the other hand, has come to Japan with a bagful of advantages. He has observed at first hand major social movements in three countries—Russia, China, and Japan. He has had invaluable experience as an underground worker and propagandist in China. He has also brought with him an impressive background in world politics and revolutionary theory. The "veterans," and especially Tokuda, wanted direct action against the evil forces which put Japan into the war. Nozaka opposed any rash actions which would bring the Communists in conflict with the U.S. Army. Tokuda regarded all American reforms with a cynical eye. Nozaka was willing to see some good in many of them. He also realized that sections of the population were grateful to the United States for the food, drugs, cotton, and other blessings. He felt it would be wrong for the party to ignore this feeling. Nozaka, finally, wanted a broader base for struggle than the Communist party. He has been the party's chief advocate of a united front of all leftist forces—the Social Democrats, the labor unions, the farmers' organizations.

I am told that there have been vigorous discussions within

the inner circles of the party, with Tokuda arguing for aggressive action, Nozaka counselling patience and moderation, and Shiga acting as a mediator. Compromises have been made by both Tokuda and Nozaka. This was especially true on the emperor issue, the party modifying its old "hang-the-villain" attitude.

Nozaka has at all times been willing to recognize Tokuda's great popularity and his ability as a mass leader. He has been content to remain in the background acting as the philosopher of the Communist movement. This has been especially true in the crises, such as the anti-Cabinet campaign in mid-spring, the "hunger" movement of May, and the "labor offensive" in October. In all of these, it was Tokuda who generalled the Communist forces.

It would be idle, however, to deduce that these differences can produce a split within the Communist party. Neither Tokuda nor Nozaka is likely to permit any divergences to develop into an open break. Lesser dissenters might be denounced. But the Big Three have been in the movement too long not to know the value of unity and discipline.

One of Nozaka's prime emphases is on the education of party members. The party today is primarily a party of emotional protest. The big job now is to rivet emotion to a base of Marxist theory. In the process of re-education, much of the marginal membership will be eliminated. But the Communist party is bound to grow. It cannot but expand in a time of crisis.

Thus far, the party has focussed its attention on urban labor. It has made significant progress. Some of the most powerful and militant unions—in transport and the electrical industry, in coal mining and communications—are dominated by Communists. There is no mystery to their success. In a time of social and economic stress, the Communists were the only ones to offer a vigorous leadership and a program of social welfare couched in one-syllable words. In Russia, thirty years earlier, Bolsheviks came to power with a program of "Bread and Peace." Japan's Communists fight on a platform almost as simple: Rice, Jobs, a Democratic Government.

Some Americans have erred in overestimating the importance of the Communist party. They have blamed it for a variety of ills, from the economic crisis to rural dislocations. Such exaggerations, if anything, have made the Communists seem stronger to the general public than they actually were. At the opposite pole, other Americans have pointed to the six Diet seats held by the Communists as "a popular rejection of extreme leftism." This conclusion is invalid, for the Communist party has grown a hundred-fold in fourteen months, and a million voters cast their ballot for the Communist ticket in the last election. Curiously, there have been some Americans—notably Atcheson—who have attacked the Communists for being both dangerous and totally unimportant.

How much help are the Japanese Communists getting from Russia? The two visitors tonight laughingly traced for us the path of a rumor, which in a year converted a report of a million-yen Russian subsidy to the Japanese Communists into a heckler's question last month: "Is it true that Nozaka brought with him from Manchuria three billion yen of Soviet money?" The fact is that no outsider—not even General Willoughby's G-2—knows. A high Japanese police official told some of us correspondents recently that both G-2 and the Japanese Government have been searching vigorously for any evidence of Russian aid to the Japanese Communists. Thus far "we've found nothing," he said sadly. I am convinced that as soon as such proof is found, the news will be broadcast to the outer edges of the world.

But though there is no aid, the political bonds are firm. The chief connecting link, of course, is Nozaka, who has spent many years in Russia and knows the policy and thought patterns of the Russian Communist leadership. As more prisoners return home to Japan from Siberia, with their inevitable contingent of Communists, the bonds will grow stronger. Moreover, the political roots of both the Russian and the Japanese parties grow out of the same Marxist soil, and their ultimate objective is the same.

I am unable to accept the argument that either the Japanese, Korean, or Chinese Communist party is an alien movement. If any of them were, it would quickly lose its mass following. But though each party is a separate identity, they must all—and that includes the Japanese Communists—act in accord on matters of broad policy. Russia is the only major ally of revolution in the world, and no Communist party can afford to spurn it.

In Japan, this becomes increasingly so, as the organized opposition to Communists gains strength. Its inspiration comes undoubtedly from Yoshida's Liberal party and its *zaibatsu* sponsors. But the following comes partly from ex-servicemen, partly from the professional patriots of the prewar days. Idle since surrender, these vehement nationalists are now beginning to band together anew. Anticommunism has become a useful slogan to Ando the racketeer and Hatoyama the purged political boss, to the men who once belonged to the "Black Dragon Society" and to the gangsters of Osaka and Tokyo. Their main weapon is terrorism.

Nozaka told us that he had been accosted recently near his house by some young hoodlums. He escaped by insisting that his name was "Yoshida." He is now changing his residences frequently, to escape possible assassination. So does Tokuda. Violence is an old feature of Japanese politics, and the leftists are unhappily preparing for its revival.

December 9, 1946   TOKYO

Hatoyama is a shrewd politician. Whatever resentment he may have for me was well concealed when he came to the house for lunch. He was just a well-fed, jovial, impeccably dressed old man dropping in for a friendly chat. He brought with him an adviser, who once served in Manchuria, and his own interpreter. With Leon Prou, the French correspondent, we sat in the living room and had drinks. Hatoyama and I drank orange juice.

To my surprise, Hatoyama was willing to talk of politics. He said he had come to Tokyo specially for the luncheon, from his "exile" at the seaside resort of Atami. "I have to be careful," he said, "because Headquarters told me to stay out of Tokyo, and out of politics. If I don't, I'm afraid they'll purge me again." He grinned. "Headquarters is keeping an eye on me. They've even tapped my wire and listen every time I talk to Premier Yoshida."

We talked of the new purge of local officials. "All the new directive will do," he said, "is produce chaos. Local governments have been crippled. The old officials who formed a barrier to communism have been removed. Now the leftists will move in."

Yoshida's name was constantly on Hatoyama's tongue. "Premier Yoshida's cabinet is in a quandary. It doesn't know what to do next, but it knows that if it doesn't do something concrete, its life is ended. The chief Secretary of the Cabinet has called on me a number of times, to ask for my advice. I told him people need hope. Promise them more rice next year, I said. Start electrifying the railways, for this will save coal. I even jokingly told him that Japan ought to import milch cows, so that a milk ration can be issued to each man, woman and child."

By his own admission, this amiable man, purged from public life, has become the hidden government of Japan. Frankly, he reeled off the names of the Cabinet ministers who had come to him to seek guidance. "The trouble with all of them," Hatoyama said, "is that they give in too easily to Headquarters." I regretted I could not fasten his words to a record, to be played every time Headquarters issued a statement on Yoshida's "democratic ideals."

We asked Hatoyama for his views on the United States policy in Japan. "At first," he said, "I thought the American Army desired to dye Japan red. There were American Communists in Headquarters, and they helped Japanese Communists to take over the radio and the press. I attributed this to MacArthur's policies. But in May and June, General MacArthur and Mr. Atcheson issued statements denouncing communism. I knew then the policy of the Occupation is to support the conservatives."

Hatoyama, however, had some sharp things to say about

the Occupation costs. They all laughed as if it was a familiar, and dirty, joke, and they all recited to me examples of extravagant spending. One mentioned a golf course for U.S. Army officers near Kyoto which cost $8,000,000 to landscape. By the time the clubhouse was built, the cost was more than doubled. They also talked of a house built for an American general in Yokohama at the cost of $800,000.

"The place had gold silk wall covering, and special material brought from Kyoto for table cloths," Hatoyama said. "The Minister of Commerce took a look at the place and said, 'I doubt if the general will be able to stand this gaudiness very long.'"

At the table, politics were dropped. We talked of Hatoyama's father, who studied at Yale and Columbia; of Hatoyama's four daughters and son; and of his religion ("I used to be a Universalist. Now I have no religion.")

He told us with delight of a book given to him by Burton Crane. "I thought the book was so excellent, I promptly sent it to Premier Yoshida and urged him to read it at once. It shows that communism and Russia are the common enemy of every democratic country. The book is Burritt's *One Big Grobe*."

It took a bit of puzzling out, but we did finally make it out. The book that delighted Hatoyama and Yoshida was William Bullitt's *One Big Globe*.

At night, ran into Colonel Kades and told him of Hatoyama's visit. Kades wanted all the details. It appears that the Government Section had learned that Yoshida has been entertaining Hatoyama, and demanded to know why. Yoshida's blithe explanation: "Mr. Hatoyama is an old friend."

What puzzles me is the look of surprise in the faces of American officers every time they discover that yet another purgee remains active in politics. The purged war criminals are so well entrenched in the business of policy-making that it has become one of the standing Japanese scandals. Hatoyama himself, for instance, played host to a flock of Liberal party bosses the night after the party's convention. One of Hatoyama's chief aides, also purged, set up a coal agency in the same building with the party headquarters. When someone asked him if this was not a violation of the purge directive, the man said: "You can't blame my friends if they drop in on me on their way upstairs, to the party headquarters."

Two weeks ago I told the Government Section of the Thought Control official who had become chief of the Labor Division in the Ministry of Welfare. Headquarters took prompt action, and the man was removed. The other day, I checked on the man. He has been promoted to a key post in the Economic Stabilization Board.

The purges have become a shameful pretence. From time to time, Headquarters issues jubilant statements, reciting the staggering figures on men *subject to* the purge. What Headquarters never mentions is the fact that thousands of men subject to the purge remain in office, and thousands of others function as the hidden government, flouting the power and authority of the United States.

December 11, 1946   TOKYO

Japan has been given free speech—with reservations. The range of these reservations has been continually growing. If originally we meant to suppress militarist propaganda alone, now we permit no word critical of the emperor, Yoshida, some of the worst war criminals, and even the *zaibatsu.*

Leading Japanese publicists met today to discuss the problem. Naturally, they are helpless, and their only hope rests on publicity abroad. The examples of censorship they cited today, I thought, mirrored not only the change in our policy in Japan, but also army mentality in general.

The classical example of censorship, of course, is the incident known here as "Hero Worship and General Willoughby." It involves an article published by a Japanese newspaper, after it had been passed by the censors. The next day the article was reprinted—again with censorial consent— in the *Nippon Times,* the English-language mouthpiece for the Japanese government. The article said in part:

"Practically every Japanese holds it a supreme fortune to find General MacArthur as the Supreme Commander of the Allied Occupation forces. . . . No wonder that General Mac-Arthur's biography has proved the postwar best seller here. . . . However, the popular reaction to this booklet which almost borders on fanatical hero worship, calls for sober reflection. . . .

"The Japanese people have long been plagued by the mistaken idea that government is something to be executed by some deity, hero, great man . . . but not by themselves. This feudalistic concept has been the very cause which prevented Japan from being democratized under the Meiji Constitution. Unless this idea is rectified, there can be no assurance of continued development of democratic government in this country. Nay, there is positive possibility that the moment General Mac-Arthur pulls out, the Japanese will pick up another 'living deity' in his stead. . . .

"Japan used to abound in ardent Hitler worshippers. . . . When the Japanese-American war started, they switched their worship to General Tojo, and, after the surrender, to General MacArthur. Japanese teachers have traditionally been bent on inspiring the children with this habit of blind worship for the ruler . . . a tendency constituting the worst enemy of democracy. . . .

"It must be emphasized that unless and until the Japanese are cleansed of this servile concept, democracy in Japan will make no progress. . . . The proper way for the Japanese to repay General MacArthur's sincere efforts to democratize this country and his wise administration is not to worship him, but to rid themselves of subservience and strive, with high self-esteem, to assume the actual authority of government by themselves. Only then will the Supreme Commander be assured that the object of the Occupation has been achieved."

When the printed paper reached Headquarters, Willoughby hit the ceiling. The *Nippon Times* presses were stopped, and the offensive editorial was yanked out. The papers already printed were hauled off the trucks. An attempt was even made to retrieve the papers sent to the Press Club.

Willoughby's angry explanation: "The article is in bad taste."

But this was merely the most spectacular case of our censorial zeal. Henry Wallace's famous speech at Madison Square Garden in mid-September was barred from the press for three days, until the American correspondents became interested. By the time the ban was raised, the speech was no longer news. The censors killed a report on President Truman's declining popularity in a Gallup Poll. They killed a story showing the rise in U.S. prices following the abolition of price controls. For two days they even withheld from the Japanese press a directive of the Far Eastern Commission on the role of labor in Japanese politics.

Under our rigid censorship, the Japanese press is not permitted to discuss Japan's own problems. It is no longer permitted to recite the war crimes of men now in authority. Specifically, the censors have killed an article quoting excerpts from the inflammatory speeches made before the war by the present Minister of Welfare. Critical comments on the new Japanese Constitution have been banned. The censors, for instance, deleted all adverse comments from a book of *parliamentary* speeches on the Constitution—though the speeches had already been printed in full in the *Official Gazette*.

No critical word is permitted of the Land Reform Bill, and no one is allowed to insinuate that the *zaibatsu* have not yet been destroyed. Nor is it permissible to mention the prewar connections between the *zaibatsu* and great foreign concerns, such as General Motors, Ford, General Electric, Westinghouse, Standard Oil, Western Electric, Siemens, Vickers-Armstrong, or even the Singer Sewing Machines and Victor Records. An article pointing out that Japan needs foreign credits and supplies, but that these must be used to bolster a democratic economy, and not private Japanese monopolies, was killed.

The censors blue-pencil all adverse comment on the emperor. Nor do they allow any disclosures of a new nationalist underground. The explanation is that "Japan is a democracy, and articles suggesting that there is an underground do not correspond to facts." Increasingly, the censors kill news reports of labor unrest, strikes, or demands for higher wages.

But none of these intrigue me as much as these three examples:

The opening portions of Leo Tolstoy's *War and Peace* have been deleted. The prewar edition, censored by the Japanese Army, was published unexpurgated.

Huge chunks have been excised from the second half of Lord Bryce's classic *Modern Democracy*. The deleted portions carried critical comments on American politics. The official explanation: "The criticism may be justified, but it's too early to present it to the Japanese." The work was published in Japan in 1931—without deletions.

A volume of Hans Christian Andersen's fairly tales was suppressed. The official explanation: "It description of a naval fight is not good for Japanese children."

December 12, 1946   TOKYO

One of our Japanese friends was at the Central Liaison Office. On a table he saw a list of names entitled "Dangerous Correspondents." The list included Joe Fromm, Bill Costello, Gordon Walker, Margaret Parton, and Hugh Deane. After my name there was a notation, "To Leave Soon."

This is just another confirmation of what most of us have known for some time. The Foreign Office is back in business, which ranges from the formulation of Japan's future foreign policy to the blacklisting of correspondents. We know for a fact that the Foreign Office holds secret "briefing sessions" with Japanese reporters, giving them an interpretation of the events abroad, telling them of the nature of reports filed by foreign correspondents stationed here, and trying to enlist their aid in spying on us. Every effort is being made to intimidate our Japanese contacts, or even assistants.

I suppose that I should feel indignant. I am not. These things are relatively unimportant when matched against the other things happening within the Japanese government. It is known, for instance, that the Foreign Office is well along on its job of drafting a policy which will play us against Russia, and vice versa. The Central Liaison Office is also acting quite openly as an Intelligence organization, spying on Headquarters and on correspondents. This is no longer temerity. This is a bold, well-considered and skillfully generaled plot to win the war despite the defeat.

December 13, 1946   TOKYO

Said goodbye to Generals Willoughby, Marquat, and Whitney. Willoughby told me I had a lot of enemies in Headquarters. I told him he did too. Marquat was in an amiable mood. He told me he saw Shirasu, the slippery vice-chief of the Central Liaison Office, and told him the Japanese protests against the Pauley Reparations Plan were only "tying the hands of the people in Headquarters who are trying to help Japan."

"We're attacked for being soft with Japan," he said. "Well, actually we feel that the only way we can take this burden off the American taxpayer is by building up Japanese economy. We want to let them build up to a certain level, and then just control certain essential industries, such as ball bearings. Without ball bearings they'll never have a war industry. The job in Japan is not to break up the *zaibatsu*. They produced goods cheaply and efficiently. The job is to redistribute wealth."

Marquat said he was opposed to the economic purge because "it has removed a number of people who were essential to industry, the guys with the know-how."

He also said the Japanese government was apparently helping to boost the costs of Occupation in the false assumption that the amount could eventually be converted into American credits at the rate of Y.15 to one dollar, and then charged against indemnities. "I told the Finance Ministry people they were nuts if they thought this would work out. They're just cutting their own throat."

December 14, 1946   TOKYO

In the morning, attended a reception at which General of the Army Douglas MacArthur became the third American ever to receive the Grand Cross of the Legion of Honor. The party, held at the residence of the one-armed Lieutenant General Zinovy Pechkoff, French Ambassador, was attended by at least thirty-six American, British, and Russian generals, two American admirals, an Apostolic Delegate, and an uncertain but large number of colonels, diplomats, bishops, and officers. Also present were Mrs. MacArthur and little Arthur.

Pechkoff's residence, the Oda House, sits comfortably atop a hill, overlooking an area burned out in our air raids. A large brick structure, it has a circular drive-in front, and a sizable Japanese garden in the rear with the inevitable pond, rocks, and dwarfed trees.

This morning the Military Police of the First Cavalry Division were turned out early, all in bright yellow helmets and spotless gloves. Their advance elements were on the main road, where they intercepted the automobiles and sent them into the maze of narrow lanes leading to the Oda House. Later, when the passengers had disembarked, the MPs saw to it that the vehicles were parked more or less according to rank.

Once past the saluting sentries, the visitors passed between two lines of young Japanese hat-check girls in bright kimonos. Beyond them was the dark lobby, where General Pechkoff stood with his aide. One of the most decorated soldiers in the French Army, Pechkoff is a compact little man with an empty right sleeve. He is reputed to have the best chef and one of the best wine cellars in town. He is also said to be related somehow to the Russian writer, Maxim Gorky, whose real name was Peshkov. The difference in spelling bothers no one, and the rumor persists. M. le General speaks both English and Russian well, though with a pronounced accent. Now he vigorously shook the hands of the arrivals with his left hand, and said unsmilingly: "How do you do?"

The guests, unless they were awfully important brass, were then left to sort themselves out, according to rank, in the rooms facing the inner garden. Mrs. MacArthur, with one or two other ranking wives and the heads of the foreign missions, was placed in the sun room on the left of the garden. The generals went into the sun room on the right. Some of the other important wives were put in a glassed-in porch of an adjoining Japanese house. The remainder sought vantage points in second- and third-floor windows and on the roof. The correspondents and the cameramen were placed in the garden, where, with the bright sun at their backs, they could take pictures to the obvious delight of the Public Relations officers.

Between the two sunrooms, on the small porch where the ceremony was to be held, a few flustered French sailors were climbing up and down unsteady ladders, putting last touches on the gay bunting and the flags. In the garden, facing the porch, twenty-four French sailors stood in two ranks. Some of them were looking up at the roof, where a young woman stood in constant danger of exposing herself. To one side of the sailors was the First Cavalry band, which played throughout the morning with considerable vigor. Next to the band was a platform on which movie cameramen were perched with their equipment. They looked very self-conscious. An army photographer kept taking pictures of them, and yelling, "Will you guys pretend you're working?" The band kept playing, the sailors shifted from foot to foot, and the cameramen made frequent trips to the sunroom to the left to photograph Mrs. MacArthur and her son. At the photographers' direction, the two turned their heads this way and that, or pretended to be talking to each other. From time to time, a false alarm came in from the house, and the sailors snapped to attention. But no one would appear, and the men would stand at ease and watch the young woman on the roof.

The band was playing, "I Can't Give You Anything But Love, Baby," when General MacArthur and General Pechkoff walked briskly onto the porch. The sailors presented arms, and the band struck up the "Marseillaise," followed by the "Star Spangled Banner." General MacArthur was wearing a well-pressed Eisenhower jacket and his customary braided cap. His trousers showed a light line where they had been folded over a hanger. He was cleanly shaven, and his chin was stuck out resolutely. All in all, it was quickly agreed in whispers, he was a fine figure of a man.

Both generals saluted while the colors were being presented. MacArthur stood facing the sun—and the cameras. Then Pechkoff, looking solemn, read the citation in both French and English from a slip of paper:

"Miraculous leader, who, during the implacable Pacific war, rendered himself illustrious in his capacity as commander-in-chief of that theater. By his magnificent victory over Japan, he was one of the principal artisans. . . . "

An aide passed a large case to General Pechkoff, who opened it and displayed its contents to General MacArthur. After a slow, stern look at it, General MacArthur passed the case to his aide, and the band struck up *"Fermez le ban."* Then in a clear, loud voice, General MacArthur responded in French. The movie cameras whirred. The young woman on the roof leaned over perilously, and a few sailors, without moving their heads, shot their eyeballs up. The contemplation ended when General Pechkoff called for "Order Arms."

Once again the band played, and the two generals came to attention. General MacArthur's arm was firm and straight in the salute, and so was the left arm of the Frenchman. But as the band went on and on, General MacArthur's arm began to tremble. It shook slightly at first, and then more and more, until everyone in the garden was watching the uncontrolled trembling with a terrible fascination. People began to nudge each other, and here and there, there was a guarded whisper.

Quite suddenly, the music ended, and the ceremony was over. The tension was broken, and everyone relaxed. General

MacArthur put his arm around General Pechkoff's shoulders and said, very audibly, "Let it always be so, old comrade." Both of them walked back to the drawing room, where the Japanese servants stood ready with champagne and appetizers. General MacArthur stopped just inside the door to receive the congratulations of the people filing through from the porch. Mrs. MacArthur pulled out a handkerchief and dabbed at her eyes.

The audience broke up into small groups. "You know," a French correspondent said excitedly, "did you notice that word 'miraculous' in the citation? The French text said *prestigieux*, which can be translated as 'outstanding.' But a couple of colonels in headquarters decided 'outstanding' was not enough. It took them a couple of days to settle on 'miraculous.' And Pechkoff, the poor fellow, had to mistranslate his own citation to conform to the official army handout."

"That's nothing," said an American radio correspondent. "According to custom, Pechkoff should've kissed MacArthur. He didn't. The reason is that a few days ago, one of MacArthur's aides wrote to Pechkoff, saying that since it was customary to dispense with the kissing when heads of State were being decorated, wouldn't it be just as well if Pechkoff skipped the kiss this time. Pechkoff naturally had to agree."

The woman who had come down from the roof kept repeating: "Did you see that grease spot on his cap? It must be pomade. Why doesn't Mrs. MacArthur see to it that his cap is cleaned?"

Now without his cap, General MacArthur stood by the door and shook the hundreds of hands passing by him. His head was cocked a little to one side, and he kept saying, "How do you do?" Behind him, in the closely packed drawing room, champagne was being served. Outside in the foyer, the Japanese girls were trying to find the guests' caps and overcoats. A little French woman with a set smile was saying to the departures: "Won't you have some more champagne?"

Two colonels and their wives were loudly exchanging impressions. "Wasn't it lovely? Wasn't he gorgeous?" said the women. "Say," one of the colonels said to the other, "I wouldn't mind getting that damned thing myself." "Yes, sir," the other said, "it sure would be a nice thing to have."

Outside, the drivers were reluctantly drifting back to their cars. A colonel was trying to find his vehicle. "Goddamn it," he kept saying to one MP after another, "haven't you seen my sedan? I got to get the hell back to my office." I offered him a ride. "No," he said, "thanks. I'll find that son of a bitch some place. I gotta get back to work. It's all right for the generals to drink champagne in the morning. Someone has got to keep things moving here."

December 15, 1946   TOKYO

The scandal on the costs of the Occupation is coming to a head. Premier Yoshida has called on General MacArthur to discuss it, and also sent him a long memorandum. Yesterday Finance Minister Tanzan Ishibashi told the gloomy details to the Diet, with the press and spectators barred.

The scandal, as Ishibashi presented it, was that the cost of maintaining the army of Occupation is wrecking Japanese economy. By March 31, 1947, the total cost will reach 50 billion yen, or more than $3,300,000,000 at the official rate of exchange. Only a quarter of this amount, Ishibashi charged, was a planned expenditure. The rest represented "extemporaneous" demands for buildings or improvements by American officers in the provinces. Since immediate compliance was demanded, Ishibashi said, the Japanese government had no choice but to buy at exorbitant prices in the black market.

Ishibashi cited some examples of what the Japanese had been required to do. A golf course near Kyoto at the cost of Y.200,000,000 ($13,000,000). A number of barracks, at the average cost of Y.40–60 millions. Eight thousand housing units for Army personnel and their families at the average cost of a million yen a unit ($66,000). A house remodelled for the

French Mission at the cost of Y.3 millions, of which a million was paid for the rugs. Close to a billion yen for the beautification of gardens in Army residences. Gold fish supplied on demand to each house, with the government paying Y.300 ($10) per fish to the contractors. Fresh flowers supplied to houses on demand, at a nominal charge. (Tokyo rumor has it that one general's flower bill ran up to Y.50,000.)

Ishibashi said that the U.S. Army was requested to plan its construction six months in advance; to allow the Japanese government to choose its own contractors; and, finally, to reduce the expenditures to a minimum.

The story is shocking, and probably everything that Ishibashi said is true. But equally significant are the things he left unsaid. Members of parliament who gave me the details of Ishibashi's speech also reported to me their belief that the government is deliberately helping to boost the costs of Occupation. The plan, they say, is to sabotage economic recovery so as to get additional aid from the United States, and, later, to use the economic crisis as an argument for softer terms at the Peace Conference. It is also widely reputed that the contractors give a substantial kickback to the government officials responsible for the letting of contracts.

December 21, 1946   SHANGHAI

At 5:22 this morning, Japan gave us an impressive send-off, with an earthquake which, I learned on arrival here, destroyed 7,000 houses in a single town in Southern Japan. Strapped in our bucket seats, we could not even get a good last look at Tokyo.

SEASON OF
RECKONING

I was glad I had gone to China. It was a good place
to make some broad deductions on our policy in Asia. It was an
even better place for seeing Japan through the eyes of her
neighbors.

For a century China has been one of the major pivots of
our foreign policy. Now the pivotal position was being shifted
to Japan. The Communist tide was sweeping China, and though
we continued to support the nationalists, we did not really
believe they could be saved. In Japan, on the other hand, we
had military bases, a closely knit and relatively undamaged
social fabric, and a government that was stable, efficient, and
friendly to us.

China was conscious of the change in our policy. She was
even more painfully aware of the fact that; while her own position was deteriorating, Japan was growing stronger—with our
help. I talked of Japan to hundreds of Chinese, in Nationalist
areas and in Red. Whatever their political coloration, the men
asked identical, uneasy question, and made identical, uneasy
forecasts of new Japanese aggression within a decade. The
Chinese resented what they called our "pampering" of Japan,
and they disliked General MacArthur with a passion directed
against few other Americans. He had tried to counter this feeling by sponsoring a tour of Japan by a group of Chinese editors.
What had worked so well and so often with others was expected to work as well with the Chinese. But what he, and his
Public Relations advisers, perhaps failed to understand was

that the fears of a nation ravaged for fifteen years could not be allayed by an all-expense junket and a few affable interviews.

Japan's face has changed little in the months I have been away. The scars of war are healing slowly, and the people still bear their look of genteel poverty. At the railroad stations thousands wait for a chance to get aboard trains. The streetcars still run, garlanded with passengers who cannot get inside. Before the Headquarters building, the usual crowd of curious GIs and Japanese wait patiently for General MacArthur's appearance on his way to lunch.

The last two days have been festive. On May Day, 400,000 people took over the Imperial Plaza, to sing, watch the dancing, and cheer demands for more food and better pay. Yesterday, 30,000 others came to the plaza to celebrate the formal inauguration of the new Constitution. It was raining, and the cynics said the crowd was drawn as much by an attachment to the new charter as by the promise of an extra sake ration. The emperor made a silent three-minute appearance on the platform. When he withdrew to his automobile, the crowd mobbed it, while the Japanese brass band, with unconscious irony, played that traditional Japanese tune, "The Stars and Stripes Forever." (The new Constitution, General McArthur noted, "reflects one of the great spiritual reformations of mankind.") Now nothing remained of yesterday's festivities but tall arches running color in the rain.

A series of local and national elections has just come to an end. The Social Democrats have managed to come in ahead of the other parties by a slim margin, but the press interprets the elections as "a conservative landslide." Put together, the rightists have close to a three-to-one majority. Tetsu Katayama, the uninspired leader of the Social Democrats, a pious Christian, a shrewd labor lawyer, and a devout feminist, is now trying to form a coalition with a band of conservatives. Diluted socialism may come to power. In the circumstances, it is not likely to halt Japan's steady postwar drift to the right.

(Mrs. Kato told me happily both she and her husband have been re-elected to the Diet. Both, I hear, have been straying to

the right. Another winner is Mrs. Tamae Fukagawa, the housewife who did not want blue-eyed babies in Japan. Shiga, the
Communist, was defeated.)

The economic crisis is at its worst. Off the record, the Japanese blame it on "fantastic bungling" in General MacArthur's
Headquarters. The Americans, in turn, blame it on the Japanese. Both are probably right. But, meanwhile, inflation grows,
wages lag far behind the rising prices, and industrial output
remains small. I am told that the index of production now stands
at one-third of the 1930–34 level.

The Far Eastern Commission has prescribed for Japan a
standard of living equal to the 1931–34 average. The Russians
wanted to take an earlier mean, but acquiesced in this, American, proposal. Meanwhile, American food continues to pour
into Japan at a steady 150,000 tons a month.

For the second time since Japan's surrender, General Mac-
Arthur has laid a restraining hand on the labor movement. On
January 31, he banned a general strike, because, he said, he
could not permit the employment of "so deadly a social weapon
in the present impoverished and emaciated condition of Japan."
The union leaders wept as they broadcast an order to labor to
abandon the strike.

There was a gory sidelight. Two young men called on
Kikunami, president of the Congress of Industrial Unions, and
demanded that he call off the strike. When Kikunami said it
was not up to him, the youths knifed him. A day later—in the
traditional style of nationalist terrorism—they were surrendered to the police by a gangster politician, who said they belonged to his "patriotic" Fresh People's Party. Kikunami is
recovering.

This is not an isolated case. With growing boldness, the
extreme right is on the march. Professional patriots wreck unions, break up strikes, hold mass meetings at which they pose
the choice: "Are you for communism or for the imperial rule?"
The funds, which once came from the Japanese Army, now
come from the *zaibatsu* and the new black market millionaires.
In Bill Costello's house, I talked to Ball and Derevyanko. Both
betrayed a deeper sense of frustration than I have detected be-

fore. By a steady whittling of the Allied Council's prerogatives, by insult and rebuff, Headquarters has reduced the Council to a humiliating impotence. Derevyanko, I thought, bore the strain better than Ball, who seems no longer sure that even his own government is fully behind him.

From many men I heard tales of the continuing feuds among General MacArthur's aides, and of the purge now in progress within Headquarters under General Willoughby's direction. Its apparent goal, correspondents say, is to remove from Headquarters all those who appear opposed to the military design for a safe and conservative Japan.

Late at night, after a day of listening, it seemed as if I had never been away. The pattern of power politics, both American and Japanese, has not changed, nor have the faces of men running the machinery of Occupation. Nor have the tales about them.

Nor, seemingly, has anything changed in Korea. Americans back from Seoul tell me General Hodge is still preparing for the coming war with Russia, and growing embittered because the Koreans do not seem to appreciate his problems. There are warnings to the Koreans to beware of "disorders and false propaganda." There are periodic alerts for the U.S. troops. In that dreary two-story courthouse in Taegu, in the single month after my visit, our military judges found 537 men guilty of rioting, sentenced 16 of them to death, released 88 others. But the warnings, the military alerts, the sternness of the courts deterred few men. Two months ago there was another wave of violence, with police stations raided, policemen killed, and the jails packed anew.

Syngman Rhee has never been so strong, and there is no longer much pretense of dislike for him. ("I love him for the enemies he's made," Hodge has said.) Kimm Kiu Sic, our avowed choice for Korea's leader, has retired to the safety of an American hospital outside Seoul. The Interim Legislative Assembly, which we advertised as a democratic instrument, has proven to be stillborn. Not even the Korean press is interested in its listless oratory.

With General MacArthur's consent, a delegation of the World Federation of Trade Unions has visited Korea. Not surprisingly, it had some difficulty meeting union leaders. But it is not easy to conceal what is happening in our zone. In its report, the delegation charged that the workers are being subjected to conditions "which are incredible in this twentieth century period of civilization." Virtually the same conclusion was reached in a survey made by an American official—a survey whose final chapter was hastily suppressed.

Arrangements are in progress in Seoul for this month's meeting of the U.S.-Soviet Joint Commission. No one expects it to succeed. Rhee even claims assurances by the State Department that a separate regime will be set up in our zone—with him at the head.

Meanwhile, in the north, the Communists continue to solidify their control. Rough edges have been rubbed off the land reform, which gave land to 750,000 sharecroppers and poor farmers. If our Intelligence reports are correct, the Communist militia is growing. Political dissidents have been pushed into the shadows. Hundreds of refugees continue to stream southward across the 38th, paying a thousand yen a head to Korean Scarlet Pimpernels. But escape is easy. The refugees are the opponents and the non-conformists—collaborators, landlords, former policemen—and the Russian border patrols make no special effort to stop them.

Korea is still two worlds, warring on each other. And in this conflict, we are still allied with the enemies of reform and freedom. "What can we do," says Seoul in self-defense, "with the red menace right across the 38th?" As if injustice is the answer to injustice, or as if democracy can be created, or defended, by denying civil liberties.

May 3, 1948   NEW YORK

This is the third spring of peace. Yet it is a restless and frightened season. Violence and passion have become the substance of politics, and each new day brings a new crisis.

In Japan, too, it is a time of stress. Security and not reform, reconstruction and not democracy have become the goals of our policy. We may long cling to a military foothold on Japanese soil. We may long retain an organ of supervision in Tokyo. But corrective Occupation is near its end.

This uneasy spring is a good time to strike the balance in Japan, to match our achievements against our failures.

The experiment in Japan is without parallel in our history, for we have sought to convert a great and aggressive nation into a democracy in our own image. We have tried it in Germany as well, but there the program of conversion had early been dissolved in international discord. In Japan, there has been no one to claim a share of our glory, and no one to share the reproach for failure.

We started well enough, with a bold and detailed blueprint. It was drawn by scholars and diplomats—all men with a clear idea of what constitutes a democratic state, and what it was in prewar Japan that precluded democracy. The men clearly understood the need for extensive wrecking. They had even allowed for the use of force by the Japanese people to sweep away groups and institutions blocking social progress.

These makers of policy prescribed the separation of the Shinto Church from the State. They ordered curbs on imperial power. They surveyed the whole range of a feudal society and economic system, and prescribed land for the sharecroppers, unions for the workers, and destruction for the huge combines, with their primordial concepts of social responsibility, their vast political power, and their grandiose appetites.

The blueprint provided for the destruction of the police state, for women's suffrage, for cleansing schools of ultra-nationalist ideas, and for the purge from public life of all those who pushed Japan along the path to war—bankers and politicians, editors, professors, generals and policemen.

We put the blueprint in the hands of our military men, and said, go ahead, the job is now yours. And the military translated the blueprint into a series of directives which sought both to wreck the old order and to build a new one.

By today, we have achieved a measure of success. Japan has a new Constitution, vesting all power in the hands of the people, and cutting the emperor down to a symbol of national unity. The Shinto Church has been separated from the public trough. A good share of the five million transferable acres has been turned over to the sharecroppers and poor farmers. Labor union strength has been built up to six million members. Anti-*zaibatsu* laws have put *zaibatsu* securities on public sale, and splintered some of the huge and predatory combines into smaller companies. Women have been given votes, speech has become relatively free, and liberal ideas of the West have been brought to the parched minds of Japan.

We have allowed the emergence of large and vigorous parties of the left—notably the Social Democratic. Together with unions, they have done a tremendous job of political education. By tilting the scale constantly in favor of the conservatives, we have deprived the progressives of an even chance in the coming struggle, but in cities as in the country there will now be thousands of men to champion reform. We shall also leave behind, as our legacy to Japan, a scepticism for the shabby doctrines of Shintoism, and a measure of disrespect for the omniscient and omnipotent police.

There are other entries on the credit side of the ledger. We have sprinkled the cities of Japan with DDT. We have taught the Japanese new methods of gathering vital statistics. We have replaced police swords with night sticks, and taught the policemen the latest methods of crime detection. We have given the crown prince an American governess. Using the best techniques of American public relations, we have helped to "sell" the new democratic emperor to his democratic subjects. We have introduced Arsene Lupin to the Japanese movie-goers, and we have made *Gone with the Wind* a Japanese classic as well. We have inspired the radio industry of Japan to emulate the ebullience, and shallowness, and the countless entertainment tricks of our own radio. We have introduced jitterbugging to the young people, and put the movie industry face to face with the crucial problem of "to kiss or not to kiss." We must have had something to do with the decision to throw the imperial palace moats open to common fishermen. After a gap of eight barren years, we have again given the Japanese access to Hemingway and Tolstoy and Karl Marx (with deletions). We have taught Japan's children the magic words of *jeep-u* and *gum-mu,* and, perhaps not too happily, we have introduced the opening word to her Anglo-Japanese dictionaries: A-Bomb.

But history is a cynic, with a passion for facts and for a second look. It can be misled neither by the boasts of Public Relations officers nor by reforms that have gone only half way. It has perspective, and patience.

Thus, history will note that on this day, Shintoism is again on the rise, a powerful religious and political force as ever linked with the imperial myth. History will note that the Old Guard is back in control of the Diet and the Cabinet, and though the people theoretically are sovereign, the premiers again report political developments to the emperor "with awe and trepidation." It will note that despite the land reform, the rural economy and local government remain under the control of landlords. It will record violations of the new land law on a scale so vast as to make the whole reform ludicrous.

History will note the steps taken to "mellow" the labor movement—from strikebreaking by twenty-year-old army sergeants in obscure towns, to punitive expeditions by Major Imboden, to last month's renewed ban on strikes by General MacArthur, to the Japanese Government's avowed plans to "modify" the labor laws.

The purge, as of this date, has become a sham. War criminals sit in the Diet, the Cabinet and the imperial court, draw new "democratic" legislation and administer the purges to fit their political ends. War criminals are "revising" the textbooks, running the press, dominating the radio and moving picture industries. Thought Control agents, purged and purged again, keep reappearing in positions of responsibility—often with American encouragement. Purged politicians and bankers and publishers continue their work through their relatives or henchmen or dummy companies.

History will take note of the new Supreme Court appointed last year by the Japanese conservatives. Its head is a lawyer who for fifteen years has served as legal counsel to the Mitsui Trust, and among its members there are many who had long and loyally served the old oligarchy. The Japanese will take canny advantage of our own blunder. For the sake of the sweet fiction that it was the Japanese themselves who were building a new democracy, General MacArthur compelled them to write all American reforms into their law books. Now, as Japanese laws, the reforms are subject to legal review by the Supreme Court.

Some landlords have already filed suits to declare the land reform unconstitutional because it deprived them of fair and just compensation. The court has taken no action, for we are still around. But the Japanese themselves guess that when the Occupation ends, the victims of democratic reform—the *zaibatsu* owners, landlords, purged officers and gendarmes—will come to the Japanese Supreme Court for redress, and get it.

History will note that some officers in Headquarters wished to void the choice of the new ultraconservative judges. These desires have been overruled by General MacArthur on the ground that tampering with the Supreme Court might attach to it an unfortunate stigma.

Few official claims have been more extravagant, or misleading, than those on the destruction of the *zaibatsu*. Painful blows, it is true, have been dealt to the combines. Many of their activities have been driven into surreptitious channels. But it must also be recorded that the major parties (with the exception of the Social Democratic), the Cabinet, the press, and the imperial court remain allied with the *zaibatsu*, and champion their cause. What is more important, the *zaibatsu* continue to control most of Japan's economy.

We ourselves have now departed so far from original policy as to absolve the *zaibatsu* of responsibility for Japan's war-making, and release most of their leaders from the Sugamo Prison "for lack of evidence."

This has been done in the face of overwhelming evidence of *zaibatsu* duplicity. As revealing as any were the facts yielded by the "scandal of the missing supplies," which rocked the Japanese Government last fall. These were the stocks that the defeated Japanese Army and Navy were required to turn over to us.

A special Diet committee headed by Kato determined that half a trillion yen's worth of supplies—ten billion dollars at the official rate of exchange—had vanished. It learned that the disposal of the goods was plotted jointly by the armed services, the government and the *zaibatsu* in the month of Japan's surrender. It found that the bulk of the supplies had gone to the *zaibatsu*, with some of the transfers made as late as the summer of 1946. The concealed stockpiles included pig and scrap iron, gold, copper, silver wire, and bullion, rubber and even shoes. On Kyushu island alone, the Tokyo press said, 5,800 railway cars were used to move the supplies to their hiding places.

None of these supplies has been funneled into that industrial revival to which the *zaibatsu* profess such warm devotion. The bulk of the stocks has been concealed, for use when the Occupation ends. Some, significantly, have been sold in the black market, and the proceeds used to buy back, through dummy owners, the *zaibatsu* securities which the government was selling to "the general public."

But the *zaibatsu* were not alone in thwarting our plans. The conservative cabinets which we entrusted with the task of democratizing Japan had worked, instead, to preserve the old order. The imperial court has fought successfully to regain its holds on Japan and her people. The "demobilization boards" have operated as disguised general staffs. And the Foreign Office has toiled secretly on an outline of a foreign policy which would regain for Japan her former glory.

Elaborate plans have been laid to play one power against another. A propaganda campaign has been organized to persuade the victors that Japan needs "living room" and "a chance to survive." Hitoshi Ashida, whose *Japan Times* in the 'thirties was one of the drumbeaters of aggression and who is now premier, has pleaded with the Allies for permission to retain "minor" islands—including Okinawa. One of his aides argued in the Diet that Japan had not been defeated, and therefore could make demands on us. And Yoshida has even asked for an army —for self-defense.

In one of the major news *coups* of the Occupation, Joe Fromm of *World Report* last year obtained the secret outline of the Foreign Office strategy at the peace conference. By playing us against Russia, the outline indicated, the Japanese would seek to end the Occupation; limit Allied supervision of Japan to the ambassadors of the four nations, with no power of direct intervention; end Allied controls on industry and foreign trade; gain the right to have aircraft; and remove restrictions on the size of armed police.

"In one conversation," Fromm reported, "a Japanese diplomat asked an Allied representative how his government would react to a proposal that Japan be permitted to have 100,000 armed police for 'security purposes.' 'I'm not in a position to express my government's attitude,' replied the Allied official. 'But if I were you, I'd suggest 90,000 or 110,000. But not 100,000. That's the number the Germans asked to have for security reasons after the first World War.' "

The measure of failure or success depends on the yardstick used. A measuring stick that can well be applied to the Occupation is the United States Initial Post-Surrender Policy, released in August, 1945. One of the great documents of American history, the statement of policy outlined in detail the path along which Japan was to be led to democracy.

If this yardstick is used, we have failed in Japan. For this yardstick cannot be applied to partial success. The success has to be complete, or else it is nonexistent. Democracy is a unit. It cannot be piecemeal. A democracy is not a democracy when its Constitution springs not out of a nation's soil, but out of the conqueror's office. A democracy is not a democracy when this democratic Constitution is served by an undemocratic government, interpreted by an undemocratic supreme court, and enforced by an undemocratic police. A democracy is not a democracy when we—its mentors—profess our devotion to free speech, and then allow our censors to bar a free discussion by the Japanese people of their own government, Constitution, and the problems of living. A democracy, finally, is a sham when a political and social system supposedly democratic is erected on a foundation of feudalism, complete with an emperor.

We have fought a costly war for the professed object of converting Japan into a state that would uphold democracy and peace. General MacArthur translated this faith into a constitutional renunciation of war and armed forces. Yet, today, few people in or out of Japan doubt that in a decade she will be ready for new military ventures. Certainly her conservative leaders, her diplomats, big businessmen, and just plain nationalists make no secret of their belief that Japan will have another chance at imperial expansion.

The Japanese have lost the war, but they are winning the peace, and they are winning it with our acquiescence. For what is happening in Japan is only partly the results of Japanese conspiracy. To a much greater degree, it is a reflection of our own policy, which in less than three years has traversed the long road from democratic reform to Japan's conversion into our military and economic bulwark in the Pacific.

What is happening in Japan is not an isolated phenomenon. It is an integral part of our foreign policy, of the new goals, fears and passions, of the global realignment of power. What is happening in Japan is also happening in Germany. What is happening in China, under our aegis, has already happened in Greece. Japan has become one of our outer redoubts, and in the process the democracy which we were to nurture has been ravished.

But the mutations of policy in Washington do not absolve General MacArthur, or his advisers, of blame. With few exceptions, these men have never relished their job of social wrecking. Nor has the situation been helped by General MacArthur's own eccentricities. Reform in Japan has moved in spurts, because the general wished to apply no pressure on Yoshida or

Shidehara; or because his heart was set on the passage of the Constitution, and he wanted nothing to interfere with it; or because a given reform might have tipped the scale against the conservatives he backed.

Americans were entitled to know of what was happening in Japan. They could learn little, because the general warred on the press, and befogged the picture with millions of adjectives. Reforms drafted in Headquarters, and then forced upon the Japanese, were extolled as expressions of Japan's yearning for democracy. Conservative victories, or even curbs on freedom, were officially hailed as triumphs of democratic practice.

The gradual change in our policy in Japan is illustrated by the stories of three meetings between General MacArthur and Emperor Hirohito. At the first encounter, the general was sternly formal. He was the representative of the victors, and Hirohito was a symbol not only of a beaten nation, but of the feudal forces which we had committed ourselves to root out.

Time passed, and at a subsequent meeting the emperor said to General MacArthur: "Our Constitution forbids us to have an army. I'm concerned over the future." General MacArthur reassured him: "The United States will assume responsibility for the defense of Japan." (The emperor's interpreter was dismissed for revealing this exchange, but it is believed that his indiscretion was ordered by the Foreign Office.)

At the following interview, General MacArthur, for the first time, addressed the emperor as "Your Majesty."

The progress from sternness to the title courteous was not important. But it was one of the countless little things which were meant to indicate the change in the nature of our relations with Japan. It was a barometer of major changes of policy and attitude—a barometer anxiously consulted both by the Americans and the Japanese.

There is another yardstick that could be employed in Japan —the yardstick of military preparedness. The men directing our national destiny foresaw a new war in which, to use the Tokyo terminology, Japan would be both a "bastion" and a "springboard." Increasingly, our national policy and conduct have been dominated by the anticipation of war.

In pursuance of this policy, we have followed two courses in Japan. We installed and maintained in power a succession of conservative regimes which would undoubtedly side with us in the next war. At the same time, we pumped money into Japan, in the form of food, cotton and vehicles. DDT sprayed over the cities, millions of people inoculated, and streets repaved.

The second course brought us friends. But there is little reason to suppose that this gratitude will be translated into support in time of war. The dominant feeling in Japan—as it must be in Germany—is dread of war. There are no inducements that would make the Japanese forget this dread.

American observers believe that if and when war comes, the Japanese government will be with us. So will the *kamikaze* youths the unemployed ex-servicemen, the fanatical officers— all those who like war for its excitement or rewards. But the common people—the miners, the sharecroppers, the railroadmen, the impoverished clerks—will stand apart. And if they are hurt, their neutrality might give place to hatred.

Had we gone through with our original reforms, turned the Old Guard out of power, and encouraged the emergence of a new and liberal leadership; had we been firm when our directives were being sabotaged; had we entrusted the job in Japan to our civilian experts, rather than the military; had we pursued our original policy without change; had we remembered that even in crisis, the welfare of the native peoples should have precedence over our own strategic designs; had we done all that, we would not only have a genuine democracy in Japan, but Washington would not have had to worry about the growth of Japanese communism.

Our worst error in Japan was our original belief that democratic reform would, or could, be carried out by men who hated it.

It is easy enough to understand why the mistake was made. The victory caught us unprepared. Early in 1945, one of the best informed U.S. Navy officers insisted in an interview with me that Japan would fight on at least until 1948. Our Intelligence was seemingly confused by the variety and contradictions of its data on Japan.

Thus, when surrender came, we were not ready for it. We had no sound estimates of Japanese morale. We had only a bare skeleton of a military government that could take over the administration of Japan. We were delighted to find that Japan had a functioning government, and we happily turned over the job to it. This was the first, and the most important, in a series of events which in the end resulted in the survival of old Japan.

Before our first Christmas in Japan, we knew that the Japanese machinery of government was geared for sabotage. We already knew that the government in Tokyo served as a buffer, to cushion and absorb the Allied pressure. But beneath it, the web of provincial government functioned without change or hindrance. We knew already of the series of palace conferences at which the master blueprint for defeating our purposes was decided. We knew that files of vital documents had been destroyed; the stocks of raw materials which Japan would need for reconstruction had been dispersed and hidden; the governing personnel had been reshuffled so that it could escape purges; vast funds had been distributed to military and nationalist groups so that they could survive the years of stress.

This—the infant days of the Occupation—was the time to start lopping off political heads, until we had reformed the whole governing body of Japan. We procrastinated, and with each day of delay the Japanese learned more of our weaknesses, and of the ways of using them to thwart our plans. And with each day, the strength of the "reformers" in Headquarters dwindled, and the influence of the "preparedness" group soared. The "reformers" had drawn the original directives, which translated the purpose and spirit of the Initial Post-Surrender Policy into blueprints for reform. But now the season of promise was over, and the season of fulfillment was on, and the "reformers," one by one, were being forced out.

Six months after Japan's surrender, one of General Mac-Arthur's key aides told me that "we're through with the punitive stage." In another two years, the tolerance had reached fantastic limits. There was Baba, the publisher of the *Yomiuri*, soliciting in writing an American general's support for a Japanese war criminal purged by another American general, and charging that the latter was swayed by "Communists around him." And, to cite an even more striking case, there was the newly purged publisher of another important daily, informing one of General MacArthur's confidantes of the way in which he, the publisher, intended to circumvent the purge. His plan, he wrote, was to transfer his stock to a dummy company, "to prevent the leftists from seizing control" of his paper. In neither case, did the American recipient take any action against the Japanese.

Today, the spirit of reform is dead, and all the Japanese know it, from the *zaibatsu* leaders, negotiating for American loans, to workers who a fortnight ago saw union leaders fired, fined or arrested by the government for calling strikes. What few reforms are still being pushed through, are but a shell of the reforms originally charted.

By now the early gap between the liberal policies of the State Department and the conservative views of Headquarters has been bridged. Curiously, the bridging has coincided with the transfer of political power in Washington from civilian to military hands. The "get-tough" foreign policy in Washington is being translated into its corollary in Japan.

Many factors affected our policy for Japan. Among them, certainly, was the Japanese sabotage. Among them was the reluctance of our own military to alter the fabric of Japan. Among them was the change in the emphasis of our Pacific policy from China to Japan. As important as any of these was the entrance of our big business on the Japanese stage.

Japan was the richest prize ever to tempt American big business. Much more now lay at stake than the renewal of the old ties with the *zaibatsu*. Japan's defeat had provided an opportunity to take over a good share of one of the world's great industrial systems.

The prime obstacle was not the Japanese. Partnership with

American concerns meant credits, patents and equipment, and most of the *zaibatsu* favored closer bonds. More bothersome was the body of controls and restraints which we ourselves had imposed on Japan in the name of reform. American big business was opposed to the entire anti-*zaibatsu* program, with its emphasis on decentralization, control of production and profits, and labor wellbeing.

The *zaibatsu* were not surprised by the appearance of a new ally. From the first day of defeat, they had courted the favor of American officialdom—with its heavy sprinkling of businessmen. As often as not, the gestures of goodwill were reciprocated. One of the earliest stories I heard in Tokyo dealt with a party given for American officers by Ryozo Asano, head of the Asano *zaibatsu*—steel, munitions, cement in China Formosa, and Manchuria. During the banquet, a U.S. Navy captain offered a toast to the host: "To the white hope of Japanese democracy. . . . " The captain was one of the officials entrusted with the job of breaking up the *zaibatsu,* and his own files must have contained the whole unsavory record of Asano operations.

Another story, equally authentic, dealt with a *zaibatsu* which for many years worked closely with one of our own great electric concerns. All through the war years, the Japanese firm maintained the residence of the American company's representative in Tokyo in readiness for his return. The building was kept in good repair, and the Americans favorite chef remained on the *zaibatsu's* payroll. Whoever won the war, business would go on as ever.

About the time I returned to Tokyo last year, the Far Eastern Commission received from the State Department a draft directive to General MacArthur, instructing him anew to break up "excessive private concentrations of economic power." As it happened, this was the last gasp of reform in Washington. A carefully engineered campaign of protest in the press and Senate forced the recall of the directive.

Subsequently, the Army Department instructed General MacArthur to modify his trust-busting. The official instructions came accompanied by a personal plea from Secretary Kenneth Royall. But by this time, the anti-*zaibatsu* program, at least on paper, had gone too far to be discarded without a loss of face. Thus, General MacArthur sharply rejected the recommendations, citing at length the earlier directives on the dissolution of the *zaibatsu*.

With no pretense at concealing the mailed fist behind it, a bill decentralizing the Japanese combines was pushed through the reluctant Diet. Then, General MacArthur met the protests on the United States Senate floor with a forecast of a "blood bath of revolutionary violence" unless the concentration of capital in Japan was broken up.

At this point, a figure long active behind the scenes appeared on the stage. This was William H. Draper, Under-Secretary of the Army and a former executive of the great Dillon, Read investment house. Draper had already helped to modify the decartelization program in Germany. Now he turned to Japan. The pressure on Tokyo was culminated with the dispatch of a mission of bankers, investors and industrialists to Japan. Draper was the head of the mission. Among its members was Paul Hoffman, President of the Studebaker Corporation and Administrator for Economic Co-operation.

Without fanfare, the mission has now in effect redrawn the policy for Japan. The new blueprint proposes to put Japan on her feet by 1953, at the estimated cost to the American taxpayer of $1,600,000,000. The Japanese press joyfully depicted the new policy as "a plan to make this nation the workshop of Asia."

Not unexpectedly, the new policy said nothing of reform. What it stressed primarily was the removal of controls on production and corporate profits. The anti-*zaibatsu* laws were to be allowed to wither by default. Labor was expected to "modify its demands." Japan was to be permitted to rebuild her merchant marine. No ceiling was to be put on her industrial expansion. Roughly half a billion dollars was to be given to Japan by the U.S. Treasury as the first installment on her recovery.

The Japanese officials reacted with alacrity. They demanded immediate changes in the labor laws, to curb the unions. They called for a sharp scaling down of reparations. They forcast the end of economic purges, and the return of men already purged.

"The prospect of greater freedom from controls, even before the peace treaty," wrote Allen Raymond of the New York *Herald Tribune*, "seems to have exhilarated Japanese businessmen and their representatives in the Diet. Leading executives of the old *zaibatsu*—purged and unpurged by a screening committee ruling on war guilt—are now converging on Tokyo to confer on how they can speed recovery."

But the Japanese pressed their advantage beyond mere business. They demanded a revision of the "hastily drawn" Constitution, starting with minor points, and ending, no doubt, with the deletion of the article in which Japan renounced war forever. And even without waiting for such revisions, the government proposed to the Diet the creation of a "Marine Peace Preservation Board," to "combat piracy and smuggling." The "pocket navy" would have 126 small vessels, including submarines, and a force of 10,000 armed men. One could well wonder how soon it would be before Japan would have an army, to "protect herself from Communist aggression."

General MacArthur was giving in to all this pressure without a struggle. His attention was focussed on the presidential elections in the United States. And, anyway, neither he nor most of his advisers had ever fought very hard to remake the old Japan. In their hearts there was neither a passionate hatred for the *zaibatsu* nor an affection for the trouble-making labor unions. What impelled them was the pressure of the early directives from Washington and a faint suspicion that a modicum of reform might lessen political and social unrest.

Even more dismal is the picture in Korea. In Japan there is at least a measure of democratic procedure, and a show of concern for public welfare. Leftist dissidence still has its organs of expression, labor unions still recruit members without hindrance, and in the Imperial Plaza men can still shout their denunciation of the government. In Korea there is no pretense. It is a battleground, on which popular right, needs and desires have been sacrificed to our conflict with Russia.

Much has happened in Korea since last year, and yet tragically little has changed. Lyuh Woon Heung, the only remaining liberal leader in our zone, has been assassinated. General Lerch died, and was succeeded by another general. In an obvious, if belated, move to match the land reform in the north, we had put our own plan—"Bunce's Folly"—into force. But no one expected it to be anything but an irritant, for it applied only to former Japanese land holdings—less than one fifth of the land—and left intact the adjoining holdings of Korea's great landowners. The sharecroppers working for Oh the landlord would remain a hungry and rebellious band.

There have been more riots; a wave last summer, and another earlier this year. The latter yielded a new crop of eight thousand prisoners, to be jammed into the overflowing jails. But when an amnesty was suggested by a United Nations' group, General Hodge denied firmly that there were any political prisoners in our zone. It was clearly a matter of definition.

As in other areas of crisis, so in Korea the United Nations has become our ally. In the face of Russian boycott, it has sent a commission to Seoul to hold elections in our zone. The Russians insisted that the only solution for Korea was an immediate withdrawal of both the Soviet and U.S. troops.

The episode made neither Russia nor us look proud. The removal of troops, proposed by Moscow, would most probably have served as a signal for a civil war. The real reason Russia opposed the elections was that the population of our zone was twice that of hers, and in any national assembly our rightists would hold twice as many seats as her leftists.

We, in turn, proclaimed our devotion to democracy, but pressed for an election that would give all power in our zone to one of the most reactionary machines known to this age. ("We have no choice," General MacArthur said to a French visitor, "but to support Syngman Rhee, as we have to support Chiang Kai-shek in China.") Moreover, we had employed a heavy hand to force other nations, such as Syria and India, to back our stand.

But no foreign observers, however friendly to us, could fail to see the three major evils of our zone. In its recommendations to General Hodge, the United Nations Commission dealt with all three. It said it was "genuinely concerned about the possible role the police might play during the elections." It insisted that the youth groups be informed that "the activities of their members are under the scrutiny of the Commission." Finally, it urged an amnesty for those very same political prisoners whose existence General Hodge had denied so blandly. Truly nothing has changed since I saw Korea.

The decision to hold elections in our zone was a personal triumph for Syngman Rhee. He celebrated it with a tremendous mass meeting, in honor of the Commission. At this rally, in full view of the police and the Commission, the rightist youths beat up the few stray leftists, tore off a few ears, gouged out an eye. When the Commission informally suggested to General Hodge that the chiefs of national and Seoul police—both Rhee's faithful henchmen—be removed for their activities, Hodge firmly rejected the suggestion.

Rhee was prepared for the election. Every organ of persuasion in our zone—the police, the young terrorists, the landlords, the Korean personnel of the Military Government—was working for him. And so certain was his overwhelming success that both his two major conservative rivals, Kim Koo, the terrorist, and Kimm Kiu Sic, the moderate whom Bertsch once hoped to see at Korea's helm, were compelled to denounce the proposed election, and urge further consultation with the Communist north. Thus, our policy was alienating even the conservatives.

Meanwhile, in the north, Russia is working out her own solutions. Preparations are afoot to set up an autonomous "Democratic People's Republic." An independent army is about to be formed. Elections have further confirmed the Communist party's hold on men's daily lives and politics. In contrast to our zone, women have been given the vote. And the flight of dissidents across the border, into our zone, continues, though on a far smaller scale.

With each day, and each action, the two powers are perpetuating that political monstrosity, the 38th Parallel. And with each day, Korea is drifting closer to internecine fighting. Once rival Korean regimes are set up in the two zones, civil war is inevitable. It may start clandestinely, with sabotage and terror. But in a time of acute stress, it is not easy to control violence. The step from blowing up a train to border raids and guerrilla warfare is very short.

There can be no doubt that we shall be caught in the middle. For in our present mood, we are not likely to retire from any of our outposts, however untenable and costly. We may withdraw part of our garrison from Korea. If we do, I am told, we shall leave behind us a "military advisory group," which will convert Korea into another Greece.

Two years ago, a general settlement of our differences with Russia could have also settled the problem of Korea. This is no longer so. The storm of history swirling across Korea has produced a political polarization. There is no middle ground left— only the irreconcilable right, led by Rhee, and the extreme, Communist-led left.

As in China, this political struggle is superimposed on the age-old struggle between the landlord and his tenant. By siding with Rhee, we have become the landlord's allies. As in China, we shall pay a heavy price for this mistake.

Since that autumn day in 1945 when I flew westward from San Francisco, I have had an opportunity to watch our foreign policy in action in three key countries of Asia. In all three, Japan, China, and Korea, the pattern of the policy did not vary.

In all three, for instance, we have pursued a negative policy. Increasingly, we have been concerned with "containing" the Russian influence, rather than with the encouragement of progressive policies which would benefit the Chinese, the Japanese, or the Koreans.

In the name of "containment," we have allied ourselves in all three countries with extreme rightists. The degrees of our intimacy with the right varied. In Japan, we have the best record, for we started with a progressive policy and, for a time in 1947–48, we worked through a relatively progressive Cabinet. But the variations did not change the pattern. In Japan, we were allied with such men as Yoshida, in Korea with such men as Rhee, in China with the extreme right wing of the Kuomintang.

It was a policy of self-imposed bankruptcy. We candidly admitted that the politicians we backed were corrupt and undemocratic. We admitted that these men neither could nor would introduce progressive reforms, and we even conceded that without such reforms internal unrest would continue. Probably the classic admission came from a Foreign Affairs Sub-Committee of the House, which stated in a report:

"It is highly preferable that the United States have a free though unmoral government in China than to have a hostile government no matter how pure and moral but dominated by Communist influences. . . . "

It was a futile and costly policy, for it ignored the well-being of the people whom we claimed to be protecting. It was doubly futile because we sought to fight Communism through feudal ideas and institutions. Social discontent in China and Korea is fed on the feudal system of land ownership. The Red armies in China and the countless rioters in Southern Korea are sharecroppers who have reached the end of their tether. In Japan, we have tried to liberate the peasant, but we have left virtually intact the feudal superstructure, topped by the emperor.

In all three countries, the Communists have associated themselves with the movements of protest. But it is naïve to think that had there been no Communists, there would have been no violent peasant revolts in China and Korea.

For a century and a half, America has been a symbol of freedom and progressive thought. In Asia, this symbol has never been as bright as it was during the last war. But in less than three years we have frittered away this treasure in goodwill. The new image of America is that of a powerful and rich and greedy nation, allied with reaction and determined to put down every mass movement left of the center, whether it is Communist, Socialist, or simply a movement of protest against injustice, corruption and oppression.

Force and repression are not the answers to unrest. The answer is an enlightened social reform. Had we supplied it, we would need have no fear of communism or Russia. The men who drew the Initial Post-Surrender Policy for Japan understood this fact. The men who took over in Washington, and the men who executed the policy did not understand.

As a result we have failed in Japan, as we have failed in China and Korea. We have succeeded merely in producing a backlog of hatred, and only the blind can now deny the possibility of Communist victory in China and Korea.

"Our greatest error," Justice William Douglas of the Supreme Court said recently, "would be to fashion our foreign policy merely in terms of anticommunism. We will fail miserably if we do no more than that. For then we will end by railing and ranting at the specter of communism, but do nothing to eliminate the conditions on which communism thrives. If we follow that course, war will soon appear as the only alternative."

The policy of "containment" and of "get tough" has proved its bankruptcy. It has committed us to alliances with feudal and undemocratic men and factions, opposed by their own peoples and surviving only with our aid. A military and political system based on such alliances rests on rotten props. It is no match for the dynamics of Communist policy and slogans.

There have been grave crises in the past in which the American people recaptured the direction of our national policy. Few of these crises could have been more serious than that which now afflicts our foreign relations. This is a time for action, and for greatness, for if we change our policy in time, we might yet save peace.

INDEX

Agapov, Boris, 95–96
Agricultural Association, 311–12, 461
agriculture, *see* land reform and economy
Agriculture, Ministry of, 19, 154
Ainus, 75
Akahata, see *Red Flag*
Akihito, Crown Prince, 493
Akita, 57, 75–80
Allied Council for Japan, 157–59, 180–82, 195, 210, 211, 217–20, 247, 300–02, 341, 344, 443–44, 453, 455–56, 490
Allied Labor News, 330
Allied Translator and Interpreter Section, 218–20
American-Korean Commission, 423
Ando, Akira, 124–25, 178, 179, 245–53, 262, 263, 304–05, 307, 309–10
Anti-Trust and Cartels Division, 238
Arahata, Kanson, 167–68, 170
"Arisue Organization," 445–46
Asahi, The, 37–38, 179, 227, 237, 244, 264, 328–34
Asano, Ryozo, 243, 503
Ashida, Hitoshi, 94, 497
Assist and Lead Society, 154–55
Associated Press, 259, 347, 350, 450
Atami, 132–34, 188
Atcheson, George, Jr., 182, 210, 217–20, 247, 301–02, 443–44, 456, 468, 471, 473
ATIS, *see* Allied Translator and Interpreter Section
Atkinson, Maj., 399, 404, 406–07, 429

Baba, Tsunego, 23, 254, 263–65, 328, 332, 340, 502
Baker, Brig. Gen. Frayne, 4, 195, 210, 211, 216, 254, 262, 328, 331–32, 342, 347, 391, 454
Ball, W. MacMahon, 157, 181, 210, 300–02, 444, 455–56, 489–90
Baltimore *Sun*, x, 126

"Bataan Boys," *see* MacArthur, men around
Behrstock, Capt. Arthur, 18
Benton, Lt. Col. H. O., 394
Bergher, M., 304, 305
Bergstrom, C. V., 395, 410
Berrigan, Darrell, 9, 19, 26, 48, 55–57
Bertsch, Lt. Leonard, 351, 353–58, 360, 362, 366, 368, 392–93
Bishop, Max, 242–43
black market, 13, 47, 172, 496
Boepple, Maj. Graf, 6
Bratton, Col. R. S., 253
Brines, Russell, 347
Brown, Maj. Gen. Albert E., 372, 431
Buchanan, Dr. Daniel C., 10
Buddhism, 319
Buddhist party, 160
Bunce, Dr. Arthur, 351, 360, 370, 431, 432, 506

Cairo Declaration, 428
censorship, 98, 102, 186–87, 235–37, 253–54, 262, 264–65, 307, 309, 334, 347, 449–50, 475–78; in Korea, 196, 391–92, 429
Central Liaison Office, 17, 128, 478–79
Central News Agency (of China), 163
Chamberlain, Prof. Basil Hall, 141
Cherne, Leo, 230
Chiang Kai-shek, 189
Chiba Prefecture, 152–55, 296
Chicago *Daily News*, 196
Chicago *Sun*, 303, 333, 347, 446
Chicago *Times*, 38
Chicago *Tribune*, 345
Chichibu, Prince, 190
Chinese Mission, 327–28
Chistiakov, Gen., 431
Christian Science Monitor, x, 196
Chu Shih-ming, Lt. Gen., 157
Civil Communications Section, 241–42

Military Government, U.S., in Korea, (*cont'd*) 363–66, 369, 371, 373–74, 386–92, 395, 401–02, 413, 414
Minpo, 264
Mito, 312, 313, 319–26
Mito Gaku (Mito School of Nationalist Thought), 320, 322, 324–25
Mitsubishi, 123, 142–52
Mitsui, 142–52, 495
Miyagi Prefecture, 50
Moon, 356, 366–71, 374
Motion Picture Division, 250
motion pictures, 304–10, 493–94
Mueller, Maj. Gen. P. J., 340
Mydans, Carl, x

Nagai, Gen, 161–62
Nagako, Empress, 11
Nagano Prefecture, 102, 105–15
Nakano, Seigo, 275
Narahashi, Wataru, 94, 125–26, 128, 131, 184, 198
National Assembly Independence Urge Youth Association, 438
Natural Resources Section, 18, 43, 338
Neighborhood Associations, 136, 183
New Japan party, 159, 161
New Republic party, 160–61
New York *Herald Tribune*, x, 3, 505
New York *Post*, 9, 449
New York *Times*, 161, 347, 361
Newspaper Union, 227, 235, 244, 264–65, 328–35
Newsweek, 347
Nichiei Studios, 307–09
Nippon Times, 25, 79, 98, 270, 301, 475–76
Nissan Trust, 305–06
Nomura, Adm. Kichisaburo, 11, 224, 434
Nozaka, Sanzo, 16, 103–05, 161, 162, 174–76, 197, 219, 220, 460, 467–72
Nugent, Lt. Col. D. R., 463

occupation costs, 66–67, 474, 479, 484–85
Official Gazette, 141, 185, 477
Okada, Adm. Keisuke, 276, 277–80, 286
Okano, Susumu, *see* Nozaka
Okawa, Shumei, 201, 207–09, 322, 326
Onjin, 378, 439–40
Osaka, 16, 116–22
Overseas News Agency, 247

Ozaki, Roy, 172, 211–12, 311–24
Ozaki, Yukio, 132–35, 221–22

Pak Heun Yung, 364
Pakchon, 377, 385, 390
Parallel, 38th, *see* Korea (North)
Parton, Margaret, x, 333, 336–37, 456, 478
Patriotic Youth Association, 383
Pauley, Ed, 5–6, 467, 479
peace conference, 497
Peace Preservation Section, 91, 94, 152
Pearl Harbor, 7, 11, 223, 259
Pechkoff, Lt. Gen. Zinovy, 480–83
Percival, Jack, 195
Peoples' party, Korea, 364, 420
Peoples' Republic, 352, 353, 362, 401
Philadelphia *Bulletin*, 176
Pickelle, Maj. F. E., 193
Police Division (U. S.), Korea 369, 387–91, 399
police, Japanese, 7, 51–52, 71, 116, 134–35, 165–68, 198, 223, 252, 313, 332–33, 335–37, 346, 471, 493, 507; *see also* Thought Control
police, Korean, 350, 353–55, 363–71, 388–91, 423–24, 429
political parties, 15–17, 145, 159–64, 184–86, 325, 458–59, 472, 493; in Korea, 359, 361
political prisoners, 44, 507; in Korea, 363–64, 388–91, 399–400, 506, 507
Potsdam Declaration, 125, 241–43, 289, 290, 292, 309
Potsdam Ordinance, 141
Pravda, 302
Press Club, 2, 3, 13, 19, 40, 41, 94, 95, 161–64, 195–96, 339, 343, 477
Press Division, 263, 453
Progressive party, 15–16, 44, 161, 179, 182, 184–85, 223
prostitution, 52, 125, 178, 212–16, 232–34
Prou, Leon, 472
Public Health and Welfare Section, 45
Public Relations Office, 3, 342
Pusan, 359, 388–90, 393–403, 426, 438

radio, 6, 295, 493
Radio Division, 330
Raymond, Allen, 505
Reader's Digest, 134
Recreation and Amusement Association, 232–34